Contributions to Management Science

More information about this series at http://www.springer.com/series/1505

Josef Windsperger • Gérard Cliquet •
George Hendrikse • Marijana Srećković

Editors

Design and Management of Interfirm Networks

Franchise Networks, Cooperatives and Alliances

 Springer

Editors

Josef Windsperger
University of Vienna
Vienna, Austria

Gérard Cliquet
Institute of Management of Rennes (IAE)
Université de Rennes 1
Rennes, France

George Hendrikse
RSM
Erasmus University Rotterdam
Leiderdorp, Zuid-Holland
The Netherlands

Marijana Srećković
Vienna University of Technology
Wien, Austria

ISSN 1431-1941   ISSN 2197-716X (electronic)
Contributions to Management Science
ISBN 978-3-030-29247-8   ISBN 978-3-030-29245-4 (eBook)
https://doi.org/10.1007/978-3-030-29245-4

This Springer imprint is published by the registered company Springer Nature Switzerland AG.
The registered company address is: Gewerbestrasse 11, 6330 Cham, Switzerland

Contents

Contributors

Jos Bijman Business Management & Organisation Group, Wageningen University & Research, Wageningen, The Netherlands

Ivo Bleeker Flynth Adviseurs & Accountants Zwolle, Zwolle, The Netherlands

Gérard Cliquet Institute of Management of Rennes (IAE), Université de Rennes 1, Rennes, France

Jean-Marie Codron INRA, UMR MOISA, INRA, CIRAD, Montpellier SupAgro, Montpellier, France

Nathalie Colasanti University of Rome Tor Vergata, Rome, Italy

Michael L. Cook Department of Agricultural and Applied Economics, University of Missouri, Columbia, MO, USA

Evelien Croonen Faculty of Economics & Business, University of Groningen, Groningen, The Netherlands

Cary Di Lernia The University of Sydney Business School, The University of Sydney, Sydney, Australia

Muriel Fadairo Université Savoie Mont Blanc, IAE Savoie Mont-Blanc (USMB/IAE) Institut de Recherche en Gestion et Economie (IREGE), Mont Blanc, France

Jason R. V. Franken School of Agriculture, Western Illinois University, Macomb, IL, USA

Rocco Frondizi University of Rome Tor Vergata, Rome, Italy

José Daniel García-Castro Escuela Politècnica Superior de Alcoy, Universitat Politècnica de València, Alcoy, Alicante, Spain

Nina Gorovaia School of Business and Law, Frederick University Cyprus, Nicosia, Cyprus

Sajjad Haider Department of Business Administration, Faculty of Economics and Administration, King Abdulaziz Universtiy, Jeddah, Kingdom of Saudi Arabia

Reinder Hamming Faculty of Economics & Business, Alumni of University of Groningen, Groningen, The Netherlands

George W. J. Hendrikse Rotterdam School of Management, Erasmus University Rotterdam, Rotterdam, The Netherlands

Julia Höhler Institute of Farm and Agribusiness Management, Justus Liebig University Giessen, Giessen, Germany

Maria Jell-Ojobor Department of Business and Management, LUISS Guido Carli University, Rome, Italy

Joanna Kuczewska Faculty of Economics, University of Gdansk, Gdansk, Poland

Francesca Mariotti Department of Business Administration, Faculty of Economics and Administration, King Abdulaziz Universtiy, Jeddah, Kingdom of Saudi Arabia

Marco Meneguzzo University of Rome Tor Vergata, Rome, Italy
Università della Svizzera Italiana, Lugano, Switzerland

Douglas Miller Rutgers Business School-Newark and New Brunswick, Piscataway, NJ, USA

Karl Morasch Bundeswehr University Munich, Neubiberg, Germany

Sylwia Morawska Collegium of Business Administration, Warsaw School of Economics, Warsaw, Poland

Josefa Mula Research Centre on Production Management and Engineering (CIGIP), Universitat Politècnica de València, Escuela Politècnica Superior de Alcoy, Alcoy, Alicante, Spain

Nguyen Minh Ngoc CREM UMR 6211CNRS, IGR-IAE Université de Rennes 1, Rennes, France

Rubens Nunes School of Animal Sc. and Food Engineering (USP/FZEA), University of São Paulo, Pirassununga, São Paulo, Brazil

Francisco Puig Dpto. Dirección de Empresas "Juan J. Renau", Facultad de Economía, Universidad de Valencia, Valencia, Spain

Noemi Rossi University of Rome Tor Vergata, Rome, Italy

Maria Sylvia Machione Saes School of Economics, Business and Accounting (USP/FEA), Center for Organization Studies (CORS), University of São Paulo, São Paulo, Brazil

Louis-Antoine Saïsset Montpellier SupAgro, UMR MOISA, Montpellier SupAgro, INRA, CIRAD, Montpellier University, Montpellier, France

Guillermo Navarro Sanfelix Dpto. Dirección de Empresas "Juan J. Renau", Facultad de Economía, Universidad de Valencia, Valencia, Spain

Vivian Lara Santos-Silva School of Animal Sc. and Food Engineering (USP/FZEA), University of São Paulo, Pirassununga, São Paulo, Brazil

Marijana Srećković Institute for Interdisciplinary Building Process Management, TU Wien, Vienna, Austria

Delelegne A. Tefera Department of Agribusiness and Value ChainManagement, Hawassa University, Awassa, Ethiopia

Eveline Corine ten Hoor University of Groningen, Groningen, The Netherlands

Andrew Terry The University of Sydney Business School, The University of Sydney, Sydney, Australia

Tomasz Tomaszewski Faculty of Economics, University of Gdansk, Gdansk, Poland

Isabel Estrada Vaquero University of Groningen, Groningen, The Netherlands

Carmen Weigelt A.B. Freeman School of Business, Tulane University, New Orleans, LA, USA

Josef Windsperger Department of Business Decisions and Analytics, University of Vienna, Vienna, Austria

Muhammad Zafar Yaqub Department of Business Administration, Faculty of Economics and Administration, King Abdulaziz Universtiy, Jeddah, Kingdom of Saudi Arabia

Design and Management of Interfirm Networks: An Introduction

Josef Windsperger, Gérard Cliquet, George W. J. Hendrikse, and Marijana Srećković

Abstract The design and management of interfirm networks has become a very important research field both in economics and management in the last two decades. The current book presents new theoretical perspectives and empirical results on the design and management of franchise networks, cooperatives, alliances, and clusters.

The design and management of interfirm networks, such as franchise chains, cooperatives, alliances, joint ventures, and licensing, has become a very important research field in organizational economics, strategic management, organization theory, and industrial marketing in the last two decades (Nooteboom 1999; Gulati 2007; Baker et al. 2008; Ménard 2013; Ehrmann et al. 2013; Hendrikse et al. 2015; Windsperger et al. 2015; Lusch et al. 2016; Hendrikse et al. 2017; Aarikka-Stenroos and Ritala 2017; Koch and Windsperger 2017). The current book addresses theoretical and empirical perspectives on the design and management of franchise networks, cooperatives, alliances and clusters by focusing on the following topics:

1. *Franchise networks*: Innovation in plural form franchise networks; role of peer trust in franchise networks; business model innovation in franchising; organizational innovation through microfranchising; CSR and competitive advantages

J. Windsperger (✉)
University of Vienna, Vienna, Austria
e-mail: josef.windsperger@univie.ac.at

G. Cliquet
Institute of Management of Rennes (IAE), Université de Rennes 1, Rennes, France
e-mail: Gerard.cliquet@univ-rennes1.fr

G. W. J. Hendrikse
Rotterdam School of Management, Erasmus University Rotterdam, Rotterdam, The Netherlands
e-mail: ghendrikse@rsm.nl

M. Srećković
Institute for Interdisciplinary Building Process Management, TU Wien, Vienna, Austria
e-mail: marijana.sreckovic@tuwien.ac.at

© Springer Nature Switzerland AG 2019   1
J. Windsperger et al. (eds.), *Design and Management of Interfirm Networks*,
Contributions to Management Science,
https://doi.org/10.1007/978-3-030-29245-4_1

of franchise chains; institutional influence of the franchise business model on competitiveness of healthcare clinics; principles for the design and management of fair Franchise Advisory Councils; and decision model for franchisee location

2. *Cooperatives:* Horizon and portfolio investment constraints in cooperatives; member heterogeneity and exit in cooperatives; demographic, economic, and institutional factors as determinants of farmers' decisions to participate in cooperatives; and opportunistic and cognitive differences between a cooperative and an investor-owned group

3. *Alliances:* Determinants of collocation for supplier-client knowledge-based coordination; tensions and governance in industry-university alliances; co-evolution of clusters and the role of trans-local linkages; effects of cluster cooperation on value creation; oligopolistic interaction and the choice between exports, FDI and strategic alliances; and public-private partnerships in the healthcare sector

A first version of the papers was initially presented at the eighth international conference on Economics and Management of Networks (*EMNet*—https://emnet. univie.ac.at/) that took place at the University of Havana, from November 15 to November 17, 2018, in Havana, Cuba.

The book is structured in three parts:

Franchise Networks
Cooperatives
Alliances

1 Franchise Networks

The study of *Nguyen and Cliquet* deals with the role of organizational forms in the innovation process of retail and service chains and more specifically within plural form networks. The authors examine how the degree of organizational mix, measured by the PCO (proportion of company-owned outlets) chosen by network operators, can influence the innovation climate considered as important criterion for innovative organization evaluation. It is hypothesized that the effects of plural form on the innovation climate are mediated by the mutual learning between franchise and company-owned outlets. Results from French networks support the mediation hypothesis and provide evidence that equilibrium in the proportion of franchised and company units is related to a high level of mutual learning, thereby positively influencing the network climate for innovation. Overall, this study contributes to the franchise literature by exploring the role of plural form as governance mechanism for creating a positive innovation climate in the franchise network.

Croonen and Hamming contribute to franchising research by developing an integrative theoretical framework on antecedents and consequences of peer trust. The authors conduct a systematic literature review on the antecedents and consequences of co-worker trust within organizations and translate these insights to a franchising context to propose their integrative framework on antecedents and consequences of franchisees' peer trust. The framework distinguishes four types of antecedents of peer trust: franchisee (i.e., trustor) characteristics, peer (i.e., trustee) characteristics, franchisor characteristics, and franchise network characteristics. Moreover, they distinguish three types of consequences of peer trust: perceptual/attitudinal outcomes, behavioral outcomes, and performance outcomes. Finally, avenues for future research on peer trust in franchise networks and potential implications for franchisors regarding the management of peer trust are discussed.

Successful franchisors build formats, devise systems, and develop network expansion models which accommodate the unique characteristics of the business and the prevailing market conditions as well as wider social trends. The study of *Di Lernia and Terry* challenges the standard franchising paradigm and suggests that there are four distinct franchising models—business format franchising, brand franchising, quasi-franchising, and flexible franchising—and presents a taxonomy to accommodate them. The focus of the study is on *flexible franchising*—a new franchise model which eschews the formulaic uniformity of conventional franchising and explicitly and intentionally embraces and incorporates as its integral feature the franchisee's flexibility to bring his or her own brand of entrepreneurship to the franchised business. The development of flexible franchising in practice is examined through case studies on two innovative Australian franchise systems.

The study of *Nunes, Silva, Fadairo, and Seas* deals with the economic rationality underlying organizational innovations in franchising and the rationale behind them. Using Brazilian primary data, they show that spatial distribution of microfranchised units is sensitive to the sector of activity. The results suggest that labor-intensive activities are suitable for microfranchised units in less populated municipalities. In addition, the empirical results indicate that the spatial distribution of microfranchising reflects network growth. Larger networks, in terms of number of units as well as territorial extension, are more likely to be present in smaller markets than smaller networks. Older networks (incumbents) that had a business experience prior to franchising tend to concentrate their franchised units in densely populated areas, while entrants that adopted microfranchising from their foundation target unexplored markets in less populated municipalities.

Although corporate social responsibility (CSR) is a widely researched topic, there is a lack of its application in the franchise literature. The integration of CSR into the franchise business model is vital as it affects the franchise firm's growth and survival. Based on resource-based and organizational capabilities theory, *Jell-Ojobor* explains how CSR strategy impacts the creation of intangible brand name assets as critical source of competitive advantage and hence increased financial performance of franchise firms. Using data from Austrian franchise firms, the results show that the CSR dimensions, such as economic, legal, ethical, and philanthropic responsibility, have a positive impact on the creation of brand name assets. Specifically, philanthropic responsibility strategy has the greatest impact on brand name assets, followed by legal, ethical, and economic responsibility strategy. Overall, this is the first study in franchising which explains the strategic role of CSR.

Gorovaia, Sanfelix, and Puig use insights from the institutional theory to study the competitiveness of healthcare clinics in Spain. The environment of the healthcare services is highly institutionalized: professional associations are state agents responsible for the extensive regulation. Recently emerged franchise chains become subject for imitation by creating institutionalized routines from within and increasing competitive pressures for other industry players. While the sector is dominated by the independent doctors, franchise organizations are becoming more popular and show steady growth rates. The franchise business model in the healthcare is evolving: while the core activity—provision of a healthcare service—cannot be standardized, as the independent judgment of a healthcare professional is legally protected, franchise chains standardize management of the healthcare clinics to achieve efficiency and economies of scale. The survey of the healthcare professionals in Spain shows how professional associations and franchise chains impact the field and provide empirical support to the hypotheses.

Franchise Advisory Councils (FACs) form an important managerial instrument for franchisors to create and/or maintain franchisees' trust in the fair and effective functioning of their franchising networks. *Croonen and Bleeker* build on procedural fairness theory and insights from studies in trade journals to develop a theoretical framework with seven core principles that affect franchisees' perceptions regarding the fair management of their FACs. These core principles are the consistency principle, the bias-suppression principle, the accuracy principle, the correctability principle, the representativeness principle, the ethicality principle, and the interactional principle. For each core principle, the authors distinguish specific managerial principles that help in fulfilling it. As a result, they present an extensive framework with principles for the design and management of fair FACs ('the fair FAC framework').

García-Castro and Mula present a franchisee location model applied to fast food restaurants. The methodology is based on research of environmental factors that influence the choice of the site. A GIS software, the determination of gravity centers, and a multicriteria matrix give a precise idea about which locations could be chosen; then an analytic hierarchy process (AHP) enables an assessment of every location alternative. An empirical application is offered in the city of Alicante in Spain.

2 Cooperatives

Cook (1995) formulates five problems which provide a challenge for cooperatives: free rider problem, horizon problem, portfolio problem, control problem, and the influence cost problem. He has argued that these problems stem from member heterogeneity. These five problems have been researched extensively. The study by *Franken and Cook* provides empirical evidence regarding two of these problems: the horizon and portfolio problem. The horizon problem entails that cooperatives will underinvest in long-term projects. The source of the problem is the limited transferability of ownership rights and member heterogeneity. Old members have a disincentive to contribute to long-term investment strategies, for example, brand promotion, market research, and new product development, because the productive life of the asset is longer than their remaining membership period. They will therefore support investment opportunities with a shorter productive life of assets than the efficient one. This logic is appealing, but various conceptual articles regarding the horizon problem have formulated arguments to question the relevance of horizon problem. For example, old members may transfer their farm to one of their children. Franken and Cook use mail surveys of three agricultural cooperatives to determine the relevance of this problem in cooperative practice. They characterize three horizon problems, i.e., the current obligation horizon problem, the classic short-term horizon problem, and the wait-to-receive horizon problem. They find some evidence for the first two horizon problems and strong support for the third horizon problem.

The portfolio problem of cooperatives captures that the diversification decision of a cooperative is influenced by the farm portfolio of members. Members tie often a substantial fraction of their farm portfolio to one cooperative because they have usually a limited number of crops and each crop is handled by one cooperative. Members will try to establish their desired farm portfolio by influencing the diversification decisions of a cooperative. Franken and Cook distinguish a vertical portfolio problem and the classical (lateral) portfolio problem. All three cooperatives show evidence of the vertical portfolio problem, and one cooperative shows strong evidence of the lateral portfolio problem.

Hoehler starts with the observation that members of cooperatives are becoming increasingly diverse and heterogeneous in terms of their farms, personal, and product characteristics. It has been argued repeatedly that this is problematic for cooperatives. A prominent example is the homogeneity hypothesis of Hansmann (1996). Increasing heterogeneity should therefore result in many members leaving the cooperative. However, this is not what happens according to Hoehler. She illustrates this claim with the cases of the cooperatives DMK and Arla. A theoretical framework is developed to formulate new hypotheses for the effect and meaning of member heterogeneity. It is inspired by the model of Hirschman (1970) and various behavioral and collective action concepts. The framework formulates hypotheses regarding cooperative exit based on performance, perceived fairness, cooperative identification, voice, loyalty, proportion of rational egoists, and the number and quality of alternatives.

Tefera and Bijman analyze the changing role and membership of cooperatives in the malt barley sector in Ethiopia. The sector has changed due to the entry of foreign brewers in the Ethiopian brewing industry. New standards did arise regarding quality, volume, and timing. Consider first the changing role of cooperatives. Cooperatives play an important role for farmers to benefit from the new opportunities by becoming more business oriented. The authors organize their data by distinguishing various roles of cooperatives.

First, the traditional role of cooperatives in the malt barley chain was the input supply function, i.e., the distribution of inputs to farmers. The entry of foreign brewers has had an impact on the input supply as well as the output marketing function of cooperatives. The results show that cooperatives facilitate the technical trainings regarding productivity and quality improvement, and organize farm management trainings, which have a positive impact on yield as well as on malt barley quality. Farmers receive price premiums of up to 20% due to the upgrading of products. The benefits materialize only when the participants are linked to brewers and malt factories.

Second, foreign brewers encourage also that cooperatives develop their output marketing function. Capacity building and management trainings provided by brewing companies enhance the management of malt barley cooperatives, which in turn improve their marketing orientation and performance. Low performance of the cooperative in marketing services was mainly attributed by the respondents to weak organizational capacities, low educated leaders, limited financial means, and a difficult relationship with the Union of 90 primary cooperatives.

Third, in modern supply chains characterized by contractual arrangements and quality requirements, cooperatives perform also a brokering role. They provide services such as collecting and distributing market information, contract negotiation, bargaining with buyers, and aggregating, transporting, and storing grains. This supports their participation in the emerging malt barley supply chains, which has a positive impact on farmers' income and livelihoods.

The membership of cooperatives has changed due to the above developments. Cooperative members differ from non-members. Members of marketing cooperatives have better access to extension services, a more entrepreneurial attitude, and show more innovativeness than non-members. Cooperative membership is biased toward farmers with more productive resources in terms of larger livestock holdings, farm size, and malt barley area and has significantly more contact with extension services than non-members. The distance to the market has a positive effect on the probability of cooperative membership. Membership has a positive effect on malt barley production and product quality and hence on malt barley prices. Cooperative membership has a positive impact on food crop income and total farm income.

Saïsset and Codron investigate the governance of organizations in the French apple industry by comparing a cooperative and an investor-owned group. The authors are inspired by the transaction cost economics approach of Williamson (1985). The subsequent development of hybrid organizational forms by Ménard (2013) is used to describe and classify the two apple groups. The cooperative is characterized as a hybrid with a strategic center, while the investor-owned group is characterized as an information-sharing hybrid.

Another development regarding transaction costs economics as initiated by Williamson is the governance of bounded rationality. Williamson distinguishes asset specificity, frequency, and uncertainty as attributes of transactions and adopts the behavioral assumptions of opportunism and bounded rationality. He highlights the implications of the behavioral assumption of opportunism in his research, but is rather silent on bounded rationality. A prominent example of the cognitive branch of transaction costs economics is Nooteboom (2009). *Saïsset and Codron* contribute to the development of the cognitive governance of organizations. It results in identifying transaction complexity as a fourth attribute of transactions. This is relevant in the apple industry due to the increase in sanitary requirements. The cognitive governance implications for the two apple groups are analyzed.

3 Alliances

Miller and Weigelt examine the impact of client niche market position and task complexity on the governance of supplier-provided knowledge work. Besides client firm size and location, the decision to collocate knowledge-based tasks depends on whether the focal client firm and its supplier need to work together closely, either so the supplier can incorporate the client's specialized knowledge about its internal operations and customers or for ongoing customization of the service to support complex operations. However, collocation of services involving software is less likely when remote service is facilitated by broadband internet infrastructure. The authors demonstrate that client positioning in the product market affects the services it receives from suppliers. Niche positioning requires specific client knowledge, such that collocation is the more efficient way to customize the supplier's product. Their findings also affirm the relationship between client task complexity and tighter governance of supplier-provided knowledge work, consistent with prior work on alliance design. They show that greater task complexity leads to collocation of supplier-provided knowledge work. In conclusion their research highlights that in knowledge-based services, particularly, entire teams may be placed at the client's location for a period of time, especially at the start of an engagement or when a new project begins.

ten Hoor and Estrada investigate tensions and governance in industry-university (IU) alliances. In their research they explore how these tensions emerge and can be effectively managed through an exploratory study of two IU alliances in the energy sector. Based on their cases, four types of dissimilarities (i.e., orientation-based, routine-based, administrative, and personal) are identified that may lead to different types of tensions (i.e., orientation, routine, transaction, and distinctive), which in turn may be addressed through different governance mechanisms (i.e., communication, flexibility, contracts, and hierarchy). Their exploratory framework provides initial insight into the connections between inter-partner dissimilarities, tension, and governance in the formation phase of IU alliances. They identify the presence of what they refer to as distinctive barriers, barriers that (1) are related to dissimilarities between industry and university partners in the alliance, but (2) do not seem to be specifically apparent in all IU alliances. They argue that these barriers can be managed through hierarchy. They conclude with the hope that future studies in the field can build upon and extend their framework to further explore the links between dissimilarities, tension, and governance in IU alliances. In addition, managers involved in the formation of these alliances should make use of their framework to timely detect problematic dissimilarities that can lead to tensions in the alliance and, thus, anticipate tension in the process of alliance design.

Mariotti, Yaqub, and Haider examine trans-local relationships and their changing dynamics over time, particularly emphasizing their knowledge flows. The underlying proposition is that the clusters are not isolated entities and that inter-cluster ties are as significant as local ties in sustaining the co-evolution of clusters. They use historical and retrospective analyses to study the interlinkages between the

NASCAR cluster and the UK's motorsport industry. Their findings highlight that the structure of the interfirm ties between the two clusters has evolved over time with a marked increase in the number of linkages established and the transfer of more sophisticated knowledge and components. At the same time, the research highlights some impediments that have delayed the transition of the NASCAR cluster to a more open entity. The authors propound that co-location and proximity are poor indicators of the structure of clusters and that the inter-cluster linkages play an important role in their co-evolution.

Kuczewska, Morawska, and Tomaszewski investigate the effects of cluster cooperation which might affect company value creation. Their study has been developed among companies cooperating and competing within two Polish business clusters: aviation and fish products. They argue that the rise in productivity co-occurs with the geographic concentration of entities, but is independent from strengthening of isolation with relation to other entities. The mere presence of the geographical concentration of enterprises is not enough to reveal the benefits of cluster cooperation affecting productivity. The closeness of formal and informal relations between enterprises and research centers and R&D organizations does not affect building relations between entities. In extreme cases, it negatively correlates with productivity. Hence the conclusion is that a strong concentration and specialization of entities in a certain region does not always result in a highly functioning cluster with global extensions but either in the development of cluster initiatives or an earlier stage of formal cluster development. They conclude that cooperation between specialized and geographically concentrated entities shows benefits affecting the increase in productivity. However, the enterprises' awareness of them benefiting from cluster cooperation, or the formalization of a cluster, is not an essential factor in the process of achieving additional benefits affecting value creation.

Morasch examines the role of oligopolistic interaction for the choice between exports, foreign direct investment, and strategic alliances. The decision over exports vs. foreign direct investment (FDI) is usually discussed in an extension of the so-called Melitz model where firms with heterogeneous costs compete in a monopolistically competitive industry. The present paper starts from a situation where a potential foreign entrant would be just indifferent between exports and FDI in such a setting. However, by assuming oligopolistic interaction, strategic considerations are also taken into account. It is shown how the strategic impact of lower marginal cost makes FDI more attractive in a Cournot setting, while exports are preferable under price competition in a market with differentiated goods. Beyond that it is also explored how a strategic alliance with a local incumbent could be a superior alternative for market entry.

The public sector has modified its financing methods, going from traditional debt instruments to new tools based on partnerships with the private sector. These are alliances between the public and the private sector regarding infrastructure investments, where the private partner cooperates in providing, managing, and financing services and structures that were traditionally a responsibility of the public sector. These collaborations are called 'public-private partnerships', and they have now become a commonly used investment strategy for all public administrations.

In their study, *Colasanti, Frondizi, Meneguzzo, and Rossi* analyze public-private partnerships, first at a more general level and then by considering their application to the healthcare sector, providing a state of the art of relevant experiences in Latin America.

References

Aarikka-Stenroos L, Ritala P (2017) Network management in the era of ecosystems: systematic review and management framework. Ind Mark Manag 67:23–36

Baker GR, Gibbons R, Murphy KJ (2008) Strategic alliances: bridges between islands of conscious power. J Jpn Int Econ 22:146–163

Cook ML (1995) The future of U.S. agricultural cooperatives: a neo-institutional approach. Am J Agric Econ 77(5):1153–1159

Ehrmann T, Windsperger J, Cliquet G, Hendrikse GWJ (eds) (2013) Network governance: alliances, cooperatives and franchise chains. Springer, Heidelberg

Gulati R (2007) Managing network resources: alliances, affiliations and other relational assets. Oxford University Press, Oxford

Hansmann HB (1996) The ownership of enterprise. The Belknap Press of Harvard University Press, Cambridge, MA

Hendrikse GWJ, Hippman P, Windsperger J (2015) Trust, transaction costs and contractual incompleteness in franchising. Small Bus Econ 44:867–888

Hendrikse GWJ, Cliquet G, Ehrmann T, Windsperger J (eds) (2017) Management and governance of networks: franchising, cooperatives and strategic alliances. Springer, Heidelberg

Hirschman AO (1970) Exit, voice, and loyalty: responses to decline in firms, organizations, and states. Harvard University Press, Cambridge, MA

Koch T, Windsperger J (2017) Seeing through the network: competitive advantage in the digital economy. J Organ Des 6(6):1–30

Lusch RF, Vargo SI, Gustafsson A (2016) Fostering a trans-disciplinary perspective of service ecosystems. J Bus Res 69(8):2957–2963

Ménard C (2013) Hybrid modes of organization: alliances, joint ventures, networks, and other 'strange' animals. In: Gibbons R, Roberts J (eds) The handbook of organizational economics. Princeton University Press, Princeton, NJ, pp 1066–1108

Nooteboom B (1999) Inter-firm alliances: analysis and design. Routledge, London, New York

Nooteboom B (2009) A cognitive theory of the firm: learning, governance and dynamic capabilities. Edward Elgar Publishing, Cheltenham, Northampton

Williamson OE (1985) The economic institutions of capitalism. Free Press, New York

Windsperger J, Cliquet G, Ehrmann T, Hendrikse GWJ (eds) (2015) Interfirm networks: franchising, cooperatives and strategic alliances. Springer, Heidelberg

Part I
Franchise Networks

Innovation Climate in Plural Form Franchise Networks: The Mediator Role of Mutual Learning

Nguyen Minh Ngoc and Gérard Cliquet

Abstract This paper deals with the role of organizational forms in the innovation activities of retail and service chains and more specifically within plural form networks where franchised and company-owned units (e.g., stores, hotels, restaurants) coexist. The main purpose of this study is to predict the influence of the organizational form of franchise networks by assessing the effect of plural form organization on the innovation climate of these networks. This paper examines how the degree of organizational mix, measured by the PCO (proportion of company-owned outlets) chosen by network operators, can influence the innovation climate considered as important criterion for innovative organization evaluation. It is hypothesized that the effects of plural form on the innovation climate are mediated by the mutual learning between franchised and company-owned outlets. Results from French networks support the mediation hypothesis and provide evidence that equilibrium in the proportion of franchised and company units is related to a high level of mutual learning, thereby positively influencing the network climate for innovation. Overall, this study contributes to the franchise literature by exploring the role of plural form as governance mechanism for creating a positive innovation climate in the franchise network.

1 Introduction

Obviously, a franchisor has a greater chance to develop a business by implementing new ideas and, then, by renewing as often as possible the innovation process. For instance, KFC uses now artificial intelligence within its customer relationship management (CRM) in its Beijing restaurants. Franchisees can also be of great help

N. Minh Ngoc
CREM UMR 6211CNRS, IGR-IAE Université Rennes 1, Rennes, France

G. Cliquet (✉)
Institute of Management of Rennes (IAE), Université de Rennes 1, Rennes, France
e-mail: gerard.cliquet@univ-rennes1.fr

© Springer Nature Switzerland AG 2019
J. Windsperger et al. (eds.), *Design and Management of Interfirm Networks*,
Contributions to Management Science,
https://doi.org/10.1007/978-3-030-29245-4_2

in this innovation process: Jim Delligatti, a *McDonald's* franchisee in Pittsburg, created the *Big Mac*, and Lou Groen, in Cincinnati, the *Filet-O-Fish*. Hence, we can pose that, in franchise networks, both franchisors and franchisees can innovate (Cliquet and Nguyen 2004).

Bradach (1998) exposes that plural form networks seem to be an efficient system in terms of innovation due to complementarities of the two forms, franchising and company arrangement, and to the mutual learning process between them. Lewin-Solomons (1999) shows that the proportion of company-owned outlets (PCO) within the network must be high enough to let the chain have a significant stake in innovation and low enough to make franchisees involved in the innovation process. However a too high PCO could scary both franchisees and potential franchisees to join the network. Franchisees could be afraid of potential conflicts and costs (Perrigot and Herrbach 2012). Potential franchisees could see a risk of too high entry fee (Cyrenne 2014) and feel a too small interest from the franchisor's part and be just considered a less costly way to fill in territory coverage within the network (Cliquet and Pénard 2012).

Like joint ventures and alliances, franchising extends organizational boundaries, and this extension affects innovativeness within organizations (Mallapragada and Srinivasan 2017) and makes innovation more difficult to implement. In franchising, this is shown by the role of franchisees which can be a strong resource for innovation as well, and many franchisors do agree with that (Cox and Mason 2007) despite Wattel's (1968–69) opinion considering that franchisors do prefer hardworking to innovative franchisees. But, most franchisees have a good understanding of their business and sometimes more than the franchisor itself (Ralston 1989). This is the reason why franchisors should better recruit franchisees with a good perceived innovativeness (Jambulingam and Nevin 1999).

Then, a dilemma appears: should the franchisor focus on standardization or on flexibility (Pardo-del-Val et al. 2014)? In other terms, should the franchisor focus on economies of scale or local adaptation, on financial issues, or on franchisees' innovative capabilities? The definition of core vs. peripheral elements (Kaufmann and Eroglu 1998) of the franchising concept becomes critical: in case of standardization priorities, the franchisor tends to enlarge core elements, whereas in the opposite case, more peripheral elements can be good bases for franchisees' innovations. Szulanski and Jensen (2008) have shown that copying exactly the original concept is more efficient for growth when the franchisor exports it, and so local adaptation can be a hinder. Hence, it would be of interest to know more about the influence of the PCO concerning this dilemma and the role of franchisees in the innovation process of a franchise network.

Based on a literature review on innovation management in retail and service networks and on an empirical research on franchise networks in France, this research examines how the PCO implemented by business format franchise network operators can influence the innovation climate as highlighted by Strutton et al. (1995) in its links with solidarity within franchise networks. Climate strength within organizations is considered an important criterion (González-Romá et al. 2002) especially for innovative organizations (Baer and Frese 2003). It is hypothesized that the effects of the plural form through the PCO on the innovation climate are mediated by the mutual learning process (Bradach 1997) between franchised and company-owned outlets. Overall, this study contributes to the franchise literature by exploring the role of plural form as mechanism for creating a positive innovation climate in the franchise network.

This article starts with a literature review on the role of plural form organization in retail and service network management to highlight the main concepts of this research—innovation climate and mutual learning—and to formulate hypotheses (Sect. 1). Section 2 describes the data and the methodology. The results are displayed in Sect. 3 and discussed in Sect. 4. The paper closes with some remarks including contributions, limits, and research perspectives.

2 Literature Review

Plural form networks are the most common organizational forms within business format franchise retail and service networks. Bradach (1997, 1998) has highlighted their role in developing innovation.

2.1 Innovation Within the Plural Form Model

A retail and/or service chain can be organized as a mono status organization, i.e., either as a purely franchised chain or as a wholly owned chain, or can be a plural form one through a mix of both franchised and company-owned units. Since the seminal article on plural form organization as a response to the threefold stake between market, hierarchy, and trust (Bradach and Eccles 1989), a considerable amount of research in franchising has investigated the plural form organization within franchised chains based on the tapered integration theory (Bradach 1997), the property rights theory (Windsperger and Dant 2006), a risk-based approach (Bürkle and Posselt 2008), or the institutional theory (Barthélemy 2011). Other articles compare various theories supposed to explain plural form organizations in franchised chains: resource-based theory, signaling theory, and tapered integration theory (Dant and Kaufmann 2003) and property rights, resource scarcity, and transaction cost theory (Windsperger 2004).

Bradach's model (1998) on US restaurant chain management was the first attempt to describe managerial implications of plural form networks. The author argued that using simultaneously company and franchise systems could help a chain to meet its four basic management challenges: (1) growing by adding units, (2) maintaining the uniformity of the concept across units, (3) responding locally to competition attacks, and (4) system-wide adaptation. The basic idea is that each structure has its strengths and weaknesses, and a plural form organization enables this arrangement mix to reinforce strengths and lower weaknesses of the chain. It has nothing to do with a hybridization (Bradach 1998) between company-owned and franchising systems which can be observed in management contract systems (Dimou et al. 2003) where the "franchisee" is just an investor and the franchisor is both the chain operator and the outlet operator like in the hotel industry (Chen and Dimou 2005). Plural form organization takes advantages of the complementary characteristics of these two arrangements. Then the overall structure will be stronger than either one operating by itself.

Every challenge enhanced in Bradach's model can be related to each other. This research is focusing on innovation within chains and is particularly related to the fourth challenge dealing with the system-wide adaptation. But it will be shown later on that it is also linked to the three other challenges. As far as the territorial expansion is concerned (Challenge 1), a fast diffusion of innovations throughout the network is a key factor of success of these innovations as Rubin (1978) raises the question of geographical dispersion in franchising. Brickley and Dark (1987) and Carney and Gedajlovic (1991) confirm the positive relationship between franchising and geographical dispersion. According to this thesis and to the agency theory (Lafontaine 1992), company-owned units are usually established near the central unit (the operator), while franchisees are rather in remote locations. Therefore, the network operator can minimize monitoring cost over company-owned units which need more control comparing to franchisees as independent partners. Other arguments focus also on cost benefits: monitoring costs (Brickley and Dark 1987), information gathering costs (Minkler 1992), and agency costs uncertainty (Ehrmann and Spranger 2004). But that does not fit with the innovation process which requires a smarter dispersion of company-owned units to facilitate the diffusion.

Store networks need therefore innovations which can be considered as a way to response locally against competitors (Challenge 3). However, this requires a stronger effort in maintaining the uniformity of the concept (Challenge 2) which is more difficult while the proportion of franchisees is higher (Manolis et al. 1995). But a better understanding of plural form advantage in system-wide adaptation needs rather a deeper study of the innovation process within retail and service networks.

2.2 Plural Form Networks and the Innovation Process

Di Benedetto (1999) finds two key success factors at the strategic level when launching a new product: (1) having cross-functional teams make decision concerning manufacturing, distribution/logistics, and marketing/sales strategy and (2) having logistics involved in formulating distribution strategies, coordinating with sales management, developing inventory strategies, and planning after-sale service. This author distinguishes also four key success factors at the tactical level: (1) high quality of selling effort, advertising, service, and technical support; (2) good management of key aspects of the launch (marketing plans, overall launch direction, and the launch itself); (3) good management of the support programs (distribution channel activities, sales force training, good pricing level, and advertising program execution); and (4) launch timing relative to competition and customers.

In a retail and service network, indeed stakes are both similar and different from those of manufacturing companies. These stakes are similar especially in case of product innovation in a retail network because of the necessity of marketing and communication plans, coordination between sales (in-store) and logistics, management of inventories, sales and customer relationships, etc., everything which needs a hierarchical management which is more difficult in a franchise system but still harder out of such a system for independent businesses having left the network (Knott 2001). And it can be immediately added that the presence of company-owned units strengthens this innovation management (Lewin-Solomons 1999) especially concerning coordination problems which are considered usually difficult to solve in a franchise system (Michael 2003). Controlling such a network during the innovation process is a real challenge (Karmeni et al. 2017) specifically when this innovation concerns the global network adaptation especially in a largely dispersed set of outlets. Innovation may be the good way to maintain competitive advantages when facing strong contenders with a large territory coverage (Wu et al. 2009).

Sorenson and Sørensen (2001) do affirm that plural form organizations reinforce the innovation process. They all argue that the dual structure is the result of synergistic effects between franchised and company-owned outlets. Conclusions derived from Bradach's research in US restaurant chains have led to a better understanding of the plural form network advantages at the marketing and strategic sides. Indeed, the plural form organization provides retail and service networks with a significant number of advantages in terms of marketing at store level: as information on local markets (Minkler 1990), concept control and product offers (Bradach 1997), brand value (Bai and Tao 2000), adaptation capacities through the concept evolution (Sorenson and Sørensen 2001), innovation stimulation (Lewin-Solomons 1999), quality respect (Michael 2000), location of units, capabilities of tactical reaction against local competition, and marketing stimulation (Bradach 1998).

Franchisors may locate their own outlets. Hence, the quality of unit location can be considered as a key factor for innovation diffusion and innovation success within a retail and service network and not only for obvious market reasons. Within a plural form network, the relative geographical position of both franchised and company-owned units in a local market is critical. Forward and Fulop (1997) consider franchising a capable form for innovation dissemination, but it is not so easy. This point has received very little attention from academic researchers so far except an attempt by Pirkul et al. (1987) but implemented far before the whole present body of knowledge about plural form organization in franchise networks. Locating smartly company-owned outlets is critical for plural form networks in so far as these outlets considered as ‚pilots" or franchisor showrooms are used by franchisors to test new products or services in a first step of the innovation process and then in a second step can be used to train franchisees specifically for service or organizational innovations (Bradach 1998). Such an effective organization constitutes a good signal to attract future franchisees (Gallini and Lutz 1992). The coexistence of franchise and company arrangements influences the quality of the point-of-sale location to improve the innovation diffusion process.

Franchisees, as independent business people, do not hesitate to tell frankly to their franchisor what they think about an innovation (Bradach 1998), but franchisees may not agree with the franchisor about an innovation (Lewin-Solomons 1997, 2000). Franchisees can be considered a source of innovation: At *McDonald's*, owner-operators (as the franchisees are called) are involved in the innovation process, and they invented very successful products like the *Big Mac*, *Egg McMuffin* (Gubman and Russell 2006), *Filet-O-Fish*, and hot apple pies (Noren 1990). Conversely, the presence of company-owned units sometimes limits deviant attempts by franchisees, i.e., new products or services initiated and introduced in market by franchisees without requiring franchisor's acceptance, hence the dilemma uniformity/adaptation (Cox and Mason 2007). Franchisors tend to operate their units to maintain and uphold the brand value that is one of the main objectives of retail and service chains. That means the proportion of company-owned units is positively correlated with the measurement of the brand value (Lafontaine and Shaw 2005). An increase of this proportion implies stronger incentives for the franchisor to promote the brand and enhance the managerial control within network. In the innovation process, such plural form management can be of great interest.

In terms of commercial stimulation and innovation, the co-presence of franchisees and company-owned units provides the network operator with different contributions: franchisees are a source of ideas (Elango and Fried 1977), whereas company outlets enable the franchisor to have new concept tested before it comes to fruition (Bradach 1998). Moreover the franchisor depends on franchisees for an important feedback because, compared to company-owned managers, they respond more effectively (Dant et al. 1992). Bradach (1998) has discussed the uniformity accomplishment of the plural form chain through ratcheting and modeling processes. In the ratcheting process, the high performance of each side sets a benchmark for the others to pursue: the franchisor uses company unit results to influence the franchisees' behavior. Conversely, the strong performance of franchisees can put pressure on company units. This double direction process is important to initiate innovation. The modeling process aims to emulate franchisees in implementing policies and practices successfully used in the company arrangement.

The literature review shows how much plural form contributes to the innovation process. After having emphasized Bradach's challenges, innovation climate is now introduced to better understand how this process works.

3   Plural Form and Innovation Climate

The conceptualization of innovation climate within a firm is derived from the broader concept of organizational climate. This concept is used to describe the day-to-day psychological environment, attitudes, feelings, and the emotional atmosphere that has profound impact on people's behavior and ability to solve problems, make decisions, and communicate (Lewin 1951). Climate was also defined as the emotional atmosphere that surrounds and envelops the interpersonal relations among and between people in the organization (Solomon et al. 1998). Some researchers have approached organizational climate as a multidimensional, organizational construct (e.g., Moran and Volkwein 1992; Ott 1989; Schneider 1975). However, others have seen it as a set of more narrowly defined constructs such as safety climate (Zohar 1980, 2000), customer service climate (Schneider et al. 1980), innovation climate (Abbey and Dickson 1983), and ethics climate (Dickson et al. 2001).

3.1 Innovation Climate and PCO

The innovation climate of an organization is something that is intangible but real (Parry 1987). Intangible means that it is difficult to define and almost impossible to evaluate in terms of costs and benefits; it is real because it affects the way people behave, their propensity to generate ideas, their willingness to share ideas with colleagues, and the motivation to develop the ideas into projects and projects into profits. Moukwa (1995) defined the creative climate as an environment where people feel free to express their ideas, serving as a solid base for innovation project of the organization.

Ekvall (1983, 1986) measured creative organizational climate in various Swedish organizations and was able to uncover a number of environmental factors that influence peoples' attitudes, feelings, and behaviors. He showed that these psychological dimensions have tremendous impact upon the success of the organization or work unit. This work clearly demonstrates that firms that can consistently and successfully innovate have more significant differences in climate than those firms that have fewer innovations. Table 1 summarizes the climate characteristics of more and less innovative organization.

This research uses ten dimensions (Isaksen et al. 2000) to determine measurement scale for the innovation climate variable in the store network. These dimensions help firms to better understand creativity areas within their workplace: (1) challenge and involvement, (2) freedom, (3) dynamism, (4) trust and openness, (5) idea time, (6) playfulness and humor, (7) conflict, (8) idea support, (9) debates, and finally (10) risk-taking.

As this research strives to link plural form and network's climate for innovation, several ideas have emerged from the literature. There are complementarities between franchise and company arrangement to maintain quality and homogeneity while promoting innovation (Bradach 1997). Lewin-Solomons (1999) justifies the existence of the two forms as a commitment device used by the franchisor to give franchisees incentives to innovate and concludes that the PCO must be low enough to make franchisees feeling innovation important and high enough to let the chain have a significant stake in the innovation process. This statement is consistent with Bradach's (1998) proposition that the most innovative chains are those where the PCO falls in the middle range, not at the extremes.

Table 1 Climate characteristics of innovative and stagnated organization[a]

Innovative organization	Stagnated organization
More open and trusting relationships	Fewer open and trusting relationships
Fewer personal conflicts	Higher frequency of personal conflicts
Higher frequency of debates and discussion about ideas	Fewer debates and less discussion
More likely to take risks	Less likely to take risks
More personal freedom in doing the job	Close and conspicuous supervision
More time to spend in idea generation/evaluation	Less time to spend in idea generation/evaluation
New ideas favorably received and encouraged	New ideas ignored or discouraged
Committed people highly involved in their work	Less commitment and involvement
More fun	Less fun
Workplace more exciting/dynamic	Workplace less exciting/dynamic

[a]http://www.innovationclimatequestionnaire.com/pages/innovation.html

We use the terms "high degree of mix" to refer to networks with a relative balanced PCO, in other words a number of franchised and company-owned stores close to 50%. The purpose is to find empirical support to the influence of the degree of mix on the network climate for innovation and leads to the following hypothesis H1:

H1 The higher the degree of mix, the higher the level of the network climate for innovation.

3.2 Mutual Learning Within a Network: A Mediation Hypothesis

Sorenson and Sørensen (2001) tackle the interactions among units within plural form chains using organizational learning perspectives through more specifically two types of learning: exploitation and exploration. Exploitation involves the incremental improvement of existing routines, whereas exploratory learning seeks to discover potentially useful untapped resources and technologies. The authors argue that in a plural form network, company-owned unit managers tend to engage in exploitation, while franchisees more frequently explore. This is confirmed by a research showing that there is no preference for the independent business compared to franchising as far as innovation is concerned (Méndez et al. 2014). Observations show that in mostly franchised chains, exploration dominated and in mainly company-owned chains, organizational learning usually took the form of exploitation. And as the balance between company-owned and franchised outlets changes, so does the balance between exploitation and exploration and that influences the chain performance.

Before Sorenson and Sørensen's article, Bradach (1998) suggests that franchising and company arrangement complement each other and the complementarities could be achieved through a mutual learning process among units. Virtually, mutual learning can be internal (within an organization) or between companies. Mutual learning involves people getting together to learn new methodologies, to share experiences, and to learn from each other's success and failure. A high level of mutual learning enhances the ability to work in group effectively (Somech and Drach-Zahavy 2013; Weiss et al. 2011), accelerates organizational learning, and avoids duplicating mistakes. Organizations with permanent mutual learning are faster growing and more flexible (Kelner and Slavin 1998).

Nowadays mutual learning referring to knowledge sharing between people and organizations is becoming a competitive strategy. Up to now no empirical work has been done on mutual learning within store networks. The purpose of the present paper is to empirically test the role of mutual learning using data collected from plural form networks. It is assumed that the higher level of the mutual learning is associated with higher level of the network climate for innovation. Mutual learning seems to play a mediator role in the relationship between the degree of mix and the innovation climate, hence the following mediation hypothesis H2:

H2 Mutual learning between franchised and company-owned units mediates the relationship between the degree of mix and the network innovation climate.

4 Methodology

The two hypotheses are tested based on data from a questionnaire survey among franchisors in France. The sample is drawn from the annual franchise directory published by the French Franchise Federation. It comprises a total of 352 plural form business format networks in various sectors, i.e., food, body equipment, home equipment, hotel, restaurant, services, etc. After several preliminary steps in questionnaire development and refinement, including exploratory interviews with franchisors, the final version of the questionnaire is reviewed, approved by franchisors, experts, and researchers in franchising. A total of 90 questionnaires results in a response rate of 25.56% with 85 usable responses.

4.1 Measurement Procedures

The "degree of mix" of the PCO is considered as an explanatory variable. It shows how is the mix of company-owned and franchised units within the retail and/or service network. Data collected on the number of franchised and company-owned

Table 2 Encoding rule of the variable "degree of mix"

Percentage of franchisees	Degree of mix
0 to 5% and 95 to 100%	1
5 to 10% and 90 to 95%	2
10 to 15% and 85 to 90%	3
15 to 20% and 80 to 85%	4
20 to 25% and 75 to 80%	5
25 to 30% and 70 to 75%	6
30 to 35% and 65 to 70%	7
35 to 40% and 60 to 65%	8
40 to 45% and 55 to 60%	9
45 to 55%	10

units enable the computation of the franchisees percentage. The "degree of mix" variable is then coded with value ranging from 1 to 10 from the percentage of franchisees (Table 2). With this encoding system, there is no difference between a mainly company-owned network and a predominantly franchise network. Using this variable, the interest is focusing first on the equilibrium between franchised and company-owned units in a plural form network.

4.2 Innovation Climate

Innovation climate is the dependent variable. The construct of innovation climate is operationalized on the basis of prior research of Ekvall (1986) who proposes a ten dimensions scale to measure creative climate (see above) already used by researchers to assess firm innovative climate. Based on these dimensions and information collected from exploratory interviews with French franchisors, several items are modified and generated to make them appropriate for this research which investigates at network level. Initial instrument to measure the network innovation climate contains 14 items (see Appendix). The respondents, all franchisors, are asked to indicate the extent to which they agree with the statement on a 9 points scale (ranging from 1 = completely disagree to 9 = completely agree). The scales are purified through an exploratory factor analysis (Churchill 1979). Nine items (from 14) showing high factor loading (>0.5) and not loading on multiple factors are retained (Table 3).

The final set of items are then tested for validity using confirmatory factor analysis. Partial least square approach fits well with small sample set (Hair et al. 2014) ($n = 85$). The initial solution of the confirmatory factor analysis does not produce satisfactory result for nine items. In fact, the loading of "dynamism" drops down to 0.1895 and this item is thus eliminated from the scale. A second attempt with eight items has been more successful (Table 4).

Finally, eight items are retained with the alpha Cronbach $\alpha = 0.8445$. The reliability of the construct is then verified. The rho convergent (ρ_{vc}) is also

Table 3 Results of exploratory factor analysis

Items retained after exploratory factor analysis	(Factor 1)
1. Idea support	0.559
2. Resources availability for idea trying	0.723
3. Financial difficulty of franchisee in adopting innovation	0.632
4. Openness and idea sharing	0.760
5. Involvement in innovation	0.739
6. Relax atmosphere	0.753
7. Risk-taking	0.549
8. Innovation adoption	0.773
9. Dynamism	0.522

Table 4 Results of confirmatory factor analysis

Items	Loading
1. Idea support	0.5592
2. Resources availability for idea trying	0.7136
3. Financial difficulty of franchisee in adopting innovation	0.5677
4. Openness and idea sharing	0.8071
5. Involvement in innovation	0.5526
6. Relax atmosphere	0.7917
7. Risk-taking	0.6429
8. Innovation adoption	0.7660

calculated (Fornell and Larcker 1981). The ρ_{vc} value equals 0.47 (quite close to the critical value of 0.5), all loadings are superior to 0.5, and the convergent validity of the construct is therefore acceptable.

4.3   Mutual Learning

Mutual learning implies the frequency to which franchised and company-owned stores learn from each other. Respondents were asked to rate this frequency on a 9 points scale (ranging from 1 = "rarely learn from each other" to 9 = "permanently learn from each other").

5   Results

The data analysis consists in testing the mediation hypothesis. The explanatory or initial variable "degree of mix" is assumed to affect the dependent variable "innovation climate." In a diagrammatic form of Hypothesis 1, the unmediated model is:

(1)

The effect of "degree of mix" on "innovation climate" is assumed to be mediated by "mutual learning" (Hypothesis 2). The mediated model is then:

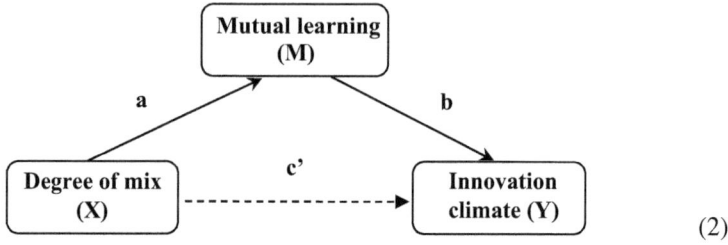

(2)

The mediation analysis follows the Baron and Kenny (1986) procedures. Results show that three preconditions are met (Table 5). First, degree of mix significantly predicts innovation climate ($\beta = 0.301$, $t = 2.875$, $p = 0.005$). This result supports H1. Second, the degree of mix significantly predicts mutual learning ($\beta = 0.464$, $t = 4.778$, $p = 0.000$). Finally, there is a significant effect of mutual learning on innovation climate ($\beta = 0.491$, $t = 4.638$, $p = 0.000$). To establish the mediation effect, the regression coefficient for innovation climate should be nonsignificant. As can be seen in Table 5, the condition is satisfied ($\beta = 0.073$, $t = 0.689$, $p = 0.493$). The variable degree of mix no longer serves as a direct and significant predictor of innovation climate when mutual learning is controlled.

Based on the loss of statistical significance in the degree of mix coefficient when mutual learning is added to the model, mutual learning is identified as potential mediator in the relationship between degree of mix and innovation climate. The Sobel test (1982) is conducted to assess the significance of the mediating effect. A z score is then calculated following all of the three versions of Sobel test (Table 6).

The mediation hypothesis H2 is supported by these tests (see Fig. 1). The percentage of the total effect that is mediated is also calculated: it indicates that

Table 5 Mediation analyses for mutual learning

Predictor	Unstd. coef.	Std. error	Std coef.	T	Sig.
Step 1: Dependent variable: CLIMAT					
MIX	0.11	0.038	0.301	2.875	0.005
Step2: Dependent variable: ML					
MIX	0.297	0.062	0.464	4.778	0.000
Step 3: Dependent variable: CLIMAT					
ML	0.281	0.061	0.491	4.638	0.000
MIX	0.026	0.039	0.073	0.689	0.493

Note: CLIMAT = innovation climate, ML = mutual learning, MIX = degree of mix

Table 6 Sobel and two Goodman tests (1960)

Test	z value	P value
Sobel	3.3203	0.00089
Goodman (I)	3.2834	0.001
Goodman (II)	3.3586	0.00078

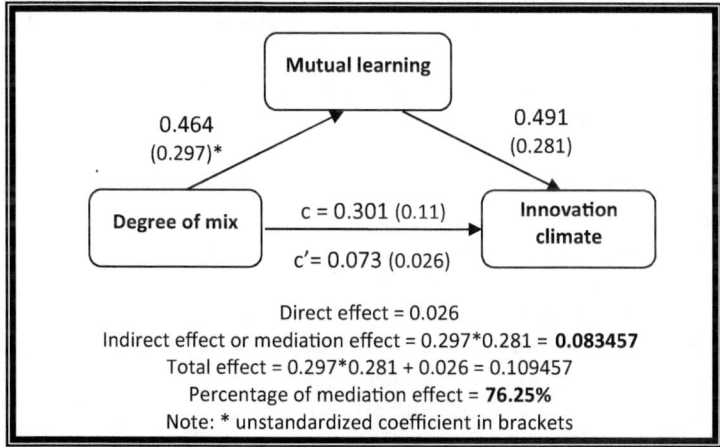

Fig. 1 Validated mediation model

Table 7 Results of correlation and regression analyses (mutual learning as independent variable)

Path	Zero-order correlation	Regression coefficient	t student	sig. t	R	R^2	F	sig. F
ML ⇨ Openness	0.432[a]	0.350	4.364	0.000	0.432	0.187	19.042	0.000
ML ⇨ Atmosphere	0.456[a]	0.337	4.663	0.000	0.456	0.208	21.740	0.000
ML ⇨ Debate	0.608[a]	0.627	6.983	0.000	0.608	0.370	48.767	0.000
ML ⇨ Idea support	0.255[b]	0.196	2.406	0.018	0.255	0.065	5.790	0.018
ML ⇨ Adoption	0.412[a]	0.320	4.119	0.000	0.412	0.170	16.970	0.000
ML ⇨ Risk-taking	0.459[a]	0.375	4.702	0.000	0.459	0.210	22.106	0.000

Note: ML = mutual learning, $N = 85$
[a]Correlation is significant at the 0.01 level (2-tailed)
[b]Correlation is significant at the 0.05 level (2-tailed)

mutual learning accounts for 76.25% of the path between degree of mix and innovation climate. The positive values of β coefficients suggest that higher level of mix chosen by a network is associated with more mutual learning between stores and so higher level of innovation climate.

To further assess the influence of mutual learning on the innovation climate, correlation and simple regression analyses are conducted between mutual learning and each element of innovation climate, such as idea support, openness, atmosphere, risk-taking, innovation adoption, and debates (Table 7).

6 Discussion

This study provides the empirical evidence from French networks that the degree of mix positively influences the network innovation climate. Actually, our results showed that the higher the degree of mix (or the more the franchisees percentage tends to 50%), the higher the level of the network climate for innovation. Moreover the relation between the degree of mix and the innovation climate is mediated by the mutual learning of company-owned and franchised units.

The findings showing that the degree of mix positively influences the innovation climate do confirm the advantage of the plural form in terms of innovation. This result is consistent with assertions in prior research by Bradach (1998), Lewin-Solomons (1999), and Sorenson and Sørensen (2001). It tends to show that the franchise network should choose a right mix for a better innovation development. Equilibrium between the number of franchised and company-owned units can lead to a high level of innovation climate within the network.

Our findings also point out the important role of mutual learning within a plural form network. Mutual learning here means franchisees and company-owned stores share and learn from each other. Bradach (1998) has stated that the plural form enabled a mutual learning that leverages the distinctive strengths of each arrangement. Actually mutual learning process is involved in many facets of the network relationships. For their own profits, franchisees strive to make the network more efficient. Sometimes, owing to the presence of franchisees, company managers become more dynamic and motivated. Through a mutual learning process, company units are aware of their responsibility to daily develop the network (Bradach 1997).

In the plural form structure, franchisees develop their capabilities to influence network performance in terms of innovation through interactions with other units. For instance, franchisee's local responses push company-owned units to be more dynamic, encourage the chain operator to develop more new products/services, or make the existing concept evolving. Franchisors often rely on information which comes from local markets to define their policies because franchisees provide solution for a better knowledge of local markets (Minkler 1990). This flow of information is usually beneficial because it stems from direct contacts of local units with consumers (Dant and Nasr 1998; Michael 2003).

A strong relation between mutual learning and the sharing and sympathetic atmosphere is found through our regression analysis. When franchised and company-owned units are conscious of learning from each other, they are ready to share knowledge and open for discussion. The willingness of sharing and opening to experience can foster a favorable environment for innovation (Rogers 1976). Based on a relational performance model, Shockley and Turner (2016) add and show that, in retail franchise networks, targeting fairness (distributive justice) helps to promote innovation and franchisees' commitment. Developing fairness toward franchisees is one of the most important challenges in a plural form network.

The mutual learning process enhances the adoption of innovations at unit (store, restaurant, hotel, etc.) level because, within a plural form network, each system has an effect on the way the other system works (Bradach 1998). The chain operator can persuade franchisees to adopt an innovation by firstly implementing it in company units. The company's adaptation directly affects the franchisee's decision-making process. The franchisor can also use company's data to demonstrate the viability of the proposed innovations. When new ideas are successfully adapted to company units, why not implementing them in franchised stores? So, the convergence of interest created by the plural form can encourage the franchisee's acceptance. In its turn, franchisee also provides feedback. The franchisor can use the franchisee performance to make pressure on company units or to set performance benchmarks for them in a stimulating and ratcheting process.

7 Conclusion

The main purpose of this study is to demonstrate the positive effect of the plural form on the innovation climate of franchise networks. Results provide empirical evidence for the mediation hypothesis under which mutual learning between franchisees and company managers mediated the relation between the degree of mix and the innovation climate. Although previous research has addressed the advantages of plural form as well as the mutual learning process, this is the first study to explore the relation between the plural form and the innovation climate and to give empirical evidence about that.

This research is subject to several limitations: The sample is rather small (85) and only one country has been studied (France). It is now difficult to obtain primary data from networks in many countries. So, further research should enlarge both the sample and the involved countries. In addition, the survey was conducted with franchisors only so that the innovation climate could not be assessed at the unit level. Interviewing franchisees and maybe company-owned unit managers could help to still better understand innovation processes in franchise networks. An ecosystem approach would probably improve the understanding of B2B relationships between the franchisor and the franchisees and between franchisees and company-owned outlet managers (Aarikka-Stenroos and Rittala 2017). Taking into account market turbulence and competition intensity would be of great interest (Kuen-Hung and Shu-Yi 2013).

The proposed model could be reinforced by several other concepts. Considering the social exchange theory could enable to introduce the ideas of franchisee entrepreneurial passion and fairness perceptions which can help to promote innovation in franchise organizations (Shockley and Turner 2016). Further research on innovation and mutual learning in complex hybrid networks like franchising could also consider motivation, opportunity, and ability to act within the corporate entrepreneurial context as they facilitate knowledge sharing and organizational learning (Turner and Wesley Pennington III 2015).

Another evolution of such research concerns communication. The importance of mutual learning leads us to take into account the role of communication within franchise networks since communication is the most important tool for creating a mutual learning environment (Kelner and Slavin 1998). Communication among partners (particularly between franchisor and franchisees, franchisees and company managers) plays a key role in overcoming resistance to innovation and in the reduction of uncertainty (Fidler and Johnson 1984). For these reasons, communication and the innovation process within plural form networks should be developed in further researches in franchising. Furthermore, future research could try to match innovation climate and innovation outcomes as it has been already done in several sectors like healthcare organizations (King et al. 2007), construction (Liu and Chan 2017), or design firms (Panuwatwanich et al. 2008).

Despite these limits, on the one hand, this study contributes to the literature by examining the role of plural form throughout the innovation process and brings some evidence to support the fourth Bradach's challenge on system-wide adaptation (1998). On the other hand, the findings seem to be interesting for practitioners in franchising. It is suggested that network operator should control the degree of mix to better manage innovation. It is necessary to pay attention to the statutory choice while implementing new stores, to insure the equilibrium between the numbers of franchised and company-owned units in a given territory in order to gain from the mutual learning effect. The spatial dispersion of these dual system outlets remains a key question.

Appendix Initial Items of the Innovation Climate Scale (14 Items)

Items	Questions	Notation scale (1 to 9)
Involvement	1. To what degree are your units available for innovations	Very weakly ⇨ Very strongly
Autonomy	2. To what degree is the autonomy of your franchisees in doing their jobs	Low autonomy ⇨ High autonomy
Openness, sharing	3. Within your network, people are open to others and share ideas	Strongly disagree ⇨ Strongly agree
Idea time	4. Your franchisees take time to think of new solutions and new ideas 5. Your owned units take time to think of new solutions and new ideas	Very rarely ⇨ Very frequently
Atmosphere	6. In general, the work atmosphere is relaxed and sympathetic	Strongly disagree ⇨ Strongly agree
Conflict	7. To what degree is there emotional tension in your network	A lot of conflict ⇨ Any conflict
Debate	8. To what degree is there the lively debate within stores	Rarely ⇨ Frequently

(continued)

Items	Questions	Notation scale (1 to 9)
Idea support	9. All new ideas are warmly welcome by franchisees 10. Resources are always available to give new idea a try	Strongly disagree ⇨ Strongly agree
Risk-taking	11. Your franchisees have tendency to take risk rather than hesitate to accept an innovation	Hesitate a lot ⇨ Usually take risk
Dynamism	12. Degree of dynamism of stores	Encoded from percentage
Financial resources	13. Your franchisees have financial difficulties to follow the network evolution	A lot of difficulties ⇨ Any difficulty
Adoption	14. In your network, innovations are accepted	Very difficultly ⇨ Very easily

References

Aarikka-Stenroos L, Rittala P (2017) Network management in the era of ecosystems: systematic review and management framework. Ind Mark Manag 67:23–36

Abbey A, Dickson JW (1983) R&D work climate and innovation in semiconductors. Acad Manag J 26:362–368

Baer M, Frese M (2003) Innovation is not enough: climates for initiative and psychological safety, process innovations, and firm performance. J Organ Behav 24(1):45–69

Bai CE, Tao Z (2000) Contract mixing in franchising as a mechanism for public good provision. J Econ Manag Strateg 9(1):85–113

Baron RM, Kenny DA (1986) The moderator-mediator variable distinction in social psychological research: conceptual, strategic, and statistical considerations. J Pers Soc Psychol 51(6):1173–1182

Barthélemy J (2011) Agency and institutional influences on franchising decisions. J Bus Ventur 26(1):93–103

Bradach JL (1997) Using plural form in the Management of Restaurant Chains. Adm Sci Q 42(2):276–303

Bradach JL (1998) Franchise organization. Harvard Business School Press, Cambridge, MA

Bradach JL, Eccles RG (1989) Price, authority, and trust: from ideal types to plural forms. Annu Rev Sociol 15:97–118

Brickley JA, Dark FH (1987) The choice of organizational form: the case of franchising. J Financ Econ 18:401–420

Bürkle T, Posselt T (2008) Franchising as a plural system: a risk based explanation. J Retail 84(1):39–47

Carney M, Gedajlovic E (1991) Vertical integration in franchise systems: agency theory and resource explanations. Strateg Manag J 12:607–629

Chen JJ, Dimou I (2005) Expansion strategy of international hotel firms. J Bus Res 58(12):1730–1740

Churchill GA (1979) A paradigm for developing better measures of marketing constructs. J Mark Res 16(1):64–73

Cliquet G, Nguyen MN (2004) Innovation management within the plural form network, in economics and Management of Franchising Networks. In: Windsperger J, Cliquet G, Hendrikse G, Tuunanen M (eds) Economics and Management of Franchising Networks. Springer, Heidelberg, pp 109–125

Cliquet G, Pénard T (2012) Plural form franchise networks: a test of Bradach's model. J Retail Consum Serv 19:159–167

Cox J, Mason C (2007) Standardization versus adaptation: geographical pressure to deviate from franchise formats. Serv Ind J 27(8):1063–1072

Cyrenne P (2014) Dual distribution and the Penrose effect. Int J Econ Bus 21(1):55–76

Dant RP, Kaufmann PJ (2003) Structural and strategic dynamics in franchising. J Retail 79:63–75

Dant RP, Nasr N (1998) Control techniques and upward flow of information in franchising in distant markets: conceptualization and preliminary evidence. J Bus Ventur 13(1):3–28

Dant RP, Kaufmann PJ, Paswan AK (1992) Ownership redirection in Franchised Channel. J Public Policy Mark 11(1):33–44

Di Benedetto CA (1999) Identifying the key success factors in new product launch. J Prod Innov Manag 16(6):530–544

Dickson MW, Smith DB, Grojean MW, Ehrhart M (2001) An organizational climate regarding ethics; the outcome of leader values and the practices that reflect them. Leadersh Q 12:197–217

Dimou I, Chen J, Archer S (2003) The choice between management contracts and franchise agreements in the corporate development of international hotel firms. J Mark Channels 10(3/4):33–52

Ehrmann T, Spranger G (2004) Successful franchising using the plural form. In: Cliquet G, Hendrikse G, Tuunanen M, Windsperger J (eds) Economics and management of franchising networks. Springer, Heidelberg

Ekvall G (1983) Climate, structure and innovativeness of organizations: a theoretical framework and experiment. Report for the Swedish Council for Management and Work Life Issues, Stockholm, Sweden

Ekvall G (1986) Working climate and creativity: a study of an innovative newspaper office. J Creat Behav 20(3):215–225

Elango B, Fried VH (1977) Franchising research: a literature review and synthesis. J Small Bus Manag 35(3):68–81

Fidler LA, Johnson JD (1984) Communication and innovation implementation. Acad Manag Serv 9(4):707–711

Fornell C, Larcker DF (1981) Evaluating structural equation models with unobservable variables and measurement error. J Mark Res 18(1):39–50

Forward J, Fulop C (1997) Insights into franchising: a review of empirical and theoretical perspectives. Serv Ind J 17:603–625

Gallini N, Lutz N (1992) Dual distribution and royalty fees in franchising. J Law Econ Org 8(3):471–501

González-Romá V, Peiró JM, Tordera N (2002) An examination of the antecedents and moderator influences of climate strength. J Appl Psychol 87(3):465–473

Goodman LA (1960) On the exact variance of products. J Am Stat Assoc 55:708–713

Gubman E, Russell S (2006) "Think big, start small, scale fast": growing customer innovation at McDonald's. Hum Resour Plan 29(3):21–22

Hair JF Jr, Hult GTM, Ringle CM, Sarstedt M (2014) A primer on partial least squares structural equation modeling (PLS-SEM). Sage, Los Angeles

Isaksen SG, Lauer KJ, Ekvall G, Britz A (2000) Perceptions of the best and worst climates for creativity: preliminary validation evidence for the situational outlook questionnaire. Creat Res J 13(2):171–184

Jambulingam T, Nevin JR (1999) Influence of franchisee selection criteria on outcomes desired by the franchisor. J Bus Ventur 14:363–395

Karmeni K, de La Villarmois O, Mansouri F (2017) Contrôle et innovation: étude de l'effet médiateur de la diffusion des connaissances dans les réseaux de franchise. Comptab Contrôl Audi 23(3):63–95

Kaufmann PJ, Eroglu S (1998) Standardization and adaptation in business format franchising. J Bus Ventur 14:69–85

Kelner SP, Slavin L (1998) The competitive strategy of mutual learning. Train Dev 52(6):72–75

King EB, de Chermont K, West W, Dawson JF, Hebl MR (2007) How innovation can alleviate negative consequences of demanding work contexts: the influence of climate for innovation on organizational outcomes. J Occup Organ Psychol 80:631–645

Knott AM (2001) The dynamic value of hierarchy. Manag Sci 47(3):430–448

Kuen-Hung T, Shu-Yi Y (2013) Firm innovativeness and business performance: the joint moderating effects of market turbulence and competition. Ind Mark Manag 42(8):1279–1294

Lafontaine F (1992) Agency theory and franchising: some empirical results. RAND J Econ 23:263–283

Lafontaine F, Shaw KL (2005) Targeting managerial control: evidence from franchising. Rand J Econ 36(1):131–150

Lewin K (1951) Field theory in social science. Harper & Row, New York

Lewin-Solomons, S. B. (1997). Innovation and authority in franchise system: toward a grounded theory of the plural form. PhD thesis, Cambridge University. http://www.econ.cam.ac.uk/dae/people/lewin/thesis.pdf. Accessed 1 Oct 2001

Lewin-Solomons SB (1999) Innovation and authority in franchise system: an empirical exploration of the plural form. Journal paper No. J-18005 of the Iowa Agriculture and Home Economics Experiment Station, Project No. 3530

Lewin-Solomons SB (2000) Innovation and authority in franchise systems: an empirical exploration of the plural form. Unpublished Working Paper. University of Cambridge, November.

Liu AMM, Chan IYS (2017) Understanding the interplay of organizational climate and leadership in construction innovation. J Manag Eng 33(3):1–10

Mallapragada G, Srinivasan R (2017) Innovativeness as an unintended outcome of franchising: insights from restaurant chains. Decis Sci 48(6):1164–1197

Manolis C, Dahlstrom R, Nygaard A (1995) A preliminary investigation of ownership conversions in franchised distribution systems. J Appl Bus Res 11(2):1–8

Méndez MT, Galindo M-A, Sastre M-A (2014) Franchise, innovation and entrepreneurship. Serv Ind J 34(9–10):843–855

Michael SC (2000) The effect of organizational form on quality: the case of franchising. J Econ Behav Organ 43:295–318

Michael SC (2003) First mover advantage through franchising. J Bus Ventur 18:61–80

Minkler AP (1990) An empirical analysis of a firm's decision to franchise. Econ Lett 34:77–82

Minkler AP (1992) Why firms franchise: a search cost theory. J Inst Theor Econ 148:240–259

Moran ET, Volkwein JF (1992) The cultural approach to the formation of organizational climate. Hum Relat 45(1):19–47

Moukwa M (1995) A structure. To Foster creativity: an industrial experience. J Creat Behav 29(1):54–63

Noren DL (1990) The economics of the Golden arches: a case study of the McDonald's system. Am Econ 34(2):60–64

Ott JS (1989) The organizational culture perspective. Brooks/Cole, Pacific Grove, CA

Panuwatwanich K, Stewart RA, Mohamed S (2008) The role of climate for innovation in enhancing business performance: the case of design firms. Eng Const Archit Manag 15(5):407–422

Pardo-del-Val M, Martinez-Fuentes C, Lopez-Sanchez I, Minguela-Rata B (2014) Franchising: the dilemma between standardisation and flexibility. Serv Ind J 34(9–10):828–842

Parry CV (1987) Creating the right climate for innovation, Director, April, p. 53

Perrigot R, Herrbach O (2012) The plural form from the inside: a study of franchisee perception of company-owned outlets within their network. Int J Retail Distrib Manag 40(7):544–563

Pirkul H, Narasimham S, De P (1987) Firm expansion through franchising: a model and solution programming. Decis Sci 18:631–645

Ralston J (1989) Franchisees who think big. Venture 11(3):55–57

Rogers CR (1976) Toward a theory of creativity. In: Rothenberg A, Hausman CR (eds) The creativity question. Duke University Press, Durham, NC, pp 296–304

Rubin PH (1978) The theory of the firm and the structure of the franchise contract. J Law Econ 21:222–233

Schneider B (1975) Organizational climates: an essay. Pers Psychol 28:447–479

Schneider B, Parkington JP, Buxton VM (1980) Employer and customer perceptions of service in banks. Adm Sci Q 25:252–257

Shockley J, Turner T (2016) A relational performance model for developing innovation and long-term orientation in retail franchise organizations. J Retail Consum Serv 32:175–188

Sobel ME (1982) Asymptotic confidence intervals for indirect effects in structural equation models. In: Leinhardt (ed) Sociological methodology. American Sociological Association, Washington DC, pp 290–312

Solomon GT, Winslow EK, Tarabishy A (1998) The role of climate in fostering innovative behavior in entrepreneurial SMEs. In: Proceedings of the 1998 USASBE annual national conference, bright horizons for small business and entrepreneurship, Clearwater, Florida, 15–18, January

Somech A, Drach-Zahavy A (2013) Translating team creativity to innovation implementation: the role of team composition and climate for innovation. J Manag 39(3):684–708

Sorenson O, Sørensen JB (2001) Finding the right mix: organizational learning, plural forms and franchise performance. Strateg Manag J 22:713–724

Strutton D, Pelton LE, Lumpkin JR (1995) Psychological climate in franchising system channels and franchisor-franchisee solidarity. J Bus Res 34(2):81–91

Szulanski G, Jensen RJ (2008) Growing through copying: the negative consequences of innovation on franchise network growth. Res Policy 37:1732–1741

Turner T, Pennington WW III (2015) Organizational networks and the process of corporate entrepreneurship: how the motivation, opportunity, and ability to act affect firm knowledge, learning, and innovation. Small Bus Econ 45:447–463

Wattel H (1968–69) Are franchisors realistic and successful in their selection of franchisees? J Retail 44(4):54–68

Weiss M, Hoegl M, Gibbert M (2011) Making virtue of necessity: the role of team climate for innovation in resource-constrained innovation projects. J Prod Innov Manag 28(S1):196–207

Windsperger J (2004) The dual network structure of the franchising firm: property rights, transaction cost and resource scarcity explanations. In: Windsperger J, Cliquet G, Hendrikse G, Tuunanen M (eds) Economics and management of franchising networks. Springer, Heidelberg

Windsperger J, Dant R (2006) Contractibility and ownership redirection in franchising: a property rights view. J Retail 82(3):259–272

Wu S-H, Chi-Tsun Huang S, Daphne Tsai C-Y, Chen Y-C (2009) Service innovation in franchising convenience store: an exploratory study. Int J Electron Bus Manag 7(2):137–148

Zohar D (1980) Safety climate in industrial organizations; theoretical and applied implications. J Appl Psychol 65:96–102

Zohar D (2000) A group-level model of safety climate: testing the effect of group climate on microaccidents in manufacturing jobs. J Appl Psychol 85(4):587–596

They Are Jolly Good Fellows! A Framework for Antecedents and Consequences of Peer Trust in Franchise Networks

Evelien P. M. Croonen and Reinder Hamming

Abstract Trust is an important topic in franchising research. However, research has neglected franchisees' trust in their fellow franchisees or 'peers' within the network ('peer trust'). Peer trust may facilitate cooperation among franchisees and hence increase unit or network performance. However, it may also negatively affect the franchisor and the network as it may facilitate franchisee coalition formation and collective actions against the franchisor. Managing peer trust within the network is therefore an important issue for franchisors. We contribute to franchising research by developing an integrative theoretical framework on antecedents and consequences of peer trust. We conduct a systematic literature review on the antecedents and consequences of coworker trust within organizations and translate these insights to a franchising context to propose our own integrative framework on antecedents and consequences of franchisees' peer trust. Our framework distinguishes four types of *antecedents* of peer trust: franchisee (i.e. trustor) characteristics, peer (i.e. trustee) characteristics, franchisor characteristics and franchise network characteristics. Moreover, we distinguish three types of *consequences* of peer trust: perceptual/attitudinal outcomes, behavioural outcomes and performance outcomes. We also discuss avenues for future scientific research on peer trust in franchise networks and potential implications for franchisors regarding the management of peer trust.

E. P. M. Croonen (✉)
Faculty of Economics & Business, University of Groningen, Groningen, The Netherlands
e-mail: e.p.m.croonen@rug.nl

R. Hamming
Faculty of Economics & Business, Alumni of University of Groningen, Groningen,
The Netherlands

© Springer Nature Switzerland AG 2019
J. Windsperger et al. (eds.), *Design and Management of Interfirm Networks*,
Contributions to Management Science,
https://doi.org/10.1007/978-3-030-29245-4_3

1 Introduction

In franchising, a franchisee engages in a contractual relationship with a franchisor and pays for the right to use the franchisor's business format in running its unit(s) while agreeing to conform to the franchisor's standards (Nijmeijer et al. 2014). Franchisees are typically part of a franchise network with fellow franchisees or 'peers' (and often company-owned units) that all operate under the same business format. The franchisor coordinates, facilitates and monitors network operations.

Trust is an important issue in franchise networks since the economic motives of franchisors and franchisees are not totally aligned (Solis-Rodriguez and Gonzales-Diaz 2012). These mixed motives create potential agency problems and relational risks and make trust an important issue among franchisors and franchisees. Most studies have focused on the franchisees' perspective and studied the antecedents and consequences of franchisees' trust in their franchisors. Franchisors typically are the dominant partner, and this may make franchisees feel vulnerable to their franchisors' actions. However, recent franchising studies (e.g. Croonen and Brand 2013; Croonen 2017) have argued that franchisees' trust can comprise different 'referents' (i.e. trustees), such as the franchise organization's CEO or regional managers. A franchisee's peers within the same franchise network comprise another group of trust referents.

Research on antecedents and consequences of franchisees' peer trust is virtually nonexistent, whereas peer trust can have both positive and negative consequences for franchisors and their franchise systems. Some studies have (implicitly) pointed at positive effects of trust or cooperation among franchisee peers, for example, by arguing or hypothesizing that cohesion among franchisees may result in more knowledge and information sharing and fewer franchisees' opportunistic behaviours (e.g. El Akremi et al. 2011).[1] However, there is also anecdotal evidence for negative outcomes or a 'dark side' of peer trust (cf. Lumineau 2017): trust among peers may result in franchisees' collective actions against the franchisor, such as collective lawsuits or exits from the network (Croonen 2006). Such collective actions may negatively affect the franchisor and the franchise network.

Given the potential scientific and practical relevance of franchisees' peer trust, it is surprising that its antecedents and consequences have been largely unstudied. We aim to contribute to literature on antecedents and consequences of franchisees'

---

[1] Some readers may wonder why it is beneficial for franchisees to trust their peers operating in other geographical locations as it may not be useful to share knowledge with them. However, knowledge sharing among franchisees does occur and affects franchisee performance (e.g. Brand et al. 2018). It is out of the scope of this paper to discuss under what conditions franchisees are most likely to share knowledge and in which conditions franchisee peer trust is thus most relevant (see Darr and Kurtzberg (2000) for such insights), but some conditions are the position centrality of the franchisee in the network and the *type* of knowledge shared. Since franchisees within a franchise network operate under one business format in largely similar types of environments, it is safe to assume that knowledge sharing will take place and can be beneficial to them. In recent years, such knowledge sharing has become even easier due to the rise of digital communication platforms.

trust by proposing an integrative theoretical framework on potential antecedents and consequences of franchisees' peer trust as an important form of trust. Since peer trust is a relatively new concept and there are similarities with coworker trust, we build on insights from studies on antecedents and consequences of coworker trust in other organizational contexts and translate them to a franchising context.

First, we define the concept of peer trust by discussing the similarities and differences with the well-known concept of coworker trust in other organizational contexts. The second step is a systematic literature review of studies in high-quality journals on antecedents and consequences of coworker trust. Building on this review, we compose an integrative framework on antecedents and consequences of coworker trust, which we use as a basis to propose an integrative framework for antecedents and consequences of franchisees' peer trust. Such an integrative framework on peer trust provides future directions for franchising research, and it provides franchisors and other practitioners initial insights in how to potentially manage peer trust and peer interactions in franchise networks.

2   Defining Peer Trust and Linking It to Coworker Trust

Trust is an important topic in all kinds of intra-organizational and inter-organizational contexts. If trust is present in a relationship, individuals can work together with a reduced need for monitoring or without engaging in self-protective behaviour (Mayer and Gavin 2005). A popular definition in the trust literature is the one by Mayer et al. (1995 p. 712) who define trust as 'the willingness of a party to be vulnerable to the actions of another party based on the expectation that the other will perform a particular action important to the trustor, irrespective of the ability to monitor or control that another party'.

We focus on franchisees' trust in their peers, which we call 'peer trust' in this study. Peer trust is defined as 'a franchisee's trust in its fellow franchisees ("peers") within the franchise system' (Croonen 2017, p. 197). More specifically, a franchisee's peer trust is the willingness of a franchisee to be vulnerable to its peers' actions based upon positive expectations of these peers' behaviours. We define franchisee peer trust as the franchisee's overall perceived level of trust in its peers within the same network, which we refer to as 'generalized peer trust'. This is typically how coworker trust is measured (e.g. Shin et al. 2014; Peng et al. 2014). Our study is not focusing on dyadic relationships between two specific peers in a network, which we refer to as 'specified peer trust'. Similarly, relatively few studies on coworker trust focus on such 'specified coworker trust' (see Appendix 1).

We build on the literature on coworker trust since there are several similarities between coworkers within organizations and franchisee peers within franchise networks. First, even though franchisees are legally independent business owners, they have to comply with contractual requirements from the franchisor, and the franchisor is monitoring their compliance (Kidwell et al. 2007; Croonen and

Broekhuizen 2019). The franchisor-franchisee relationship has some hierarchical element in which the franchisor is typically the more dominant partner (cf. employer). All franchisees in a network have such a hierarchical relationship with the franchisor, and as such they are part of a network (cf. organization) with the franchisor (cf. management) as the leader. Moreover, just as coworkers, franchisees are embedded in a network of peers. Franchisee peers are interdependent since the behaviour and performance of individual franchisees may influence the performance of their peers (Combs and Ketchen 2003; Kidwell et al. 2007). This means that the performance of the franchise network is dependent on the behaviour of the franchisees. This is also the case in intra-organizational contexts with employers and employees/coworkers.

3 A Systematic Literature Review on Antecedents and Consequences of Coworker Trust: Methodology

We conducted a systematic literature review (cf. Dada 2018; Nijmeijer et al. 2014) focusing on the antecedents and consequences of coworker trust. A systematic literature review helps in synthesizing reliable knowledge from earlier research in a transparent and scientific way.

3.1 Selection of Studies

The studies included in this review investigated the antecedents and/or consequences of coworker trust in organizations. We conducted our search in an electronic database, namely, Web of Science InCites™. We searched in four categories of journals: Business, Management, Industrial Relations and Labor and Applied Psychology. Each of the four categories resulted in a list of peer-reviewed journals ranked according to their 5-year impact scores (Eigenfactor). The first 15 journals in each specific category were included in this review, which means that this review is based on the most influential journals. The search criteria were 'coworker trust' and 'co-worker trust', since both terms are used in the literature. The search took place on May 28, 2018, and we searched on 'Topic' in the Web of Science database. The coverage period includes articles published up to June 2018, without other limitations with reference to the publishing date. The search process was limited to articles published in English. Only journal articles were included in the searching procedure (i.e. no books or chapters).

The overall search strategy generated a total sample of 32 articles. Of the initial sample of 32 articles, the title and abstracts were reviewed since the title and abstracts of articles contain often the keywords of the article (Dada 2018). Seven articles were excluded because they did not meet the inclusion criteria. The inclusion criteria include articles that focus on antecedents and consequences of coworker trust. Excluded articles mentioned one of the search terms in the text, but were not focusing on the antecedents or consequences of coworker trust in detail. The new sample was further evaluated, and five articles that did not meet the inclusion criteria were removed. This full text reading reduced the selection to 20 articles. Finally, one article was added because it was mentioned in several articles. Ultimately, 21 articles were included in the analysis.

3.2   Summary of Studies

The selected studies represent a heterogeneous literature stream, with many different theories, variables, conceptualizations and methodologies. Appendix 1 presents a summary of the 21 articles that were included in the final sample.[2] They are published between 2002 and 2018. The antecedents and consequences of coworker trust received almost equal attention in the included articles. Of the final sample, ten articles paid attention to both the antecedents and consequences of coworker trust. Six of the studies paid only attention to the antecedents of coworker trust and five articles only to the consequences of coworker trust.

The far majority of the studies in Appendix 1 used a quantitative research design ($n = 20$). None of the articles adopted a qualitative research design, and one article was a conceptual article (i.e. Lau and Cobb 2010). Most of the studies on coworker trust in the review used the finance industry as empirical setting ($n = 6$). These are followed by articles that used the manufacturing industry ($n = 4$) and education ($n = 5$). The other articles do not specify the industry. The studies were conducted in more than 12 different countries, most of them in North America, followed by countries in Europe. Appendix 1 shows that various theoretical perspectives were used in the different articles. The majority of studies builds on the social exchange theory ($n = 6$)[3] or on the trust literature ($n = 5$). These findings are in line with the arguments that trust has an important role in the emergence and maintenance of social exchange relationships (Blau 1964). Furthermore, the social exchange theory is one of the most influential theories for understanding workplace behaviour (Cropanzano and Mitchell 2005).

---

[2]A more detailed overview of the articles is available upon request at e.p.m.croonen@rug.nl.

[3]Social exchange theory is a broad theory and includes socialization theory, fairness heuristic literature, social cognitive theory, network theory and reciprocity theory. These different theories are included in the social exchange theory because these theories are focusing on the emergence and maintenance of social exchange relationships (Blau 1964).

4 An Integrative Framework on Antecedents and Consequences of Coworker Trust

4.1 The Concept of Coworker Trust

Trust can be divided into two main forms: cognition- or calculative-based trust, on the one hand, and affect- or relational-based trust, on the other hand (McAllister 1995; Schilke and Cook 2015). Cognition-based trust reflects the trustor's instrumental evaluation of the trustee's characteristics, whereas affect-based trust reflects the emotional bond between individuals, leading to personal care. As described in Appendix 1, four studies in the review focused solely on affect-based coworker trust (i.e. Settoon and Mossholder 2002; Parker et al. 2006; Lapointe et al. 2014; Peng et al. 2014), whereas no study focused solely on cognition-based coworker trust. Two of the reviewed studies were using both cognition-based and affect-based trust (Ladebo 2006; Lau and Cobb 2010). The other 15 reviewed studies were not focusing on a specific form of trust.

It is important to note that the quantitative studies ($n = 20$) measured coworker trust in different ways. Some studies used a matched/dyadic approach ($n = 6$), thus focusing on 'specified coworker trust'. This means that coworker trust is measured between two employees who regularly interact on a work-related basis. The other quantitative studies in the review ($n = 14$) used a more general approach of coworker trust focusing on 'generalized coworker trust'. Such studies were focusing on coworker trust within the organization in general, based on the perception of the trustor.

4.2 Antecedents of Coworker Trust

Our review identifies four main types of antecedents of coworker trust:

A. Employee (i.e. trustor) characteristics
B. Coworker (i.e. trustee) characteristics
C. Leadership characteristics
D. Organizational characteristics

These types of antecedents are presented in the integrative framework in Appendix 2, together with the variables belonging to each type and the direction of the relationship with coworker trust (indicated with pluses and minuses). It is important to note that the coworker, leadership and organizational characteristics mostly refer to the employee's *perception* of these characteristics (an exception is Lau and Liden 2008). Below, we discuss each type of antecedent in more detail. Please note that only few studies (Yakovleva et al. 2010; Roussin and Webber 2012; Svensson 2018) have taken into account potential moderating and mediating variables in studying the antecedents of coworker trust. For the sake of simplicity, we have excluded the moderators and mediators from the literature review.

4.2.1 Type A Antecedents: Employee (i.e. Trustor) Characteristics

The employee characteristics can be divided into 'soft' and 'hard' characteristics. 'Soft' characteristics refer to trustor characteristics that are relatively difficult to measure, and they include trustors' personal traits, perceptions and/or attitudes. The 'hard' characteristics are the trustor's measurable characteristics, including for example, the trustor's time in the organization.

'Soft' Characteristics

Propensity to Trust (+): Propensity to trust is a personality trait reflecting an individual's perception of the general trustworthiness of others (Mayer et al. 1995; Colquitt et al. 2007). Three of the 21 studies of the final sample argued and found that employees' propensity to trust is positively related to their coworker trust (Van der Werff and Buckley 2017; Yakovleva et al. 2010; Roussin and Webber 2012).

Self-Estrangement (−): Building on social exchange theory, Golden and Veiga (2018) found that higher levels of employees' self-estrangement are negatively related to their coworker trust. Self-estrangement can be defined as a psychological separation from the self, which means that there is a difference between a person's self-image in the workplace and a person's ideal self-image. According to Golden and Veiga, higher levels of self-estrangement lead to separation of workers and fewer social exchanges among them, which leads to passive and indifferent behaviour of workers to their coworkers. As a result, self-estranged employees invest less time in their relations with coworkers and are less willing to share resources.

Skills Development (+): In a study among 711 employees in the public sector in Sweden, Svensson (2018) found that employees' perceived skills development is positively related to their coworker trust. According to Svensson (2018), higher levels of skills and competencies lead to employment security, which in turn decreases the vulnerability of an employee in his or her position. Employees with more skills are less afraid of losing their position, which is creating trust for both internal and external workers (Svensson 2018). Therefore, perceived skills development is positively related to coworker trust.

'Hard' Characteristics

Time in Organization (+): The effect of an employee's time in the organization on coworker trust was reported in Van der Werff and Buckley (2017). Their empirical study among 193 employees of an international accountancy and consultancy firm found that the time of an individual in the organization was positively related to coworker trust. The level of coworker trust increases over time as a result of the socialization process (Wilson et al. 2006). Positive experiences of the trustor and trustee will lead to more interactions and the building of social resources, which will lead to an increase in the level of coworker trust.

Type of Employment (External (−) vs. Internal (+)): Svensson (2018) distinguished between internal and external workers: internal workers are directly hired by the organization, whereas external workers are working *for* the organization but they are not employed by it. Social integration in an organization is more difficult for external workers since they are often working there for a shorter time period. This is negatively related to a sense of belonging and shared norms, which has a negative influence on coworker trust (Liden et al. 2003). Internal workers have a higher sense of belonging and shared norms, which positively affects coworker trust.

4.2.2 Type B Antecedents: Coworker (i.e. Trustee) Characteristics

Six studies showed that trustors' perceived coworker characteristics have an influence on their coworker trust (Dirks and Skarlicki 2009; Lau and Cobb 2010; Yakovleva et al. 2010; Colquitt et al. 2011; Scott et al. 2013; Halbesleben and Wheeler 2015).

Trustworthiness (+) Two studies considered the influence of employees' perceived coworker trustworthiness on their coworker trust (Dirks and Skarlicki 2009; Colquitt et al. 2011). Trustworthiness typically comprises three characteristics of the trustee: ability, benevolence and integrity (Mayer et al. 1995; Colquitt et al. 2011). Dirks and Skarlicki (2009) and Colquitt et al. (2011) found that employees' perceived ability, benevolence and integrity of coworkers are positively related to their coworker trust. Yakovleva et al. (2010) found these results only for benevolence and integrity. The studies are building on the social exchange theory and trust literature, which provides support that social exchanges are necessary to build coworker trust.

Relationship Conflict (−) The only conceptual study in this systematic review is the one by Lau and Cobb (2010). They developed a conceptual model building on the social exchange theory that explores the impact of relationship conflict between coworkers on coworker trust. Such relationship conflict will lead to negative sentiments in the relationship, which leads to differences in values, perspectives and attitudes (Williams 2001). Therefore, Lau and Cobb (2010) propose that relationship conflict has a negative effect on coworker trust.

Uncivil Behaviours (−) The study of Scott et al. (2013) showed that trustors' perceived uncivil behaviour of coworkers has a negative influence on their coworker trust. The study took place among more than 400 individuals in different industries in the Philippines. Uncivil behaviour of coworkers will make the trustor doubt about the benefits of the relationship. This has a negative influence on the social exchanges and the perceived trustworthiness of coworkers and will decrease the level of coworker trust.

Resource Investments (+) Halbesleben and Wheeler (2015) consider the influence of employees' perceived resource investments on their coworker trust. They showed that higher coworkers' resource investment leads to an increase in coworker support. The authors build on the conservation of resource theory: as employees acquire personal resources, they can invest these resources as a means to gain additional resources (Hobfoll 2001). Close coworkers develop reciprocal resource gain cycles, where helping behaviours increase perceived coworker support and the subsequent trust that the coworker will reciprocate helping behaviours (Halbesleben and Wheeler 2015).

4.2.3   Type C Antecedents: Leadership Characteristics

Two studies (i.e. Peng et al. 2014; Gill and Caza 2018) showed that coworker trust is a result of trustors' perceived leadership characteristics. Additionally, Lau and Liden (2008) focused on the impact of trust by the leader in coworkers on coworker trust.

Authentic Leadership (+) Gill and Caza (2018) found a relation between trustors' perceived authentic leadership and social exchanges between coworkers, which generates higher levels of coworker trust. Authentic leadership is the combination of interrelated behaviours, which emphasizes the behaviour of leaders in acting to their workers. An authentic leader will have workers who are more likely to follow, trust and identify themselves with their leader (Gill and Caza 2018). This will positively influence the employees' group behaviours, and it will lead to a more positive group climate, which increases the level of coworker trust.

Abusive Supervision (−) Peng et al. (2014) found that employees' perceived abusive supervision by their leaders is negatively related to their coworker trust. Their analysis among 411 employees in 23 different Chinese companies shows that trustors' perceived abusive supervision is negatively related to affect-based trust between coworkers. Workers who perceive to be treated unfairly by their leaders do not have the feeling that they are part of the group. Building on the social exchange theory, trustors' perceived abusive supervision will lead to less social exchanges among coworkers and hence lower levels of coworker trust.

Leader's Trust in Coworkers (+) Lau and Liden (2008) found in their matching survey among 146 individuals in different organizations that the level of trust of leaders in specific coworkers is positively related to coworker trust. Leaders of an organization have more influence than coworkers in an organization, because they have a higher formal status. Therefore, leaders have a bigger role in the creation of a positive attitude among coworkers, which helps in creating trust between coworkers (Liden et al. 2004). Trusted employees often have more responsibilities and confidential information and obtain more advice from the leader (Lau et al. 2007). This leads to higher performance, and coworkers see the trustor as more capable. As a result of this, trust of the leader in coworkers leads to higher coworker trust (Lau and Liden 2008).

4.2.4 Type D Antecedents: Organizational Characteristics

Four studies (i.e. Roussin and Webber 2012; Lapointe et al. 2014; Shin et al. 2014; Svensson 2018) showed that trustors' perceived organizational characteristics influence coworker trust in organizations. These characteristics can be divided into cultural characteristics and procedural characteristics.

Cultural Characteristics
Psychological Safety (+): Only one study (i.e. Roussin and Webber 2012) found a relationship between employees' perceived psychological safety and their coworker trust. Roussin and Webber's study among managers in the technology and manufacturing industry found that psychological safety is positively related to coworker trust. Psychological safety leads to more trust between employees. Employees who perceive a higher level of psychological safety are more willing to take risks and are less afraid of being locked out or being embarrassed, which positively influences coworker trust (Roussin and Webber 2012).

Shared Norms (+): Svensson (2018) found that employees' perceived shared norms have a positive relationship with their coworker trust. The feeling of familiarity with shared norms facilitates predictability in a relationship, which increases the level of trust between coworkers. This coherence among peers makes coworkers known with their way of thinking and acting, which has a positive effect on the level of coworker trust (Svensson 2018).

Procedural Characteristics
Organizational Socialization Tactics (+): The analysis of Lapointe et al. (2014) among 224 participants in different organizations found that newcomers' perceived organizational socialization tactics lead to higher coworker trust. Organizational socialization tactics are part of a process in which new employees are introduced to their new environment, by learning the behaviours, attitudes and skills that are necessary for their function in the organization. Building on the social exchange theory, higher levels of organizational socialization tactics give newcomers more ways to build social exchanges with their coworkers. An increase in social exchanges among employees leads to more affect-based trust in peers (Lapointe et al. 2014).

Procedural Justice (+): The analysis of Shin et al. (2014) among employees of 107 different teams of an electronic company in Korea found that perceived procedural justice is positively related to coworker trust. A procedural justice climate reflects the fairness level of the decision-making processes in an organization. Workers who feel that an organization is making fair decisions think that they are working in a team that is following the same ethical principles (Frazier et al. 2010). Higher levels of procedural justice will lead to more cohesion among coworkers, which leads to a higher level of coworker trust.

4.3   Consequences of Coworker Trust

Our review identifies three main types of consequences of coworker trust:

E. Perceptual/attitudinal outcomes
F. Behavioural outcomes
G. Performance outcomes

These types of consequences represent different 'hierarchical levels' of outcomes that ultimately affect performance. Perceptual/attitudinal outcomes reflect employees' perceptions, feelings and valuations of situations, which may in turn affect these employees' actual actions (behavioural outcomes). In turn, the behavioural outcomes may affect performance at different levels, such as the individual, team or organizational level. The articles in our review do not explicitly distinguish these different outcome levels, but we argue that it is important to understand the 'causal chain' of different outcomes affecting firm performance as the ultimate outcome (cf. Becker and Gerhart 1996). The three main types of consequences and the variables belonging to each type are presented in the integrative framework in Appendix 2. The direction of the relationships between coworker trust and the specific outcomes is indicated with pluses and minuses.

4.3.1   Type E Consequences: Perceptual/Attitudinal Outcomes

Six studies focused on the impact of coworker trust on employees' perceptions ($n = 2$, Ladebo 2006; May et al. 2004) or attitudes ($n = 4$, Ferres et al. 2004; Ladebo 2006; Parker et al. 2006; Lapointe et al. 2014).

Perceptual Outcomes
Group Cohesion (+): Group cohesion is an individual's feeling of being part of a group (Ladebo 2006). Ladebo's study among participants of an agricultural development program in Nigeria found that coworker trust is positively related to group cohesion. Higher levels of coworker trust lead to more cohesion among individuals in a group (Webber 2002), because workers have positive expectations about the behaviour of their coworkers and leaders. In turn, individuals perceiving group cohesion are willing to make sacrifices towards the achievement of goals and are motivated to stay in the work group (Ladebo 2006). Group cohesion is therefore related to affective commitment (see below), which is the extent an employee feels an emotional attachment to the organization (Ladebo 2006).

Psychological Safety (+): Of the reviewed articles, one study considers psychological safety as an antecedent of co-worker trust, whereas another study (i.e. May et al. 2004) considers it a consequence of coworker trust. This study showed that coworker trust has a positive influence on a feeling of safety by the trustor. This result was found in a survey of 213 employees in a large insurance company in the United States. An increase in coworker trust leads to the feelings of safety at work and leads to coworkers who are more willing to take risk without the fear of negative consequences (Colquitt et al. 2011; May et al. 2004).

Attitudinal Outcomes

Affective Commitment (+): Four studies showed that coworker trust has a positive impact on the affective commitment of workers with the organization (i.e. Ferres et al. 2004; Ladebo 2006; Lapointe et al. 2014; Parker et al. 2006). Affective commitment is the emotional attachment of an employee towards the organization (Ladebo 2006). Most of the studies were building on the social exchange theory ($n = 2$). All studies found a positive relationship between coworker trust and affective commitment. Relatedly, Ferres et al. (2004) found a negative direct relationship between coworker trust and employees' turnover intentions.

4.3.2 Type F Consequences: Behavioural Outcomes

Ten studies focused on the impact of coworker trust on employee behaviours, with citizenship behaviour as the most important type of behaviour.

Citizenship Behaviour (+) A consequence of coworker trust is an increase in citizenship behaviour. This relationship is reported in nine studies (i.e. Settoon and Mossholder 2002; Parker et al. 2006; Dirks and Skarlicki 2009; Yakovleva et al. 2010; Peng et al. 2014; Shin et al. 2014; Halbesleben and Wheeler 2015; McGuire and Bielby 2016; Golden and Veiga 2018). Most of them are building on the social exchange theory. Irrespective of the industry and country, all studies showed that workers citizenship behaviour increases as a result of higher levels of coworker trust. Organizational citizenship behaviour (OCB) is a behaviour that is not directly related to the main task activity; it supports the organizational, social and psychological context of work. The literature review showed different subfactors of citizenship behaviour between coworkers, which are all related to helping behaviour and proactive working behaviour towards coworkers and towards the organization. This is also shown by Williams and Anderson (1991) who distinguished two types of citizenship behaviours: these are proactive cooperation and assistance between coworkers ('individual CB') and proactive work behaviour for the organization ('organizational CB'). Taken together, coworker trust has a positive influence on individual and organizational CB.

Exclusion of Coworkers (−) One study found that a decrease in coworker trust leads to exclusion of coworkers (Scott et al. 2013). Violated trust relationships lead to workers who are less willing to work together and who are afraid of a vulnerable position (Mayer et al. 1995). Lower levels of coworker trust will lead to less social exchanges between coworkers and coworkers who are more focused on their own survival in an organization (Scott et al. 2013). This results in the exclusion of coworkers.

4.3.3 Type G Consequences: Performance Outcomes

Performance (+) Five of the 21 studies argued or found that coworker trust has a positive influence on the level of performance (i.e. Colquitt et al. 2011; Dirks and

Skarlicki 2009; Golden and Veiga 2018; Lau and Cobb 2010; Peng et al. 2014). All these studies defined performance at the individual level, that is, the individual's task performance (Peng et al. 2014), job performance (Colquitt et al. 2011; Golden and Veiga 2018), or role performance (Lau and Cobb 2010). This relationship is found in several industries and countries, and the studies are mainly building on the social exchange theory.

5   A Proposed Integrative Framework on Antecedents and Consequences of Peer Trust in Franchise Networks

5.1   Introduction to the Framework

This section proposes an integrative framework on peer trust in franchise networks on the basis of the abovementioned framework of coworker trust. Our review on coworker trust showed that the coworker trust literature is still quite fragmented; so far, researchers have studied different (types of) antecedents and consequences adopting different theoretical perspectives. A next step in research on coworker trust would be to develop and test more comprehensive frameworks that include multiple types of antecedents (i.e. employee, coworker, leadership and organizational characteristics) and/or multiple types of consequences (i.e. perceptual/attitudinal, behavioural and performance outcomes). Moreover, only a few studies on coworker trust have included moderating and mediating variables, which also seems to be a fruitful avenue for future research on coworker trust.

In the remainder of this paper, we focus on franchisees' peer trust in franchise networks rather than coworker trust. Given the similarities between coworkers and franchisees, the insights from our literature review may largely be applicable to franchisees' peer trust; however, there are also some differences. Most importantly, franchisees are independent business owners operating in their own local markets and may therefore be more inclined than coworkers to act in their own interests (e.g. Dant and Gundlach 1999) and to have fewer interactions (e.g. Darr et al. 1995), and they may be more sensitive to potential 'peer competition' or 'intra-brand competition' (Croonen and Broekhuizen 2019). We combine the broad overview on the basis of the coworker trust literature with insights from franchising research to propose an integrative and more comprehensive framework on antecedents and consequences of peer trust in franchise networks (see Appendix 3 for our broad framework). Since there is hardly any research on peer trust in franchise networks, such a framework provides some potentially fruitful avenues for future research in franchise networks. As pointed out, we keep it simple here by focusing solely on potential antecedents and consequences of franchisees' peer trust and by excluding potential moderating or mediating variables.

5.2   Antecedents of Peer Trust

5.2.1   Type A Antecedents: Franchisee (Trustor) Characteristics

Franchisee characteristics can also comprise both 'soft' and 'hard' characteristics.

'Soft' Characteristics
The soft characteristics can include franchisee personal traits, such as the franchisee's propensity to trust or the franchisee's self-estrangement. Croonen and Brand (2013) already pointed at the relevance of a franchisee's propensity to trust for understanding a franchisee's trust in the franchisor and its organization, but it is likely that it also affects a franchisee's peer trust since propensity to trust is a general disposition. Regarding self-estrangement as another soft characteristic, to the best of our knowledge, there are no franchising studies that have looked into the effects of franchisees' self-estrangement on their trust or any other variable. Such research could be very useful given the potential consequences for the network of having self-estranged franchisees (cf. Golden and Veiga 2018). For example, self-estranged franchisees may not attend social gatherings or regional meetings, and they may be less willing to share information and knowledge with peers and even with the franchisor. A third and final 'soft' antecedent of franchisees' peer trust could be franchisees' perceived skills development. In the coworker context, employees' skills development was found to positively affect coworker trust due to perceived employment security (Svensson 2018); however, for franchisees—as independent business owners who value their autonomy (cf. Dant and Gundlach 1999)—franchisees' perceived increased skills may also lead to a willingness to break free from the network to continue as fully independent business owners. This may ultimately result in less commitment to the franchisees' peers and even a decrease in peer trust.

'Hard' Characteristics
Regarding the hard characteristics that we derived from the coworker trust review, only the franchisee's time in the network may be a relevant antecedent of franchisees' peer trust as Svensson's distinction between internal and external employees does not apply to a franchising context. Following the reasoning of Van der Werff and Buckley (2017), it can be argued that franchisees that have been in the network for a long time period may have undergone a socialization process that positively affects their trust in their peers. Anecdotal evidence from the franchising literature confirms such a relationship; long-time franchisees sometimes even described their peers as family members or as friends because of the shared history (cf. Croonen 2006).

5.2.2   Type B Antecedents: Peer (i.e. Trustee) Characteristics

We expect the peer characteristics to be applicable to franchising contexts as well. The effects may even be stronger in a franchising context since franchisees' performance may be directly affected by the actions of their peers (cf. horizontal risks as mentioned by Combs et al. 2004). We thus argue that franchisees will assess their peers' trustworthiness (i.e. ability, integrity and benevolence) and that a positive assessment positively affects their level of peer trust (cf. Mayer et al. 1995; Colquitt et al. 2011). In a similar vein, it can be argued that franchisees' positive assessments of their peers' resource investments will positively affect their peer trust (cf. Halbesleben and Wheeler 2015).

However, besides these positive effects, franchisees can also negatively affect their peers through 'uncivil' behaviours and/or conflicts (cf. Scott et al. 2013; Lau and Cobb 2010). The integrative framework of coworker trust showed that uncivil behaviour of coworkers and conflicts with coworkers have negative influences on coworker trust. These authors focus on uncivil behaviours in relationships among coworkers, such as being unfriendly or disrespectful. These may be relevant in a franchise context as well; however, for franchisees there is even more at stake. They expect their peers to comply with the franchisor's business format and not to harm the network's reputation in the outside world. In other words, franchisees expect their peers not to behave opportunistically. Even though monitoring of the franchisees in order to prevent such behaviours is an important task for franchisors (Combs et al. 2004; Croonen and Broekhuizen 2019), monitoring can never be perfect, and therefore franchisees always need to have some trust that their peers will not behave opportunistically. The effect of peer opportunistic behaviours on franchisees' peer trust would therefore be an important topic in franchising research.

5.2.3   Type C Antecedents: Franchisor Characteristics

The franchisor is the leader of the franchise network, and therefore the franchisees' perceived franchisor characteristics are likely to affect franchisees' peer trust. The franchisor can positively or negatively affect franchisees' peer trust.

The literature review on coworker trust showed that leaders can positively affect coworker trust by showing authentic leadership (Gill and Caza 2018) and by trusting employees (Lau and Liden 2008). The positive effect of authentic leadership on coworker trust is also likely to occur in a franchising context, since authentic leadership generally leads to a positive organizational climate. The relationship between the leader's trust in employees and coworker trust may be a bit more complicated than suggested by Lau and Liden (2008). They argue that employees that are trusted by their leaders will often have more responsibilities and more confidential information and get more advice from the leader and that they will behave according to the leader's expectations to continue receiving the leader's trust. According to Lau and Liden, such trustworthy behaviours are also noticed by other employees, which leads to coworker trust in the organization. However, we can think of situations in which a leader's trust in employees can 'backfire': some employees can consider the leader's behaviours as 'preferential treatments' for the trusted employees, which may result in perceptions of unfairness. In such situations, a leader's trust in specific employees can create a distance between coworkers that are clearly trusted by the leader and those who are not. Such a distance may ultimately result in lower coworker trust. Franchisees may be even more sensitive to peers receiving preferential treatments than coworkers because franchisees are independent business owners and their incomes may (partly) depend on their franchisor's and peers' behaviours. Some franchising literature has already presented evidence of franchisee preferential treatments and resulting perceptions of unfairness among fellow franchisees, for example, because some franchisees were asked to join a committee or received special deals (cf. Croonen 2010). This preferential treatment could ultimately negatively influence peer trust in the network. All in all, we expect that a franchisor's trust in *specific* franchisees may negatively affect franchisees' peer trust because of the perceived preferential treatment and resulting unfairness perceptions among peers. This should probably be contrasted with a more 'generalized' level of trust of the franchisor; if the franchisor demonstrates that it trusts the group, then franchisees' peer trust may be more likely.

A third and final franchisor characteristic that can affect franchisees' peer trust is abusive supervision. Peng et al. (2014) found that employees perceiving abusive supervision from their leader are less likely to trust their peers because they feel that they do not belong to the group. In a similar vein, franchisees could have the feeling that they are treated unfairly by the franchisor, which could negatively influence their interactions with their peers. Therefore, we overall expect that a franchisee's perceived abusive supervision negatively affects its peer trust. However, this relationship is likely to be less strong (or may even be positive) if the other franchisees also feel treated unfairly by the franchisor. In that case, peers may be triggered to interact and to form coalitions to jointly 'fight' their franchisor, and these interactions regarding a 'common enemy' may positively affect peer trust. Even though we do see such franchisee coalition formation processes in franchising practice, such processes are still a black box in the franchising literature.

5.2.4   Type D Antecedents: Franchise Network Characteristics

Similar to organizational characteristics in a coworker context, the franchise network characteristics can comprise both cultural and procedural characteristics. Regarding the cultural characteristics, there is no reason to assume that the relationships between cultural characteristics (i.e. psychological safety and shared norms) and coworker trust will be different in a franchising context. Since research on coworker trust does not agree on whether employees' perceived psychological safety is an antecedent or a consequence of coworker trust (cf. May et al. 2004; Roussin and Webber 2012), it is important for (franchising) researchers to take this ambiguity into account first.

Regarding the procedural characteristics, the finding of Lapointe et al. (2014) on the positive effects of socialization tactics on coworker trust is very likely to be applicable to franchising contexts as well. Franchising researchers could investigate the effects of different tactics on franchisees' peer trust; for example, studies could focus on the effect of different types of franchisee training on franchisees' peer trust. Additionally, a franchise network's 'procedural justice climate' (cf. Shin et al. 2014) is likely to be a very important characteristic that affects franchisees' peer trust. This is related to the above discussion on preferential treatments. In a franchise network with fair procedures, it is less likely that franchisees perceive unfair preferential treatments of peers (cf. Croonen 2010), which may thus positively affect franchisees' peer trust. Finally, an important procedural and formal element of franchise networks that may affect franchisees' peer trust is the franchise contract. The franchise contract is an important governance mechanism that steers franchisees' behaviours, for example, through reducing opportunism and increasing compliance (Hajdini and Windsperger 2019). More specifically, some contractual provisions (e.g. resale price maintenance and exclusive territory arrangements) may reduce intra-brand competition which may in turn facilitate the development of franchisees' peer trust. In other words, if franchisees perceive a high level of intra-brand competition, they may be less inclined to trust each other. The way in which different contractual provisions may affect franchisees' peer trust is a black box that warrants further research. The contractual clauses distinguished by Hajdini and Windsperger (2019) could be a useful starting point in that.

5.3   Consequences of Franchisees' Peer Trust

In the review on coworker trust, we already argued that consequences of coworker trust form a 'causal chain' of variables, in which perceptual/attitudinal outcomes affect behavioural outcomes that in turn affect performance outcomes at different levels (cf. Becker and Gerhart 1996). The reasoning is the same in a franchising context.

5.3.1   Type E Consequences: Perceptual/Attitudinal Outcomes

The review on coworker trust showed positive effects of coworker trust on employees' perceived group cohesion and their affective commitment to their organizations (cf. Ferres et al. 2004; Ladebo 2006; Parker et al. 2006; Lapointe et al. 2014). Such relationships between franchisees' peer trust and their affective commitment to their franchise networks may also be found in franchise contexts. However, in recent years (franchising) researchers have distinguished different forms of commitment (see Meek et al. 2011; Mignonac et al. 2015). An important question is *if* and *how exactly* franchisees' peer trust would affect these different forms of commitment.

5.3.2   Type F Consequences: Behavioural Outcomes

Our literature review demonstrated that researchers mostly focus on the positive effects of coworker trust on employee behaviours, more specifically on their citizenship behaviours. These behaviours are constructive to the organization. In the franchising literature, we have one study by El Akremi et al. (2011) that found that cohesion among franchisees (cf. peer trust) leads to fewer franchisees' opportunistic behaviours (i.e. deviation from standards and less information withholding). Researchers thus largely seem to assume and find that trust among coworkers or peers has positive effects.

In Sect. 5.3.1 we already hinted at the need for a more elaborate understanding of the effects of franchisees' peer trust on different forms of franchisee commitment, but such a need definitely also exists for understanding the relationships between franchisees' peer trust and franchisees' behaviours in the franchise network. We base this statement on several observations in franchise practice of franchisees joining forces against their franchisors, such as via filing collective lawsuits or by jointly leaving their franchise networks (to start a competing network). Such behaviours are destructive to the franchise network, but they only seem possible because of trust among the peers. Depending on the level of analysis, franchisees' peer trust can thus have positive or negative outcomes (cf. Lumineau 2017), and it is important to study the conditions under which these positive or negative outcomes arise.

We can think of two possible situations in which franchisees' peer trust can lead to behaviours that are destructive to the network. The first situation is franchisees' 'collective' distrust in the franchisor (collective = at least a group of franchisees). In case of franchisees' lack of trust in the franchisor, it is likely that franchisees form coalitions to create some 'countervailing power' against the franchisor. These coalitions are only possible in case of franchisees' peer trust. In situations of problematic relationships with the franchisor, franchisees' peer trust can thus lead to joint behaviours that are destructive to the franchisor and the franchise network. In practice, we therefore sometimes see that franchisors try to apply 'divide and conquer' strategies, for example, by trying to prevent franchisee interactions.[4] A second situation in which franchisees' peer trust can be destructive to the franchise network is when peer trust leads to information and knowledge sharing among franchisees (cf. Halbesleben and Wheeler 2015), which may ultimately increase the franchisees' perceived skills and self-efficacy and in turn may increase their desire for autonomy (cf. Dant and Gundlach 1999). Even when there is trust in the franchisor, their increased skills and need for autonomy may cause franchisees to be inclined to leave their network to continue the business on their own or with a newly started network with some peers. We have recently seen some examples of the latter in Dutch retailing (e.g. drugstores and sports fashion). Of course, a combination of the two abovementioned reasons (i.e. distrust in the franchisor and building of skills and self-efficacy in combination with a need for autonomy) is possible as well.

5.3.3 Type G Consequences: Performance Outcomes

As pointed out in Sect. 4.3.3, only five of the reviewed studies have incorporated performance consequences of coworker trust, and these all focused on individuals'

---

[4]Such franchisor 'divide and conquer strategies' typically do not seem very effective because franchisees always find a way to interact.

task, job or role performance as opposed to performance at the team/group or organizational level (cf. Fulmer and Gelfand 2012). In a franchising context, these different levels may also be relevant. Some previous studies (e.g. Meiseberg et al. 2017; Brand et al. 2018) have focused on the effects of 'peer networking' on franchisee unit performance, but it is not yet known how exactly franchisees' peer trust affects unit performance, let alone how it affects team or network performance. Peer trust may facilitate networking and hence performance, but there is no scientific knowledge yet on how peer trust facilitates peer networking (e.g. Are there differences regarding the types and dimensions of knowledge on which peers aim to interact? Who is networking with whom? Is more peer trust needed for sharing tacit knowledge rather than tangible knowledge?) and ultimately performance (e.g. how do peer trust and networking affect different dimensions of performance?). A next step would be to focus on the effects of franchisees' peer trust on performance of subgroups within the franchise networks (e.g. specific countries or regions) or networks as a whole (e.g. do franchise networks with high levels of peer trust outperform the ones with lower levels of peer trust?).

6   Conclusion

The aim of this paper was to develop an integrative framework on antecedents and consequences of franchisees' peer trust within franchise networks. Given the mixed motives that are present in franchise networks, this is an important managerial issue for franchisors. Our framework provides insights into potential types of antecedents and consequences of franchisees' peer trust. The coworker trust literature can serve as a useful source of inspiration; however, our systematic literature review has shown that this literature is still fragmented and sometimes even inconsistent (e.g. the role of psychological safety). Moreover, there may be some differences between employment and franchising contexts; compared to coworkers, franchisees may have a higher desire for autonomy, they may have fewer interactions with each other, they may be more critical to their peers' actions, and the legal context for franchise relationships is different compared to that for employment relationships. For future research, it is important to take such franchise-specific contingencies into account in developing and testing theoretical frameworks on antecedents and/or consequences of franchisees' peer trust. For franchisors and their consultants, such frameworks can really help in managing peer trust: they can help in understanding when and how franchisees' being 'jolly good fellows' is beneficial or not and the type of actions that franchisors can undertake to actively manage peer trust.

Appendix 1 Summary of Research on the Antecedents and Consequences of Coworker Trust

	Number of studies[a]		Number of studies[a]		Number of studies[a]
Total sample	21				
Methodology		**Theoretical perspective**		**Consequences**	
Quantitative	20	Authentic leadership theory	1	Perceptual/attitudinal outcomes	6
Qualitative	0	Conservation of resource theory	1	Behavioural outcomes	10
Conceptual	1	Organizational behaviour and social psychology	1	Performance outcomes	5
Industries		Social exchange theory	11	**Trust definition**	
Agricultural	1	Social information processing theory	1	Cook and Wall (1980)	2
Education	5	Theory of psychological engagement	1	Mayer and Davis (1999)	4
Engineering	2	Transformational leadership literature	1	Mayer et al. (1995)	5
Finance	6	Trust literature	5	McAllister (1995)	3
Firefighters	1	**Antecedents**		Other definitions	8
Healthcare	3	Employee characteristics	6	**Forms of trust**	
Manufacturing	4	Coworker characteristics	6	Affect-based trust	4
Retail	1	Leadership characteristics	3	Cognition-based trust	0
Not specified	6	Organizational characteristics	4	Affect- and cognition-based trust	2
Countries				Not specified	15
Australia	2			**Measurement of trust**	
Canada	2			Matching/dyadic approach	6
China	1			Overall	14
Europe	1			Not relevant	1
Ireland	1				
Korea	1				
Nigeria	1				
Philippines	1				
Sweden	1				
United Kingdom	1				
United States	9				

[a]Some of the studies were focusing on more than one antecedent, consequence, industry, country, etc.

Appendix 2 Integrative Framework on the Antecedents and Consequences of Coworker Trust

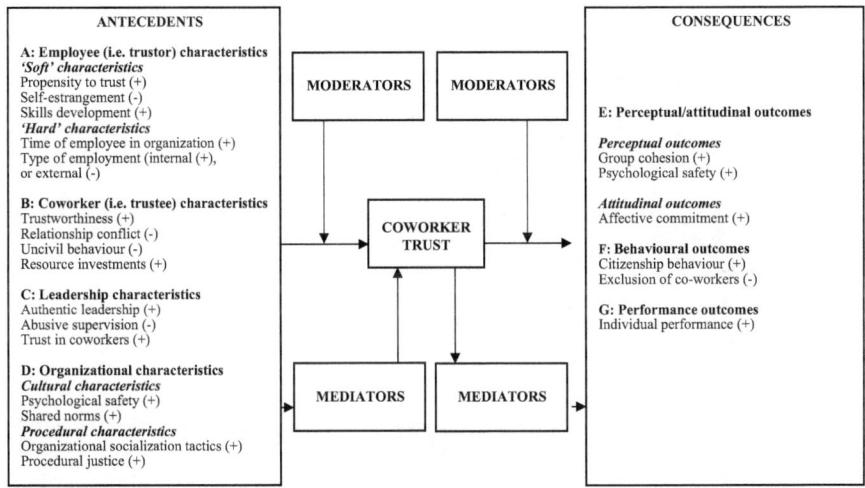

Appendix 3 Proposed Integrative Framework on the Antecedents and Consequences of Franchisees' Peer Trust

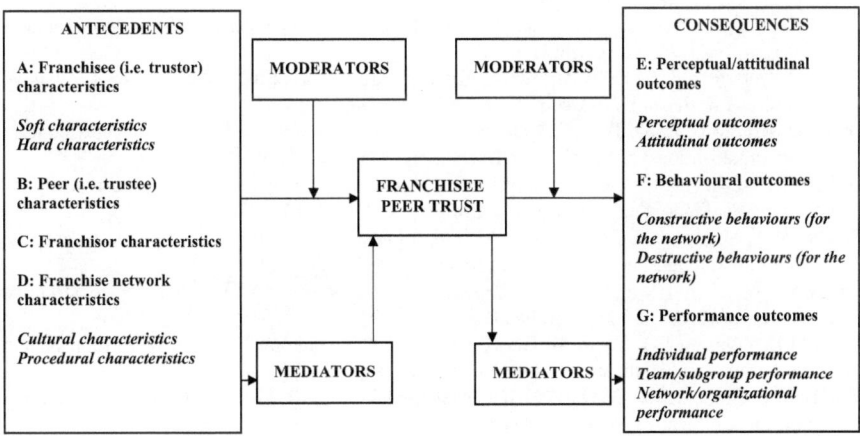

References

Becker B, Gerhart B (1996) The impact of human resource management on organizational performance; progress and prospects. Acad Manag J 39(4):779–801

Blau PM (1964) Exchange and power in social life. Transaction, New Brunswick, NJ

Brand MJ, Croonen EPM, Leenders RTAJ (2018) Entrepreneurial networking; a blessing or a curse? Differential effects for low, medium and high performing franchisees. Small Bus Econ 50(4):783–805

Colquitt JA, Scott BA, LePine JA (2007) Trust, trustworthiness, and trust propensity: a meta-analytic test of their unique relationships with risk taking and job performance. J Appl Psychol 92(4):909–927

Colquitt JA, LePine JA, Zapata CP, Wild RE (2011*) Trust in typical and high-reliability contexts: building and reacting to trust among firefighters. Acad Manag J 54(5):999–1015

Combs JG, Ketchen DJ (2003) Why do firms use franchising as an entrepreneurial strategy? A meta-analysis. J Manag 29(3):443–465

Combs JG, Michael SC, Castrogiovanni GJ (2004) Franchising; a review and avenues to greater theoretical diversity. J Manag 30(6):907–931

Cook J, Wall T (1980) New work attitude measures of trust, organizational commitment and personal need non-fulfilment. J Occup Organ Psychol 53(1):39–52

Croonen EPM (2006) Strategic interactions in franchise relationships. University of Groningen, PhD Thesis Faculty of Business Administration

Croonen EPM (2010) Trust and fairness during strategic change processes in franchise systems. J Bus Ethics 95(2):191–209

Croonen EPM (2017) Understanding antecedents of franchisee trust. In: Hoy F, Perrigot R, Terry A (eds) Handbook of research on franchising. Edward Elgar Publishing, Cheltenham, UK

Croonen EPM, Brand MJ (2013) Antecedents of franchisee trust. J Mark Channels 20(1–2):141–168

Croonen EPM, Broekhuizen TLJ (2019) How do franchisees assess franchisor trustworthiness? J Small Bus Manag 57(3):845–871

Cropanzano R, Mitchell MS (2005) Social exchange theory: an interdisciplinary review. J Manag 31(6):874–900

Dada O (2018) A model of entrepreneurial autonomy in franchised outlets: a systematic review of the empirical evidence. Int J Manag Rev 20(2):206–226

Dant RP, Gundlach GT (1999) The challenge of autonomy and dependence in franchised channels of distribution. J Bus Ventur 14(1):35–67

Darr ED, Kurtzberg TR (2000) An investigation of partner similarity dimensions on knowledge transfer. Organ Behav Hum Decis Process 82(1):28–44

Darr ED, Argote L, Epple D (1995) The acquisition, transfer and depreciation of knowledge in service organizations; productivity in franchises. Manag Sci 41(11):1750–1762

Dirks KT, Skarlicki DP (2009*) The relationship between being perceived as trustworthy by coworkers and individual performance. J Manag 35(1):136–157

El Akremi A, Mignonac K, Perrigot R (2011) Opportunistic behaviors in franchise chains: the role of cohesion among franchisees. Strateg Manag J 32(9):930–948

Ferres N, Connell J, Travaglione A (2004*) Co-worker trust as a social catalyst for constructive employee attitudes. J Manag Psychol 19(6):608–622

Frazier ML, Johnson PD, Gavin M, Gooty S (2010) Organizational justice, trustworthiness, and trust: A multifoci examination. Group Org Manag 35(1):39–76

Fulmer CA, Gelfand MJ (2012) At what level (and in whom) we trust; trust across multiple organizational levels. J Manag 38(4):1167–1230

Gill C, Caza A (2018*) An investigation of authentic leadership's individual and group influences on follower responses. J Manag 44(2):530–554

Golden TD, Veiga, JF (2018*) Self-estrangement's toll on job performance: the pivotal role of social exchange relationships with coworkers. J Manag 44(4):1573–1597

Hajdini I, Windsperger J (2019) Contractual restraints and performance in franchise networks. Ind Mark Manag. https://doi.org/10.1016/j.indmarman.2019.02.011

Halbesleben JR, Wheeler AR (2015*) To invest or not? The role of coworker support and trust in daily reciprocal gain spirals of helping behavior. J Manag 41(6):1628–1650

Hobfoll SE (2001) The influence of culture, community, and the nested-self in the stress process: advancing conservation of resources theory. Appl Psychol 50(3):337–421

Kidwell RE, Nygaard A, Silkoset R (2007) Antecedents and effects of free riding in the franchisor–franchisee relationship. J Bus Ventur 22(4):522–544

Ladebo OJ (2006*) Perceptions of trust and employees' attitudes: a look at Nigeria's agricultural extension workers. J Bus Psychol 20(3):409–427

Lapointe É, Vandenberghe C, Boudrias JS (2014*) Organizational socialization tactics and newcomer adjustment: the mediating role of role clarity and affect-based trust relationships. J Occup Organ Psychol 87(3):599–624

Lau RS, Cobb AT (2010*) Understanding the connections between relationship conflict and performance: the intervening roles of trust and exchange. J Organ Behav 31(6):898–917

Lau DC, Liden RC (2008*) Antecedents of coworker trust: leaders' blessings. J Appl Psychol 93(5): 1130–1138

Lau DC, Liu J, Fu PP (2007) Feeling trusted by business leaders in China: antecedents and the mediating role of value congruence. Asia Pac J Manag 24(3):321–340

Liden RC, Wayne SJ, Kraimer ML, Sparrowe RT (2003) The dual commitments of contingent workers: an examination of contingents' commitment to the agency and the organization. J Organ Behav 24(5):609–625

Liden RC, Bauer TN, Erdogan B (2004) The role of leader-member exchange in the dynamic relationship between employer and employee: implications for employee socialization, leaders, and organizations. In: Coyle-Shapiro JAM, Shore LM, Taylor MS, Tetrick LE (eds) The employment relationship: examining psychological and contextual perspectives. Oxford University Press, Oxford UK, pp 226–250

Lumineau F (2017) How contracts influence trust and distrust. J Manag 43(5):1553–1577

May DR, Gilson RL, Harter LM (2004*) The psychological conditions of meaningfulness, safety and availability and the engagement of the human spirit at work. J Occup Organ Psychol 77(1):11–37

Mayer RC, Davis JH (1999) The effect of the performance appraisal system on trust for management: a field quasi-experiment. J Appl Psychol 84(1):123–136

Mayer RC, Gavin MB (2005) Trust in management and performance: who minds the shop while the employees watch the boss? Acad Manag J 48(5):874–888

Mayer RC, Davis JH, Schoorman FD (1995) An integrative model of organizational trust. Acad Manag Rev 20(3):709–734

McAllister DJ (1995) Affect-and cognition-based trust as foundations for interpersonal cooperation in organizations. Acad Manag J 38(1):24–59

McGuire GM, Bielby WT (2016*) The variable effects of tie strength and social resources: how type of support matters. Work Occup 43(1):38–74

Meek WR, Davis-Sramek B, Baucus MS, Germain RN (2011) Commitment in franchising: the role of collaborative communication and a franchisee's propensity to leave. Enterp Theory Pract 35(3):559–581

Meiseberg B, Mignonac K, Perrigot R, El Akremi A (2017) Performance implications of centrality in franchisee advice networks. Manag Decis Econ 38:1227–1236

Mignonac K, Vandenberghe C, Perrigot R, El Akremi A, Herrbach O (2015) A multi-study investigation of outcomes of franchisees' affective commitment to their franchise organization. Enterp Theory Pract 39(3):1–28

Nijmeijer KJ, Fabbricotti IN, Huijsman R (2014) Making franchising work: a framework based on a systematic review. Int J Manag Rev 16(1):62–83

Parker SK, Williams HM, Turner N (2006*) Modeling the antecedents of proactive behavior at work. J Appl Psychol 91(3):636

Peng AC, Schaubroeck JM, Li Y (2014*) Social exchange implications of own and coworkers' experiences of supervisory abuse. Acad Manag J 57(5):1385–1405

Roussin CJ, Webber SS (2012*) Impact of organizational identification and psychological safety on initial perceptions of coworker trustworthiness. J Bus Psychol 27(3):317–329

Schilke O, Cook KS (2015) Sources of alliance partner trustworthiness: integrating calculative and relational perspectives. Strateg Manag J 36(2):276–297

Scott KL, Restubog SLD, Zagenczyk TJ (2013*). A social exchange-based model of the antecedents of workplace exclusion. J Appl Psychol 98(1):37–48

Settoon RP, Mossholder KW (2002*) Relationship quality and relationship context as antecedents of person-and task-focused interpersonal citizenship behavior. J Appl Psychol 87(2):255

Shin Y, Du J, Choi JN (2014*) Multi-level longitudinal dynamics between procedural justice and interpersonal helping in organizational teams. J Bus Psychol 30(3):513–528

Solis-Rodriguez V, Gonzalez-Diaz M (2012) How to design franchise contracts: the role of contractual hazards and experience. J Small Bus Manag 50(4):652–677

Svensson S (2018*) Organizational trust: how to include the division of labour? Econ Ind Democr 39(2):272–293

Van der Werff L, Buckley F (2017*) Getting to know you: a longitudinal examination of trust cues and trust development during socialization. J Manag, 43(3):742–770

Webber SS (2002) Leadership and trust facilitating cross-functional team success. J Manag Dev 21(3):201–214

Williams M (2001) In whom we trust: group membership as an affective context for trust development. Acad Manag Rev 26(3):377–396

Williams LJ, Anderson SE (1991) Job satisfaction and organizational commitment as predictors of organizational citizenship and in-role behaviors. J Manag 17(3):601–617

Wilson JM, Straus SG, McEvily B (2006) All in due time: the development of trust in computer-mediated and face-to-face teams. Organ Behav Hum Decis Process 99(1):16–33

Yakovleva M, Reilly RR, Werko R (2010*) Why do we trust? Moving beyond individual to dyadic perceptions. J Appl Psychol 95(1):79–91

Business Model Innovation in Franchising: Rethinking the Franchising Taxonomy

Cary Di Lernia and Andrew Terry

Abstract The business format franchise is the gold standard for franchising. It delivers a uniform, standardised and consistent product, and this is indeed one of its key strengths. Franchising is nevertheless a practical commercial strategy. Successful franchisors build formats, devise systems and develop network expansion models which accommodate the unique characteristics of the business and the prevailing market conditions as well as wider social trends. This paper challenges the standard franchising paradigm and suggests that there are four distinct franchising models—business format franchising, brand franchising, quasi-franchising and flexible franchising—and presents a taxonomy to accommodate them. The focus of this paper is nevertheless on *flexible franchising*—a new franchise model which eschews the formulaic uniformity of conventional franchising and explicitly and intentionally embraces and incorporates as its integral feature the franchisee's flexibility to bring his or her own brand of entrepreneurship to the franchised business. The development of flexible franchising in practice is examined through case studies on two innovative Australian franchise systems.

1 Introduction

Almost three decades ago, William Davidow and Michael Malone in *The Virtual Corporation* (1992) identified driving forces that were transforming the marketplace and corporations. Contemporary commercial models needed to become adaptable, flexible and responsive. Franchising provides a textbook example. Since its development in the 1950s under the influence of franchising pioneers such as Ray Kroc (McDonald's) and Harland Sanders (KFC) who were searching for practical solutions to the challenges they faced in the expansion of their licensed networks, business format franchising has revolutionised the distribution of goods and services

C. Di Lernia (✉) · A. Terry
The University of Sydney Business School, The University of Sydney, Sydney, Australia
e-mail: cary.dilernia@sydney.edu.au; andrew.terry@sydney.edu.au

© Springer Nature Switzerland AG 2019
J. Windsperger et al. (eds.), *Design and Management of Interfirm Networks*,
Contributions to Management Science,
https://doi.org/10.1007/978-3-030-29245-4_4

in virtually all industry sectors and has transformed the business landscape of most countries. It has been franchising's capacity for reinventing itself—its continual adaptation to accommodate changing circumstances and market conditions—which has guaranteed its increasing influence as a business model throughout the world.

Franchising is essentially a strategy for business cloning. The franchising relationship is based on a prescribed business model developed by the franchisor and carried out under the franchisor's guidance and oversight by franchisees who are granted the right to trade under the franchisor's brand and system. The appeal of franchising for a franchisee lies in 'the potential benefits of being able to conduct the business under an established brand name using tested operational systems' (Parliamentary Joint Committee 2008, p xiii). The essence of franchising is, in the words of Kos (1990, p. 1), 'to convey the appearance of a single entity largely indistinguishable from a single owner chain comprising branches at separate locations'. It is the resulting formulaic uniformity—disparagingly captured in the title of George Ritzer's book *The McDonaldization of Society* (2004)—which has been responsible for the spectacular development of franchising.

It is nevertheless a retreat from such formulaic uniformity which, this paper argues, will be an increasingly significant factor in franchising's future development. While independence and individualism have traditionally been seen as the enemies of franchising, the paradigm is shifting as increasing commercial pressures come to disrupt the standard model. Streed and Cliquet acknowledge that 'research in this regard is still scarce and the impact of autonomy in the franchise network is still untested for the most part' but observe that 'the market appears to be changing and the traditional business format franchising model based on uniformity is being challenged on multiple fronts' (2017, p. 52). Extant research in relation to the standardisation/customisation dichotomy has been explored in relation location (Cox and Mason 2007), product offerings (Pardo-del-Val et al. 2014), particular operational aspects (Grünhagen et al. 2014) and service personalisation (Streed and Cliquet 2008), but these are simply particular aspects of a wider franchisee autonomy presented in this paper. While business format franchising accommodates intrapreneurial franchisees prepared to work within the system, the opportunities for entrepreneurial franchisees who require an outlet for their individuality beyond the confines of the brand and system are of course limited. For the typical franchisee, standardisation is a necessary, and virtually inevitable, reality. Nevertheless, there are increasing commercial pressures (discussed below, and see Terry and Di Lernia 2013) to allow greater franchisee autonomy—and to reconsider the appropriate balance between adaptation and standardisation—making this a phenomenon of increasing commercial significance.

This paper challenges the standard franchising paradigm. It identifies four discrete franchise models with a particular focus on a novel iteration in the form of *flexible franchising* and presents a case study of two Australian flexible franchise systems.

2   Rethinking the Franchise Model and Redefining the Franchising Taxonomy

Isaac Singer is generally credited as the founder of franchising (Dicke 1992). In 1851 he invented not only the world's first viable domestic sewing machine but also a new method of distribution under which independent salesmen paid fees to acquire exclusive territorial rights to sell his branded products. By the 1930s in the USA, franchising was entrenched as the preferred method of distributing motor vehicles and gasoline, and its presence was being felt in retail marketing and the emerging services sector. However, in terms of growth and innovation, the decade of the 1950s was the most significant period. The growth of franchising in that period is explained by the expanding postwar economy and a growing interstate highway system. This was the era in which Harland Sanders (KFC) and Ray Kroc (McDonald's) built national chains along the developing interstate networks. The innovation in franchising in that period is explained by the evolution of franchising from product and trade name franchising (referred to in this paper as *brand franchising*), characterised by a relationship between supplier and dealer in which franchised dealers concentrate on one company's product line and to some extent identify their business with that of the supplier, to the more sophisticated *business format franchising* model. The latter is characterised by an ongoing business relationship between franchisor and franchisee which includes product, service and trademark, as well as the entire business concept itself, training and a continuing process of assistance, guidance and supervision.

It is business format franchising that has driven the relentless development of franchising in the USA and internationally to the extent that the terms 'franchising' and 'business format franchising' are usually used interchangeably. This paper nevertheless suggests that there are four distinct franchise models—*brand franchising*, *business format franchising*, *flexible franchising* and *quasi-franchising*. Business format franchising for obvious reasons dominates franchising practice[1]—but it is not the only model. While the unique advantages of business format franchising make it the preferred and appropriate model in most cases, it is not the exclusive reserve of franchising strategy. This paper argues that there are in fact viable, discrete and alternative models which harness in different ways, and in different

---

[1] A convenient summary of the benefits of business format franchising is set out in the Report by the House of Representatives Standing Committee on Industry, Science and Technology, *Finding a Balance: Towards Fair Trading in Australia*, May 1997, p. 84:

> Substantial benefits exist for both franchisees and franchisors under the system. The franchisor derives income from any initial franchising fee and from access to a continuing cash flow through product sales and from licence fees without having to provide additional capital or to directly manage the franchisee. The franchisor gains from access to established business systems, developed products or services, training and business advice, group advertising and lower risk.

combinations, the brand ('front-of-house' features—the brand, the image, the standardised consumer experience, the look and feel, the trade dress, the appearance, the servicescape) and system ('back-of-house' features—the items underlying the external manifestation of the chain, including specifications, processes, policies and procedures which make the business work efficiently) architecture.

The power of franchising derives from the innovative packaging of the franchisor's brands, systems, management, technologies, networks and economies of scale in combination with the committed proprietorship of the franchisee. However there is scope for massive variety in the manner in which these elements are packaged. Klein argues that 'control, exclusivity and standardisation' are the distinguishing features of franchise relationships and that there is a 'continuum of contract arrangements along these dimensions' (Klein 1995, p. 12). The search for a definitive line between brand franchising and business format franchising, and between business format franchising and more flexible iterations of it, is elusive (Marnoto 2013, p. 38). This may suggest that discrete model recognition and classification is a pointless exercise. It is nevertheless argued that despite blurred boundaries there are distinct models. It is not a matter of a 'best' model, but the appropriate model which is likely to provide the best outcomes in particular circumstances. Recognition of the discrete and distinct models, of their strengths and weaknesses and of their utility in different contexts, can facilitate the development of franchising and the appropriate deployment of these models in appropriate contexts. Figure 1 below presents a new taxonomy of the four franchising models discussed below along the axes of brand and system primacy.

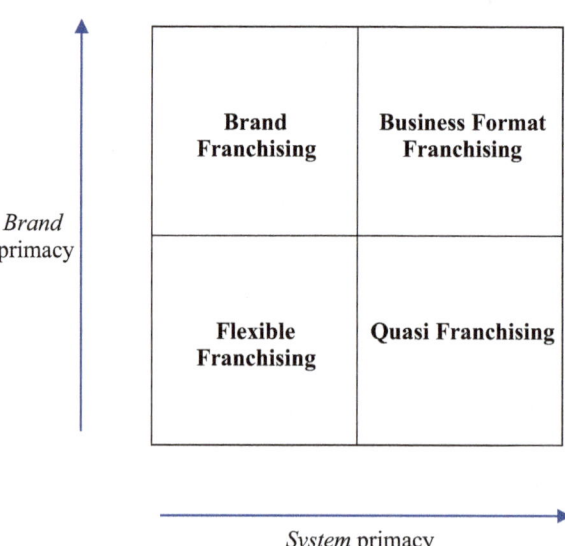

Fig. 1 Franchise model taxonomy

2.1 Business Format Franchising

Standardisation, consistency and uniformity across all aspects of the business is the key to business format franchising with 'virtually every aspect of such systems is regulated via contract in order to ensure system wide standardisation' (Grünhagen et al. 2014, p. 828). Business format franchising synergistically harnesses brand and system—front-of-house and back-of-house—architecture. It is a sophisticated business relationship whereby a franchisor who has developed a unique or individual manner of doing business permits the franchisee to use that system, in a controlled fashion, in the operation of the franchisee's independently owned business. Business format franchising is characterised by an ongoing business relationship between franchisor and franchisee which includes the product, service and trademark, as well as the entire business concept itself—a marketing strategy and plan, image, comprehensive operational standards, systems and formats, operating manuals, training, quality control and a continuing process of assistance, guidance and supervision. It is a 'symbiotic relationship in which the needs of the franchisor and the franchisee blend in a commercial marriage of convenience' (Terry and Giugni 2019, p. 641). In the words of the US House of Representatives Committee on Small Business (1990, p. 13), business format franchising 'has provided the means for merging the seemingly conflicting interests of existing businesses with those of aspiring entrepreneurs in a single process that promotes business expansion, entrepreneurial opportunity and shared cost and risk'. It is business format franchising that is driving the development of franchising and expanding its influence to virtually every industry sector and in most countries around the world.

2.2 Brand Franchising

First-generation franchising—that for which Isaac Singer is credited with introducing in the 1860s—is variously referred to as 'traditional franchising' (Blair and Lafontaine 2005), 'product and trade name franchising' (Justis and Judd 1989), 'product name franchising' (Price 1997), 'product distribution franchising' (Blair and Lafontaine 2005) and 'product-driven franchising' (Sherman 2011). This paper adopts the term 'brand franchising' to describe what are essentially exclusive branded distributorship arrangements where the franchisor provides either the product (as in new motor vehicle distributorships) or the essential ingredient or know-how to a manufacturer or processor (as in soft-drink bottling) for distribution in an exclusive territory under the franchisor's trademarks. In this form of franchising, there is an absence of any real format beyond the branded product which is distributed, processed and/or manufactured.

Brand franchising fits uneasily into the modern franchising picture. The examples of brand franchising usually cited—petroleum retailing, new motor vehicle retailing and soft-drink bottling—are, at least in the first two cases, well advanced in their metamorphosis to business format franchise systems. Interestingly, franchising statistics generally exclude franchising activities in motor vehicle and fuel retailing—in Australia because of the 'unique characteristics of these industries' (Frazer et al. 2016).[2] Motor vehicle and fuel turnover data is nevertheless included in sector turnover data presumably because in dollar terms they far outweigh the turnover from business format franchising and thus inflate considerably the entire franchise sector turnover.[3]

If fuel and new motor vehicle franchises are indeed brand franchises, this form of franchising has the greatest share of the entire franchising sector in terms of turnover, although not in franchisor and franchisee numbers. Business format franchising is nevertheless the most rapidly growing model. It is not only the preferred and most appropriate model for the majority of new franchise systems, but is also the product of an evolutionary process for many older brand franchise systems.

Outside the fuel, motor vehicle and soft-drink bottling sectors, brand franchising is nevertheless very much the poor relation to business format franchising in the franchising world. But while the business format franchise is the preferred model for franchise development because it offers a complete business format (including initial training, operational and managerial systems and ongoing assistance and support), resulting in a cloned network, it remains an aspiration for many developing countries. The commercial, social, cultural, economic and regulatory infrastructure may not be sufficiently advanced for the effective development of business format franchising (Binh and Terry 2014). The simplicity of brand franchising works well in this environment. It should not be seen as a lesser franchising model—simply as a different model that accommodates contemporary business conditions and makes viable a form of franchising which could not properly or effectively be achieved through a business format model.

2.3   Quasi-franchising

Terry and Di Lernia (2013) suggest a role for a form of franchising which incorporates only back-of-house elements—the tried, tested and proven systems and procedures which are not directly visible to the customer—and eschews brand and

---

[2]Frazer et al. (2016) estimate that in 2016 there were '70,700 business format franchised units and 8300 company owned units, producing a total of 79,000 units operating in business format franchises in Australia'. This number represented almost 4% of small businesses in Australia. The survey estimated an additional 6500 fuel retail and 4618 motor vehicle retail outlets (Frazer et al. 2016, p. 6).

[3]Frazer et al. (2016) estimate that in 2016 'the total sales revenue of business format franchises was $66.5 billion (compared with $65 billion in 2014). Together with motor vehicle sales of $43.4 billion and fuel retail of $36 billion, the total sales revenue for the entire franchising sector was estimated to be $146 billion (compared with $144 billion in 2014)' (Frazer et al. 2016 p. 6).

other visible manifestations of a standardised 'one-size-fits-all' approach to service provision. They propose a form of quasi-franchising where brand and related front-of-house features are removed or, at least, significantly reduced. The 'franchisee' acquires the right, and the obligation, to use the 'franchisor's' back-of-house system while retaining flexibility for entrepreneurial endeavour in building an idiosyncratic, eclectic and individualised business.

The essence of this type of quasi-franchising is simply franchising without the brand and associated trade dress, image and external indicia that symbolise membership of a standardised chain. It is a form of B2B franchising under which the business proprietor benefits from a range of back-of-house systems which remove many of the challenges in establishing a business—and without which business entry is difficult if not impossible—while retaining discretion in relation to front-of-house features. The underlying arrangements are imperceptible to consumers. Back-of-house franchising provides the opportunity for 'franchisees'—who need a 'trusted guide'—to be able to express their entrepreneurial individuality, the scope for which is limited in a conventional business format franchise (McCrindle n.d.). This option may be particularly attractive to Generation Y who are believed to be more entrepreneurial than previous generations but who want to establish their own businesses which express their own individuality (Milman 2010). Whereas brand franchising removes or substantially reduces system architecture, quasi-franchising removes or severely limits brand architecture. It is a model which currently has limited scope but which is set to grow in future, especially in market segments in which a unique individual experience may trump standardisation—hotels, pubs, cafes, restaurants and boutique fashion. The Australian experience in relation to cafes is instructive:

> The quest to be different and offer customers a boutique experience has driven radical changes in store sizes and locations . . . The standard coffee shop doesn't exist any more . . . Everyone's looking for baristas with the biggest tattoos, biggest beard and best cut-off T-shirt. It's gone from a typical coffee shop with table and chairs to a little hole in the wall, 20 to 30 square metres in size with exposed brickwork and a couple of milk crates for stools out front. (Johnston 2013)

Given that franchising, as usually understood, incorporates brand and system, front-of-house and back-of-house, characteristics, it may seem inconsistent to label back-of-house franchising as quasi-franchising, but not brand franchising which is essentially its opposite—front-of-house franchising. Although legal definition should not drive commercial practice, it is accepted that as every definition of franchising throughout the world includes a brand element, it is inappropriate to use the term 'franchise' to define this extreme iteration of 'franchising'.

2.4   Flexible Franchising

The term flexible franchising is used to describe a franchise model which incorporates as a deliberate strategy a degree of freedom on the part of the franchisee to localise and customise both brand and system architecture. It differs from brand franchising in that there is a format, albeit less prescriptive than business format franchising, and which incorporates franchisee discretion. It differs from quasi-franchising in that there is a brand architecture—albeit incorporating franchisee freedom to adapt, customise and localise. It differs from business format franchising in that the usual prescriptions in relation to brand and system are not absolute. Flexibility and freedom to customise, accommodate local conditions and give effect to the franchisee's notions of entrepreneurialism are encouraged. This form of franchising has been referred to as 'freedom franchising' (Streed and Cliquet 2017), 'no-format franchising' (Marnoto 2013) and 'customised or personalised business format franchising' (Terry and Di Lernia 2013), but it is suggested that the term 'flexible franchising' best captures the essence of this model. It is this model which is discussed in the following sections of the paper.

3 The Flexible Franchise Model

The accepted strength of business format franchising is that it delivers a uniform, standardised and consistent product. As explained by Myers (2013), 'franchising by its nature discourages innovation on the part of franchisees, who are required by their franchisors to follow very specific policies and procedures spelling out exactly what they will sell, how they will make or deliver it, and even what their stores or restaurants will look like'. There is nevertheless considerable diversity in the scope and sophistication of business format franchising systems. Grünhagen et al. comment that 'anecdotal evidence . . . suggests that specific areas of franchise systems may remain almost entirely unregulated by the franchisor, hence, leaving substantial freedoms for franchisees' (2014, p. 828). The concept of allowing franchisees a degree of flexibility in the operation of their franchised businesses is not a new phenomenon. Two decades ago Kaufmann and Eroglu (1999) raised the issue of the appropriate limits of uniformity in business format franchising. They recognised that franchise systems incorporate both core and peripheral elements and suggested that 'finding the balance between standardisation of the core elements and permitted local market adaptation of the peripheral elements remains one of the greatest challenges for the franchisor' (Kaufmann and Eroglu 1999, p. 83).

Flexible franchising might simplistically be regarded as a looser, less disciplined, less structured form of business format franchising. However, there are massive differences in the level of sophistication of business format franchise systems—from the highly prescriptive McDonald's model to much less sophisticated arrangements—the authors nevertheless suggest that flexible franchising is a separate and discrete franchising model in which franchisee flexibility is an integral rather than an incidental part of the agreement. It is not as extreme as quasi-franchising in which brand architecture is largely irrelevant or brand franchising in which system architecture is largely irrelevant, but it nevertheless incorporates as an integral and essential element a degree of franchisee flexibility in both brand and system architecture which is anathema to contemporary business format franchising.

This form of franchising has received little attention in the franchising literature. Streed and Cliquet (2008) discuss the need for franchisors to evaluate trade-offs between standardisation and adaptation of the business concept in order to satisfy their customers and identify potential guidelines for franchisors who are trying to conciliate brand uniformity and adaptation to consumer demand. They accept that 'service personalisation, and more specifically customised personalisation, presents . . . an effective opportunity for chains to adapt to local customer needs without jeopardizing brand integrity' (Streed and Cliquet 2008, p. 220) and argue that 'local responsiveness is more efficient in a franchise system than a company system' (Streed and Cliquet 2017, p. 51). Marnoto goes further to recognise a new form of franchising where franchisees are given greater autonomy and decision-making power than business format franchisees (2013, p. 38). Marnoto describes this 'new form of franchising' as one in which franchisors are 'deeply involved in the relationship with the franchisees, but give them more autonomy and decision power than business format franchisors do' (2013, p. 36). Terry and Di Lernia also discuss a form of customised business franchising allowing franchisee flexibility in the provision of system services (Terry and Di Lernia 2013). Each paper discusses the Great Harvest Bread Co. system which its founder describes as a 'freedom franchise' because of the 'extreme freedom' given to franchisees. Franchisees trade under the Great Harvest Bread Co. banner, but the franchisor 'welcomes and rewards entrepreneurial spirit', and although 'know how such as recipes and management processes are provided each store [can] build its own identity for a better fit in the local business landscape'. The Great Harvest Bread Co. website states:

> If you look at most franchises, they began when some smart person figured out a way to make some money by writing a recipe down and inviting others to copy it. The great thing about these sorts of franchises is that they aren't very risky for the person joining the franchise. The business is, after all, proven.
>
> Most franchises of this variety require owners to do things the franchise's way, with little or no variation. Cookie cutter-style. That's because the franchisor is trying to build a national brand, the foundation of which is consistency. The problem with this sort of franchise, if you're an entrepreneur-type, is that they aren't very much fun.
>
> At the other end of the spectrum is starting up and running your own independent start-up. There you have all the freedom in the world to create this thing just the way you want, but you're flying solo, with no one else to lean on. That's why so many start-ups fail.
>
> We provide an alternative with some of the advantages of a traditional franchise and some of the fun of a "let's-do-it-all-ourselves" start-up. Our philosophy is simple: let's create unique neighborhood bakery cafes that are a reflection of the Great Harvest brand and the bakery cafe owner. We are no cookie cutter franchise. We are a freedom-based, healthy franchise that encourages excellence and individuality (not to mention a spirit of fun and generosity).

The franchising literature's recognition of franchisee personalisation is nevertheless limited by the sovereignty of the brand architecture and servicescape. While brand integrity is critical in business format franchising, the extent to which franchisors can tolerate departure from system standards without concept infringement is a developing issue driven by practical commercial considerations.

Great Harvest Bread Co. is one of the few case studies of flexible franchising in the literature. There are more limited examples of allowing certain freedoms to customise in relation to geography (Cox and Mason 2007), to product (Pardo-del-Val et al. 2014) or to particular operational aspects such as human resource management (Grünhagen et al. 2014) and service personalisation (Streed and Cliquet 2008), but these are limited and particular instances. In no instance does it appear that the allowed flexibility is driven by the characteristics of the franchisee or to harness their entrepreneurial abilities and apply it beyond these limited categories. Where flexibility is allowed, the outcome appears extremely favourable. Grunhagen et al. note that '"pockets" of freedom may foster entrepreneurial activities by franchisees that in turn, might enhance the performance not only of the individual owners, but that of the entire franchise system [and that] allowing franchisees such freedoms strategically may offer a distinct competitive advantage to franchisors who capitalise on the benefits of such arrangements' (Grünhagen et al. 2014, p. 828).

There is indeed increasing recognition that allowing franchisees some discretion over discrete and invariably non-core elements of the business can exist within business format franchising and indeed operate to enhance operational efficiencies and profitability in areas such as human resource management (Grünhagen et al. 2014). An unintended consequence of a flexible franchise model is that it reduces the likelihood of a franchisor being vicariously liable for the conduct of its franchisees (Terry and Huan 2013).

The franchising literature offers many examples of franchisees as critical sources of novel ideas. Kaufmann and Eroglu note that it is often franchisees who create new products, modify existing ones and come up with solutions to system problems in their efforts to adapt to local market conditions. Franchisee ingenuity has, for example, led to many of McDonald's iconic menu items including the Big Mac (Love 1995, p. 293). Such innovations are considered, debated, tested, assessed and trialled before being rolled out system-wide. The franchising literature also offers examples of customisation particularly in relation to expansion to offshore markets to accommodate commercial, social and cultural characteristics (see generally Watson 1997 and Liu 2008). It is the franchise partner—usually master franchisee or area developer—in the host country which drives the necessary customisation.

The large cities which provide the most fertile ground for franchising span massive demographic, social, income, cultural divides—in some cases very similar to the challenges faced by offshore expansion. As with all developments in franchising, the driver is not academic theory but business reality. Franchisors customise and localise when they go overseas and should do when they enter new locales. Franchisees with local knowledge are well equipped to do this (Gorovaia 2017).

Despite the acknowledgement of such franchisee innovation, there is, under the contemporary business format franchising model, little opportunity or scope for such franchisee creativity and entrepreneurship to be encouraged within his or her own business. This is the distinguishing feature of flexible franchising. The freedom and flexibility to innovate is not accepted only or even primarily on a system-wide basis, but is encouraged, even expected, for introduction by individual franchisees within their own businesses.

In their 2013 paper, Terry and Di Lernia argue that the trait of individuality impacts on franchising from two angles—consumer and business. From the consumer's perspective, a consumer who places a premium on individuality of consumption may prefer a customised as opposed to a standardised experience. From the entrepreneur's perspective, a prospective franchisee who has the opportunity to express entrepreneurial individuality—the scope for which is limited in the conventional business format franchise—may be encouraged to take up a business opportunity that might not have been taken up in the absence of any option other than franchisee indenturement under a business format franchise model or the other extreme, completely independent business proprietorship. It perhaps reflects the supposed irreverent Australian character trait that flexibility is more likely to gain traction in Australia than the USA or Europe. It has been suggested that:

> Americans view chains as comforting. No matter where you are, Starbucks will always be there and taste the same. Australians prefer one-offs that are a bit quirkier. The fact that every shop is different is a fun part of the challenge. The Down Under demise of Krispy Kreme says more about our attitude to chains than our attitudes to the US. (Urban quoting Garrett 2010)

It is nevertheless suggested that these issues transcend those of national character.

A flexible franchise model may be embraced as a reactive strategy or as a proactive strategy. The reactive route may be activated as part of a transition from a brand franchise model to a more systematic model. The reactive route is most obviously seen in branded distribution or service arrangements in transition to more comprehensive franchise systems. It will often be commercially unviable for a distributor to impose—whether unilaterally or bilaterally—a comprehensive system on a looser arrangement. The distributor must sell the benefits of a more structured system to a business customer reluctant to accept the obligation to pay royalties in addition to product supply, in return for the promoted benefits that flow from comprehensive front- and back-of-house systems. The necessary compromise may be to allow the franchisee, who in the past has operated very much as an independent—albeit with some branding architecture associated with the product— a degree of flexibility and discretion to apply their own style of entrepreneurship to customising their business.

This paper nevertheless suggests there is scope to embrace flexible franchising as a proactive strategy—a deliberate and calculated strategy—to harness individual franchisee entrepreneurship. This strategy recognises and establishes flexible franchising as a deliberately and unambiguously flexible model to a much greater extent than in relation to the peripheral factors in the Kaufmann-Eroglu model. It is driven not as a commercial reaction to franchisee reluctance to commit to prescriptive systems, nor as a consequence of problems in the practical enforcement of system prescriptions. It is driven proactively to harness franchisee entrepreneurship expressed in localising and customising their business. It is believed that support for the adoption of a flexible franchise model is also found in the 'long tail' that characterises franchising operations in all countries which embrace franchising. Australia is not atypical. Two-thirds of its 1089 systems have less than 50 units, with over 41% holding up to 20 units (Frazer et al. 2016). Many such small systems will not achieve the critical mass necessary for effective business format operation. To allow, indeed require, franchisees to embrace customisation and localisation and personalisation may present their best opportunity for effective, continued operation and the retention of good franchisees.

4   Flexible Franchising in Practice: Examples from Australia

It was suggested above that the embrace of a flexible franchise model may be reactive or proactive. The reactive route is demonstrated by Degani—a coffee shop chain which faced predictable challenges in evolving from a branded coffee distribution system to a more comprehensive coffee shop system. The proactive route is exemplified by Eview Property Group—a real estate group focussed on service differentiation through a customised approach.

4.1   Degani

Founded in 1999, Degani until recently operated in effect as an exclusive branded distributor of its own coffee, essentially as a brand franchise in which coffee was supplied to a network of coffee shops which loosely branded themselves as Degani. With the growth of the business came the decision to move to a more comprehensive franchise system, a move which has faced predictable problems in dealing with the entrenched resistance of the current network who are not particularly sympathetic to the embrace of systematisation with the accompanying imposition of royalties as the quid pro quo for the alleged benefits of a business format franchise system (Gordon 2014). Degani's strategic solution to this commercial challenge has been to allow a substantial measure of franchisee flexibility and discretion in relation to both front-of-house and back-of-house elements. Degani franchisees retain a level of flexibility which is both foreign and anathema to contemporary business format franchise systems.

Degani's website describes its mission as to 'offer a unique customer experience that is individually designed and tailored to meet the needs of the clientele and area in which it serves' (Degani.com.au). Degani believes that its value proposition lies in the customisation and sophistication of its offering. Allowing what might be termed a 'creative licence' under the Degani brand, franchisees are permitted freedom in their particular offering which allows them to develop a distinctive business which fits the neighbourhood it operates within: 'every café design and every menu is created to meet the needs of the local community and the café owner'

(Degani.com.au), resulting, it is claimed, in Degani being 'more relevant in the market' (Rickert 2014).

Former franchise development manager Tanya Kanaris has suggested that the imperative to innovate is the biggest challenge to coffee chains, noting it would be 'dangerous' for chains to ignore gains being made by independent operators in the café sector through their unique offerings (Franchise Business 2015; Heffernan 2015). There is a focus on avoiding the label of a 'cookie cutter' operation and on maintaining excellent operational standards rather than strict replication (Franchise Business 2014). Flexibility for franchisees ranges from everything from the model chosen, the menu offered and various aspects of the store fitout and décor.

Evident here is the delineation of a strict replicative focus from the building of trust in a brand—concepts which have been enmeshed so tightly in the development of many successful business format franchises throughout the history of franchising. Essentially Degani believes that customer loyalty will result from the maintenance of high operational standards rather than formulaic conformity and uniformity— and further that interest from prospective franchisees who are willing to work hard to extend the brand and their own personalised iteration of it will come from extending trust and autonomy to them, rather than insisting on one highly specified, non-customisable model which franchisees may feel no empowerment within and therefore no strong commitment to. Founder George Pezaros states 'when you combine the passionate people with the right premises and a supportive, but non-interfering infrastructure, it works. You must have flexibility. Why say no to ideas, passion and vision?' (Gordon 2014). He believes this freedom to customise and personalise has assisted in Degani's expansion.

Degani's aim is to shape the business 'into a unique franchise model, bringing consistency across all stores, but allowing our franchise business partners the freedom of individuality, which remains true to the brand' (Foster 2014). Degani's flexible business model, low royalties and a personalised support structure constitute key value propositions for prospective franchisees (Franchise Business 2015). Deriving the benefits of franchisee entrepreneurialism, ingenuity and local knowledge nevertheless comes with a responsibility to select franchisees who will flourish in the flexible structure. According to Degani's senior management:

> We show due diligence when it comes to franchise partner selection by evaluating firstly if an individual should be in retail; and secondly should they be in retail with us. Our brand is unique. It has exclusivity and flexibility, but [we] know the realities of operation and what it takes to be successful, so our screening process is very detailed. (Gordon 2014)

Empowering franchisees to become active managers in the sculpting of their particular outlet demonstrates Degani's flexible, collaborative approach. Chefs at each café are given flexibility and ownership over the food served:

> They've given us a rough menu but we create it our way. It gives us the opportunity to experiment and put our own stamp on the food... I can do whatever I want here, within reason. We've even got customers telling us their ideas of what they'd like to see in the shop so we try to look at them, we try and see how we can make it to suit everybody. We've come up with some pretty good ideas. (Silvini 2015)

By embracing individuality, Degani allows franchisees the freedom to offer services suited to their local customer base with Degani providing a dedicated national support.

4.2 Eview Property Group

In the proactive vein stands Eview Property Group, a non-traditional real estate franchise group, which has also seen the merits of a more flexible approach to franchised business ownership established and built on the principle that franchisee autonomy within a system is an essential feature of the system.

Developed in 2006 and designed to give members a personalised edge over their competitors, member agents (currently circa 40) are able to offer a customised service with the support of a corporate back-office system. Dubbed 'a new concept in real estate business ownership', the 'your brand your business' approach allows franchisee agents to tailor their business to their experience and desired position in the market (Eview 2015). This includes the personalisation of the member agent's trading name to feature their own name and colours with the Eview logo displayed in the background, and the freedom to work and list wherever one's client base finds itself, with systems and support available for the agent to 'run their own business their own way' (Eview 2015). Members have complete flexibility to operate from standalone, shared or home offices and thereby accommodate their particular market niche and personal operational preferences. This innovative model has been designed to compete with 'tired models [whose] market relevance is quickly and dramatically being eroded [in a market where] technology and consumer behaviour is undergoing massive change' (Eview 2015). Like Degani, Eview appears willing to trust the potential of its member agents to grow and maintain business relationships and add value to them over time. Eview claims that:

> Real estate is about people. People buy from people, not from a brand. The Eview Group's *YBYB* platform literally turns the traditional franchising model on its head. How? Because it's making the agent and the business synonymous with one another. In other words, as part of the Eview Group, you are the brand. (Eview 2015)

Eview is pitching its model to an untapped source of potential franchisees which conventional real estate models would find it difficult to attract. Allowing member agents to customise their business model and offering and to harness Eview's centralised business support services provides a base for agents who are confident in their selling and customer service ability but who may not be so well versed in, or even excited about, running the back end of a business which is conventionally non-client facing. Member payments to Eview are determined having regard to the extent of support chosen from the franchisor's suite of services. Member agents are able, but are not required, to access centralised back-office functions provided by Eview Group including marketing, training, access to networks, administration, IT support, human resources, continuing education, finance and accounts and online accessibility to corporate resources. Key financial metrics are provided by a cloud-based reporting system offered by Eview for member agents to maintain detailed knowledge of their operations. Eview also offers the services of its centralised human resources department to streamline the employment of staff and all the administrative effort around it, including regulatory compliance. These services are designed to allow agents to focus their attention on vendors and purchasers and 'do what you do best—sell and manage real estate'.

Eview permits choice around income streams and management and offers several options around membership levels which can themselves be tailored to appeal to a broad range of potential franchisees. Importantly, member agents choose the level of back-office support they require and pay an appropriate fee based on the number and type of services contracted for. This flexible approach allows franchisee members to customise their business offering and the precise nature and extent of their involvement in it, which is a potential value proposition for agents looking to defect from more structured systems and those who seek independence as well as support. Attracting such potential value adding franchisees through the provision of a 'middle of the road' path in this industry may provide agents in this position with the support they need to compete distinctly and successfully with more established conventional franchise model competitors.

5   Conclusion

Franchising's capacity for reinventing itself is a matter of record. Indeed its continual adaptation to accommodate changing circumstances and market conditions is a major factor in its increasing influence throughout the world. The manner in which franchising is implemented is nevertheless capable of infinite variation. Franchising is not a business in itself but is a method of doing business—an innovative and dynamic method of distributing goods and services. It encompasses a wide variety of different practices that are used in different ways, and with varying degrees of sophistication, in virtually all industry sectors. It is an essentially practical strategy which, in the words of Martin Mendelsohn, 'did not derive from one moment of inventiveness by an imaginative individual [but from] the solutions developed by businessmen, in response to the problems with which they were confronted in their business operations' (Mendelsohn 2004). It is franchising's capacity for adaptation and innovation which drives its relentless development.

It is perhaps ironic that standardisation and uniformity—the foundations on which franchising has been built—provide a real challenge to the ongoing march of franchising. Gen X and Gen Y—the increasingly significant market segment— are increasingly demanding an increasingly personalised experience both as consumers and as entrepreneurs. McDonald's recent experience—'how very un-McDonald's'—highlights the demands of today's Gen X and Gen Y consumers and the challenge of balancing standardisation with customisation and localisation. Less well documented is the challenge that today's Gen X and Gen Y entrepreneurs pose for franchisee recruitment—the demand for much greater autonomy and freedom and the opportunity to express their individuality within the confines of the franchise system. Changing demographics provide exciting opportunities for those systems able to embrace them.

While both Degani and Eview may be simplistically thought of as a looser, less disciplined, less structured form of business format franchising, it is argued that such assessments miss the point. These systems have consciously (either reactively or proactively) embraced a model which unequivocally allows, and indeed encourages, franchisee customisation and personalisation of the product and service provided. In the words of Degani's former franchise development manager:

> We are creating an innovative, flexible approach to franchising and ultimately I believe that companies who don't move towards that model will find it hard to survive in an increasingly competitive market. We are steering clear of the cookie-cutter mentality where all stores look and feel the same, serve the same food, and sell the same products. (Stowe 2015)

In the words of Eview's founder:

> The challenge most real estate agents face is that current options available have been around for decades. They are the same tired models which lack innovation and their market relevance is quickly and dramatically being eroded as technology and consumer behavior is undergoing massive change. (Eview.com.au)

These businesses are pioneers in what is becoming an important area for the development of franchising, albeit in an unfamiliar flexible guise. It is not surprising that they have sought comfort in recognisable elements of business formats, but they nevertheless constitute harbingers of successful future franchise operations. While business format franchising accommodates intrapreneurial franchisees prepared to work within the system, the opportunities for entrepreneurial franchisees who require an outlet for their individuality beyond the confines of the brand and system are of course limited. Flexible franchising is a strategy which provides this opportunity while also being attractive to a growing number of consumers for whom a more personalised experience may trump formulaic uniformity (Terry and Di Lernia 2013).

Stephen Giles, when Chairman of the Franchise Council of Australia, suggested over a decade ago that 'it is likely that franchising as a business method will need to be dismantled and reconstructed. It will be franchising techniques, not franchising, that will be relevant. Old formats may no longer be relevant or may not deliver the same competitive advantage' (Giles 2008). Internationally expanding franchisors to a developing country introduce not only new brands and products and technologies and standards but a new way of thinking about doing business. The concept of flexible franchising provides the opportunity for the franchising sector to think about a new way of franchising. Franchising is not a business—it is a method of doing business. The franchise model has proven to be innovative and dynamic, but its evolution to date has been almost exclusively within the existing paradigm of the business format model and rigid adherence to systems both back- and front-of-house. This paper suggests that the future development of franchising is likely to involve a rethinking of the extent to which formulaic uniformity is an appropriate or effective aspiration.

References

Binh B, Terry A (2014) Meeting the challenges for franchising in developing countries: the Vietnamese experience. J Mark Channels 21(3):210

Blair R, Lafontaine F (2005) The economics of franchising. Cambridge University Press, Cambridge

Cox J, Mason C (2007) Standardisation versus adaptation: geographical pressures to deviate from franchise formats. Serv Ind J 27(8):1053–1072

Davidow WH, Malone MS (1992) The Virtual Corporation: Structuring and revitalizing the corporation for the 21st century. HarperCollins, New York

Dicke TS (1992) Franchising in America: the development of a business method 1840–1980. University of North Carolina Press, Chapel Hill NC

Eview Property Group (2015) 'Your brand your business'

Foster S (2014) Degani dreams big up north with plans for 30 outlets in Queensland. The Courier-Mail. http://www.couriermail.com.au/business/degani-dreams-big-up-north-with-plans-for-30-outlets-in-queensland/story-fnfli675-1226997936108

Frazer L, Weaven S, Grace A, Selvanathan S (2016) Franchising Australia 2016. Griffith University, Brisbane

Franchise Business (2014) Degani's fresh approach to the café business. http://www.franchisebusiness.com.au/news/degani-s-fresh-approach-to-the-cafe-business

Franchise Business (2015) 20 questions about the franchise: Degani. 26 November 2015. http://www.franchisebusiness.com.au/news/20-questions-about-the-franchise-degani

Giles S (2008) Unpublished speech as Chairman of the Franchise Council of Australia,

Gordon TL (2014, November 1) Spilling the beans. Success: Business Magazine. http://successbusinessmag.com.au/spilling-beans-george-pezaros/

Gorovaia N (2017) Knowledge transfer in franchising. In: Hoy F, Perrigot R, Terry A (eds) Handbook of research on franchising. Edward Elgar, Cheltenham

Grünhagen M, Wollan M, Dada L, Watson A (2014) The moderating influence of HR operational autonomy on the entrepreneurial orientation–performance link in franchise systems. Int Entrep Manag J 10(4):827–828

Heffernan M (2015) Booming coffee market moves into consolidation phase. The Sydney Morning Herald. http://www.smh.com.au/business/retail/booming-coffee-market-moves-into-consolidation-phase-20150317-1m1g1p.html

Johnston E (2013) Small blessings: hole-in-the-wall trend for cafes. Sydney Morning Herald quoting Michael Vranic, leasing manager for City Commercial in Sydney

Justis R, Judd R (1989) Franchising. South Western Publishing Co, Boston, MA

Kaufmann P, Eroglu S (1999) Standardisation and adaptation in business format franchising. J Bus Ventur 14(1):69

Kos S (1990) Franchisor liability for franchisee misconduct, Legal Forums. Franchisor's Association of Australasia, 1

Klein B (1995) The economics of franchise contracts. J Corporate Fin: Contracting, Governance and Organisation 2. 9 at p 12

Liu WK (2008) KFC in China. Wiley, Singapore

Love JF (1995) McDonald's: behind the Golden Arches. Bantam Books, New York

Marnoto S (2013) No-format franchising: a new form of entrepreneurship and sustainable growth. 1:1 Stud Organisation Manag Sustain at p 38

Mendelsohn M (2004) The guide to franchising, 7th edn. Thomson Learning, UK

McCrindle M (n.d.) Understanding generation Y. The Australian Leadership Foundation. http://www.communicationcache.com/uploads/1/0/8/8/10887248/understanding_generation_y.pdf

Milman O (2010) Generation Y keen to start businesses: Survey. 20 September 2010. http://www.smartcompany.com.au/start-up/20100921-generation-y-keen-to-start-new-businessessurvey.html

Myers R (2013) How franchisees can find room for innovation. http://www.entrepreneur.com/article/225992 March 7, 2013

Pardo-del-Val M, Martínez-Fuentes C, López-Sánchez J I, Minguela-Rata B (2014) Franchising: the dilemma between standardisation and flexibility. 34:9–10 Serv Ind J 828–842

Parliamentary Joint Committee on Corporations and Financial Services, Parliament of Australia (2008, December) Opportunity not opportunism: improving conduct in Australian franchising. p xiii

Price S (1997) The Franchise Paradox. Cassell

Rickert K (2014, July 25) Degani brews expansion plans. Business News Australia.http://www.businessnewsaus.com.au/articles/degani-brews-expansion-plans.html

Ritzer G (2004) The McDonaldization of Society. Pine Forge Press, Sage, Thousand Oaks, CA

Sherman A (2011) Franchising and licensing, 4th edn. Amacom, New York

Silvini C (2015) 'Yes, chef'. Townsville Eye. 12 December 2015

Stowe S (2015) New appointment to help grow Degani brand. Franchise Business. http://www.franchisebusiness.com.au/news/new-appointment-to-help-grow-degani-brand

Streed O, Cliquet G (2008) Concept uniformity: control versus freedom in business format franchising. In: Hendrikse G, Tuunanen M, Windsperger J, Cliquet G (eds) Strategy and governance of networks: cooperatives, franchising and strategic alliances. Springer, Berlin, pp 205–220

Streed O, Cliquet G (2017) Autonomy in franchising. In: Hoy F, Perrigot R, Terry A (eds) Handbook of research on franchising. Edward Elgar, Cheltenham

Terry A, Di Lernia C (2013) Quasi-franchising: a new model for strategic business cooperation. In: Ehrmann T, Windsperger J, Cliquet G, Hendrikse G (eds) Network governance: alliances, cooperatives and franchise chains. Physica, Berlin, Germany, pp 269–286

Terry A, Huan JL (2013) Franchisor liability for franchisee conduct. Monash Univ Law Rev 39(2):388–410

Terry A, Giugni D (2019) Business and the Law, 7th edn. Thomson Reuters, Sydney

Urban R (2010) Changing tastes too fast for food chains. Weekend Australian, quoting professor Geoffrey Garrett, Dean of The Wharton School of Business at the University of Pennsylvania

US House of Representatives Committee on Small Business (1990) Franchising in the US Economy: Prospects and problems

Watson JL (1997) Golden Arches East: McDonald's in East Asia. Stanford University Press, Stanford California

Websites

Degani Website: https://degani.com.au/
Eview Website: http://www.eview.com.au/
Great Harvest Bread Co Website: https://www.greatharvest.com/

Why Adopt Microfranchising? Evidence from Brazil on an Organizational Innovation Designed to Face New Challenges

Rubens Nunes, Vivian-Lara S. Silva, Muriel Fadairo, and Maria Sylvia M. Saes

Abstract This paper deals with the economic rationality underlying organizational innovations in franchising and the rationale behind them. Using Brazilian primary data, we obtain evidence that spatial distribution of microfranchised units is sensitive to the sector of activity. Our results suggest that labor-intensive activities are suitable for microfranchised units in less populated municipalities. In addition, we provide evidence that the spatial distribution of microfranchising reflects network growth. Indeed, larger networks, in terms of number of units as well as territorial extension, are more likely to be present in smaller markets than smaller networks. Older networks (incumbents) that had a business experience prior to franchising tend to concentrate their franchised units in densely populated areas, while entrants that adopted microfranchising from their foundation target unexplored markets in less populated municipalities.

1 Introduction

Franchising networks contractually bind an upstream party, the franchisor, to a network of retailers using its brand name and business format, the franchisees. Used internationally in all retail and services sectors, this organizational form

R. Nunes · V.-L. S. Silva
School of Animal Science and Food Engineering (USP/FZEA), University of São Paulo, Pirassununga, São Paulo, Brazil
e-mail: rnunes@usp.br; vivianlara@usp.br

M. Fadairo (✉)
IAE Savoie Mont Blanc (USMB/IAE) Institut de Recherche en Gestion et Economie (IREGE), Université Savoie Mont Blanc, Annecy, France
e-mail: Muriel.Fadairo@univ-savoie.fr

M. S. M. Saes
School of Economics, Business and Accounting (USP/FEA), Center for Organization Studies (CORS), University of São Paulo, Butantã, São Paulo, Brazil
e-mail: ssaes@usp.br

© Springer Nature Switzerland AG 2019
J. Windsperger et al. (eds.), *Design and Management of Interfirm Networks*, Contributions to Management Science,
https://doi.org/10.1007/978-3-030-29245-4_5

stands out as a dominant model of trade in the twenty-first century. Due to its peculiar structure and behavioral aspects, franchising represents a rich context of investigation. Comparing Brazil with the USA and France, Dant et al. (2008) showed the importance of franchising in this country.

In Brazil, the economic crisis that started in 2014, coupled with the saturation of specific location areas, has raised new challenges related to organizational innovations in franchising. In this continent-sized country, spatial dynamics play a key role, for example, the allocation of sector performances when considering the different regions. As reported by the media, many networks find in the favelas their most profitable units. In addition, other studies have observed an interest of the networks in exploring areas outside the southeast usual circuits, specifically in the north, northeast, and midwest (Bitti et al. 2019).

Additional issues arise from the contemporary franchising landscape in Brazil, regarding the evolution of the prevailing system and the attractiveness to new franchisees. In that direction, the design of a new generation of franchising systems has begun to emerge in Brazil: microfranchising, a small business model which replicates proven marketing and operational concepts. It is common to associate such a business model with the idea of empowerment of the poor (e.g., Burand and Koch 2010; Lehr 2008), although in some cases opportunities for self-employment and increasing incomes emerge as unintended consequences of for-profit franchising network expansion (Kukec and Erceg 2017).

According to the Brazilian Franchising Association (ABF), a microfranchise is defined as a business concept whose total investment does not exceed three times the Brazilian annual income per capita (of approximately USD 25,000). This new generation has already attracted interest from some conventional franchise networks. For these reasons, there is the need to properly and systematically explore this alternative format, motivating the research interests of this paper.

To sum up, the current competitive context of franchising in Brazil generates organizational innovations associated with growth strategies facing new challenges. Focusing more precisely on microfranchising, the following research question arises: from the Brazilian current experience, what do we learn about the economic rationality of microfranchising? In other words, taking into account spatial and sector-based dynamics, in which cases is this innovative format relevant? We provide here the first quantitative exploration of microfranchising in the literature. Econometrics allows us to test hypotheses that can be generalized to better understand this new format and go beyond extant information and descriptive case studies.

Our estimation results, based on a new and unique dataset, show that the choice of microfranchising as a business format is mainly related to locational aspects (places difficult to reach, social vulnerability, and logistical aspects). We discuss interesting practical and research implications of our findings.

The rest of the paper is organized as follows: Section 2 presents the analytical background, dealing with the definition of microfranchising and the related hypotheses. In Sect. 3, we specify the Brazilian context, before presenting the data and the methodology in Sect. 4. Section 5 contains our empirical results and the related comments. Finally, we offer a conclusion in Sect. 6.

2 Analytical Background and Hypotheses

2.1 Microfranchising and Social Franchising Versus Business Format Franchising

While business format franchising is a well-known and successful organizational format in retailing, the literature on microfranchising and social franchising is scarce but developing (Alon and Naatu 2019). Recent advances concern case studies (e.g., Alon 2014) and discussion of the links and differences between the three concepts (Crawford-Spencer 2015; Du Toit 2017; Zafeiropoulou 2017). Yet, the concepts and definitions are still not used in the same way and with the same meaning in all the articles on the topic.

Asemota and Chahine (2017) distinguish social from microfranchising on the grounds of business model design: while the former aims to achieve social goals by incorporating people at the bottom of the pyramid as franchisees, the second seeks to promote well-being by offering products and services accessible to people who would have otherwise been out of the market. Du Toit (2017) emphasizes the relationship between microfranchising and microfinance, with the term "micro" in microfranchising referring to the concept of microfinance which consists of loans granted to help poor individuals to start a business. Poverty reduction is thus central and links the two concepts. Microfranchising can thus be defined as a specific format of franchising enabling impoverished people to start a business. Christensen et al. (2010) show that microfranchising is linked to social goals, namely, poverty reduction, via the reduction of unemployment. Indeed, microfranchising facilitates access to employment, enabling impoverished individuals to become self-employed and eventually hire people in their communities. Asemota and Chahine (2017) recognize the effect of microfranchising on employment but stress access to basic goods and services at affordable costs. Brodie et al. (2002) study the direct sale of branded products as a specific form of franchising and identify some unintentional positive effects on the welfare of part-time workers most of whom are women, since it is a low-cost and low-entry barrier business opportunity. This business model benefits the selling firms by grouping an "army of individuals" around friendship circles, without advertising expenses and special premises. The idea of women empowerment through microfranchising is also emphasized by Chatnani (2010).

Finally, microfranchising has at least two different meanings: on one hand, a financially sustainable model that provides affordable goods and services in response to the failure of the formerly structured market to supply these and, on the other hand, just a down-sized business, with comparatively low fixed capital and cash investments. The first concept encompasses explicit social goals and financial constraints in order to attain sustainability, while the second departs from a profit-oriented firm that produces social benefits, either intentionally or unintentionally.

These two opposing views are consistent with the definitions by Zafeiropoulou (2017), who considers microfranchising as being part of social franchising and emphasizes an inclusion relationship, and by Du Toit (2017), who highlights intersections between micro- and social franchising. Defending the idea that microfranchising is an organizational form like business format franchising or a plural form organization, whereas social franchising offers a specific content, we agree with the last view (Du Toit 2017), which underlines the complementarities between micro- and social franchising and corresponds to our focus in this study.[1]

As with business format franchising, the social franchisee uses the brand name and business concept of the upstream party, the franchisor. In both cases, business format and social franchising, the franchisee and the franchisor are legally independent entrepreneurs, related by a franchise contract defining their rights and obligations. As with business format franchising, a branded network is thus created, with the franchisor being in charge of brand promotion and reputation preservation. Yet, there is a central difference: social franchising is just a means that uses market-based solutions to achieve social goals. Thus, social franchising merges goals of different natures: economic efficiency (efficiency with respect to the market) and social efficiency (efficiency with respect to the whole society—including poverty reduction, improvement of living conditions, and environmental concerns).

The emerging academic literature on social franchising is ambiguous regarding this duality of goals. Some authors, such as Du Toit (2017), assert that social franchising networks can sometimes be defined as nonprofit organizations supported by public programs and donors. On the other hand, Aliouche and Bonet Fernandez (2017) insist on the necessity to generate revenues, at least to achieve long-term sustainability.

In Brazil, microfranchising is defined by the ABF as a format for small businesses, requiring a low initial investment by the franchisee. This definition does not explicitly take social goals into consideration, yet those are implicit in our study. In addition, Brazilian microfranchising networks are usually for profit-oriented firms. The Brazilian experience is rich in lessons as the microfranchising format proves to be economically efficient, sometimes even more than the commercial business format. Our goal in this paper is to precisely explore the conditions of this economic rationality.

---

[1]The authors are grateful to editor Gérard Cliquet for his help in removing ambiguities and clarifying the concepts.

2.2 Microfranchising and Social Entrepreneurship as Partially Overlapping Concepts

Because of complementarities between micro- and social franchising, the literature on microfranchising overlaps the literature on social entrepreneurship. While we have identified ambiguities in the extant conceptual framework distinguishing micro-, social, and business format franchising, the relationship between franchising and social entrepreneurship is clearly stated in the literature.

Firstly, fostered by the impacts of the global economic crisis of 2008, intractable poverty, and environmental issues, scholarly interest in social enterprise has progressed. A large amount of research is now available (e.g., Davies et al. 2019; Doherty et al. 2014; Fayolle and Matlay 2010; Short 2014; Short et al. 2009; Stevens et al. 2015; Tracey and Jarvis 2007). In this literature, the goal of societal value creation is inseparable from financial sustainability. A dual mission thus explicitly defines social enterprises. The main issue of this underlined hybridity is to succeed in combining social purposes with economic rationality.

In this context, social franchising is "simply" defined as a scaling strategy for social entrepreneurship, the application of franchising to social entrepreneurship (Aliouche and Bonet Fernandez 2017; Alon 2014; Kistruck et al. 2011; Volery and Hackl 2010; Zafeiropoulou 2017). Both are therefore complementary. With the replication process inherent in franchising, challenges to the economic sustainability of the micro- or social franchisor and the overall micro- or social franchising model are stressed.

2.3 Hypothesis Development

Based on the previous discussion, we assume that each microfranchising network chooses where its units will be located, with the aim to maximize expected profits or at least to achieve economic sustainability (Sivakumar and Schoormans 2011). The latter depends on the franchisee's performance. We also assume that the size of the market is relevant to this decision-making process. Large markets offer the possibility to exploit economies of scale, though in this context the new units face fierce competition (Bitti et al. 2019). As an organizational innovation, microfranchising can be considered as an attempt to solve this trade-off.

From this analytical context, we argue that microfranchising in the Brazilian market is relevant when the product or service is complex. For such types of goods, consumer utility increases when the purchase is complemented with information provided by the franchisee. In addition, the franchisee has more information than the franchisor about the consumers. The theoretical background for these flows of information is the theory of information asymmetry, drawn from the field of contract theory (Akerlof 1970). Following this reasoning, microfranchising is suitable for sectors where the utility of products and services depends on complementary information provided to the consumer, such as new features of innovative electronic products. The related hypothesis is as follows:

Hypothesis 1 Microfranchising is relevant in specific sectors, related to the product complexity.

In addition, microfranchising is relevant in locations difficult to reach by traditional formats. This argument is related to the idea that microfranchising is the result of a rescaling of an already proven business model, with the purpose of making it feasible in smaller markets, that is, in less populated municipalities where the exploitation of economies of scale is limited. For this reason, we formulate the following hypothesis:

Hypothesis 2 Microfranchising is relevant to explore markets in less populated municipalities where conventional franchised units would be inefficient.

Finally, even in large metropolises in developing countries, there are potential markets partially isolated from major urban centers, such as the "favelas" in Brazil and "misery villages" in Argentina. Microfranchised units, especially when conducted by local residents (Zafeiropoulou and Koufopoulos 2013), can be instruments to exploit such market segments. From this reasoning, we derive the following hypothesis:

Hypothesis 3 Microfranchising is relevant to explore hidden markets in dense urban places.

3   Franchising and Microfranchising in Brazil

Well established in North America and Europe, franchise networks are growing strongly in emerging economies, despite the social, economic, and political crises. Indeed, statistics show a remarkable dynamism in several African countries, China, Turkey, Mexico, and Brazil (Fadairo and Lanchimba 2017; Perrigot 2017).

Regarding the number of brands, Brazil occupies a central place in Latin American franchising: in 2013, there were 2703 franchised brands in the country, 80% more than in Mexico which is the second largest market for franchising in the region. This predominance is confirmed by per capita changes.

Yet, statistics presented in Fig. 1 highlight a contrasted evolution of Brazilian franchising (ABF 2017). Since the economic crisis, the growth of the system has changed from its level prior to the crisis. Indeed, recent changes are characterized by a smoother growth in sales (from 8%, e.g., between 2016 and 2017), units (2%), and employment (1%) and even a decrease in the number of chains (−6%).

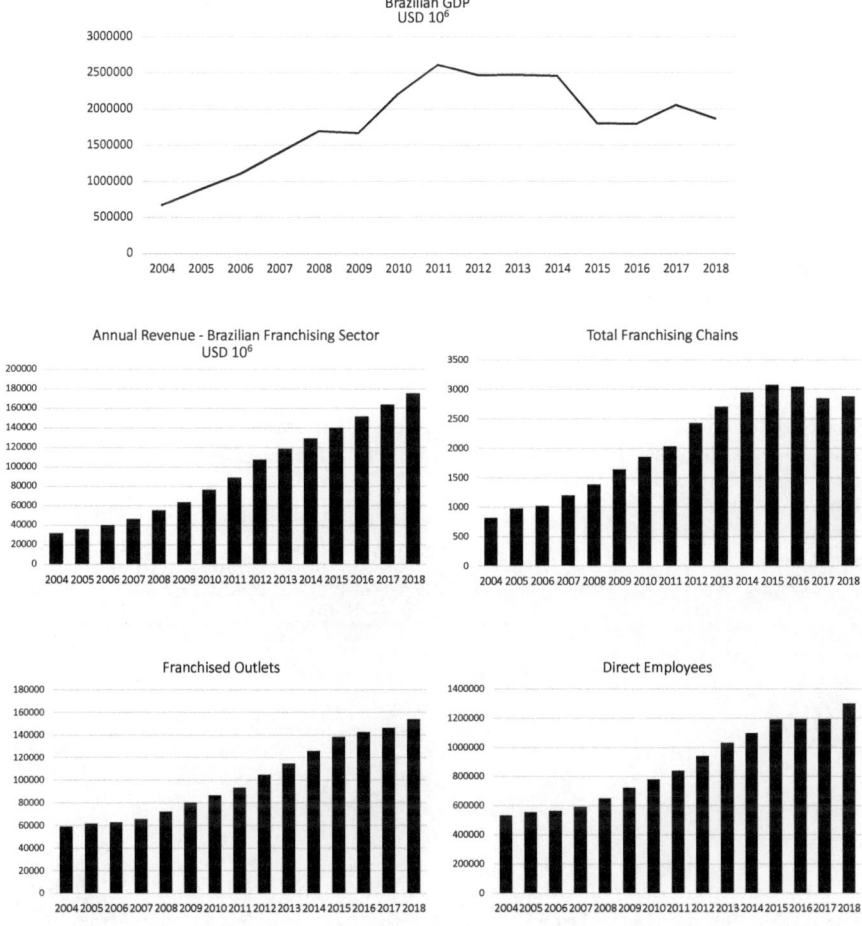

Fig. 1 Evolution of Brazilian franchising (2004–2017). Source: Based on IPEA-Data and ABF

A closer look at sector performances reveals some important features. The food sector appears as one of the important sectors in Brazilian franchising (Table 1). As shown in Table 1, the growth of franchising in this emblematic sector has known no slowdown since the Brazilian crisis.

However, the impact of the Brazilian economic crisis on the franchised food sector is clearly suggested by Table 2. All the big international brands in Brazilian food franchising presented a slowdown in the number of stores opened between 2014 and 2015. In addition, with the crisis impact, the hypothesis of a saturation process regarding the expansion of well-established brands is relevant, at least in some Brazilian locations. Whatever the argument, it is pertinent to note that the crisis compelled companies to reconsider their strategies.

Table 1 Sector-based allocation of Brazilian franchising (2013–2017)

Sectors	2013 (%)	2017 (%)
Business and other retails	21.1	5.6
Food	20.0	28.3
Health, beauty, and well-being	NC	21.7
Clothing	7.4	12.6
Hotel and tourism	7.3	3.0
Educational services	6.6	11.6
Entertainment and leisure	NC	1.0
Home/building and construction	5.1	7.1
Automotive services	3.5	3.5
Communication, computer, and electronics	3.0	2.5
Cleanliness and conservation	0.9	3.0

Source: Based on CNS and ABF. NC, non-comparative statistics resulting from changes in the methodology used by the ABF in the nomenclature of the sectors

Table 2 Number of franchising fast-food stores opened in Brazil

Source: Chain websites	2014	2015
Subway	414	354
Burger King	130	104
Bob's	74	55
McDonald's	86	44
Giraffas	12	25
Pizza Hut	17	22
Spoleto	51	16
Habib's	25	7
KFC	7	3

The search for adaptive paths goes directly through the microfranchising sector. The ABF pointed out a total of 557 franchise chains employing the microfranchising model in Brazil in 2016, either exclusively or concomitant with the traditional model (Fig. 2).

Of this total, 79.8% are employed exclusively with microfranchises, and 20.2% operate with both formats, i.e., conventional and microfranchises. In turn, the ABF revealed that among the chains that still do not operate with microfranchising, 36% indicated their intention to develop this format in the coming years.

The current interest in microfranchising is also related to a better performance of this organizational innovation compared with the conventional model. Indeed, according to the ABF, microfranchising has recorded a growth in sales of 22% against 16% of business format franchising during the period 2016/2017.

A better performance was also recorded in terms of growth in both the number of new networks and the number of new units, with microfranchises in Brazil growing by 10 and 6%, respectively, over the period 2016 and 2017, while the conventional model slowed down, respectively, by 6 and 2%.

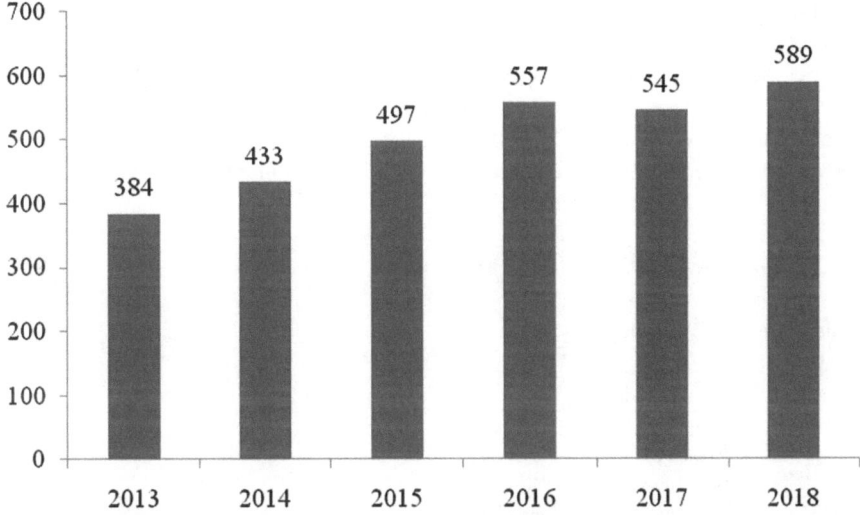

Fig. 2 Number of networks operating microfranchising units (2013–2018). Source: ABF (2018)

4 Data and Measurement

4.1 Data Collection and Sample

We use cross-sectional data on microfranchising networks in Brazil covering the year 2017. The data source is the ABF. The unit of analysis is the franchise network. Our sample consists of 132 observations of "pure microfranchised chains," that is, networks constituted only by microfranchised units. For each brand, the data contains information regarding the location of the units. This is a new and unique dataset. Moreover, the data was collected for this specific research.

4.2 Variables of Interest

4.2.1 Dependent Variables

The dependent variables are the number of microfranchised units belonging to a given network settled in municipalities. Municipalities are classified into six groups, according to their population. The thresholds are established aiming both to avoid an unbalanced distribution in the sample and to capture different profiles of municipalities. This implies that a municipality with about 100,000 inhabitants is not just five times more populated than one with 20,000 inhabitants, but it offers in addition qualitative differences in terms of infrastructure and services.

Thus, we distinguish six dependent variables. Each of them refers to the number of franchised units per network (NUM) in a specific class of municipalities: municipalities with 20,000 inhabitants (NUM20); between 20,001 and 40,000 inhabitants (NUM40); and successively 100,000 (NUM100), 250,000 (NUM250), and 1 million inhabitants (NUM1000). NUMMORE refers to the number of franchised units per network in municipalities with more than 1 million inhabitants.

4.2.2   Summary Statistics (See Table 3)

Table 3 The study variables

Exploratory variables	Description	Average	Median	Min.	Max.	SD
NBRMUN	Number of municipalities in which the franchise brand is present—counting variables	45.20	20.5	1	600	83.94
UNITMUN	Average number of units per municipality—number of units divided by NBRMUN	1.85	1.33	1	28	2.54
OWNUNIT	Percentage of own units in the network—%	19.49	0.47	0	100	65.49
LAGFRAN	Time until the adoption of franchising model—years	5.83	3	0	40	8.11
STARTBUS	Time since the business started—years	14.34	10	0	60	11.56
PLFORM	Adoption of either a single- (0) or multiple (1)-franchise format	0.26	0	0	1	0.44
PAYFRANC	Payment of franchise fee (0 = absence; 1 = presence)	0.90	1	0	1	0.30
PAYROYAL	Payment of royalties (0 = absence; 1 = presence)	0.96	1	0	1	0.19
SECFOOD	Sector: Food (1 if the network belongs to the sector, if not 0)	0.11	0	0	1	0.32
SECHOME	Sector: Utilities and services for home	0.06	0	0	1	0.24
SECCOMM	Sector: Communications and electronics	0.14	0	0	1	0.35
SECHOTUR	Sector: Hotels and tourism	0.04	0	0	1	0.19
SECCLEAN	Sector: Cleaning and maintenance services	0.08	0	0	1	0.27
SECFASH	Sector: Fashion	0.05	0	0	1	0.21
SECAUTO	Sector: Automotive services	0.04	0	0	1	0.19
SECEDUC	Sector: Educational services	0.14	0	0	1	0.35

5 Estimations, Results, and Discussion

The statistics in Table 4 are consistent with Hypothesis 1, which relates the use of microfranchising to the sector. These preliminary results justify the inclusion of sector dummies in the econometric models. Indeed, the chi-square test in Table 4 leads to the rejection of the independence hypothesis ($p < 0.001$), implying that the spatial distribution of franchised units depends on the sector in which they operate.

Six regressions—one for each type of municipality—are estimated, using the OLS method. We control for heteroscedasticity with the White test and multi-collinearity by means of the variance inflation factor (VIF).

The estimation results presented in Table 5 highlight the factors underlying the spatial pattern of microfranchising, taking into account the population classes. These results are of great interest for expansion strategies within franchising networks.

Thus, if a franchise unit of a brand is settled in a municipality of up to 20,000 inhabitants, it is probably the only one (NBRMUN, $p < 0,001$). The average number of units per municipality (UNITMUN) is statistically noticeable only in municipalities with more than 1 million inhabitants, suggesting that microfranchising is a format used both to reach small municipalities—in this case the size of the market limits the exploitation of economies of scale—(Hypothesis 2) and to target markets hidden within dense urban areas (Hypothesis 3).

In Table 5, the dependent variable is the number of franchise units in municipalities included in population class.

As suggested by preliminary results (Table 4), the business sector of a microfranchising network exerts a significant influence on the spatial distribution of its units. Automotive services microfranchised units are more abundant in municipalities with less than 250,000 inhabitants. One possible explanation is the real estate rental differentials between larger and smaller municipalities, reducing the minimal efficient scale in small towns. Labor-intensive activities such as automotive services are apparently suitable to less populated municipalities.

Additional results concern first the number of franchisor-owned units. This variable appears to be irrelevant in explaining the spatial distribution of microfranchised units. Yet, some caveats are required. Indeed, the ABF's data repository contains only formal ownership of franchise units, not the effective control exerted by the franchisor over units formally belonging to third parties, but closely tied to the franchisor.

A year of increased activity in the franchise network tends to increase by double the number of units in cities with more than 1 million inhabitants (STARTBUS, $\beta > 0$ and $p < 0.001$), but decreases the presence of old brands in smaller municipalities (STARTBUS, $\beta < 0$ and $p < 0.05$). Businesses that from the beginning started as franchise networks tend to have a more noticeable presence in small municipalities (LAGFRAN, $\beta > 0$ and $p < 0.001$) than businesses that took time to be converted to the franchise model (LAGFRAN, $\beta < 0$ and $p < 0,001$).

The incidence of franchise fees (PAYFRANC) and the payment of royalties (PAYROYAL) did not reveal clear influence on the spatial allocation of microfran-

Table 4 Franchised units per sector and municipality population

	NUM20	NUM40	NUM100	NUM250	NUM1000	NUM MORE	Total	%
Food	5	8	28	111	249	464	865	8.0
For home	1	0	8	13	30	50	102	0.9
Communications/electronics	20	58	111	209	437	474	1309	12.1
Entertainment and leisure	0	0	1	1	3	4	9	0.1
Hotels and tourism	2	1	17	55	105	109	289	2.7
Cleaning and maintenance	15	22	99	176	286	448	1046	9.6
Fashion	4	9	36	78	131	132	390	3.6
Health and beauty	9	28	94	141	206	282	760	7.0
Automotive services	84	121	259	315	443	474	1696	15.6
Business services	66	78	190	240	363	365	1302	12.0
Educational services	102	243	454	519	731	1034	3083	28.4
TOTAL	308	568	1297	1858	2984	3836	10,851	
%	2.8	5.2	12.0	17.1	27.5	35.4		100

Table 5 OLS regression coefficients

	NUM20	NUM40	NUM100	NUM250	NUM1000	NUM MORE
Const	0.008	−0.905	−2.665	−0.944	−13.122	−52.303***
NBRMUN	0.096***	0.171***	0.338***	0.412***	0.613***	0.631***
UNITMUN	−0.102	0.009	−0.122	0.046	0.552	3.240***
OWNUNIT	0.004	0.010	0.011	0.013	0.020	0.031
LAGFRAN	0.252***	0.245***	0.480***	0.315 **	0.008	−2.258***
STARTBUS	−0.100 **	−0.154 **	−0.299***	−0.082	0.315	2.082***
PLFORM	0.152	−0.135	0.225	0.451	−1.117	0.952
PAYFRANC	−1.458	−1.845	−1.787	−2.495	−1.676	2.769
PAYROYAL	−0.181	−0.031	1.378	−2.445	3.029	24.678
SECFOOD	−0.621	−0.955	−2.960	0.985	6.942	16.815*
SECHOME	1.226	1.621	2.167	3.179	6.471	7.182
SECCOMM	−1.465	−0.834	−3.816*	−0.263	7.324	11.792
SECHOTUR	−2.650	−3.714	−6.377*	−2.743	−0.716	−8.230
SECCLEAN	−1.652	−3.303*	−3.310	0.038	0.435	4.833
SECFASH	−2.592	−3.710*	−5.812*	−1.423	1.370	1.862
SECAUTO	5.228***	4.438*	10.951***	12.130***	10.851	6.978
SECEDUC	−1.325	1.231	−1.019	−5.911 **	−14.466***	−14.688
R^2	0.861	0.917	0.942	0.952	0.908	0.834
Adjusted R^2	0.840	0.904	0.934	0.945	0.894	0.809
F statistics	41.075***	73.084***	108.2 * **	132.5 ***	65.36 ***	33.21 ***

Note: *Significant at $p < 0.05$; ** 0.005; *** 0.001

chised units. The same result holds for the simultaneous adoption of more than one channel (PLFORM): store, kiosk, home-based activity, and mobile units. Regarding educational services, microfranchised units are scarcer than the average microfranchising presence in medium- and large-sized municipalities.

6 Conclusion

Microfranchising is innovative in the sense that franchisees do not bring massive capital inflows to franchising brands, but franchisees' local market knowledge and personal networks. These are features of the microfranchising model fitted to entry strategies of franchising brands in new markets, especially small ones. These markets are placed not only in less populated municipalities but also in the densely populated metropolitan areas.

Location decisions attempt to solve the trade-off between the exploration of economies of scale and information costs in pristine markets.

The coexistence of more than one business format in a franchising network does not seemingly play any relevant role in location decisions. The same stands for contractual mechanisms for rent transference such as franchising fees and royalties.

We found evidence that the spatial distribution of microfranchised units is sensitive to the sector of activity. Labor-intensive activities seem to be suitable to microfranchised units in less populated municipalities. Spatial distribution also reflects the growth of franchising networks. Larger networks in terms of number of units as well as in territorial extension are more likely to be present in smaller markets than smaller networks. Older networks (incumbents) that started franchising after developing a business model in single firms concentrate their franchised units in densely populated areas, while entrants that adopted franchising just from their foundation targeted unexplored markets in less populated municipalities.

As a device to make use of local market knowledge, microfranchising competes with direct sales, a contractual relationship in which there is no investment in fixed capital. Direct sales are suitable to the distribution of finished goods with which the consumer is unfamiliar. Direct sales and franchising networks that combine traditional and microfranchising are promising subjects for future research.

Acknowledgement We gratefully acknowledge the support of the University of São Paulo—Comité Français d'Evaluation de la Coopération Universitaire et Scientifique avec le Brésil Programme (USP-COFECUB 2017–2020) under grant agreement no. Uc Sh 165-17. We would like to thank Professor Gérard Cliquet for insightful comments. Additional thanks go to the Brazilian Franchising Association (Associação Brasileira de Franchising—ABF) for its collaboration in the data collection process. The usual caveats apply.

References

ABF (2016) Desempenho do franchising brasileiro. Associação Brasileira de Franchising. https://www.abf.com.br/wp-content/uploads/2017/02/Perfil-das-Microfranquias.pdf. Accessed 17 Jan 2019

ABF (2017) Desempenho do franchising 2017. Associação Brasileira de Franchising. https://www.abf.com.br/wp-content/uploads/2018/03/Desempenho-do-Franchising-2017.pdf. Accessed 17 Jan 2019

Akerlof G (1970) The market for 'lemons': quality uncertainty and the market mechanism. Q J Econ 84:353–374

Aliouche H, Bonet Fernandez D (2017) Social entrepreneurship and franchising: a panacea for emerging countries? In: GWJ H et al (eds) Management and governance of networks. Springer, Cham, pp 75–90

Alon I (ed) (2014) Social franchising. Palgrave, Macmillan. 99 p

Alon I, Naatu F (2019) Social franchising: a bibliometric and theoretical review. J Promot Manag 25:738. https://doi.org/10.1080/10496491.2019.1584777

Asemota J, Chahine T (2017) Social franchising as an option for scale. Volunt Int J Volunt Nonprofit Org 28(6):2734–2762. https://doi.org/10.1007/s11266-016-9763-7

Bitti EJS, Fadairo M, Lanchimba C, Silva VLS (2019) Should I stay or should I go? Geographic entrepreneurial choices in Brazilian franchising. J Small Bus Manag. https://doi.org/10.1111/jsbm.12469

Brodie S, Stanworth J, Wotruba TR (2002) Direct sales franchises in the UK: a self-employment grey area. Int Small Bus J: Researching Entrepreneurship 20(1):53–76

Burand D, Koch D (2010) Microfranchising: a business approach to fighting poverty. Franchise Law Journal 30(1):24–34

Chatnani NN (2010) Women's empowerment through microfranchising. Amity Global Bus Rev 5(1):24–37

Christensen LJ, Parsons H, Fairbourne J (2010) Building entrepreneurship in subsistence markets: microfranchising as an employment incubator. J Bus Res 63:595–601

Crawford-Spencer E (2015) Deriving meaning for social franchising from commercial franchising and social franchising. J Mark Channels 22:163–174

Dant RP, Perrigot R, Cliquet G (2008) A cross-cultural comparison of the plural forms in franchise networks: United States, France, and Brazil. J Small Bus Manag 46(2):286–311. https://doi.org/10.1111/j.1540-627X.2008.00244.x

Davies IA, Haugh H, Chambers L (2019) Barriers to social enterprise growth. J Small Bus Manag. 57(4):1616–1636 https://doi.org/10.1111/jsbm.12429

Doherty B, Haugh BH, Lyon F (2014) Social enterprises as hybrid organizations: a review and research agenda. Int J Manag Rev 16:417–436. https://doi.org/10.1111/ijmr.12028

Du Toit A (2017) In: Hoy F, Perrigot R, Terry A (eds) An introduction to social franchising, handbook of research on franchising. Edward Elgar, Cheltenham, pp 559–577

Fadairo M, Lanchimba C (2017) Franchising in Latin America. In: Hoy F, Perrigot R, Terry A (eds) Handbook of research on franchising. Edward Elgar, Cheltenham, pp 482–414

Fayolle A, Matlay H (2010) Handbook of research on social entrepreneurship. Edward Elgar, Cheltenham. 352 p

Kistruck MG, Webb JW, Sutter CJ, Ireland RD (2011) Microfranchising in base-of-the-pyramid markets: institutional challenges and adaptations to the franchise model. Entrep Theory Pract 35(3):503–531

Kukec L, Erceg A (2017) Micro franchising as a tool for increasing self-employment and competitiveness: Croatian examples. Ekonomski Vjesnik 30(1):181–191

Lehr D (2008) Microfranchising at the base of the pyramid. Working paper. Acumen Fund

Perrigot R (2017) An exploration of franchising in Africa. In: Hoy F, Perrigot R, Terry A (eds) Handbook of research on franchising. Edward Elgar, Cheltenham, pp 515–535

Short J (Ed) (2014) Social entrepreneurship and research methods. Research methodology in strategy and management, Vol. 9. Emerald, Bingley

Short JC, Moss TW, Lumpkin GT (2009) Research in social entrepreneurship: past contributions and future opportunities. Strateg Entrep J 3:161–194

Sivakumar A, Schoormans JPL (2011) Franchisee selection for social franchising. J Nonprofit Publ Sect Market 23:213–225

Stevens R, Moray N, Bruneel J (2015) The Social and Economic Mission of social enterprises: dimensions, measurement, validation, and relation. Entrep Theory Pract 39(5):1051–1082

Tracey P, Jarvis O (2007) Toward a theory of social venture franchising. Entrep Theory Pract 31(5):667–685

Volery T, Hackl V (2010) The promise of social franchising as a model to achieve social goals. In: Fayolle A, Matlay H (eds) Handbook of research in social entrepreneurship. Edward Elgar, Cheltenham, pp 155–179

Zafeiropoulou FA (2017) The social franchise model: a systems approach of the dynamics of institutions and embeddedness in social franchise formation. In: Hoy F, Perrigot R, Terry A (eds) Handbook of research on franchising. Edward Elgar, Cheltenham, pp 578–607

Zafeiropoulou FA, Koufopoulos DN (2013) The influence of relational embeddedness on the formation and performance of social franchising. J Mark Channels 20:73–98

Strategic CSR and the Competitive Advantage of Franchise Firms

Maria Jell-Ojobor

Abstract Although corporate social responsibility (CSR) is a widely researched topic, there is a lack of its application in the franchise literature. The integration of CSR into the franchise business model is vital as it affects the franchise firm's growth and survival. Based on resource-based and organizational capabilities theories, our study explains how CSR strategy impacts the creation of intangible brand name assets as critical source of sustainable competitive advantage and, hence, increased financial performance. We adopt a multi-stakeholder-oriented CSR construct of economic, legal, ethical, and philanthropic responsibility dimensions. Using data from Austrian franchise firms, our results show that those CSR dimensions have a positive impact on brand name asset creation. Specifically, philanthropic responsibility strategy has the greatest impact on brand name assets, followed by legal, ethical, and economic responsibility strategies. Overall, this is the first study in franchising which explains the strategic role of CSR.

1 Introduction

Franchising is a form of strategic alliance whereby a brand owner of a product or service (the franchisor) grants exclusive rights to independent entrepreneurs (franchise network partners or franchisees) to implement and operate the standardized business format or package over a predetermined period in a particular territory. In the last decades, franchising has experienced steady growth in different industries all over the world such as retailing, restaurant, lodging, construction, insurance, and healthcare. In the USA, franchise businesses grew faster than the rest of the

M. Jell-Ojobor (✉)
Department of Business and Management, LUISS Guido Carli University, Rome, Italy
e-mail: mjellojobor@luiss.it

© Springer Nature Switzerland AG 2019
J. Windsperger et al. (eds.), *Design and Management of Interfirm Networks*,
Contributions to Management Science,
https://doi.org/10.1007/978-3-030-29245-4_6

economy in 2017.[1] In Europe, the annual franchise growth rate is predicted to be over 8%, promoting the creation of enterprises and small business ownership and, as a consequence, of employment and of turnover.[2]

The most critical assets for franchise system growth and survival are its brand name and reputation (e.g., Contractor and Kundu 1998a, b; Erramilli et al. 2002). Franchise branding binds the firm's stakeholders to its brand (Werther and Chandler 2005). It secures favorable supplier conditions and attracts customers by promising an outstanding product and service quality. Furthermore, it is a strategic asset for the management of the franchise partners who are the "key elements" of successful franchise system growth. A well-known franchise brand signals system quality to potential partners which reduces the franchisor's recruitment costs, such as searching and screening, and adverse selection (Preble et al. 2000; Elango 2007). Furthermore, it enables the setting of specific contract terms regarding higher initial fees, royalty rates, and advertising fees (Choo 2005). Also, a strong franchise brand increases bonding between partners (Contractor and Kundu 1998a, b). Finally, the franchisees' threat of brand withdrawal in case of opportunistic behavior reduces the franchisor's ex post holdup risk (Fladmoe-Lindquist and Jacque 1995; Quinn and Doherty 2000; Pizanti and Lerner 2003). Corporate social behavior can "make or break" a firm by directly impacting on its intangible assets, such as brand name, image, and reputation (e.g., Hillman and Keim 2001; Barnett 2007; De la Cruz and De Saá-Pérez 2003). Even though the relevance of "corporate social responsibility" (CSR) investment for intangible asset management has been acknowledged by the scientific as well as corporate community, its analysis in the franchise literature is scarce (Combs et al. 2011; Dant et al. 2012).

Based on the resource-based and organizational capabilities theories, our study explains the strategic role of CSR for the achievement of sustainable competitive advantage of franchise firms. Thereby, we link corporate stakeholder and brand management with strategic CSR (Werther and Chandler 2005). We adopt Carroll's (1991) CSR dimensions of economic, legal, ethical, and philanthropic responsibility to institutionalize stakeholders' issues as an integral part of corporate culture and strategy of franchise firms. We show that such stakeholder-oriented CSR strategy impacts the creation of intangible "CSR-related" assets, such as brand name assets, in franchising.

Our study makes several important contributions. First, it contributes to the scarce literature on CSR applied in the field of franchising. Thereby, we provide new theoretical insights by demonstrating how the strategic management perspective (the resource-based theory and organizational capabilities theory) extends our understanding of creating intangible assets and building competitive advantage through the franchise firm's CSR strategy. Second, our study develops and tests a

---

[1]Franchise Business Outlook January 2018, published by the International Franchise Association (IFA) Foundation.

[2]Report published in 2011 by the European Franchise Association: "Franchising: A Vector for Economic Growth in Europe."

new CSR construct in franchising which is based on Carroll's multi-stakeholder-oriented CSR dimensions. Third, our study contributes to the findings on the business case for CSR (Carroll and Shabana 2010) by emphasizing the importance of a diversified CSR strategy for the achievement of intangible assets and sustainable competitiveness and hence increased financial performance.

In the following, we review the literature on CSR in franchising and explain the stakeholder approach to CSR. We proceed with the development of our research model and hypotheses on the relationship of CSR and intangible assets. Thereafter, we present the methodology used and our empirical findings. We conclude with the discussion of results, implications, limitations, and suggestions for future research areas.

2 Relevant Literature

2.1 Franchising and CSR

In the franchising literature, CSR is a widely unexplored research area (Combs et al. 2011; Dant et al. 2012). Existent franchise studies that focus on CSR address two main areas: one being the institutionalized or standardized aspects of CSR in the franchise sector such as laws, ethics codes, and disclosure and the other explaining the impact of CSR on firm performance. Referring to the first research area, Storholm and Scheuing (1994) summarize legal standards that regulate the franchisor-franchisee relationship, i.e., antitrust laws, disclosure rules, standards on advertising, encroachment, termination, mandatory purchases, and property rights protection. Preble and Hoffman (1999) examine the franchise firm's stakeholders and topics addressed with ethics codes of 23 national franchise associations in North and South America, Asia, and Europe. Gámez-González et al.'s (2010) review of ethics codes from 46 national and international franchise associations results in 40 ethical topics. Perrigot et al. (2013) find that two factors positively impact the level of corporate social disclosure on companies' websites, i.e., chain size and the percentage of company-owned units of French franchise systems.

While Perrigot et al. (2013) use corporate social disclosure as a proxy for a franchise firm's CSR engagement, Meiseberg and Ehrmann (2012) develop a CSR construct based on the several dimensions from Kinder, Lydenberg, and Domini (KLD Research & Analytics, Inc.) as well as subjective measures on CSR activities. Their findings contribute to the second research area and show that factors, such as system size, experience, and multiunit ownership, increase CSR activity, which in turn enhances financial performance of German franchise firms.

Similarly, Croonen (2010) investigates the benefits from CSR, through already looking at CSR's positive impact on creating intangible assets, specifically the franchisees' commitment in the franchise relationship. Croonen's (2010) case study in the Dutch drugstore industry demonstrates that ethical franchisor behavior based on trust and fairness toward franchisees increases the franchisees' commitment during proposed strategic change processes. Nygaard and Biong (2010) shed light on the franchisor's necessity to exercise control over franchisees in order to ensure compliance with CSR standards and ethical values. Franchisor "CSR" control enhances franchisees' commitment and loyalty toward the franchise system. Lee et al. (2012, 2014) adopt Carroll's (1991) CSR model and differentiate CSR into economic, legal, ethical, and philanthropic responsibility dimensions. They show that franchisor's CSR strategy positively impacts the relationship quality between the franchisor and franchisees and, consequently, relationship outcomes, such as commitment and turnover intention, within franchised food service enterprises in South Korea. More recently, Rhou et al. (2016) reveal that the positive relationship between CSR and increased corporate financial performance (CFP) in the franchised restaurant industry also depends on the consumer's CSR awareness. Furthermore, Youn et al. (2016) find that the impact of CSR on CFP is "service" or "context" specific, that is, greater for fast-food restaurants than full-service restaurants.

2.2 The Stakeholder Approach to CSR

Corporate social responsibility is defined as "situations where the firm goes beyond compliance and engages in actions that appear to further some social good, beyond the interests of the firm and that which is required by law" (McWilliams et al. 2006, p. 3). Wood (1991, p. 703ff) defines CSR as the firm-specific processes and capabilities of environmental assessment (e.g., detecting shifts in the social, economic, political, and technological environment, such as stakeholder interests, regulatory environment, new technologies), stakeholder management (e.g., garner legitimacy benefits and reputation by balancing conflicting stakeholder interests and creating trust and interorganizational relationships), and issues management (e.g., developing legitimate responses) (Sirsly and Lamertz 2007).

There is consensus in CSR literature that management of CSR has become stakeholder management (e.g., Chakravarthy 1986; Donaldson and Preston 1995; Clarkson 1995; Wood and Jones 1995; McWilliams and Siegel 2001). The stakeholder approach to CSR recognizes various primary and secondary stakeholder groups. These are defined as "any identifiable group or individual who can affect the achievement of an organization's objectives or who is affected by the achievement of an organization's objectives" (Freeman and Reed 1983, p. 91). Therefore, besides shareholders and investors, the corporate environment is made up by consumers, employees, governments and institutions, the natural environment, suppliers and network partners, communities and activist groups, and competitors.

Important approaches have been developed for firms to classify and prioritize stakeholders' (CSR) issues (e.g., Mitchell et al. 1997; Rowley and Berman 2000), thereby acknowledging the challenges of industry-specific stakeholder constellations (e.g., Brammer and Pavelin 2006; Bhattacharya et al. 2009), information asymmetry (e.g., McWilliams and Siegel 2001; Servaes and Tamayo 2013), and opportunistic behavior (e.g., Rowley 1997; Rowley and Moldoveanu 2003). The critical task for firms is to identify the primary stakeholders and attend to their sometimes fluctuating, competing demands through the development of superior CSR strategies.

The firm's identification and management of stakeholders is widely explained by the resource dependency theory and the institutional theory (Oliver 1991; Greening and Gray 1994; Rowley 1997; Rowley and Moldoveanu 2003). Specifically, those stakeholders who have a legitimate claim on the firm can exercise power over the firm to coerce it to act in their favor (Rowley and Moldoveanu 2003). According to resource dependency theory (e.g., Pfeffer and Salancik 1978), resources are allocated between the stakeholders (e.g., consumers, owners, employees, suppliers, and competitors) and the firm. Because firms are not self-contained or self-sufficient and given that any kind of strategic change and adaption results in additional costs, firms prioritize issues and strategically respond to those stakeholders who have more power, control, and leverage over the critical resources (such as monetary, physical, knowledge, information, and social legitimacy). This leverage, exercised through exit threats and resource withdrawal, can jeopardize the success and survival of the firm (Ullmann 1985; Oliver 1991; Hill and Jones 1992; Frooman 1999). A failure to respond appropriately can result in negative corporate associations and make consumers buy elsewhere, stockholders sell their stocks, or employees quit their jobs (Hill and Jones 1992, p. 141).

Furthermore, according to Aguilera et al. (2007), "firms within a given industry are confined by the specific norms, values, and beliefs of that industry"; and firms engage in CSR to preserve their social legitimacy and social license to operate (2007, p. 845). Based on the institutional theory (e.g., Meyer and Rowan 1977; DiMaggio and Powell 1983), corporate behavior and socially responsible management depends on the institutional contexts of the firm's organizational environment characterized by different constituents and actors such as market and nonmarket actors (Delmas and Toffel 2008). Within organizational environments, common and accepted values, standards, rules, and norms develop, formed by formal and informal institutions such as the state, government, society, and cultures (Oliver 1991; Delmas and Toffel 2008). Therefore, under normative, intrinsic stakeholder management, firms adhere to institutional pressures and shape their CSR strategy according to the formal and informal rules prevailing in their environment. Failure in doing so will be sanctioned by the stakeholders' resource contribution withdrawal, in turn negatively affecting the shareholders' objectives.

3   Research Model and Hypotheses

Grounded in resource-based and organizational capabilities theories, our study explains the impact of the franchise firm's CSR strategy on its ability to develop intangible CSR-related assets which can become the source of sustainable competitive advantage (see Fig. 1). CSR investment is a multidimensional construct of

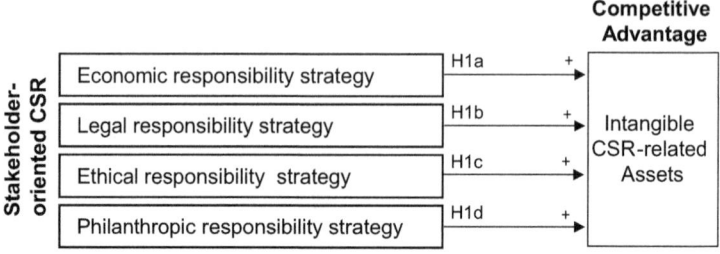

Fig. 1 CSR strategy and competitive advantage of the franchise firm

economic, legal, ethical, and philanthropic responsibility which addresses different stakeholder issues.

3.1 Intangible CSR-Related Assets as Source of Competitive Advantage

Based on resource-based and organizational capabilities theories (e.g., Nelson and Winter 1982; Wernerfelt 1984; Rumelt 1984; Barney 1991; Conner 1991; Foss 1993; Madhok 1996), franchise firms that create and exploit complementary intangible assets, know-how, resources, and capabilities from their CSR activities will realize competitive advantage.

CSR management is a continuous investment with a long-term perspective, for instance, through an everyday interaction with stakeholders. It positively impacts the development of intangible assets such as brand name value, reputation, trust, satisfaction, and commitment. These complementary intangible, CSR-related assets are characterized as being valuable, rare, inimitable, and non-substitutable (Barney 1991). They cannot be acquired on the market or easily imitated by others and hence become the source of competitive advantage (Hillman and Keim 2001; De la Cruz and De Saá-Pérez 2003; McWilliams and Siegel 2011; Hult 2011).

In franchising, the creation and maintenance of brand name value and reputation is critical—facilitating the rapid expansion and diffusion of the franchise network (e.g., Julian and Castrogiovanni 1995; Pak 2002). Therefore, CSR and intangible asset management become an inseparable strategy for gaining competitive advantage (Fombrun et al. 2000; Werther and Chandler 2005; Lacey and Kennett-Hensel 2010). Ultimately, intangible CSR-related assets, such as brand name, reputation, and trust, result in lower capital costs, decreased hiring and training costs, premium pricing through product innovation and differentiation, repeat purchase customers and word of mouth, favorable contracts and other benefits by governments and public institutions, and entry barriers for competitors (Turban and Greening 1997; Brown and Dacin 1997; Christmann 2000; Roberts and Dowling 2002; McWilliams and Siegel 2011).

3.2 Creation of Intangible Assets with CSR Strategy

Adopting a resource-based and organizational capabilities approach to CSR (e.g., Sharma and Vredenburg 1998; Branco and Rodrigues 2006; Husted and de Jesus 2006; Sirsly and Lamertz 2007; Surroca et al. 2010; Carroll and Shabana 2010; McWilliams and Siegel 2011), stakeholders become an integral part of the firm's strategic planning (Hult 2011; Husted et al. 2012), and "CSR management" becomes "stakeholder management." Thereby, firms achieve sustainable competitive advantage through their adaptive capability to manage the CSR issues of their stakeholders (e.g., Berman et al. 1999; Hillman and Keim 2001; Bansal 2005; Barnett 2007; Darnall et al. 2008; De la Cruz and De Saá-Pérez 2003).

Investing into CSR to achieve legitimacy among stakeholders and firm survival is not a guarantor for improving competitive advantage. The impact of the firm's CSR investments on the exploration of intangible CSR-related assets is both contingent upon which type of CSR investment is undertaken and which industrial sector the firm is primarily associated with. For example, CSR management with no relation to a firm's business and industry may be interpreted by stakeholders as a misdirected investment effort, negatively influencing the firm's reputation (Brammer and Pavelin 2006; Bhattacharya et al. 2009; Peloza and Shang 2011). Porter and Kramer (2002, 2006) go even further by arguing that a value-creating CSR strategy should look beyond immediate stakeholder interests and cause-related marketing altogether. Above all, CSR should be concerned with social needs that either are affected by a firm's value chain activities or affect the firm's competitive context.

Carroll (1979, 1991) differentiates CSR into economic, legal, ethical, and philanthropic dimensions to account for the complex stakeholder constellations and expectations inherent in the firm's environment. Different CSR strategies target different stakeholders, resulting in different benefits for the firm (Lee et al. 2012; Kim et al. 2017). Accordingly, *economic responsibilities* of business reflect the belief that business should provide goods and services to meet consumer needs of society and create jobs and fair workers' pay, ultimately with the goal of increasing productivity, profitability, and return on investment for shareholders. *Legal responsibilities* of business indicate a concern that economic responsibilities are pursued within the framework of the codified law. *Ethical responsibilities* of business go beyond what is required by law. They reflect the firm's unwritten codes, norms, and values implicitly derived from society. Finally, *philanthropic responsibilities* are volitional in nature and not expected in an ethical or moral sense, wherein firms contribute financial and human resources to the community to improve the quality of life.

Therefore, a strategic approach to CSR will capture the benefits from CSR investments, which are the intangible CSR-related assets such as brand name, reputation, and trust that build the franchise firm's competitive advantage in the long run. Based on Carroll (1979, 1991), such CSR strategy is multidimensional and addresses the social expectations and needs of the firm's multiple stakeholder groups. We can formulate the following hypotheses (see Fig. 1):

Hypothesis H1 *The franchise firm's CSR strategy impacts the creation of intangible CSR-related assets.*

Specifically:

Hypothesis H1a *The franchise firm's economic responsibility strategy positively impacts its brand name assets.*

Hypothesis H1b *The franchise firm's legal responsibility strategy positively impacts its brand name assets.*

Hypothesis H1c *The franchise firm's ethical responsibility strategy positively impacts its brand name assets.*

Hypothesis H1d *The franchise firm's philanthropic responsibility strategy positively impacts its brand name assets.*

4 Research Methodology

4.1 Data

We test our hypotheses by conducting a survey in the Austrian franchise sector, where, starting from the 1970s, business format franchising became a popular business model. In 1986, the Austrian Franchise Association (AFA) was established. In 2012, Austria counted 445 franchise systems and 7150 franchise partners with 8720 outlets and 66,000 employees. In collaboration with the AFA, we distributed the questionnaire to 311 Austrian franchise companies in several survey rounds via mailing, online, and email during the period of February–June 2014. It turned out that 31 companies were not franchising any longer, and after data cleaning, the final sample includes 65 responses accounting for a 23% response rate. 52% of the responding franchise firms belong to the service industry and 40% to the retailing industry, and the rest were production franchises. Respondents, mainly franchisors or franchise managers, were asked to provide information on topics related to the CSR strategy, brand competitiveness, decision-making, financial performance, as well as general characteristics of the franchise firm, among others. The average age of Austrian franchise systems was 16 years, and the average chain size contained 68 franchise and company-owned outlets.

To trace nonresponse bias, we examine whether the results obtained from the analysis are influenced by early vs. late respondents (Armstrong and Overton 1977). No significant differences emerged between the two respondent groups. We applied

Harman's one-factor test to check the presence of common method bias, which could not be corroborated (Podsakoff et al. 2003).

4.2   Measurement

The principal component factor analysis with varimax rotation on all subjective items of the independent variables confirmed a four-factor solution explaining 69% of the variance. Therefore, common method bias is unlikely to affect the interpretations of our results. We employed multiple measures of construct reliability including Cronbach's alpha, composite reliability (CR), and average variance extracted (AVE). As shown in Table 1, Cronbach's alpha, CR, and AVE values for all latent predictor variables (ECONOMICcsr, LEGALcsr, ETHICALcsr, and PHILANTROPICcsr) and the dependent variable (BRAND) were above the recommended thresholds of 0.70, 0.60, and 0.50, respectively. Furthermore, we used AVE to assess construct discriminant validity of the latent predictor and dependent variables. As suggested by Fornell and Larcker (1981), we compared the shared variance (squared correlation) between each pair of constructs against the corresponding AVE from each construct. The squared correlations are also summarized in Table 1.

To operationalize our dependent and independent variables, we developed multiple-item constructs measured on seven-point Likert scales (1 = do not agree at all, 7 = totally agree). Our measurement constructs are summarized in the appendix.

4.2.1   Dependent Variable

Our dependent variable is the franchise firm's brand name assets *(BRAND)*. Brand name assets are intangible assets considered to be central to the franchise firm's success and the building of competitive advantage (e.g., Contractor and Kundu 1998a, 1998b; Quinn and Doherty 2000). Similarly, existent studies use brand name and reputation as measures for intangible assets in the context of CSR (e.g., Brown and Dacin 1997; Sharma and Vredenburg 1998; Marcus and Geffen 1998;

Table 1 Construct reliability and discriminant validity

| | Cronbach's-α | CR | AVE | Squared correlations | | | | |
				1	2	3	4	5
1. BRAND	0.738	0.932	0.776	1				
2. ECONOMICcsr	0.787	0.913	0.783	0.023	1			
3. LEGALcsr	0.835	0.931	0.73	0.050	0.212	1		
4. ETHICALcsr	0.815	0.939	0.757	0.042	0.327	0.058	1	
5. PHILANTROPICcsr	0.830	0.921	0.746	0.120	0.353	0.133	0.331	1

Hillman and Keim 2001; Roberts and Dowling 2002; De la Cruz and De Saá-Pérez 2003; Branco and Rodrigues 2006; Husted and de Jesus 2006; Surroca et al. 2010; McWilliams and Siegel 2011; Servaes and Tamayo 2013). Therefore, adopted from previous franchise studies (Combs and Ketchen Jr 1999; Erramilli et al. 2002; Barthélemy 2008), we used four items that measure the CSR-related brand name assets *(BRAND)* of the franchise firm on seven-point Likert scales (see appendix).

4.2.2 Independent Variables

Our independent variables are the stakeholder-oriented CSR strategies applied by franchise firms. We use Carroll's (1991) multidimensional CSR construct of economic, legal, ethical, and philanthropic responsibility to portray the complex stakeholder environment of franchise firms. Similarly, existent studies adopt those CSR dimensions to measure CSR activities targeted toward franchisees in the food service industry (Lee et al. 2012) or toward customers in the gaming industry (Kim et al. 2017). In collaboration with Austrian consultants specialized in CSR and franchising, we developed several seven-point Likert scale items for each dimension. *Economic responsibility strategy (ECONOMICcsr)* consists of three items. *Legal responsibility strategy (LEGALcsr)* is measured on a five-item scale. *Ethical responsibility strategy (ETHICALcsr)* is defined by five items. *Philanthropic responsibility strategy (PHILANTROPICcsr)* consists of four items (see appendix).

4.2.3 Control Variables

As control variables, we included an industry variable *(INDUSTRY)* which differentiates between service, manufacturing, and retail franchising. CSR activities are industry specific, and the "fit" between industry and CSR (Brammer and Pavelin 2006) is critical for the exploration of intangible CSR-related assets and the competitive advantage of the firm. Furthermore, we controlled for the influence of franchise system age *(AGE)* on the exploration of intangible CSR-related assets. This is a frequently used proxy variable in franchise studies (e.g., Huszagh et al. 1992; Kedia et al. 1994; Contractor and Kundu 1998a, 1998b; Burton et al. 2000; Erramilli et al. 2002; Castrogiovanni et al. 2006; Dunning et al. 2007). It captures the franchise system's accumulation of specific assets, resources, know-how, and capabilities over time, such as superior CSR strategy, that positively impacts the creation of intangible CSR-related assets. System age *(AGE)* was measured the by the number of years since the franchise system was founded.

4.3 Results

Table 2 reports the descriptive statistics and Pearson correlation coefficients of the variables used in the regression model. None of the correlations indicate problems of

Table 2 Descriptive statistics

Variable	Mean	SD	N	Correlations						
				1	2	3	4	5	6	7
1. BRAND	5.823	1.098	65	1						
2. ECONOMICcsr	5.754	1.146	65	0.151	1					
3. LEGALcsr	4.785	1.586	65	0.224	0.460**	1				
4. ETHICALcsr	5.923	1.020	65	0.204	0.572**	0.241	1			
5. PHILANTROPICcsr	5.046	1.325	65	0.347**	0.594**	0.365**	0.575**	1		
6. AGE	15.983	15.085	59	0.162	−0.271*	−0.242	−0.430**	−0.203	1	
7. INDUSTRY	2.585	0.635	65	−0.073	0.072	0.205	0.046	0.051	−0.145	1

$**p < 0.01; *p < 0.05$

Table 3 The impact of multidimensional CSR strategy (economic responsibility, legal responsibility, ethical responsibility, and philanthropic responsibility) on brand name assets

Brand name assets			
	Constant	0.031(0.493)	0.151(0.367)
	AGE	0.176(0.120)	0.362_{**}(0.102)
	INDUSTRY	0.030(0.188)	−0.010(0.141)
H1a	ECONOMICcsr		0.174_{*}(0.086)
H1b	LEGALcsr		0.283_{**}(0.094)
H1c	ETHICALcsr		0.222_{*}(0.106)
H1d	PHILANTROPICcsr		0.478_{**}(0.084)
	N	59	59
	R^2	0.042	0.530
	Adjusted R^2	0.003	0.467

$_{**}p < 0.01$; $_{*}p < 0.05$
Values in parentheses represent standard errors

multicollinearity as the correlation matrix shows relatively low correlations among the seven variables and the multicollinearity test shows that these data are not confounded by overlapping covariations (min and max VIF of 1.009 and 1.40, respectively).

We apply linear regression to test our hypotheses on the impact of CSR strategy on the exploration of intangible CSR-related assets (see Fig. 1). Our predictor variables are the franchise firm's economic responsibility strategy *(ECONOMICcsr)*, legal responsibility strategy *(LEGALcsr)*, ethical responsibility strategy *(ETHI-CALcsr)*, and philanthropic responsibility strategy *(PHILANTROPICcsr)*. They impact the franchise firm's brand name assets (BRAND). In addition, our regression model controls for franchise system age *(AGE)* and industry *(INDUSTRY)*.

Table 3 displays our estimation results. Our data provide support for the overall hypothesis (H1) that CSR strategy increases the franchise firm's brand name assets. More specifically, the positive and significant impact on franchise firm's brand name assets can be observed for all four CSR dimensions. Hence, our analysis supports H1a, H1b, H1c, and H1d. Comparing the standardized beta coefficients of the predictor variables shows the relative importance of CSR dimensions on brand name assets. First, our results reveal that compared to the other three dimensions, economic responsibility strategy (H1a) exerts the smallest positive impact on brand name assets. Second, legal responsibility (H1b) and ethical responsibility (H1c) have a fairly similar positive impact on brand name assets. Third, the greatest positive impact on brand name assets is achieved with philanthropic responsibility strategy (H1d). Regarding control variables, franchise firm's age *(AGE)* positively and significantly impacts brand name assets. Conversely, industry *(INDUSTRY)* is not significant in our model. To summarize the test of the research model, all hypotheses (H1a–H1d) are supported by our data.

5   Discussion and Implications

Our study explains the strategic role of CSR in franchising. Based on Carroll (1991), we define the franchise firm's CSR strategy as a multidimensional construct. Being differentiated into economic, legal, ethical, and philanthropic responsibility dimensions, it targets the interests of multiple stakeholders of the franchise firm. Based on resource-based and organizational capabilities theories, the adoption of such a CSR strategy influences the creation of intangible CSR-related assets, such as brand name and reputation assets, which are the main source of sustainable competitive advantage of franchise firms.

Our regression analysis with data from the Austrian franchise sector supports the hypotheses of our research model. Overall, our results shed light on the positive relationship of CSR strategy and the generation of intangible assets which are the brand name assets of Austrian franchise firms. More specifically, our findings demonstrate that the four CSR dimensions have a discriminating impact on the value creation of those assets for franchise firms. Particularly, the philanthropic responsibility strategy has the greatest impact, followed by legal and ethical responsibility strategy, while economic responsibility strategy exerts the smallest impact on the brand name assets of franchise firms.

First, Austrian franchise firms adopt an *economic responsibility* strategy with the primary goal of increasing economic benefits, such as productivity and profitability. Austrian franchisors are cognizant that shared social values create bonding and trust among partners, an important determinant for the long-lasting success and survival of franchise relationships. In this context, also existent franchise studies discuss the relevance of trust for successful franchise partnerships (e.g., Pizanti and Lerner 2003). Second, Austrian franchise firms strictly adhere to the law and existing regulations to avoid penalty payments and other adverse sanctions due to legal violations. Therefore, they implemented a compliance system as part of their *legal responsibility* strategy and monitor franchisees' adherence to established system standards and existent legislation. Works by Storholm and Scheuing (1994), Gámez-González et al. (2010), and Perrigot et al. (2013) also summarize legal franchise standards and ethics codes and highlight their relevance for franchising. Third, Austrian franchise firms believe in their *ethical responsibility* to create progress for the society and a balance between social, environmental, and economic values. Through the codification of ethical values in system manuals and the like, those become part of corporate strategy to be complied with by franchisees. Finally, Austrian franchise systems regard themselves as "corporate citizens" who integrate social and environmental interests of stakeholders into their *philanthropic responsibility* strategy. Such engagement should be communicated to the public to increase the reputation of Austrian franchise firms. Similarly, Lee et al. (2012) find that franchise firms' philanthropic CSR investments are motivated by image considerations.

The findings of our study contribute to the scarce literature on CSR in franchising (Jeon and Gleiberman 2017). Franchising is characterized by a strong emphasis on intangible asset management. Intangible assets, such as brand name and reputation, not only attract customers. They are also the fundamental criteria for franchise partners to join and facilitate rapid expansion and diffusion of the franchise network. Our study also contributes to explanations of the business case for CSR (Carroll and Shabana 2010), which defines how firms can derive economic and financial benefits from CSR investments. By testing the impact of CSR on financial performance (Griffin and Mahon 1997; Margolis and Walsh 2003; Orlitzky et al. 2003), empirical studies found positive relationships (e.g., Clarkson et al. 2008), some provided contrary findings (e.g., Cordeiro and Sarkis 1997), while others argued that the relationship is neutral (Nelling and Webb 2009). Grounded in resource-based and organizational capabilities theories, we explain how franchise firms can create intangible assets and hence capture sustainable competitive advantage through stakeholder-oriented CSR strategies. Thereby, we conceptualize CSR strategy by a multidimensional CSR construct that differentiates economic, legal, ethical, and philanthropic responsibility.

Our empirical results may guide franchisors and franchise managers in the adoption of a strategic CSR approach. While CSR strategy has an overall positive impact on brand name assets of franchise firms, we find that philanthropic responsibility strategy achieves the greatest value-creating impact, followed by legal, ethical, and at last economic responsibility strategies. Therefore, franchise firms need to be cognizant of their corporate responsible behavior, which may have different effects on their intangible assets, ultimately impacting their competitive advantage and financial performance. Moreover, our study can assist public policy makers in the development of initiatives, programs, and regulations that are tailored to the industry-specific environment of franchise firms. This is vital to support the franchise firm's achievement of competitive advantage with CSR and prevent adverse corporate political influence tactics, such as manipulation strategies and lobbying, as a response to unfavorably considered public policies (McWilliams et al. 2002; Hillman et al. 2004). Finally, enhancing a strategic understanding of CSR which can be the source of competitive advantage of the firm is imperative as governments increasingly transfer CSR responsibility to the authority of the firm (Van Marrewijk 2003). Consequently, a strategic CSR approach not only impacts growth and survival of the franchise firm itself but also growth and competitiveness of a country's economy (Vallentin and Murillo 2012).

Our study faces some limitations and recommends some future research topics. We only analyzed the impact of CSR strategy on the franchise firm's most critical intangible assets, namely, its brand name assets. It is worth exploring a more sophisticated set of intangible assets such as commitment, trust, and satisfaction, which all have the potential to create value and competitive advantage for the firm. Furthermore, CSR scholars criticize the fragmented, mainly unilateral CSR analysis which results in an incomplete explanation of the business case for CSR and, ultimately, inconsistent findings regarding financial performance (Margolis and Walsh 2003; Marquis et al. 2007). Therefore, combining resource-based and organizational capabilities theories with transaction cost and agency theory (e.g., Hill and Jones 1992; Russo 1992; Jones 1995; Ruf et al. 2001) may provide further explanations on the relationship between CSR, intangible asset management, and competitive advantage. Finally, due to the data based on Austrian franchise firms, the results may be subject to cultural bias and hence unsuitable for generalization. Accordingly, we would like to motivate researchers to extend this study to other countries and advance the strategic CSR approach through a multi-theoretical perspective. In addition, adopting a cross-country perspective to CSR may also affect the implementation of effective CSR strategy within international franchise systems. In this context, an important future research question might address standardization vs. local adaptation of CSR strategy, in order to gain legitimacy among global stakeholders.

6 Conclusion

The aim of this study is to explain the strategic role of CSR for the creation of intangible assets in franchising. We adopt a multidimensional CSR construct including economic, legal, ethical, and philanthropic responsibility strategies, which addresses the issues of multiple stakeholders. Our results show that CSR strategies have a positive but discriminating impact on brand name assets of franchise firms. Franchise firms need to be cognizant of their choice of CSR strategy, which impacts the creation of brand name assets as critical source of sustainable competitive advantage and hence financial performance.

Appendix Summary Measures on CSR Strategy and Brand Name Assets

Constructs	Items	Description of measures
Brand name assets Cronbach's-$\alpha = 0.738$ CR = 0.932 AVE = 0.776	Four seven-point items, anchored by "do not agree at all" [1] and "totally agree" [7], adopted from Combs and Ketchen, 1999; Erramilli et al., 2002; Barthélemy, 2008	1. Our franchise brand is very strong as compared to our competitors. 2. Our franchise system is very recognized as compared to our competitors. 3. The quality of our franchise system is very high as compared to our competitors. 4. Our brand name is very important for the achievement of competitive advantage.

(continued)

Constructs	Items	Description of measures
Economic responsibility strategy Cronbach's-α = 0.787 CR = 0.913 AVE = 0.783	Three seven-point items, "do not agree at all" [1] and "totally agree" [7], developed by franchise consultants	1. Shared values create trust and bonding in franchise relationships. 2. Social interests beyond minimum legal requirements should be considered after economic interests only. 3. Commitment to social and environmental standards should be consistent with economic objectives.
Legal responsibility strategy Cronbach's-α = 0.835 CR = 0.931 AVE = 0.730	Five seven-point items, "do not agree at all" [1] and "totally agree" [7], developed by franchise consultants	1. We have implemented a compliance system to guarantee the recognition of applicable law. 2. We monitor our franchisees' compliance with the law. 3. We impose sanctions on franchisees for violating the law. 4. We monitor our franchisees' compliance with system standards and values. 5. We impose sanctions on our franchisees for breaching system standards and values.
Ethical responsibility strategy Cronbach's-α = 0.815 CR = 0.939 AVE = 0.757	Five seven-point items, "do not agree at all" [1] and "totally agree" [7], developed by franchise consultants	1. Through sustainable corporate operations, we create progress and benefit for the whole society. 2. Our franchise system aims to add economic as well as social and environmental value with its business operations. 3. If economic and social interests are inconsistent with our corporate operations, we try to find a balance between them. 4. Our franchise system upholds fundamental values which are codified in system manuals, codes of conduct, and similar documents. 5. We expect from our franchisees to comply with our system values.

(continued)

Constructs	Items	Description of measures
Philanthropic responsibility strategy Cronbach's-α = 0.830 CR = 0.921 AVE = 0.746	Four seven-point items, "do not agree at all" [1] and "totally agree" [7], developed by franchise consultants	1. Integration of social and environmental interests into corporate strategy is the responsibility of a corporate citizen. 2. As corporate citizens, we consider social engagement as self-purpose and independent of economic interests. 3. Our franchise system's reputation is increased by our proven social and environmental engagement. 4. A franchise system should communicate its social and environmental positioning and engagement to the public.

References

Aguilera RV, Rupp DE, Williams CA, Ganapathi J (2007) Putting the S back in corporate social responsibility: a multilevel theory of social change in organizations. Acad Manag Rev 32(3):836–863

Armstrong JS, Overton TS (1977) Estimating non-response bias in mail survey. Avenues to greater theoretical diversity. J Manag 30(6):907–931

Bansal P (2005) Evolving sustainably: a longitudinal study of corporate sustainable development. Strateg Manag J 26(3):197–218

Barnett ML (2007) Stakeholder influence capacity and the variability of financial returns to corporate social responsibility. Acad Manag Rev 32(3):794–816

Barney J (1991) Firm resources and sustained competitive advantage. J Manag 17(1):99–120

Barthélemy J (2008) Opportunism knowledge and the performance of franchise chains. Strateg Manag J 29(13):1451–1463

Berman SL, Wicks AC, Kotha S, Jones TM (1999) Does stakeholder orientation matter? The relationship between stakeholder management models and firm financial performance. Acad Manag J 42(5):488–506

Bhattacharya CB, Korschun D, Sen S (2009) Strengthening stakeholder–company relationships through mutually beneficial corporate social responsibility initiatives. J Bus Ethics 85(2):257–272

Brammer SJ, Pavelin S (2006) Corporate reputation and social performance: the importance of fit. J Manag Stud 43(3):435–455

Branco MC, Rodrigues LL (2006) Corporate social responsibility and resource-based perspectives. J Bus Ethics 69(2):111–132

Brown TJ, Dacin PA (1997) The company and the product: corporate associations and consumer product responses. J Mark 61(1):68–84

Burton F, Cross AR, Rhodes M (2000) Foreign market servicing strategies of UK franchisors: an empirical enquiry from a transactions cost perspective. Manag Int Rev 40(4):373–400

Carroll AB (1979) A three-dimensional conceptual model of corporate performance. Acad Manag Rev 4(4):497–505

Carroll AB (1991) The pyramid of corporate social responsibility: toward the moral management of organizational stakeholders. Bus Horiz 34(4):39–48

Carroll AB, Shabana KM (2010) The business case for corporate social responsibility: a review of concepts research and practice. Int J Manag Rev 12(1):85–105

Castrogiovanni GJ, Combs JG, Justis RT (2006) Resource scarcity and agency theory predictions concerning the continued use of franchising in multi-outlet networks. J Small Bus Manag 44(1):27–44

Chakravarthy BS (1986) Measuring strategic performance. Strateg Manag J 7(5):437–458

Choo S (2005) Determinants of monitoring capabilities in international franchising: foodservice firms within East Asia. Asia Pac J Manag 22(2):159–177

Christmann P (2000) Effects of "best practices" of environmental management on cost advantage: the role of complementary assets. Acad Manag J 43(4):663–680

Clarkson ME (1995) A stakeholder framework for analyzing and evaluating corporate social performance. Acad Manag Rev 20(1):92–117

Clarkson PM, Li Y, Richardson GD, Vasvari FP (2008) Revisiting the relation between environmental performance and environmental disclosure: an empirical analysis. Acc Org Soc 33(4-5):303–327

Combs JG, Ketchen DJ Jr (1999) Explaining interfirm cooperation and performance: toward a reconciliation of predictions from the resource-based view and organizational economics. Strateg Manag J 20(9):867–888

Combs JG, Ketchen DJ Jr, Shook CL, Short JC (2011) Antecedents and consequences of franchising: past accomplishments and future challenges. J Manag 37(1):99–126

Conner KR (1991) A historical comparison of resource-based theory and five schools of thought within industrial organization economics: do we have a new theory of the firm? J Manag 17(1):121–154

Contractor FJ, Kundu SK (1998a) Franchising versus company-run operations: modal choice in the global hotel sector. J Int Mark 6(2):28–53

Contractor FJ, Kundu SK (1998b) Modal choice in a world of alliances: analysing organisational forms in the international hotel sector. J Int Bus Stud 29(2):325–358

Cordeiro JJ, Sarkis J (1997) Environmental proactivism and firm performance: evidence from security analyst earnings forecasts. Bus Strateg Environ 6(2):104–114

Croonen E (2010) Trust and fairness during strategic change processes in franchise systems. J Bus Ethics 95(2):191–209

Dant RP, Grünhagen M, Kaufmann PJ, Brown JR, Cliquet G, Robicheaux RA (2012) Chronicling the saga of 25 years of International Society of Franchising. J Small Bus Manag 50(4):525–538

Darnall N, Henriques I, Sadorsky P (2008) Do environmental management systems improve business performance in an international setting? J Int Manag 14(4):364–376

De la Cruz D-DM, De Saá-Pérez P (2003) A resource-based view of corporate responsiveness toward employees. Organ Stud 24(2):299–319

Delmas MA, Toffel MW (2008) Organizational responses to environmental demands: opening the black box. Strateg Manag J 29(10):1027–1055

DiMaggio PJ, Powell WW (1983) The iron cage revisited: institutional isomorphism and collective rationality in organizational fields. Am Sociol Rev 48:147–160

Donaldson T, Preston LE (1995) The stakeholder theory of the corporation: concepts evidence and implications. Acad Manag Rev 20(1):65–91

Dunning JH, Pak YS, Beldona S (2007) Foreign ownership strategies of UK and US international franchisors: an exploratory application of Dunning's envelope paradigm. Int Bus Rev 16(5):531–548

Elango B (2007) Are franchisors with international operations different from those who are domestic market oriented? J Small Bus Manag 54(2):179–193

Erramilli KM, Agarwal S, Dev CS (2002) Choice between non-equity entry modes: an organisational capability perspective. J Int Bus Stud 33(2):223–242

Fladmoe-Lindquist K, Jacque LL (1995) Control modes in international service operations: the propensity to franchise. Manag Sci 41(7):1238–1249

Fombrun CJ, Gardberg NA, Barnett ML (2000) Opportunity platforms and safety nets: corporate citizenship and reputational risk. Bus Soc Rev 105(1):85–106

Fornell C, Larcker DF (1981) Structural equation models with unobservable variables and measurement error: algebra and statistics. J Mark Res 18:382–388

Foss NJ (1993) Theories of the firm: contractual and competence perspectives. J Evol Econ 3(2):127–144

Freeman RE, Reed DL (1983) Stockholders and stakeholders: a new perspective in corporate governance. Calif Manag Rev 25(3):88–106

Frooman J (1999) Stakeholder influence strategies. Acad Manag Rev 24(2):191–205

Gámez-González J, Rondan-Cataluña FJ, Diez-de Castro EC, Navarro-Garcia A (2010) Toward an international code of franchising. Manag Decis 48(10):1568–1595

Greening DW, Gray B (1994) Testing a model of organizational response to social and political issues. Acad Manag J 37(3):467–498

Griffin JJ, Mahon JF (1997) The corporate social performance and corporate financial performance debate twenty-five years of incomparable research. Bus Soc 36(1):5–31

Hill CW, Jones TM (1992) Stakeholder-agency theory. J Manag Stud 29(2):131–154

Hillman AJ, Keim GD (2001) Shareholder value stakeholder management and social issues: what's the bottom line? Strateg Manag J 22(2):125–139

Hillman AJ, Keim GD, Schuler D (2004) Corporate political activity: a review and research agenda. J Manag 30(6):837–857

Hult GTM (2011) Market-focused sustainability: market orientation plus! J Acad Mark Sci 39(1):1–6

Husted BW, de Jesus SJ (2006) Taking Friedman seriously: maximizing profits and social performance. J Manag Stud 43(1):75–91

Husted BW, Allen DB, Kock N (2012) Value creation through social strategy. Bus Soc 54(2):147–186

Huszagh SM, Huszagh FW, McIntyre FS (1992) International franchising in the context of competitive strategy and the theory of the firm. Int Mark Rev 9(5). https://doi.org/10.1108/02651339210020268

Jeon HJ, Gleiberman A (2017) Examining the role of sustainability and green strategies in channels: evidence from the franchise industry. J Mark Theory Pract 25(2):189–199

Jones TM (1995) Instrumental stakeholder theory: a synthesis of ethics and economics. Acad Manag Rev 20(2):404–437

Julian SD, Castrogiovanni GJ (1995) Franchisor geographic expansion. J Small Bus Manag 33(2):1

Kedia BL, Ackerman DJ, Bush DE, Justice RT (1994) Study note: determinants of international-ization of franchise operations by US franchisors. Int Mark Rev 11(4):56–68

Kim JS, Song H, Lee CK, Lee JY (2017) The impact of four CSR dimensions on a gaming company's image and customers' revisit intentions. Int J Hosp Manag 61:73–81

Lacey R, Kennett-Hensel PA (2010) Longitudinal effects of corporate social responsibility on customer relationships. J Bus Ethics 97(4):581–597

Lee YK, Lee KH, Li DX (2012) The impact of CSR on relationship quality and relationship outcomes: a perspective of service employees. Int J Hosp Manag 31(3):745–756

Lee YK, Kim SH, Banks HSC, Lee KH (2014) An ethical work climate and its consequences among food-service franchise employees. Asia Pac J Tour Res 20(11):1286–1312

Madhok A (1996) Crossroads-the organization of economic activity: transaction costs firm capabilities and the nature of governance. Organ Sci 7(5):577–590

Marcus A, Geffen D (1998) The dialectics of competency acquisition: pollution prevention in electric generation. Strateg Manag J 19(12):1145–1168

Margolis JD, Walsh JP (2003) Misery loves companies: rethinking social initiatives by business. Adm Sci Q 48(2):268–305

Marquis C, Glynn MA, Davis GF (2007) Community isomorphism and corporate social action. Acad Manag Rev 32(3):925–945

McWilliams A, Siegel D (2001) Corporate social responsibility: a theory of the firm perspective. Acad Manag Rev 26(1):117–127

McWilliams A, Siegel DS (2011) Creating and capturing value: strategic corporate social responsi-bility resource-based theory and sustainable competitive advantage. J Manag 37(5):1480–1495

McWilliams A, Van Fleet DD, Cory KD (2002) Raising rivals' costs through political strategy: an extension of resource-based theory. J Manag Stud 39(5):707–724

McWilliams A, Siegel DS, Wright PM (2006) Corporate social responsibility: strategic implications. J Manag Stud 43(1):1–18

Meiseberg B, Ehrmann T (2012) Lost in translation? The prevalence and performance impact of corporate social responsibility in franchising. J Small Bus Manag 50(4):566–595

Meyer JW, Rowan B (1977) Institutionalized organizations: formal structure as myth and ceremony. Am J Sociol 83(2):340–363

Mitchell RK, Agle BR, Wood DJ (1997) Toward a theory of stakeholder identification and salience: defining the principle of who and what really counts. Acad Manag Rev 22(4):853–886

Nelling E, Webb E (2009) Corporate social responsibility and financial performance: the 'virtuous circle' revisited. Rev Quant Finan Acc 32(2):197–209

Nelson RR, Winter SG (1982) An evolutionary theory of economic behavior and capabilities. Harvard University Press, Cambridge MA, pp 195–307

Nygaard A, Biong H (2010) The influence of retail management's use of social power on corporate ethical values employee commitment and performance. J Bus Ethics 97(1):87–108

Oliver C (1991) Strategic responses to institutional processes. Acad Manag Rev 16(1):145–179

Orlitzky M, Schmidt FL, Rynes SL (2003) Corporate social and financial performance: a meta-analysis. Organ Stud 24(3):403–441

Pak YS (2002) The effect of strategic motives on the choice of entry modes: an empirical test of international franchisers. Multinatl Bus Rev 10(1):28

Peloza J, Shang J (2011) How can corporate social responsibility activities create value for stakeholders? A systematic review. J Acad Mark Sci 39(1):117–135

Perrigot R, Oxibar B, Déjean F (2013) Corporate social disclosure in the franchising sector: insights from French franchisors' websites. J Small Bus Manag 53(2):321–339

Pfeffer JS, Salancik G (1978) The external control of organizations: a resource dependence perspective. Harper and Row, New York

Pizanti I, Lerner M (2003) Examining control and autonomy in the franchisor-franchisee relationship. Int Small Bus J 21(2):131–159

Podsakoff PM, MacKenzie SB, Lee JY, Podsakoff NP (2003) Common method biases in behavioral research: a critical review of the literature and recommended remedies. J Appl Psychol 88(5):879

Porter ME, Kramer MR (2002) The competitive advantage of corporate philanthropy. Harv Bus Rev 80(12):56–68

Porter ME, Kramer MR (2006) Strategy and society the link between competitive advantage and corporate social responsibility. Harv Bus Rev 84:78–92

Preble JF, Hoffman RC (1999) The nature of ethics codes in franchise associations around the globe. J Bus Ethics 18(3):239–253

Preble JF, Reichel A, Hoffman RC (2000) Strategic alliances for competitive advantage: evidence from Israel's hospitality and tourism industry. Int J Hosp Manag 19(3):327–341

Quinn B, Doherty AM (2000) Power and control in international retail franchising - evidence from theory and practice. Int Mark Rev 17(4/5):354–372

Rhou Y, Singal M, Koh Y (2016) CSR and financial performance: the role of CSR awareness in the restaurant industry. Int J Hosp Manag 57:30–39

Roberts PW, Dowling GR (2002) Corporate reputation and sustained superior financial performance. Strateg Manag J 23(12):1077–1093

Rowley TJ (1997) Moving beyond dyadic ties: a network theory of stakeholder influences. Acad Manag Rev 22(4):887–910

Rowley T, Berman S (2000) A brand new brand of corporate social performance. Bus Soc 39(4):397–418

Rowley TI, Moldoveanu M (2003) When will stakeholder groups act? An interest- and identity-based model of stakeholder group mobilization. Acad Manag Rev 28(2):204–219

Ruf BM, Muralidhar K, Brown RM, Janney JJ, Paul K (2001) An empirical investigation of the relationship between change in corporate social performance and financial performance: a stakeholder theory perspective. J Bus Ethics 32(2):143–156

Rumelt RP (1984) Towards a strategic theory of the firm. Compet Strategic Manag 26:556–570

Russo MV (1992) Power plays: regulation diversification and backward integration in the electric utility industry. Strateg Manag J 13(1):13–27

Servaes H, Tamayo A (2013) The impact of corporate social responsibility on firm value: the role of customer awareness. Manag Sci 59(5):1045–1061

Sharma S, Vredenburg H (1998) Proactive corporate environmental strategy and the development of competitively valuable organizational capabilities. Strateg Manag J 19(8):729–753

Sirsly CAT, Lamertz K (2007) When does a corporate social responsibility initiative provide a first-mover advantage? Bus Soc 47(3):343–369

Storholm G, Scheuing EE (1994) Ethical implications of business format franchising. J Bus Ethics 13(3):181–188

Surroca J, Tribó JA, Waddock S (2010) Corporate responsibility and financial performance: the role of intangible resources. Strateg Manag J 31(5):463–490

Turban DB, Greening DW (1997) Corporate social performance and organizational attractiveness to prospective employees. Acad Manag J 40(3):658–672

Ullmann AA (1985) Data in search of a theory: a critical examination of the relationships among social performance social disclosure and economic performance of US firms. Acad Manag Rev 10(3):540–557

Vallentin S, Murillo D (2012) Governmentality and the politics of CSR. Organization 19(6):825–843

Van Marrewijk M (2003) Concepts and definitions of CSR and corporate sustainability: between agency and communion. J Bus Ethics 44(2-3):95–105

Wernerfelt B (1984) A resource-based view of the firm. Strateg Manag J 5(2):171–180

Werther WB, Chandler D (2005) Strategic corporate social responsibility as global brand insurance. Bus Horiz 48(4):317–324

Wood DJ (1991) Corporate social performance revisited. Acad Manag Rev 16(4):691–718

Wood DJ, Jones RE (1995) Stakeholder mismatching: a theoretical problem in empirical research on corporate social performance. Int J Org Anal 3(3):229–267

Youn H, Song S, Lee S, Kim JH (2016) Does the restaurant type matter for investment in corporate social responsibility? Int J Hosp Manag 58:24–33

Institutional Influences of Professional Associations and Franchise Organizations on Competitiveness of the Healthcare Clinics

Nina Gorovaia, Guillermo Navarro Sanfelix, and Francisco Puig

Abstract This paper uses insights from the institutional theory to study the competitiveness of the healthcare clinics in Spain. The environment of the healthcare services is highly institutionalized: professional associations are state agents responsible for the extensive regulation. Recently emerged franchise chains become subject for imitation by creating institutionalized routines from within and increasing competitive pressures for other industry players. While the sector is dominated by the independent doctors, franchise organizations are becoming more popular and show steady growth rates. The franchise business model in healthcare is evolving: while the core activity—provision of a healthcare service—cannot be standardized, as the independent judgment of a healthcare professional is legally protected, franchise chains standardize management of the healthcare clinics to achieve efficiency and economies of scale. The survey of the healthcare professionals in Spain shows how professional associations and franchise chains impact the field and provide empirical support to the hypotheses.

1 Introduction

Although franchising is used in more than 80 industries, it is highly concentrated just in a few industries, like retailing, fast food, and hospitality (Shane 2005: p. 1). Studies on franchising typically use data from the fast-food industry, retailing, and hotels, creating a so-called McDonald's effect (Dant 2008). Franchising is not limited to fast food though. Kaufmann and Dant (1999) name several nontraditional US

N. Gorovaia (✉)
School of Business and Law, Frederick University Cyprus, Nicosia, Cyprus
e-mail: n.gorovaia@frederick.ac.cy

G. Navarro Sanfelix · F. Puig
Dpto. Dirección de Empresas "Juan J. Renau", Facultad de Economía, Universidad de Valencia (Spain), Valencia, Spain
e-mail: guinasan@alumni.uv.es; francisco.puig@uv.es

© Springer Nature Switzerland AG 2019   113
J. Windsperger et al. (eds.), *Design and Management of Interfirm Networks*,
Contributions to Management Science,
https://doi.org/10.1007/978-3-030-29245-4_7

sectors where franchising became increasingly popular, e.g., telecommunications, financial planning and business consulting, medical and dental services, travel and transportation services, and internet providers. Most of the research articles on franchising do not report any specific industry scope, which creates a serious gap in industry studies (Rosado-Serrano et al. 2018). While the knowledge of the North American fast-food industry cannot be comfortably generalized to other franchising sectors, we also cannot be sure that franchising theories universally apply to cross-cultural and cross-sectional settings (Dant 2008.)

In response to a call for more research on franchising in nontraditional sectors (Dant 2008; Rosado-Serrano et al. 2018), we focus in this study on dentistry, physiotherapy, and optics sectors in Spain. These sectors are dominated by the self-employed doctors, independent healthcare professionals, and public clinics and are highly institutionalized. The reason of this choice is the recent unprecedented emergence of franchise chains and their steady growth rates. For example, in 2006, *Times* magazine called a Spanish dental clinic company *Vitaldent* "McDentist" for impressive growth and expansion of the brand abroad to Portugal, Italy, Poland, and the USA. Although this specific company eventually stopped franchising as it got embroiled in legal problems, franchising companies are emerging within sectors that were traditionally dominated by independent doctors and public clinics.

According to the Spanish Franchise Registry, there are 21 franchise chains in dental care services, 13 in optics, 6 in physiotherapy, and 9 in other health-related services (e.g., clinics for Alzheimer patients, fertility clinics, audiology clinics, podiatrists, seniors' care, etc.). Emergence and popularity of these chains deserve scholarly attention. The environment of the healthcare services is highly institutionalized, and professional associations are state agents responsible for extensive regulation. The paper's aim is to analyze the institutional influences of professional associations and newly emerging franchise chains on competitiveness of the healthcare professionals. Furthermore, the paper discusses the evolution of a franchise model in the context of healthcare services. It utilizes the insights from the institutional theory and primary data from Spain to study the competitiveness of independent healthcare professionals and interplay of institutions to regulate their activities.

2 Franchising and Institutional Influences in the Healthcare Sector

2.1 The Franchise Model in the Healthcare Sector

Very few studies in the franchise literature focus on franchising in nontraditional sectors. Davies and Aurini (2006) report the use of franchising in private tutoring centers in Canada; Sekliuckienė and Langvinienė (2012) study the emergence of the franchise business model in the property and real estate sector in Lithuania;

Warraich and Perrigot (2017) investigate the franchising chains operating in Pakistan's education system; Perrigot (2017) describes a case study in the healthcare sector in Kenya. Other examples of less traditional franchising can be found in the sectors like travel and tourism agencies, repairs, IT, and real estate.

Training and education of franchisees and their employees are the main point of difference between traditional and nontraditional franchising. Franchising requires an industry in which an average person can learn the business operations with the franchisor's training (Shane 2005: p. 13). Typically, the initial training takes from several days to a few weeks. For example, Subway provides 2 weeks' training before sending franchisees to run their businesses. In traditional industries, trainings are usually short, and any employees without higher education can be trained to perform the tasks. Previous studies in the context of different countries report the following average duration of the initial trainings of the franchisees: in the USA 17 days (Lafontaine and Shaw 1999), in Austria 23 days (Windsperger 2004), and 1–4 weeks in the UK (Brickley et al. 2006). Traditional franchise chains usually hire unskilled labor but use advanced management practices and sophisticated training techniques to transfer job-related skills (Cappelli and Hamori 2008).

The situation is very different in medicine and education, where specialized professional skills are required. Franchise chains in education and healthcare services hire employees with at least a bachelor degree, while in the case of dental and physiotherapy clinics, they hire qualified doctors, whose professional training lasts from 6 to 10 years fulltime. Training as a dentist in the EU requires at least 300 ECTS credits, and further specialization increases it to 420 ECTS credits. Another distinctive feature is that healthcare professionals are members of professional associations that give them license to practice and ensure compliance with professional protocols and codes of ethics.

Though doctors receive extensive education and practical training, they almost completely lack business training. This might be less of a problem for doctors employed in public hospitals, but creates a serious impediment for doctors wishing to operate their own private clinics as they have to manage business operations as well. The franchise model resolves this problem by allowing medical and nonmedical personnel to specialize in running healthcare clinics and share co-ownership. For doctors, there are numerous advantages of the franchise model: they can devote their attention to treating patients and avoid the business and administrative duties that go with their practice for which they usually lack training and skills.

The sector of healthcare services is traditionally dominated by independent healthcare professionals and doctors. Recently, successful franchise systems emerged within this sector in Spain, e.g., Vitaldent, Open Dental, and Millenium Dental in dentistry; General Optica, Vistalia, and Alain Afflelou in optics; and Fisi-On and Praxia Body Repair in physiotherapy. Factors contributing to the emergence and growth of franchise chains within the healthcare sector are the steady increase of healthcare expenditures, rising cost of healthcare, and aging population. Franchise companies that streamline their operations and reduce costs for the patients provide a valuable alternative to private and more expensive health clinics.

2.2 Professional Associations

Franchisees in the healthcare sector and employees of the franchisees, additionally to possessing highly specialized skills gained through extensive education, are required to be members of professional associations to exercise their professions. Our focus is on professional associations that aim to advance a specific profession, through research, practice, and professional development (Thackeray et al. 2005; Greenwood et al. 2002). Professional associations are instrumental in giving a license to operate. A common reason to become a member of such a professional association is to maintain certification to perform health-related services, advancing profession, and networking. Professional associations typically set knowledge and educational requirements for their members and provide a legal barrier to entry. The setting examined here is highly institutionalized. It is thus an interesting context for two reasons. On one hand, although independent doctors joining a franchise system and becoming franchisees are legally obliged to adhere to the conditions of a franchise contract, on the other hand, they are also members of the professional associations, which impose important regulatory requirements (DiMaggio and Powell 1983; Ruef and Scott 1998).

In Spain, the relationship between companies and professional associations is regulated by Article 3 of Law 2/1974 about professional associations. For professions related to healthcare services—doctors, nurses, pharmacists, veterinarians, physiotherapists, opticians, dentists, chiropodists, and psychologists—membership in professional associations is mandatory. Biologists, physicists, and chemists are also required to become members of professional associations, if their activities are related to the healthcare sector.

Professional associations maintain public lists of all professionals authorized to practice. Professionals must pay a membership fee. In return, professional associations provide the following services to their members: training, professional insurance, legal consulting, meetings and conferences, and social networks. Professional associations are important regulatory agents and especially in times of crises can lead and host the public discourse through which the change is debated and endorsed (Greenwood et al. 2002).

2.3 Core and Peripheral Elements of a Franchise

The franchise model as applied to the healthcare sector has evolved compared to traditional franchising. The main difference is the definition of core and peripheral activities to balance requirement for the standardization and uniformity with the need to allow a certain degree of freedom while performing health-related services. Kaufmann and Eroglu's (1999) model offers a valuable framework for understanding how franchisors achieve efficiency and uniformity through standardization. This model has to be revisited in the case of healthcare, as core activities—provision of healthcare services—performed by highly skilled professionals cannot be fully standardized.

There is a trade-off in business format franchising between standardization requirements to achieve uniformity of product and service offerings and adaptation to the local market environment, consumer tastes, and cultural imperatives. Previous research has demonstrated that standardization is necessary for success of franchising because it permits image continuity and brings cost savings through scale economies due to joint purchasing, marketing, advertising, and R&D (Kaufmann and Eroglu 1999; Szulanski and Jensen 2006). Components of the franchise business format such as product/service deliverables, benefit communicators, system identifiers, and format facilitators are identified as either core or peripheral in Kaufmann and Eroglu's model (Kaufmann and Eroglu 1999). Core elements are usually standardized, while peripheral elements of the franchise business format can be adapted. Finding balance between standardization of the core elements and permitting local market adaptation of the peripheral elements remains one of the greatest challenges facing franchisors (Kaufmann and Eroglu 1999).

Various empirical studies shed more light on the delicate balance between the standardization and adaptation. Research by Szulanski and Jensen (2006) shows that presumptive adaptation stalls franchise network growth, while a conservative approach to adaptation, which basically entails close adherence to the original practice, results in remarkably rapid network growth. Cox and Mason's (2007) study reports that franchisors gave permission to modify some of the peripheral components of the format, while none of the franchisors in the sample permitted the adaptation of core format components. For example, franchisees were able to alter the product mix, set prices competitively, implement local marketing campaigns, and perform recruitment procedures. However, franchisors would not allow franchisees' adaptations that could distort the core components of the format. Streed and Cliquet (2008) on the example of McDonald's and Great Harvest cases show that both companies made similar choices in preserving the integrity of their core format components. The key difference, however, was in the definition of these core components. While Great Harvest limited the number of core components to essential elements such as trademark, logo, brand image, and positioning, McDonald's developed a complex multilayered system of brand and "sub-brand" components as part of their core components. Winter et al. (2012) tested survival consequences of precise replication and local adaptation in franchising organizations and found that nonstandard products sizably and significantly increased franchise units' likelihood of exit, thus offering support to the standardization hypothesis.

In the case of franchise systems in dentistry, optics, and physiotherapy, it is apparent that the core activity, namely, the provision of a healthcare service, cannot be fully standardized by the franchisor. It is the task of a professional association to establish protocols for the provision of the health-related services. And still even in this case, a healthcare professional is able to exercise a great degree of judgment and autonomy in the treatment of each patient. What attract healthcare professionals into franchise chains are peripheral activities, like chain-wide advertisements, recognized brand name, centralized supplies of equipment and raw materials, and trainings related to new equipment, materials, and procedures. Professionals retain their autonomy in provision of healthcare, but at the same time are supported by standardized management practices, trainings, and innovations (Nijmeijer et al. 2014). Thus, franchise chains in the healthcare sector define differently their core and peripheral activities; and while their core activities—provision of healthcare services—cannot be standardized by the franchisor, their peripheral activities like advertisements and promotion, supplies of equipment and raw materials, trainings related to new developments in healthcare, R&D, accounting, and management of patients are centralized to achieve economies of scale.

The franchise business model evolves when applied to the healthcare services. The institutional influences of health laws and professional rules create a need to develop structures that are not typical for many traditional franchised businesses. As Gilliland et al. (2014) point out, the corporate practice of medicine doctrine, which is designed to protect the healthcare professional's independent judgment, results in a very substantial restructuring of the franchise business model. It is not the healthcare business that is being franchised nor the medical, dental, or healthcare practice that provides healthcare to a patient, but rather the management of the medical, dental, and physiotherapy clinics.

3 Theoretical Framework

In the following section, we use insights from the institutional theory to develop hypotheses relating to institutional influences on the competitiveness of healthcare clinics in Spain.

3.1 Institutional Influences of Professional Associations

Institutional theory is a leading theoretical framework that explains how environmental influences shape organizations (Meyer and Rowan 1977; Zucker 1987; DiMaggio and Powell 1983). Organizations are expected to conform to social expectations to secure legitimacy and exhibit similar features and patterns of behavior (isomorphism). Institutional theory considers the processes by which structures, schemas, rules, norms, and routines become established as authoritative guidelines for social behavior (Scott 2004: 462). Compared to theories grounded in economic rationalism that consider efficiency as a driving force for organizational governance, institutional theory focuses on legitimacy and conformity.

According to DiMaggio and Powell (1983: 148), the process of institutionalization emerges for four reasons: to increase the interaction among organizations in the same field, to establish accepted structures and patterns of a coalition, to increase the information exchange between the members, and, finally, to develop mutual awareness and protection mechanisms. Hence, institutional forces transform organizations and make them more homogeneous. According to DiMaggio and

Powell, there are three forms of institutional pressures: coercive, mimetic, and normative. While coercive pressures regularly come from large actors, e.g., the state, to adopt specific practices, mimetic pressures usually come from more successful and influential peers. Normative pressures develop as a result of similar professional values and training and encourage adoption of appropriate practices.

There are two theoretical approaches to study institutions according to Zucker (1987): first, to study the environment as an institution and, second, to study the organizations as institutions. While *environment as institution* assumes that organizations reproduce sector-wide or system-wide rules, *organization as institution* takes central role in generation of rules at the organizational level. In the first case, institutions are created as a consequence of a state project and represent agreements shared by the members of organizational fields. Thus, institutional influences come from outside of the organization. Conformity of the organizations to this normative order increases the flow of societal resources to the organizations and improves long-term survival prospects (Zucker 1987).

Professional associations are state agents and exercise great influence over healthcare professionals in Spain who are required to join them in order to get their operational licenses and conform to their protocols and codes of ethics. Membership in the professional associations creates an opportunity for the healthcare professionals to participate in the public discourse regarding standards of the profession, but also provides training opportunities and socialization and informs about new trends. Professional associations are source of both coercive and normative pressures for healthcare professionals, because they legislate the activity of healthcare professionals and establish ethical norms of profession. Professional employees typically subscribe to explicit professional norms (Combs et al. 2009). Conforming to the rules of the game set by professional associations increases survival prospects of healthcare professionals and improves their performance. Hence, we can formulate the following hypothesis:

Hypothesis 1 *Professional associations positively influence competitiveness of healthcare clinics.*

3.2 Institutional Influences of Franchise Organizations

Zucker's second approach to study *organization as institution* assumes that institutional elements arise from within the organization itself and become subject to imitation by other organizations in the field. If routines are more formalized and contribute to organizational success, they are likely to be adapted and replicated by other organizations. Thus, the most successful business organizations in the sector can be also a source of institutional influence (Delmas and Toffel 2004; Lieberman and Asaba 2006) and set an example for other companies to follow. In this case, the legitimacy is motivated by market efficiency considerations, rather than by legal framework. Mimetic pressures come from peer organizations who are perceived to be successful.

Franchise companies are famous for using advanced management techniques to manage chain-wide operations and sophisticated training practices. Due to centralization of some of their activities, like development of the brand name, chain-wide advertisements and promotions, wholesale purchases of equipment and supplies, chain-wide training of franchisees in new techniques and materials, standardization, and codification of their know-how, they are able to enjoy economies of scale that lead to efficiency and faster growth. Existence of successful franchise organizations in the sector sets example for independent businesses to follow and contributes to the replication of successful practices. Knowledge exchange is facilitated by employees' turnover and rehiring of qualified specialists from the franchise organizations. Kraatz and Moore (2002) show empirical support for mimetic pressures through hiring executives from competing organizations.

Barthélemy (2011) warns of the dangers of mimetic isomorphism: organizations may imitate superficial features and fail to replicate more subtle features that are likely to impact performance. For example, an independent clinic may imitate special promotions like the free mouth cleaning offered by a franchise chain that ultimately will have little or no effect on the clinic's profitability and fail to see that trainings in new dental treatments and procedures that a franchise clinic offers to its doctors significantly improve the quality of service and the outcome of the treatment.

Hence, we can formulate the following hypothesis:

Hypothesis 2 *Franchise organizations positively influence the competitiveness of healthcare clinics.*

4 Empirical Study

4.1 Survey of Healthcare Professionals

The empirical setting for testing the hypotheses are healthcare professionals in Spain, members of three professional associations—dentists, opticians, and physiotherapists. We started our empirical work by obtaining the consent of three professional associations to distribute the questionnaire to their registered members. The questionnaire was posted online, and the healthcare professionals received a link to answer it electronically. The questionnaire took approximately 15 minutes to complete on the average. We received 108 usable responses with a response rate of 24.65%. The healthcare professionals (dentists, physiotherapists, and opticians) were respondents of the survey. They were considered knowledgeable to respond because they are running their own practices or are franchisees of the established franchise organizations or are employed by public clinics. Majority of respondents were independent, 9% were employed by public clinics, and 5% were employed by franchise organizations.

4.2   Professional Associations

Our empirical sample is defined by membership in professional associations. Three professional associations supported our study and distributed a survey instrument to their members. Table 1 summarizes key facts about these professional associations.

Table 1 Professional associations

	Dentistry	Optics	Physiotherapy
Legal framework	Law 2/2000, March 31st, by Generalitat Valenciana	Law 2/2007, February 5th, by Generalitat Valenciana	Law 1/2000, March 30th, by Generalitat Valenciana
Year of foundation	2000	2007	2000
Goals	NA	To share values, ethical standards, and professional commitment. To serve the community and ensure ethical and professional conduct with patients, colleagues, and other healthcare professionals	To provide a better healthcare to the population. To defend and represent the members
Ethical code	Yes	Yes	Yes
Vacancies	Yes	Yes	Yes
Judicial proceedings	5 court cases, 5 favorable judgments, 8 complaints, 83 claims	NA	Application form to report the incidents is available
Required level of education	High education in medicine	Heterogeneous profiles	High education in medicine
Management	Professional dentists	Professional opticians and optics managers	Professional physiotherapists
Services to members	Retraining, conferences, consulting, insurance, grants, retirement, library	Retraining, conferences, consulting, insurance, library	Insurance, consulting, library
Public relations	All the information is for members only	Interactive tools on the webpage to communicate with the public	List of approved clinics and information for patients on the web
Communication with members	Circular letters, professional journal	Press office, information board, blog	Blog
Position	Extremely defensive	Conciliatory position	Defensive position

Source: Professional associations' websites and sector reports

The following differences can be observed: Dentists' and physiotherapists' associations seem to be more defensive and protect the profession from external threats. Both associations often issue complaints and defend their position in court. Optics association has a more conciliatory position and provides a meeting point for public discourse of profession. Optics association is open to the public and maintains various blogs and boards. Dentists' association is on the contrary more closed: all the services are for members only. Dentists' association publishes a journal with a key focus on retraining, new materials, and new techniques. All the three associations defend their members: dentists' association uses coercive power to defend the profession, physiotherapists' association is defensive but tries to maintain good public relations, and, finally, optics association is open to a dialogue with all the stakeholders.

4.3 Franchise Organizations

Following Zucker's (1987) argument of *organization as institution*, franchise companies impact the sector through advanced management practices and sophisticated training techniques. It is likely that other companies in the industry imitate successful practices which in turn will increase their survival prospects and performance. Furthermore, collaboration and rehiring of workers from franchise organizations facilitates knowledge sharing and exchange. Table 2 summarizes information about some of the successful examples of franchise companies in dental care, physiotherapy, and optics sectors.

Table 2 summarizes the characteristics of some of the prominent examples of franchise systems in the healthcare sector. Franchised outlets are typically run by the professional managers, not doctors. Similarly to franchising in traditional sectors, franchise chains in healthcare use aggressive advertising of their brand names. Some of the chains have a large number of franchise establishments in Spain and abroad. Franchise chains regularly offer promotions to their patients and provide financing for treatments. Franchise companies offer lower prices to the patients and have more bargaining power to negotiate agreements with the insurance companies. As a result of the emergence of successful franchise companies within the sector, competition intensifies.

4.4 Measurement

To test the hypotheses, we use the following variables: Competitiveness of healthcare clinics is our dependent variable. Institutional influences of professional associations and institutional influences of franchising companies are our explanatory variables. We use human capital of the healthcare professionals, number of

Table 2 Franchise companies in dental care, physiotherapy, and optics

Name of the company	Vitaldent	Davida Rehabilitación	General Óptica
Activity	Dentistry	Physiotherapy	Optics
Year of foundation	1997	2000	1955
Number of outlets	354	23	300
Initial investment	€520.000	€60.101	€76.000
Entry fee	€0	€9.015	€0
Advertising fee	6%	€601 p.a.	0%
Royalty fee	5%	15%	3%
Contract duration (years)	10	10	3
Services	Implantology, dental prostheses, orthodontics, invisible orthodontics, dental veneers, dental aesthetics, advanced dental cleaning, periodontics, endodontics, halitosis, caries, snoring	Physiotherapy, speech therapy, occupational therapy, brain damage, home rehabilitation, Pilates, pregnancy, traffic accidents, home treatments available	Low vision, orthokeratology, eye prostheses
Chain-wide offers and promotions	Treatment financing available, free mouth cleaning, special offers in some of the treatments	Contracts with most important insurance companies	Licensing to sell premium glasses

Source: Companies' websites and Sabi and Alimarket databases (checked 15/02/2019)

the healthcare professionals in an establishment, and sectoral dummies as control variables.

4.4.1 Competitiveness of Healthcare Clinics

Competitiveness of healthcare clinics (Comp) was operationalized using a four-item scale. Healthcare professionals were asked to rate whether the reputation of their establishment was better than that of the competitors, whether the quality of service provided was better than that of their competitors, whether the financial situation of the clinic was more solid than that of their competitors, and whether their clinic could respond to customer demands faster than the competitors.

4.4.2 Institutional Influences of Professional Associations

A two-item scale was used to test the institutional influences of professional associations (PA) on competitiveness of healthcare professionals. Healthcare professionals were asked whether professional association works actively to protect and improve the profession and whether they see advantages to collaborate with professional associations and other governmental bodies. This is a formative construct representing domain of content; therefore, "internal consistency reliability is not an appropriate standard for evaluating the adequacy of the measures" (Jarvis et al. 2003: 202; Diamantopoulos and Winkelhofer 2001).

4.4.3 Institutional Influences of Franchise Organizations

Institutional influences of franchise organizations (FRA) were measured with one-item construct. The healthcare professionals were asked whether franchise chains operating in the sector positively impact professional activity exercised by the healthcare professionals. While there are some concerns with single-item scales, due to their low construct validity, sensitivity, and reliability, research has shown that single-item measures are often reasonable substitutes for multi-item scales (Wanous and Reichers 1996; McKenzie and Marks 1999; Bergkvist and Rossiter 2007).

4.4.4 Control Variables

We used the following controls in the study: human capital of the healthcare professionals, number of professional employees (ProfEmpl) to control for the size of the clinic, and sectoral dummies.

Human capital refers to "skills, experiences, attitudes, ideas, values and competencies of the people in the firm" (Watson and Stanworth 2006: 339). The skills, experience, and competences of the doctors are likely to improve the service quality, success of the treatment, and patients' satisfaction. Human capital is considered to be a source of competitive advantage. Human capital (HC) construct was measured by three items. Healthcare professionals were asked whether professionals of the clinic have lots of experience, whether the establishment permits them to organize the work activities autonomously, and whether the wages/salaries the clinic pays are higher than the industry average.

To control for the size of the clinic, we used the number of professional employees. The bigger size of the clinic can indicate more experience, more resources, and higher competitiveness. Finally, sectoral dummies were used to control for sectoral-specific effects.

4.4.5   Factor Analysis and Construct Validation

For each multi-item construct, the items were subjected to factor analysis to ensure single-factor structure. For unidimensional construct measures, all the items should load heavily on the first factor than on any other factor. Only one factor emerged from a factor analysis conducted on each multi-item construct, confirming the unidimensional nature of the items. Subsequently, inter-item reliability analysis using Cronbach's alpha was done on multi-item scales. Alpha coefficients are reported in the Appendix.

4.5   Regression Analysis

Descriptive statistics and correlations are reported in Table 3. The average clinic employs 12 professional doctors. The sample used in the regression analysis consists of 61 dental, 31 optics, and 14 physiotherapy clinics. Seventy percent of the sample are independent doctors, 5% of doctors are employed by franchised organizations, 5% of doctors are members of cooperatives, 9% are employed by public clinics, and the rest specified their status as "other." It is apparent that franchising is not the most popular business model within these sectors and independent clinics continue to dominate the sector of healthcare services. However, young age of franchise chains entering these sectors and steady growth of the number of franchise outlets indicate that franchising as a business model ventures into the healthcare sector.

To test the hypotheses (H1 and H2), we carry out a regression analysis. We conduct an OLS regression analysis with competitiveness of healthcare clinics as a dependent variable. Competitiveness of healthcare clinics is defined as better reputation, better quality of service, better financial standing, and faster reaction to customers' requests. The explanatory variables refer to institutional influences of professional associations (PA) and institutional influences of franchise organizations (FRA). Control variables refer to human capital of healthcare professionals (HC), sectoral dummies, and number of healthcare professionals in the clinic (ProfEmpl). The control variable measuring the number of healthcare professionals in a clinic ProfEmpl was log transformed due to a skewed distribution.

Table 3 Descriptive statistics and correlations

	Min	Max	Mean	St. Dev.	Comp	PA	FRA	HC	ProfEmpl
Comp	2.25	7	5.08	1.04	1				
PA	1	7	3.93	1.55	0.336_{**}	1			
FRA	1	7	1.89	1.33	0.165	0.077	1		
HC	1	7	4.97	1.25	0.383_{**}	0.267_{**}	−0.098	1	
ProfEmpl	1	500	12.32	40.37	0.085	−0.009	0.190_{*}	−0.091	1

$_{**}p < 0.01$ (two tailed)
$_{*}p < 0.05$ (two tailed)

We estimate the following regression equation:

$$COMP = \alpha + \beta_1 PA + \beta_2 FRA + \beta_3 HC + \beta_4 \ln ProfEmpl + \beta_5 Physiotherapists + \beta_6 Optitians$$

According to the institutional theory, professional associations create the rules of the game for the healthcare professionals and establish standards for practicing a profession. Professional associations also set legal barriers for entering the field and take disciplinary action against those who engage in misconduct. Professional associations positively impact the competitiveness of healthcare clinics; thus, we expect the coefficient of the PA variable to have a positive sign. Furthermore, according to the institutional theory, successful franchise organizations impact the competitiveness of the healthcare clinics by introducing more advanced management practices and sophisticated training techniques. Independent health clinics are imitating some practices of the franchise organizations they perceive successful. Thus, we expect the sign of the coefficient of the FRA variable to be positive.

According to the intellectual capital perspective, the human capital of healthcare professionals positively impacts the competitiveness of the clinic and is a source of competitive advantage. Patients are more satisfied with their treatment if the doctor is skilled and experienced. In addition, larger clinics that employ more professionals are likely to have more experience and be more competitive. Table 4 reports the results of the regression analysis.

Table 4 Regression results

DV: Competitiveness	Model 1	Model 2
Intercept	3.071_{***}	2.239_{***}
	(0.452)	(0.457)
Physiotherapists	0.143	−0.022
	(0.273)	(0.263)
Opticians	0.350_{*}	0.285
	(0.208)	(0.201)
LnProfEmpl	0.039	−0.026
	(0.082)	(0.082)
HC	0.357_{***}	0.372_{***}
	(0.078)	(0.078)
PA		0.154_{***}
		(0.057)
FRA		0.136_{*}
		(0.078)
N	108	108
Model F	$F = 5.600_{***}$	$F = 7.688_{***}$
R^2	$R^2 = 0.172$	$R^2 = 0.311$
Adjusted R^2	Adj. $R^2 = 0.141$	Adj. $R^2 = 0.271$
Adj. $R^2 = 0.141$		

$_{***}p < 0.01$; $_{**}p < 0.05$; $_{*}p < 0.1$; values in parentheses are standard errors

First, we conduct an OLS regression analysis with only control variables (Model 1). The coefficient of the human capital (HC) variable is positive and highly significant, indicating that more skilled and experienced professionals provide better healthcare treatments and, thus, increase their clinics' competitiveness. Second, we add the institutional variables to Model 1. The results of the regression analysis are presented in Table 4 (Model 2). The coefficient of professional associations (PA) is positive and highly significant. This is consistent with our hypothesis (H1) that institutional influences of professional associations positively impact competitiveness of the healthcare clinics. The coefficient of franchise organizations (FRA) is also positive and slightly significant, providing moderate support to the argument that franchise organizations set an example for independent clinics and are being imitated. The presence of successful franchise organizations within the sector impacts competitiveness of the healthcare clinics. The omitted sectoral dummy variable "dentists" represents a reference category. Compared to dentists, opticians are likely to be more competitive (Model 1); however, this effect disappears in Model 2.

5   Conclusions and Future Research

The goal of this research is to explain how institutions regulate activities of the healthcare clinics and improve their competitiveness. Drawing on Zucker's (1987) concepts *environment as institution* and *organization as institution*, we hypothesized that professional associations and newly emerged franchise chains impact competitiveness of the healthcare professionals through coercive, normative, and mimetic pressures. The empirical setting of the study is the healthcare sector in Spain. Using data from a survey of professional dentists, opticians, and physiotherapists—members of three professional associations—we show that institutional influences of professional associations and franchise organizations positively impact competitiveness of the healthcare clinics. In addition, we find that human capital is positively related to competitiveness. These findings are important given the deficit of sectoral studies in franchising and more specifically lack of focus on franchising in healthcare.

Firstly, we investigate the impact of professional associations on competitiveness of the healthcare clinics. Professional associations are state agents responsible for the regulation of the medical profession, but also set ethical and professional standards and lead public discourse on the future of the profession. They exert coercive and normative pressures on their members. Our study shows that professional associations positively impact competitiveness of the clinics measured as quality of service, reaction to patients' demands, and reputation.

Secondly, we investigate the impact of newly emerged franchise companies on competitiveness of the healthcare clinics. Successful franchise chains recently emerged within the sector of healthcare services (Nijmeijer et al. 2014) and set example for other companies to follow. Franchise companies use advanced management techniques and provide extensive trainings for doctors, which allow them to offer an excellent service for a fair price. Furthermore, through centralization of their activities like promotion and advertising, purchasing, supplies, IT, standardization, and codification of know-how, they achieve economies of scale. Franchise companies are likely to exercise mimetic pressures on independent clinics. Our findings show moderate support for this argument.

Thirdly, the paper discusses the evolution of the franchise model as applied to healthcare. Because the corporate practice of medicine is designed to insulate a healthcare professional's independent judgment, it limits the control a franchisor can assert over the delivery services and products offered by the healthcare franchise (Gilliland et al. 2014). The healthcare services instead are regulated by laws, protocols, and codes of ethics of the professional associations. Healthcare franchises define differently their core and peripheral activities as compared to franchising in traditional sectors and hire highly qualified professionals. The peripheral activities in healthcare franchises—those relating to advertising, promotion, accounting, IT, patients' management, material and equipment sourcing, and training in new techniques and materials—are standardized to achieve economies of scale. To conclude, it is the management of the healthcare clinic that is standardized, not the healthcare service itself.

The main contribution of this study is to show that the healthcare clinics can improve their competitiveness by complying to coercive and normative pressures of professional associations and by imitating successful practices of the franchise companies that guarantee market efficiency. The study adds to the institutional literature by empirically testing Zucker's (1987) concepts *environment as institution* and *organization as institution*. Setting this study in the context of dentistry, optics, and physiotherapy, we respond to a recent call for more research on franchising in nontraditional sectors (Dant 2008; Rosado-Serrano et al. 2018).

The study has important implications for the independent healthcare professionals. They can improve the quality of their services to the patients and competitiveness of their clinics by complying with the legal, professional, and ethical norms of professional associations. They should take advantage of the trainings, knowledge exchange, conferences, and networking opportunities, provided by their professional associations in order to leverage their skills and to advance their profession. Furthermore, the healthcare professionals should adapt some of the successful practices of the franchise companies that are likely to improve the market performance of their clinics and satisfaction of their patients. Specifically, they should pay attention to the training opportunities provided by the healthcare franchises.

This research is not without limitations. While coercive, normative, and mimetic pressures are theoretically distinct concepts, they are more difficult to distinguish empirically. Future studies should consider investigating the impact of coercive, normative, and mimetic pressures separately and their interaction effects. Due to a small number of franchise chains within the healthcare sector and their relatively young age, quantitative research methodology is difficult to implement. While the survey of healthcare professionals achieved satisfactory response rates, the small absolute number of employees of franchise organizations does not permit to compare them with independent doctors. Qualitative interviews with franchisors and franchisees operating in dental care, physiotherapy, and optics could shed more light on how franchise organizations standardize their business activities, satisfy the institutional requirements of professional associations, and respond to economic pressures.

Appendix

Operationalization of the variables:
Competitiveness of the healthcare clinics, Cronbach's-$a = 0.751$

1. The reputation of our company is greater than that of our competitors.
2. The quality of the service we provide is very much better than that of our competitors.
3. The financial situation of the clinic where I develop my professional activity is much more solid and stable than that of the main competitors.
4. When we detect an unmet need of customers, we react faster than our competitors.

Institutional influences of professional associations

1. The professional association works actively to protect and improve our profession.
2. We obtain advantages when collaborating with professional associations.

Institutional influences of franchise organizations

1. The franchised organizations positively influence the sector where I develop my professional activity.

Human capital of healthcare professionals, Cronbach's-$a = 0.651$

1. Professional employees of the clinic have lots of experience.
2. The clinic permits me to organize my work autonomously.
3. The salaries paid by our clinic are higher than the industry average.

References

Barthélemy J (2011) Agency and institutional influences on franchising decisions. J Bus Ventur 26(1):93–103

Bergkvist L, Rossiter JR (2007) The predictive validity of multiple-item versus single-item measures of the same constructs. J Mark Res 44(2):175–184

Brickley JA, Misra S, Horn RLV (2006) Contract duration: evidence from franchising. J Law Econ 49(1):173–196

Cappelli P, Hamori M (2008) Are franchises bad employers? ILR Rev 61(2):147–162

Combs JG, Michael SC, Castrogiovanni GJ (2009) Institutional influences on the choice of organizational form: the case of franchising. J Manag 35(5):1268–1290

Cox J, Mason C (2007) Standardisation versus adaptation: geographical pressures to deviate from franchise formats. Serv Ind J 27(8):1053–1072

Dant RP (2008) A futuristic research agenda for the field of franchising. J Small Bus Manag 46(1):91–98

Davies S, Aurini J (2006) The franchising of private tutoring: a view from Canada. Phi Delta Kappan 88(2):123–128

Delmas M, Toffel MW (2004) Stakeholders and environmental management practices: an institutional framework. Bus Strateg Environ 13(4):209–222

Diamantopoulos A, Winkelhofer H (2001) Index construction with formative indicators: an alternative to scale development. J Mark Res 38(2):269–277

DiMaggio PJ, Powell WW (1983) The iron cage revisited: institutional isomorphism and collective rationality in organizational fields. Am Sociol Rev 48(2):147–160

Gilliland J, Kirsch MA, Siebert M (2014) Legal complexities of franchising in the health care industry. Working paper presented at the American Bar Association Forum on Franchising, October 15–17, 2014 Seattle, WA

Greenwood R, Suddaby R, Hinings CR (2002) Theorizing change: the role of professional associations in the transformation of institutionalized fields. Acad Manag J 45(1):58–80

Jarvis CB, Mackenzie SB, Podsakoff PM (2003) A critical review of construct indicators and measurement model misspecification in marketing and consumer research. J Consum Res 30(2):199–218

Kaufmann PJ, Dant RP (1999) Franchising and the domain of entrepreneurship research. J Bus Ventur 14(1):5–16

Kaufmann PJ, Eroglu S (1999) Standardization and adaptation in business format franchising. J Bus Ventur 14(1):69–85

Kraatz M, Moore J (2002) Executive migration and institutional change. Acad Manag J 45(1):120–143

Lafontaine F, Shaw KL (1999) The dynamics of franchise contracting: evidence from panel data. J Polit Econ 107(5):1041–1080

Lieberman MB, Asaba S (2006) Why do firms imitate each other? Acad Manag Rev 31(2):366–385

McKenzie N, Marks I (1999) Quick rating of depressed mood in patients with anxiety disorders. Br J Psychiatry 174(3):266–269

Meyer JW, Rowan B (1977) Institutionalized organizations: formal structure as myth and ceremony. Am J Sociol 83(2):340–363

Nijmeijer KJ, Huijsman R, Fabbricotti I (2014) Creating advantages through franchising in health care: a qualitative, multiple embedded case study on the role of the business format. BMC Health Serv Res 14(1):485–500

Perrigot R (2017) An exploration of franchising in Africa. In: Hoy F, Perrigot R, Terry A (eds) Handbook of research on franchising. Edward Elgar, Northampton MA, pp 515–535

Rosado-Serrano A, Paul J, Dikova D (2018) International franchising: a literature review and research agenda. J Bus Res 85(1):238–257

Ruef M, Scott WR (1998) A multidimensional model of organizational legitimacy: hospital survival in changing institutional environments. Admin Sci Q 43(4):877–904

Scott WR (2004) Institutional theory: contributing to a theoretical research program. In: Smith KG, Hitt MA (eds) Great minds in management: the process of theory development. Oxford University Press, Oxford, pp 460–484

Sekliuckienė J, Langvinienė N (2012) Development of franchising as a business model in the Lithuanian real estate services market. Bus Syst Econ 2(2):107–119

Shane S (2005) From ice cream to the internet: using franchising to drive the growth and profits of your company. PH Professional Business

Streed O, Cliquet G (2008) Concept uniformity: control versus freedom in business format franchising. In: Hendrikse G, Tuunanen M, Windsperger J, Cliquet G (eds) Strategy and governance of networks. Contributions to management science. Physica-Verlag, Heidelberg, pp 205–220

Szulanski G, Jensen RJ (2006) Presumptive adaptation and the effectiveness of knowledge transfer. Strateg Manag J 27(10):937–957

Thackeray R, Neiger BL, Roe KM (2005) Certified health education specialists' participation in professional associations: implications for marketing and membership. Am J Health Educ 36(6):337–344

Wanous JP, Reichers AE (1996) Estimating the reliability of a single-item measure. Psychol Rep 78(2):631–634

Warraich MA, Perrigot R (2017) Franchising in the education sector: how do Pakistani customers perceive this new phenomenon? In: Hendrikse G, Cliquet G, Ehrmann T, Windsperger J (eds) Management and governance of networks. Contributions to management science. Springer, Cham, pp 91–108

Watson A, Stanworth J (2006) Franchising and intellectual capital: a franchisee's perspective. Int Entrep Manag J 2(3):337–349

Windsperger J (2004) Centralization of franchising networks: evidence from the Austrian franchise sector. J Bus Res 57(12):1361–1369

Winter SG, Szulanski G, Ringov D, Jensen RJ (2012) Reproducing knowledge: inaccurate replication and failure in franchise organizations. Organ Sci 23(3):672–685

Zucker LG (1987) Institutional theories of organization. Annu Rev Sociol 13:443–464

Management of Franchising Networks: Seven Principles for Fair Franchise Advisory Councils

Evelien P. M. Croonen and Ivo Bleeker

Abstract Franchise Advisory Councils (FACs) form an important managerial instrument for franchisors to create and/or maintain franchisees' trust in the fair and effective functioning of their franchising networks. We build on procedural fairness theory and insights from articles in trade journals to develop a theoretical framework with seven core principles that affect franchisees' perceptions regarding the fair management of their FACs. These core principles are the consistency principle, the bias suppression principle, the accuracy principle, the correctability principle, the representativeness principle, the ethicality principle, and the interactional principle. For each core principle, we distinguish specific managerial principles that help in fulfilling it. This discussion results in an extensive framework with principles for the design and management of fair FACs ("the fair FAC framework"). We end the chapter by discussing theoretical implications and avenues for future research.

1 Introduction

> First and foremost, the "my way or the highway" approach does no one any good. Brand leadership must remain cognizant of the fact that their franchisees have invested what is likely their life savings in their business. Giving them an opportunity to provide feedback is very important.
>
> Quote by Steven Beagelman - April 29, 2019

Franchising networks—consisting of a franchisor owning a business format and multiple franchisees who pay for the right to use this format—are characterized by a strong interdependence among the franchise partners (Cumberland 2015).

E. P. M. Croonen (✉)
Faculty of Economics & Business, University of Groningen, Groningen, The Netherlands
e-mail: e.p.m.croonen@rug.nl

I. Bleeker
Flynth Adviseurs & Accountants Zwolle, Zwolle, The Netherlands
e-mail: ivo.bleeker@flynth.nl

© Springer Nature Switzerland AG 2019   133
J. Windsperger et al. (eds.), *Design and Management of Interfirm Networks*,
Contributions to Management Science,
https://doi.org/10.1007/978-3-030-29245-4_8

The franchisor develops, owns, and maintains a business format reflecting a strategic positioning in the market (Kaufmann and Eroglu 1998) and engages into contractual relationships with individual franchisees who adopt the franchisor's business format in their own businesses. The franchisor is responsible for the overall strategy and branding of the network and coordinates, facilitates, and monitors the network's operations (Croonen and Broekhuizen 2019). One important managerial challenge for franchisors is to build and maintain franchisees' trust in the fair and effective functioning of the franchising network ("franchise system trust," Croonen 2010). Such franchisees' trust is important because franchise contracts are often characterized by an imbalanced relationship in favor of the franchisor in order to protect the business format (Storholm and Scheuing 1994). Thus, franchisors typically are the dominant partner, and this may make franchisees feel vulnerable to their franchisors' decisions and actions. When franchisees trust their franchisors and the functioning of their franchising networks, they feel less vulnerable, which may lead to higher compliance with franchisor decisions (Croonen 2010; Davies et al. 2011).

Franchise Advisory Councils (FACs) can serve as an important instrument for franchisors to build and maintain the franchisees' trust in the functioning of their franchising networks (e.g., Dandridge and Falbe 1994; Cochet and Ehrmann 2007; Croonen 2010). The FAC is *an elected or selected group of franchisees who meet with representatives of the franchise headquarters to discuss and provide advice on issues of importance to all franchisees* (Dandridge and Falbe 1994, p. 43). The FAC serves as a communication platform where franchisor delegates and FAC representatives (franchisees) can (1) discuss new ideas concerning the network's value proposition, (2) informally provide input into different operational aspects, and (3) negotiate compromises on precarious issues in mutually beneficial ways (Cochet and Ehrmann 2007). The FAC is an important institutional arrangement in franchising networks by which franchisors can signal to their franchisees that they are considering franchisees' interests (Cochet and Ehrmann 2007).

Despite the importance of FACs for effective network management, very few scientific researchers have actually studied the role of FACs in franchising networks, their working mechanisms, and their influence on franchisees' franchise system trust (Croonen 2010). So far, no studies have aimed to explain what principles are exactly needed to effectively manage an FAC. This chapter contributes to literature on the design and management of franchising networks by proposing a theoretical framework on the management of Franchise Advisory Councils (FACs). Integrating insights from procedural fairness theory (e.g., Leventhal 1980; Cohen-Charash and Spector 2001; Colquitt 2001) with practical insights from articles published in trade journals and our own interactions with franchise practitioners, we propose a framework with seven core principles that affect franchisees' perceptions regarding the fair management of their FACs. We aim to provide knowledge to franchisors on how to design and manage their FACs in order to ultimately manage their franchisees' trust in the franchise system. Moreover, we provide knowledge to franchisees on how they might use FACs to have their interests represented in their franchising networks.

2   A Fairness Perspective on FACs: A Framework for Fair FAC Management

2.1   Introduction to the Framework

We adopt fairness theory to develop our fair FAC management framework. The concepts of fairness and justice have gained considerable attention by business and management scholars in the early 1960s and even more after the 1990s (Cohen-Charash and Spector 2001). The terms fairness and justice have been used interchangeably in the literature; however, for the sake of consistency, we use the term "fairness" throughout this paper. Fairness comprises three dimensions, namely, (1) distributive fairness, (2) procedural fairness, and (3) interactional fairness (Adams 1963; Lind and Tyler 1988; Cohen-Charash and Spector 2001; Colquitt 2001; Colquitt et al. 2001; Pfeifer 2007; van Dijke et al. 2018).

The first fairness dimension is distributive fairness and comprises an actor's perceived fairness of decision *outcomes* (Cohen-Charash and Spector 2001). In the context of franchising, franchisees' perceived distributive fairness is typically related to the *financial* outcomes of their franchisors' decisions since franchisees are independent business owners (Croonen 2010). The second fairness dimension is procedural fairness and refers to an actor's perceived *process* by which outcomes are determined (Lind and Tyler 1988). In the context of franchising, procedural fairness comprises the franchisees' perceived fairness of their franchisors' decision-making processes. The process refers to the principles, procedures, and governance mechanisms that have been used to make decisions (Cohen-Charash and Spector 2001). There are six rules or principles which are considered to increase procedural fairness when implemented and followed correctly (Leventhal 1980; Colquitt 2001). These are (1) the consistency principle, (2) the bias suppression principle, (3) the accuracy principle, (4) the correctability principle, (5) the representativeness principle, and (6) the ethicality principle. In the context of franchising, the FAC is an institutionalized arrangement through which franchisees are "involved" (i.e., by giving advice and in some cases by having a vote) in the franchisor's decision-making. The design and application of the FAC's principles are very likely to affect franchisees' perceptions of fair decision-making in the network. The third and final fairness dimension is interactional fairness and refers to the way in which a decision-maker is behaving toward affected individuals (Cohen-Charash and Spector 2001). According to Greenberg (1990, 1993), interactional fairness consists of interpersonal and informational aspects. The interpersonal aspects comprise the respectful treatment of affected actors (cf. franchisees), while informational aspects consider providing knowledge about the procedures that demonstrate regards for actors' (cf. franchisees') concerns.

Previous fairness research has found that actors are more likely to accept unfavorable decision outcomes if they judge the process prior to a decision to be fair (Brockner and Wiesenfeld 1996). Thus, procedural fairness might to some extent reduce negative effects of unfavorable decision outcomes when a decision-making process is considered fair (cf. Brockner and Wiesenfeld 1996). Similarly, we argue that franchisees may be more willing to accept franchisor decisions if the decision-making process was managed fairly in the FAC (cf. Dwyer 2008). In this paper, we focus on Leventhal's six principles of procedural fairness that can be applied to FACs so franchisees experience a fair FAC management. Moreover, Cohen-Charash and Spector (2001) argue that interactional fairness is not an independent fairness dimension, but rather a principle of procedural fairness and an additional principle to Leventhal's six fairness principles (Leventhal 1980). We therefore distinguish seven core principles for fair FAC management.

In sum, our fair FAC management framework (Fig. 1) distinguishes seven core principles from the fairness literature that are likely to affect franchisees' perceptions regarding the fairness of the management of their FACs and will ultimately affect franchisees' franchise system trust (Croonen 2010). The seven core principles are (1) the consistency principle, (2) the bias suppression principle, (3) the accuracy principle, (4) the correctability principle, (5) the representativeness principle, (6) the ethicality principle, and (7) the interactional principle. Below, we elaborate on each core principle, and we discuss the specific managerial principles that help in attaining it. We build on insights from franchising practitioners to elaborate on the principles.

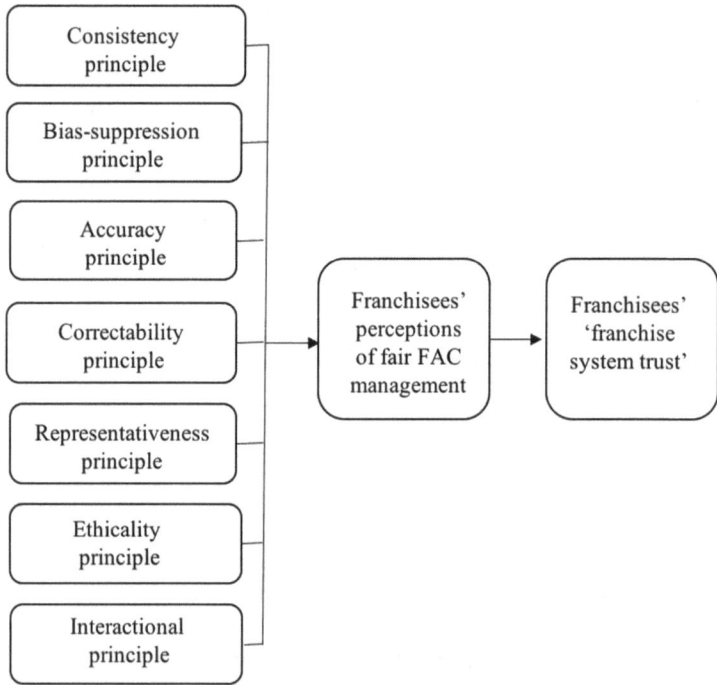

Fig. 1 The fair FAC management framework

2.2   The Consistency Principle

The consistency principle states that the procedures of an FAC should be consistent across franchisees and consistent over time (Croonen 2010). Franchise practitioners (e.g., Dwyer 2008; Hackel 2011) argue that making use of bylaws with clear clauses on several issues can help in improving FAC consistency. The bylaws can be basic or complex and are clearly written in concise legal language to cover all dealings of the FAC to make sure that everyone involved has similar expectations (Dwyer 2008). The potential evolution of circumstances and problems over time explains the importance of bylaws. Namely, the bylaws explicitly list provisions and procedures which are required to stay consistent over time to secure the viability and procedural consistency of an FAC (Dwyer 2008). FAC bylaws consist of essential clauses which specify the (1) purpose of the FAC, (2) decision-making authority of the FAC, (3) membership of the FAC, (4) general meeting clauses, (5) franchisor's role in the FAC, and (6) FAC expenses. Below, we outline the specific managerial principles related to these six essential clauses.

Principle 1: Clear FAC Purpose
The first managerial principle that needs to be considered in managing an FAC is developing a clear FAC purpose that incorporates the FAC's goals and objectives. The basic purpose of an FAC is improving communication between the franchisor and franchisees; however, broader objectives may be included depending on the specific characteristics of the franchising network (Dwyer 2008). Dwyer (2008) mentions several examples of broad FAC objectives such as the generation of promotional ideas or ensuring the maintenance of high standards and business practices throughout the system. The reasoning behind the clear formulation of an FAC purpose is to make sure that everyone involved in the FAC has similar and realistic expectations.

Principle 2: Decision-Making Authority
FACs may have voting power on a limited number of important issues (Cumberland 2012b; Flaherty 2016). A clause in the bylaws could state on what topics (e.g., major strategic changes or changes in fee structures) an FAC has voting power. On the other hand, topics that are outside the FAC's decision-making authority may be discussed for advice only (Cumberland 2012b). In case FAC members have voting powers, there should be a formal voting procedure (Cumberland 2012b). Unfortunately, the literature does not argue how this voting procedure should be regulated. Nevertheless, one could argue that a franchisor should follow a certain FAC advice if a majority of franchisees—a percentage which has been determined in advance—vote in favor of this advice. The voting power of FAC representatives represents a trade-off for franchisors; on the one hand, voting power could increase the FAC's credibility; but on the other hand, it may delay decision-making processes.

Principle 3: FAC Membership

The FAC bylaws should include a membership clause with several guidelines. A first guideline that should be considered is based on *how* franchisees become FAC representatives (e.g., appointment by franchisor or elections by fellow franchisees). In addition to this, guidelines are needed on *who* can become FAC representatives. Both these guidelines can be related to the representativeness of FAC membership. Therefore, it will receive more attention under "the representativeness principle." Another managerial principle that should be considered to ensure FAC consistency over time is the registration of formal FAC membership roles (e.g., chairperson and secretary) with additional information concerning their duties. Cumberland (2012b) recommends that the roles of FAC members should be regularly outlined for the FAC representatives and their constituents. This prevents a situation where FAC member roles are unclear, which could lead to political processes taking precedence over the governing process (Cumberland 2012b) and thereby negatively impacting perceptions of fairness. In addition, the amount of FAC representatives should be determined to strengthen consistency over time.

While Perry (1993) states that FACs typically consist of 5–11 FAC representatives, Hackel (2011) proposes that FACs should have a minimum of 9 and a maximum of 21 representatives. This difference in the amount of FAC representatives could be explained by the fact that it is not clear in what size of franchising networks these authors developed these insights. Next to that, Dwyer (2008) suggests that the number of franchisees represented by each FAC representative should be limited to a maximum of 50 franchisees. For each suggestion, one could argue that the amount of FAC representatives and number of franchisees represented by each representative is dependent on the number of franchisees in a network. Additionally, the term length of FAC representatives is also critical for the effective functioning of an FAC (Hackel 2011). If a franchisee has been an FAC representative for too long, the amount of new information gained will diminish, and the FAC representative may feel like she/he has more power than its constituents. To avoid this inconsistency, 3-year terms are recommended by Hackel (2011) to achieve one-third new and one-third retiring FAC representatives each year. Dwyer (2008) proposes that FAC representatives should hold no more than two terms consecutively. In other words, they can only be appointed or elected for two times. The length of each term will then consequently determine how long franchisees can be an FAC representative.

Principle 4: Organization of FAC Meetings

A clause regarding the organization of FAC meetings should also be included in terms of how often and how long FAC meetings should be held. Hackel (2011) suggests having shorter meetings that occur more frequently when FAC representatives and franchisor delegates are located fairly close to each other. However, when the costs of traveling to an FAC meeting are relatively high, it is better to meet more frequently via web conferences and less frequently in person in FAC meetings that will last longer. As a general guideline, FAC meetings should be held in a mix of live meetings and web conferences at least once a month to ensure FAC representatives and possibly the franchisor's representatives are aware of the progression. Also, it is advised as a basic rule to have no more than one-third franchisor delegates of all attendees present during FAC meetings (Hackel 2011). The explanation for this will be given in the discussion on the "bias suppression principle." Next to this, it is important to build in some flexibility and time at the end of each FAC meeting. This allows for discussion of ideas and other topics emerging from the FAC meeting conversation, but were not on the meeting agenda (Hackel 2011). Each FAC meeting should be closed with specific plans and a timetable to make sure all FAC members know their responsibilities for follow-up progressions (Dwyer 2008).

Principle 5: Franchisor's Role
Another issue that should be considered as part of the FAC bylaws is whether franchisor delegates should become formal members of the FAC (Wulff 2005). In favor of this statement, one could argue that formal participation of the franchisor in an FAC avoids an "us" vs. "them" attitude by establishing a jointly two-way communication platform. In contrary, one could also argue that an FAC may generate more credibility in the eyes of franchisees if the franchisor is not a formal member. Wulff (2005) explains this by the tendency of FAC representatives to speak more freely when the franchisor is not always present. In addition to this explanation, one could argue that franchisees will perceive the FAC more as their own device that exists with support of the franchisor, rather than a device of the franchisor for one-way communication as mentioned by Lawrence and Kaufmann (2010). Next to that, FAC representatives and franchisees will meet among themselves in formal and informal ways to share their own views before matters are discussed with franchisor delegates and executives in an FAC meeting. Thus, one could argue that an FAC without formal membership of franchisor delegates seems more logical, as long as there is commitment by the franchisor to listen to FAC representatives (Wulff 2005).

Principle 6: FAC Expenses
FAC bylaws also require a clause to determine in advance which FAC expenses are paid by whom (Wulff 2005). It appears that FACs are either subsidized by the franchisor or funded by franchisees themselves. The first possibility indicates that an FAC is supported by the franchisor. However, a drawback of franchisor-funded FACs is that the franchisor can exert influence and control on an FAC's activities. When an FAC is funded by franchisees, one could argue that it is more independent. As a result, it would generate more credibility in the eyes of franchisees because the franchisor could exert less control. However, a drawback of a franchisee-funded FAC is that a franchisor could perceive it as a threat. Namely, one could argue that the independence is associated with the characteristics of an independent franchise association (IndFA; see Lawrence and Kaufmann [2010] for a discussion). Having an FAC which is funded by both the franchisor and its franchisees could be a solution for solving both drawbacks. In other words, FAC co-funding allows to reap the benefits of both franchisor support and franchisees' perceived credibility. In support of this, Dwyer (2008) states that the common practice for FAC representatives is to

pay their own expenses, while the franchisor generally provides a meeting facility and secretarial staff for administrative use (e.g., FAC meeting minutes). Another possibility is to include the expenses of the FAC as a portion of the marketing fund fees, which are paid by all franchisees (Dwyer 2008). In either case, how expenses are paid should be clearly defined in the bylaws (Dwyer 2008).

Practical Illustrations: The Consistency Principle

Several franchisees of *Sports Unlimited** argued that their FAC was not very consistent in its functioning. There were FAC bylaws which stated that it was the FAC's task to provide advice to the franchisor about a range of important issues. However, FAC representatives felt that they only gave advice on marketing issues and that the advice was not taken seriously by the franchisor in the decision-making process. They felt that their roles were not always consistent over time. Moreover, there was no fixed schedule for the planning of the FAC meetings, so the meetings were sometimes scheduled last minute and at inconvenient moments. FAC representatives therefore often did not have enough time to prepare for the FAC meetings. One franchisee also said about the lack of time to prepare: *They sent us the agenda right before the meeting, and that was actually it.*

According to the franchise manager of BeautyWorx, the consistency of the FAC also depends on the franchisor's management. In their franchising network, there were relatively frequent changes of the franchisor's management, which caused some inconsistencies in FAC operations due to differences in management styles.

**All names in the practical illustrations are pseudonyms. All practical illustrations are based on in-depth interviews or frequent interactions with franchise practitioners.*

2.3   The Bias Suppression Principle

The bias suppression principle states that personal self-interests of the franchisor and its delegates should be prevented from operating the FAC.

Principle 1: Private FAC Representative Meetings

Hackel (2011) argues that FAC representatives should be allowed to have private meetings without the attendance of franchisor delegates. These meetings should stimulate FAC representatives to speak freely about issues without the franchisor management being present. It is expected that in such a way an FAC will increase fairness perceptions among franchisees because they will see that the FAC is not just a management "rubber stamp" (Hackel 2011). Franchisors should avoid that the FAC is just a one-way communication device in which the franchisor is only focused on informing and educating franchisees to promote their own agenda. The FAC representatives simply become indoctrinated by self-serving benefits while the power is being held by the franchisor. In short, in support of the bias suppression principle, one could argue that private meetings are in favor of avoiding potential self-interests of the franchisor and its delegates.

Principle 2: Control of Franchisor's Presence

In the discussion on the consistency principle, we already mentioned that practitioners recommend that no more than one-third of franchisor delegates should be present during FAC meetings (Hackel 2011). The reason for this can be explained by the bias suppression principle. Namely, it is important to avoid franchisor dominance during FAC meetings (Hackel 2011). Such dominance could encourage the franchisor to put forward their own interests, known as "one-way communication" (Lawrence and Kaufmann 2011), instead of listening to franchisees. In support of effective two-way communication, it is advised to only seat the franchisor's essential delegates in a "U"- or square-shaped meeting configuration. When there is need for more franchisor delegates, they could attend the meeting outside the "U"- or square-shaped meeting configuration (Hackel 2011). One could also argue that the presence of franchisor delegates can be controlled by making sure each FAC meeting is chaired by an FAC representative or by an independent chairperson and not by a franchisor delegate. This principle also applies to web conferences.

Practical Illustrations: The Bias Suppression Principle

Some franchisees at *Sports Unlimited* felt overwhelmed by the presence of too many franchisor delegates during their FAC meetings. The number of franchisor delegates was too high in their view. At one point, the franchisor decided to outsource the position of the FAC's chairperson to an external consultant. This was a costly, but effective, solution: it really reduced the franchisees' perceived dominance of the franchisor delegates during the FAC meetings.

One franchisee who used to chair the FAC at Bookstores Unlimited pointed at one of his most important rules: the FAC representatives have to be able to operate independently in order to prevent the FAC from becoming a "rubber stamp" to just promote the franchisor's interests. According to this franchisee, this means that FAC representatives should never accept financial payments* from the franchisor and they should never accept fancy FAC dinners and FAC meetings in exotic locations. This is all to make sure that FAC representatives remain critical toward the franchisor's decision-making process and keep their credibility among their constituents.

A reimbursement of actual expenses is fine, but FAC representatives should not receive a "salary" for their FAC involvement.

2.4 The Accuracy Principle

The accuracy principle refers to the principle that advice given by FAC representatives should be based on as much good information and informed opinions as possible. Broadly speaking, the managerial principles in support of the accuracy principle should hold the franchisor delegates and FAC representatives accountable for meeting with their constituents, respectively, the franchisor and fellow franchisees (Cumberland 2012b). Accuracy can also be facilitated/controlled by tight adherence to agenda items and decisions for action as opposed to open discussion or at least a strong chairperson who directs opinionated disaffected discussion to the "open discussion" end part of the meeting.

Principle 1: Transparency and Openness
The franchisor should avoid secrets by being open and transparent to FAC representatives in terms of franchising network information and franchisor's dealings (Modell 2010). Anderson (2002) states that an FAC should at least have full access to franchisor's management and staff to collect information. This is expected to avoid franchisees' time in second-guessing the franchisor (Modell 2010). The transparency and openness could, for example, enable the FAC to design, monitor, and report the results of a supplier audit (Grueneberg 2004). In return, Dwyer (2008) and Grueneberg (2004) suggest implementation of a requirement for FAC representatives to sign a confidentiality agreement. This would prevent FAC representatives from distributing confidential franchising network information. As a result, one could argue that the franchisor would feel more comfortable in offering transparency and openness in sensitive information. Transparency can be facilitated through communication channels such as (1) encrypted/password-protected intranet or (2) secure email.

Principle 2: FAC Meeting Agenda
The preparation of an FAC meeting through an agenda contributes to effective meetings, rather than being informal discussion sessions among FAC representatives and the franchisor delegates (Grueneberg 2004; Wulff 2005). The planned FAC agenda can be prepared by FAC representatives based on input from franchisees or jointly between the franchisees and franchisor in which each committee submits discussion subjects for the meeting. Hackel (2011) expects that FAC representatives will receive little response from their constituents, but one could argue that the ability to provide input fosters satisfaction with the FAC on its own.

Furthermore, one could argue that the amount of input from franchisees is dependent on the importance of the FAC meeting agenda topics. Generating input for the meeting agenda can be achieved by sending out an email prior to building the agenda. Once there is a draft agenda, it should be sent out one last time to ask if any members have additional issues to add (i.e., Grueneberg 2004; Hackel 2011). In either case, FAC meeting agendas typically include topics such as operations, marketing, technology, finance and management, strategic planning, new concept development, products and services, and company reviews (i.e., Bloom 2003;

Grueneberg 2004; Dwyer 2008). When the final FAC agenda is finished, it should be circulated to all FAC members well in advance of a meeting (i.e., Wulff 2005; Dwyer 2008; Hackel 2011).

Principle 3: FAC Meeting Minutes

It is suggested that a member of each FAC meeting is responsible for taking detailed minutes that will be distributed to stakeholders such as FAC representatives, their constituents, and the franchisor. The best person to do this would be an independent person, and otherwise we would suggest an FAC representative to take care of the minutes to avoid franchisees' suspicions of their franchisor's misrepresentation of information. The minutes will ensure that everyone is informed about the progress and occurrences of each FAC meeting (Wulff 2005; Dwyer 2008) and that a clear record of proceedings is kept for later reference.

Principle 4: Follow-Up Mechanism

A follow-up mechanism allows franchisor delegates, FAC representatives, and their constituents to be informed about the progression of activities (Wulff 2005). To achieve this, each FAC meeting should be closed with specific plans/action items and a timetable so that each FAC member knows his/her responsibilities (Grueneberg 2004; Dwyer 2008). In this manner, everyone should know what is expected of them and when (Grueneberg 2004). The follow-up mechanism would contribute to the FAC's reputation as an effective mechanism in representing franchisees' interests in the decision-making of the franchisor. More specifically, informing the franchisee community about progressions is expected to build support for the FAC and triggers the franchisor to show how it is following up suggestions made by the FAC. Next to the closing of each FAC meeting with specific plans and a timetable, other possibilities for follow-up mechanisms could be (1) a regular (e.g., monthly) FAC newsletter, (2) an internet-based discussion board, and/or (3) a franchise intranet news bulletin.

Principle 5: Digital (Private) FAC Communication

The use of digital tools in a private environment can greatly enhance the effectiveness of FACs. It is a digital place which can be visited by FAC representatives, and possibly also their constituents and the franchisor, for discussions on certain topics that might lead to useful advice. Also, the digital area can be used to post a calendar of events, FAC meeting agendas, and FAC meeting notes (Hackel 2011). Meanwhile, one could argue that the franchisor might consider a private digital communication by FAC representatives and their constituents as a threat which potentially fosters franchisee coalitions. When franchisee constituents are also involved in a so-called "nonpublic communication forum," it should be led in order to make sure the content of active conversations is meaningful and positive (Hackel 2012). In fact, a committee could be created in support of the FAC which helps to develop topics and ensure conversations to get started (Hackel 2012). According to Hackel (2011), the digital communication could take place on the intranet of the franchising network. However, one could argue that the franchisor has the possibility to access digital areas which are solely meant to be private for

FAC representatives. Therefore, the FAC could also consider making use of other digital tools such as (1) a Facebook private group and (2) a private discussion board of an external party.

> **Practical Illustration: The Accuracy Principle**
> The franchise manager of BeautyWorx pointed out the following about the accuracy of his information in his communications with the FAC during the implementation of a strategic change: *I do not come forward with anything before I know for sure that my information for the franchisees is correct, and I know for sure that the amount of renovating costs that has to be covered by the franchisees is correct. You always need to give the right information.*

2.5 The Correctability Principle

The correctability principle states that it should be possible for the FAC to modify and reverse FAC decisions that are perceived as unfair by the FAC representatives and their constituents.

Principle 1: Clause on Change in Bylaws
It is recommended to include a statement in FAC bylaws about the possibility to change one of the essential FAC clauses (Wulff 2005). In addition to this, one could argue that the statement should give the possibility to modify or reverse decisions that are perceived unfair by the FAC representatives and their constituents. This seems reasonable given that potential changes occur over time, which could result in required adjustments in the FAC bylaws or decisions (Wulff 2005). However, one could argue that all FAC members (or at least a significant majority) have to agree with changes in FAC bylaws. Grueneberg (2004) therefore suggests letting the FAC conduct surveys to make sure that all franchisees' voices are heard. Next to that, Cumberland (2012b) proposes that a periodical FAC evaluation conducted by an objective party could help to see whether the FAC is managed effectively.

Principle 2: Presenting Ideas in Concept Stage
A suggestion can be made in favor of avoiding the actual reversal of decisions made by a franchisor that are perceived unfair by franchisees. According to Hackel (2011), it is key for the franchisor to present ideas to FAC representatives at the beginning of the concept stage. This would allow the FAC representatives to give advice for potential modifications by considering franchisees' interests. In other words, the collective discussion between franchisor and franchisees could help to improve the quality of ideas and decision-making. Also, involving FAC representatives at the beginning of a concept stage makes them feel valued and engaged, which has a positive influence on their loyalty toward the franchisor (Hackel 2011).

Practical Illustrations: The Correctability Principle

One franchisee at *Sports Unlimited* pointed at the importance of the correctability principle: *It is not so bad to make wrong decisions; what is worse is to lack the ability to actually make or modify decisions.* At the time we interviewed this franchisee, there was a process going on to redesign the FAC bylaws. Since the start of the FAC a couple of years before that, there were only two pieces of paper on the governance of the FAC. At the moment we interviewed him, the FAC had just sent out a survey to the franchisees to see how they could improve the functioning of the FAC.

Another example is at BeautyWorx: the franchisor wanted to implement a new business format, and the franchisees had to invest quite some money in a new store interior. Already in an early stage, the FAC representatives indicated that they considered the costs of renovating as too high, which is why the franchisor started to experiment with cheaper materials for the store interior. These cheaper materials were eventually used by the franchisees in their store renovations.

2.6 The Representativeness Principle

The representativeness principle states that the needs and opinions of all franchisees should be represented when FAC representatives provide a binding or nonbinding advice in the franchisor's decision-making process.

Principle 1: Member Selection Procedures

The membership of an FAC is important to achieve a broad FAC representation where the interests of all franchisees are considered (Hackel 2011; Croonen 2010). There are two typical ways in determining FAC membership. The first possibility is that the franchisor is responsible for appointing the FAC representatives. Here the franchisor could select franchisees based on several criteria such as (1) balancing experienced with relatively new franchisees, (2) a balanced location/region representation, and (3) a balance between single-unit and multiunit franchisees (i.e., Wulff 2005; Dwyer 2008). Hackel (2011) extends these criteria by the inclusion of less loyal franchisees who have issues to be heard. More specifically, this would prevent the creation of an overly supportive FAC with less critical input (cf. Cumberland 2012a). Also, giving voice to less loyal franchisees is considered beneficial for winning them over by making them more engaged (Hackel 2011). Furthermore, a balance in gender of FAC representatives and the size (small/large) of franchisees' establishments could also be considered as a criterion for appointing FAC representatives (Hackel 2011). Thus, the main goal for striking a balance in the FAC membership appointment is to have adequate representations of all franchisees on dimensions that are relevant for the respective network (Dwyer 2008).

However, one could argue that the appointment of franchisees by the franchisor can be biased toward the franchisor's self-interests. Namely, it could foster the threat of appointing FAC representatives who are prone to become so-called rubber stamps in exchange for self-serving benefits (Cumberland 2012a). As a result, Anderson (2002) and Croonen (2010) indicate that the potential bias of appointed FACs leads to diminished credibility in the eyes of franchisees. Therefore, it is also considered important to discuss the second possibility for the membership composition of an FAC. Namely, elections can be used in which FAC representatives are elected by their peers by means of votes (cf. Anderson 2002; Cumberland 2012b). A potential issue that might arise in elections is whether to give multiunit franchisees just one vote or one vote for each unit owned. Namely, the elections can result in disproportionate outcomes in which either single-unit or multiunit franchisees are overrepresented. Also, one could argue that elections make it harder to achieve a balanced FAC composition in which there is an adequate representation of the abovementioned criteria. Therefore, Cumberland (2012b) proposes that elections should be based on some system (e.g., geographic or by some other criteria appropriate for the organization). In practice, it appears that if the franchisor is doing a good job, franchisees won't feel the need for elections (Hackel 2011). In short, there appear to be both advantages and disadvantages for both appointing and electing FAC representatives. Hackel (2011) proposes that it is also possible to create a mix of both appointed and elected FAC representatives. This would require some experimentation by the franchisor in order to get the balance between appointed and elected members right.

Principle 2: Extension with Committees
It is suggested that the FAC can be extended with multiple franchisee committees in order to maximize franchisees' involvement (Hackel 2012). Each franchisee committee is focused on the examination of a particular problem, issue, or initiative in a specific subject area, such as operations, technology, marketing, or finance (i.e., Wulff 2005; Dwyer 2008). The examination leads to possible solutions, which can be used to make recommendations to the FAC in representing franchisees' interests. Committees can meet via web conferences to cut costs. When there are conferences or other live meetings, they can meet in person. Committees should be populated by franchisees who are not serving the FAC and one FAC representative who will act as a communication link (or boundary spanner) between the committee and the FAC. As a result, the committees are an extension of the FAC and help to hear more voices in the franchise system and therefore increase franchisees' overall involvement (Hackel 2012).

Principle 3: Input from Franchisees
It can be said that an FAC is no stronger than the support it receives from its franchisee constituents (Anderson 2002). Therefore, the FAC representatives need

input from the franchisees in the franchising network to make sure their needs and opinions are represented in the decision-making process of a franchisor. Anderson (2002) proposes that there must be regular communication between FAC representatives and franchisees expressing their needs, questions, and concerns. Several suggestions have been made in trade journals about how to collect franchisees' voices in a systematic way. First of all, one could think of coupling each FAC representative as a direct contact person with a group of franchisees. So, if those franchisees have certain interests that need to be represented by the FAC, they can contact this specific FAC representative through possible communication channels such as (1) in person, (2) email, (3) telephone, and (4) a discussion forum through intranet or other social networks. Second, Grueneberg (2004) suggests allowing the FAC to conduct system surveys to collect opinions in a systematic way. Third, the FAC could organize an annual franchisee conference to foster even broader perspectives of franchisees (Grueneberg 2004).

> **Practical Illustrations: The Representativeness Principle**
> Franchisors of different networks often point at problems with finding potential FAC representatives who are willing to be a candidate in FAC member elections. For example, multiunit franchisees typically have a higher interest and more time to become FAC members than single-unit franchisees, which could lead to biased representation. Single-unit franchisees typically manage their own stores and are not willing or able to leave the work floor. In theory, having elections thus sounds great, but in practice this turns out to be much more difficult.
>
> One franchisee of BeautyWorx pointed out that it is very difficult to provide input and to make yourself heard and thus to make sure that your interests are represented via the FAC: *In earlier years, you could discuss matters with smaller groups, but now when there is a meeting with the FAC, you have to write down your questions on a piece of paper and hand it in before the meeting. It has become "one-way traffic." You are in a room with 300 people, and then there are problems with the microphones; and when you ask a question, they [the FAC representatives] say: "We will come back to the subject later."*

2.7 The Ethicality Principle

The ethicality principle states that the FAC management should be compatible with fundamental moral and ethical values of franchisees.

Principle 1: Freedom to Speak
A first principle in favor of the ethicality principle is suggested by Hackel (2011). He suggests that everyone should be allowed to speak freely, honestly, and frankly during FAC meetings without fear of upsetting management. In other words, fear of reprisal by franchisor delegates will be excluded through this procedure. This procedure supports the earlier argumentation of Cumberland (2012b) that possibilities for open communication, without fear of reprisal, will contribute to the participation in the strategic decision-making of the franchisor.

Principle 2: Personal Confidentiality
A second principle that should be considered states that everything said in FAC meetings needs to be held in confidence, which means that no person shall quote any member of the FAC (Hackel 2011). One could propose to make general references to the FAC representatives or franchisor delegates when sensitive information about a problem will be shared with outsiders. Also, clear announcements should be made when information about FAC meetings (e.g., FAC meeting minutes as mentioned in the accuracy principle) will be shared with outsiders. FAC bylaws could contain clauses that specify penalties for those members who do not adhere to the principle (e.g., paying a fine).

Practical Illustration: The Ethicality Principle
According to the franchise manager of BeautyWorx, the way the franchisor delegates and the FAC representatives interact really depends on the persons who are involved. A franchisee of *Sports Unlimited* confirmed this; he felt that the franchisor delegate at the FAC meetings had basically a *low level of trust in everyone and everything**, which really affected his interactions with the FAC representatives. FAC representatives became very careful because of that. Another franchisee from the same network framed the behavior of the franchisor delegate like this: *Mr. Johnson is the big boss! There is no "together" in his vocabulary.*

**In the scientific literature, we would say this person has a low "'propensity to trust."*

2.8 The Interactional Principle

The interactional principle states that FAC members should behave in a respectful manner toward each other.

Principle 1: Active Listening
The first managerial principle regarding interactions is based on the respectful behavior of the franchisor delegates toward FAC representatives and vice versa.

Grueneberg (2004) proposes that the franchisor delegates should practice active listening to FAC representatives. Listening to what FAC representatives consider important enough to discuss in the FAC meeting is more important for a franchisor than solely providing information to FAC representatives (Grueneberg 2004). In addition, the franchisor delegates should repeat what was said by FAC representatives to reinforce retention and to make sure the correct message was received (Grueneberg 2004).

Principle 2: Respectful Behavior
The FAC members should behave in a respectful, polite, and honest manner toward each other (cf. Bies and Moag 1986). The International Franchise Association (IFA) has devoted considerable attention to respectful behavior in the IFA's code of ethics. It states that franchisor delegates and FAC representatives are committed to show mutual respect for each other and to those with whom they do business. Furthermore, the IFA code of ethics also considers honesty, which embodies openness, candor, and truthfulness in explaining effective communications as an integral component of a successful franchising network. Both parties need to be sincere in word, act, and character (i.e., reputable and without deception) when there is commitment to sharing ideas and information and to face challenges in clear and direct terms.

Principle 3: Provide Knowledge on Procedures
The third principle states that the franchisor delegates should provide knowledge to FAC representatives about the procedures that demonstrate regards for franchisees' concerns regarding franchisor decisions. It is argued that the provision of knowledge by franchisor delegates about the franchisor's decision-making steps will contribute to franchisees' understanding that regards for their concerns are showed during decision-making processes. A reasonable explanation about the decision-making steps will also contribute to franchisees' acceptance of these steps (cf. Greenberg 1990, 1993).

Principle 4: Training and Social Capital
A fourth managerial principle could be added to the interactional principle by considering training and the development of social capital in the FAC. It is suggested by Modell (2010) and Cumberland (2012b) that the FAC chairperson and FAC representatives should receive training and guidance in listening skills, engaging in constructive conflict, and communicating with the people they represent. Since there is potential dynamic tension between franchisor delegates and FAC representatives in an FAC, knowing how to be professional in handling that tension is considered a key component for building a strong relationship. Professional training could be the answer for that (i.e., Modell 2010; Cumberland 2012b), and franchisors can promote that (new) FAC members periodically receive skills training.

Practical Illustrations: The Interactional Principle

One franchisee of Body&Care illustrated the importance of active listening when talking about the recently established FAC in his franchising network: *It started off really well, and it was necessary. The franchisees were able to take a look behind the scenes at the franchisor's organization and expected that the management would listen to them. But then you really do have to listen to them, and the franchisees thought they were not really listened to ... "*

The franchisor of Service@Home pointed at a problem in his FAC, which was that—in his point of view—FAC representatives in his network were not able to represent their constituents because they were too much focused on their own businesses and interests rather than on issues that concerned the network as a whole. The franchisor considered training for the FAC representatives to promote their understanding of strategic and operational tensions at the network level and to provide them with the skills and motivation to adequately represent their constituents.

3 Conclusion, Discussion, and Directions for Future Research

Even though franchising scholars have pointed at Franchise Advisory Councils (FACs) as a potentially important instrument in the management of franchising networks (e.g., Dandridge and Falbe 1994; Cochet and Ehrmann 2007; Croonen 2010; Cumberland 2015), there is very little scientific research on the exact roles of FACs in franchising networks and on the mechanisms that affect franchisees' perceptions of the functioning of FACs. This chapter's main contribution to the franchising literature is thus the development of a theoretical framework on the antecedents of fair FACs ("the fair FAC framework").

Drawing on fairness theory literature, we distinguish and describe the operation of seven core principles of procedural fairness that can be applied to FACs, namely, (1) the consistency principle, (2) the bias suppression principle, (3) the accuracy principle, (4) the correctability principle, (5) the representativeness principle, (6) the ethicality principle, and (7) the interactional principle. Since these theoretical principles are quite broad, we draw on multiple insights offered by franchising practitioners on specific principles that may help in achieving fair FACs. The inclusion of these specific principles leads to an extended fair FAC management framework. The extended framework is presented in Appendix A.

This framework provides franchisors with insights regarding the management of their FACs and serves as a solid basis for future franchising research. The next step in such research is to empirically test the framework in a variety of franchising contexts. First of all, future empirical research should study the relative importance of the core fairness principles in explaining franchisees' fairness perceptions regarding their FACs. Moreover, these principles are solely based on the *management* of the FAC, and our framework does not yet include other factors that may directly or indirectly affect franchisees' FAC fairness perceptions, such as franchisees' individual characteristics and the general atmosphere in the franchising network. Fairness literature has argued that fairness perceptions are "in the eyes of the beholder," meaning that individual characteristics, such as propensity to perceive fairness, can directly or indirectly affect fairness perceptions and individuals' responses to unfair outcomes and process (Colquitt et al. 2018; Bobocel 2013). Moreover, when there generally is a positive atmosphere in the franchising network, it is more likely that franchisees will perceive the FAC as fair and credible, whereas when there is already a level of distrust within the network, franchisees may be very suspicious in their interpretations of the functioning of their FACs.

A second step in future empirical research would be to delve deeper into the specific managerial principles for each core principle to study their relative importance in franchisees' perceptions of the application of the principles and ultimately the fair management of their FACs. More in-depth knowledge on the most effective principles and how to fulfill them helps FACs (i.e., franchisor delegates and FAC representatives) in setting their priorities in designing and managing fair and credible FACs. Especially regarding the actual fulfillment of the principles, there may be some practical problems that show that organizing a fair FAC is easier in theory than it is in practice, as our practical illustrations already showed. For example, how can franchisors make sure that franchisees want to make themselves available for becoming an FAC representative? How can franchisors make sure that the FAC representatives are indeed a good representation of their constituents (e.g., that the FAC representatives are not only the most successful franchisees)? What should a training for FAC representatives look like? All these questions show that there is still a lot to learn about the fair and effective design and management of FACs. We hope that franchising researchers will devote much more attention to FACs as they form an important instrument in the effective management of franchising networks.

Appendix: Extended Fair FAC Management Framework

The fair FAC management framework

The consistency principle	The bias-suppression principle	The accuracy principle	The correctability principle	The representativeness principle	The ethicality principle	The interactional principle
1: Clear FAC purpose	1: Private FAC representative meetings	1: Transparancy and openness	1: Clause on change in bylaws	1: Member selection procedures	1: Freedom to speak	1: Active listening
2: Decision-making authority	2: Control of franchisor's presence	2: FAC meeting agenda	2: Presenting ideas in concept stage	2: Extension with committees	2: Personal confidentiality	2: Respectful behavior
3: FAC membership		3: FAC meeting minutes		3: Input from franchisees		3: Providing knowledge on procedures
4: Organization of FAC meetings		4: Follow-up mechanism				4: Training and social capital
5: Franchisor's role		5: Digital (private) FAC communication				
6: FAC expenses						

References

Adams JS (1963) Toward an understanding of inequity. J Abnorm Soc Psychol 67:422–436

Anderson B (2002) Franchisee advisory councils serve as effective conduits. Franchising World 34(6):9–10

Bies RJ, Moag JF (1986) Interactional justice: communication criteria of fairness. In: Lewicki R, Sheppard BH, Bazerman MH (eds) Research on negotiations in organizations, vol 1, pp 43–55

Bloom BV (2003) Cooperation: the key to building lasting franchise relationships. Franchis World 35(6):27–28

Bobocel DR (2013) Coping with unfair events constructively or destructively: the effects of overall justice and self-other orientation. J Appl Psychol 98(2):720–731

Brockner J, Wiesenfeld BM (1996) An integrative framework for explaining reactions to decisions: interactive effects of outcomes and procedures. Psychol Bull 120:189–208

Cochet O, Ehrmann T (2007) Preliminary evidence on the appointment of institutional solutions to franchisor moral hazard – the case of franchise councils. Manag Decis Econ 28(1):41–55

Cohen-Charash Y, Spector PE (2001) The role of justice in organizations: a meta-analysis. Organ Behav Hum Decis Process 86(2):278–321

Colquitt JA (2001) On the dimensionality of organizational justice: a construct validation of a measure. J Appl Psychol 86(3):386–400

Colquitt JA, Conlon DE, Wesson MJ (2001) Justice at the millennium: a meta-analytic review of 25 years of organizational justice research. J Appl Psychol 86(3):425–445

Colquitt JA, Zipay KP, Lynch JW, Outlaw R (2018) Bringing "the beholder" center stage: on the propensity to perceive overall fairness. Organ Behav Hum Decis Process 148:159–177

Croonen EPM (2010) Trust and fairness during strategic change processes in franchise systems. J Bus Ethics 95(2):191–209

Croonen EPM, Broekhuizen TLJ (2019) How do franchisees assess franchisor trustworthiness? J Small Bus Manag 57(3):845–871

Cumberland DM (2012a) Franchise advisory boards and councils: mapping your relationship. Franchising World 44(9):31–33

Cumberland DM (2012b) Part 3: franchise advisory boards and councils: mapping your future. Franchising World 44(12):72–73

Cumberland DM (2015) Advisory councils in franchising: advancing a theory-based typology. J Mark Channels 22:175–191

Dandridge TC, Falbe CM (1994) The influence of franchisees beyond their local domains. Int Small Bus J 12(2):39–49

Davies MAP, Lassar W, Manolis C, Prince M, Winsor RD (2011) A model of trust and compliance in franchise relationships. J Bus Ventur 26:321–340

Dwyer JM (2008) No franchise is an island: franchisees and franchisors rely on each other. Franchising World 40(7):80–81

Flaherty T (2016) Strategies for working with franchise advisory councils. Franchising World 48(8):35–37

Greenberg J (1990) Organizational justice: yesterday, today, and tomorrow. J Manag 16(2):399–432

Greenberg J (1993) The social side of fairness: interpersonal and informational classes of organizational justice. In: Cropanzano R (ed) Justice in the workplace. Lawrence Erlbaum Associates, London

Grueneberg S (2004) Creating and maintain effective relations with franchisee advisory councils. Franchis World 36(6):22–23

Hackel E (2011) Getting better results from your franchisee advisory councils. Franchis World 43:22–24

Hackel E (2012) Creating empowerment: enabling franchisees to be heard. Franchising World 44(9):26–27

Kaufmann PJ, Eroglu S (1998) Standardization and adaptation in business format franchising. J Bus Ventur 14(1):69–85

Lawrence B, Kaufmann PJ (2010) Franchisee associations: strategic focus or response to franchisor opportunism. J Market Channel 17(2):137–155

Lawrence B, Kaufmann PJ (2011) Identity in franchise systems: the role of franchisee associations. J Retail 87(3):285–305

Leventhal GS (1980) What should be done with equity theory? New approaches to the study of fairness in social relationships. In: Gergen KJ, Gereenberg MS, Willis RH (eds) Social exchange: advances in theory and research. Plenum, New York, pp 27–55

Lind EA, Tyler TR (1988) The social psychology of procedural justice. Springer, New York, NY

Modell CS (2010) Trust: key to successful franchise relationships. Franchis World 42(9):9–10

Perry R (1993) The facts about FAC's: they work! Franchis World 25(4):12–14

Pfeifer C (2007) The perceived fairness of layoffs in Germany: participation, compensation, or avoidance? J Bus Ethics 74:25–36

Storholm G, Scheuing EE (1994) Ethical implications of business format franchising. J Bus Ethics 13(3):181–188

van Dijke M, de Cremer D, Langendijk G, Anderson C (2018) Ranking low, feeling high: how hierarchical position and experienced power promote prosocial behaviour in response to procedural justice. J Appl Psychol 103(2):164–181

Wulff E (2005) Advisory councils: effective two-way communications for franchise systems (revised version of 2005). International Franchise Association, Washington, DC. Retrieved from www.franchise.org

Decision Model to Locate a Franchisee Applied to a Fast-Food Restaurant

José Daniel García-Castro and Josefa Mula

Abstract This paper proposes and develops a decision model that allows fast-food restaurants to be located in urban areas. This decision model starts by preselecting a city as the study area, calculates the centre of gravity of the points of interest that positively affect the restaurant's demand in the busiest thoroughfares and runs an analytic hierarchy process (AHP) to evaluate the location alternatives. Finally, it selects the most appropriate alternative for this type of restaurant in the chosen city. The proposed methodology has been applied and validated in a real case study and compared with alternative approaches.

1 Introduction

Franchises are business models designed to quickly expand without owners having to make large capital investments (Caves and Murphy 1976). The basis of these models lies in sharing the know-how of a product or service, the brand and products with third parties. The cost of acquiring a franchise comes as an entry fee and as percentages of royalties of the net sales made from the given products (Lafontaine and Shaw 1999). In this context, the fast-food concept applies to restaurants that do not prepare food, but serve readymade meals. The purpose of these restaurants is to serve products that offer a low-cost service in the shortest possible time that meet safety requirements. The success of a fast-food restaurant relies on serving high-calorie meals at the lowest cost to reduce operating costs in relation to both labour and materials by standardising processes and continuous improvement (Kaufmann and Lafontaine 1994). In parallel, these restaurants centre on hard price negotiations

J. D. García-Castro
Universitat Politècnica de València, Escuela Politècnica Superior de Alcoy, Alcoy, Alicante, Spain

J. Mula (✉)
Research Centre on Production Management and Engineering (CIGIP), Universitat Politècnica de València, Escuela Politècnica Superior de Alcoy, Alcoy, Alicante, Spain
e-mail: fmula@cigip.upv.es

© Springer Nature Switzerland AG 2019
J. Windsperger et al. (eds.), *Design and Management of Interfirm Networks*,
Contributions to Management Science,
https://doi.org/10.1007/978-3-030-29245-4_9

for the prices they pay for raw materials. This is based on their advantage of owning large networks of restaurants worldwide that come as franchises or own chains. Rodríguez-Sirgado (2011) states that the success of fast-food businesses rests, on the one hand, on their fast service and, on the other hand, in their low prices and flexible opening hours. For all these reasons, people tend to eat in these fast-food restaurants due to lack of time, being able to afford them, and because they are open any time of the day. Therefore, the fast-food sector is an appealing market niche for investors. However, for a fast-food franchisee to be profitable, it must be located in strategic places. Thus, investing in fast-food restaurants involves making two main strategic decisions: firstly, selecting the chain of restaurants one wishes to invest in and, secondly, solving the unknown matter of where to locate the restaurant. The present work focuses on the second of these decisions.

Location models are processes that select a given location by eliminating one alternative or more (Ghosh and McLafferty 1987; Cliquet 2006). Carro-Paz and Gómez-González (2012) believe that strategic decision making about locations involves selecting among many sites where criteria are generally restricted to matters of cost, profitability, response times (Kaufmann et al. 2000), closeness to certain places, or any others depending on the company's characteristics or its activity. Such problems are extremely important as these decisions entail tying up financial resources in the long term, and any mistake made in these decisions may mean large losses for companies. These decisions also affect companies' competitiveness, so sound selections efficiently favour operations, while bad decisions imply considerably limited operations. It is worth stressing that most of the methodologies which propose locating fast-food restaurants start by assessing preselected alternatives, like Tzeng et al. (2002), whose authors hierarchise their options by a multicriteria selection method. The study by Widaningrum et al. (2018) considers employing a geographical information system (GIS) to understand how the fast-food restaurant market performs when not selecting an exact location as the final outcome.

This study proposes and applies a new methodology based on quantitative methods for decision making about the location of fast-food restaurants in urban areas. The overall objective of the proposed methodology comes as the following specific objectives: (1) collect and analyse the necessary spatial, numerical and qualitative data to calculate the possible locations and to make a final decision; (2) calculate alternatives for locations using the location centre of gravity method; (3) calculate the hierarchisation of all the location alternatives by the analytic hierarchy process (AHP) method; (4) select the best alternative for locations from all the possible options. In order to test and validate the proposed methodology, it was applied in a case study.

The rest of the article is arranged as follows: Section 2 presents the state of the art of the problem. Section 3 considers a work methodology proposal. Section 4 validates the proposal by applying it to a practical case. Section 5 compares the proposed approach with alternative methods. Finally, Sect. 6 offers the conclusions and future research lines identified while this work was underway.

2 Literature Review

Many location decision models have been proposed based on the multiplicative interaction competitive model (Nakanishi and Cooper 1974) and the location-allocation model (Weber 1909; Ghosh and Rushton 1987) like MULTILOC (Achabal et al. 1982) with specific heuristics. Chasco-Lafuente (2000) applies the commercial gravitation methods of Reilly (1931) and Huff (1963), which are very useful for explaining how people behave when faced with choice situations to determine market areas in commercial subareas in order to outline the expansion plan strategy of shopping centres. Tzeng et al. (2002) propose a multicriteria decision-making method to select the best possible options from four different alternatives for the location of a fast-food restaurant in the city of Taipei. To do so, the authors resort to AHP with 5 aspects and 11 criteria, which allows them to make a decision and obtain a quantitative result.

Sevtsuk (2014) uses 14,000 buildings of Cambridge and Somerville, Massachusetts, to analyse location patterns of retail and food establishments. The author tests five hypotheses about retail locations and estimates the impacts of different location characteristics. The results show how specific location attributes impact the probabilities of finding retailers.

Widaningrum (2015) uses GIS and Thiessen polygons as tools to determine the potential areas to obtain convenient locations for shops in a city. This study is based on tracing polygons on a map of a city by taking already existing shops as a reference. Along with attributes (sources to generate customers), it is possible to observe shops' market characteristics within an area of influence demarcated by Thiessen polygons. Widaningrum et al. (2018) conclude that the locations of the fast-food restaurants in the city of Jakarta are not the most populated places of this city, but tend to be in places occupied more by places of interest.

Chen and Sai (2016) propose a data mining framework based on rough set theory to support location selection decisions. This framework consists of four stages: (1) problem definition and data collection, (2) RST analysis, (3) rule validation and (4) knowledge extraction and usage. A restaurant chain case study is used to validate the proposal. Thronton et al. (2016) show the relation of locations of fast-food restaurants to their surroundings in areas with less spending power near secondary and primary education schools in Victoria (Australia). Yıldız and Tüysüz (2018) develop a hesitant analytic hierarchy process (H-AHP) and grey relational analysis (GRA) for food retailing from a strategic decision level.

Other location selection applications can be found in Hong and Xiaohua (2011), who focus on emergency logistics centres based on AHP; Chauhan and Singh (2016), who address healthcare waste disposal locations; Asakereh et al. (2017), who consider solar farm locations; Kazazi et al. (2018), who determine the location of parking lot sites; and Zhao et al. (2018), who are oriented to the location selection problem of distribution hubs.

One conclusion to be drawn is that the methodologies proposed to date do not completely cover the requirement of an investor who plans to locate a fast-food franchisee business by starting only by preselecting a city. The works by Widaningrum (2015) and Widaningrum et al. (2018) serve as a basis to start this research as they have developed a methodology that employs GIS and traces Thiessen polygons to analyse the areas of influence around the points of sale in the study. The problem with this methodology is that, although it allows us to understand how the market performs around areas of influence, it does not provide tools to select specific points on a geographical map to locate alternatives for locations.

The work by Tzeng et al. (2002) is a fundamental guide for the decision-making system as it proposes the AHP method as a tool. The problem here is that these authors start with preselected alternatives and only apply AHP for each preselected point of sale.

For all these reasons, the present work proposes a new work methodology to help future investors in the decision-making process they follow to select the location for a fast-food franchisee. This new approach combines the proposals by Widaningrum (2015), Widaningrum et al. (2018) and Tzeng et al. (2002) and adds new tools, such as the location centre of gravity method by Weber (1909) and other methods developed by the authors of the present work.

3 Methodology Proposal

Proposing a quantitative methodology to select the location of fast-food restaurants is no easy task because qualitative methods tend to be used, and these depend on the experience and knowledge of those who wish to locate restaurants. Moreover, franchises do not tend to facilitate any structured methods to choose locations because investors shoulder the main correct decision-making responsibility. This book chapter proposes a new methodology that intends to provide investors in fast-food restaurants with a qualitative and quantitative tool so they can select a suitable location for their restaurants by starting by only preselecting a city.

The proposed methodology consists in three main phases and five steps or sub-phases (Fig. 1): (1) data collection, (2) data analysis and processing and (3) decision making.

Each phase comprises a set of steps taken to reach the decision-making stage. A description of the proposed methodology follows.

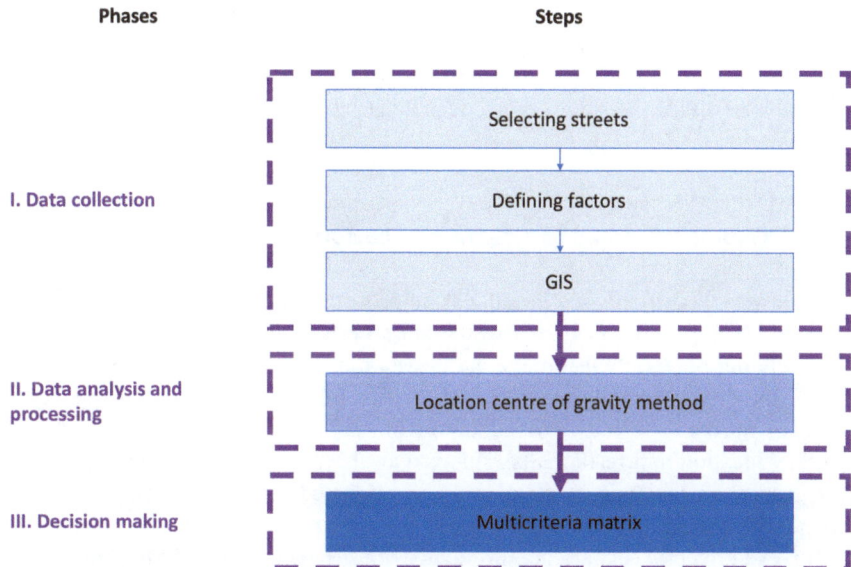

Fig. 1 Proposed methodology

3.1 Data Collection Phase

Research commences by collecting the data needed to use the location centre of gravity method. In this case, it is necessary to consider the following three steps:

3.1.1 Selecting Streets or Avenues

Fast food is a restaurant type that came about from having to attend to many people in a few minutes and who must eat quickly (Rodríguez-Sirgado 2011). This is mainly due to today's rapid pace of living as occupational demands increasingly grow and, therefore, people have less free time to eat. Fast-food units are either located close to pedestrian traffic downtown or along high-traffic roads in suburbia or within shopping centres with large parking lots. This is because it helps potential customers to find restaurant options around their workplaces or on their way to perform daily living activities. Widaningrum et al. (2018) conclude that fast-food restaurants are not located in high-density-population areas. By using GIS, these authors determine that certain factors, like closeness to places of public interest and competitors, are more relevant than the location of points of sale in densely populated places. In this sense, public interest places can attract tourists when competitors' presence is very important for both concrete and theoretical reasons (Hotelling 1929).

Accordingly, the first step is to select the busiest avenues and streets with places of public interest or other fast-food restaurants in the studied city with a maximum street/avenue length of 500 m, which is based on the authors' experience. One proposal is to divide the streets or avenues longer than 500 m into as many sections as necessary.

3.1.2 Defining Influential Environmental Factors

This is a very important step because it helps to define the factors that positively or negatively affect the fast-food restaurant's performance (potential customers). After defining potential customers, we move on to locate them on a geographical map of the city. Widaningrum (2015) uses five influential environmental factors and many attributes to locate shops: points of public use, medical centres, offices, leisure, education and restaurants. This proposal recommends conducting surveys with experts on the type of restaurant to be located and, in this way, to define influential environmental factors. This is a very important step that depends on the surveyed experts' experience in identifying the factors that may positively or negatively affect the restaurant's economic results.

3.1.3 Geographical Information System (GIS)

Widaningrum (2015) defines GIS as a data collection method for running spatial analyses that combines and manages data and attributes, like searching for characteristics in a given region. It allows users to store, edit, consult and analyse any kind of data about the geography of a given place. Application of technology has no limits and is increasingly used for decision making about archaeology, logistics, politics, town planning, economy, etc. Hence, it is a spatial search tool that enables users to find and analyse attributes to help them to understand how markets, economies, etc. perform. For this type of urban study on the location of fast-food restaurants, the location of influential environmental factors in a rectangular area of height is proposed (a line lying perpendicularly to the street) that equals 200 m, whose base equals the street length that is 500 m long or shorter. Everything must be reflected on the geographical map of the city.

3.2 Data Analysis and Processing Phase

The next phase of the proposed methodology consists in analysing and processing the data collected in the previous phase. To do so, it is necessary to define and use a method that processes data and generates possible locations on a geographical map. Here, we propose using the location centre of gravity method according to Weber (1909). It is based on the idea that, if we wish to minimise total transport costs, then the bigger the demand of a point, the better it is to be located near it. The same occurs with points with very high transport unit costs. Each demand or production point attracts a warehouse to it with a force directly proportional to the product of the transport unit cost and the material flow that leaves or reaches this point. This centre of gravity method is reflected on the point of two axes (X, Y). Equation (1) expresses its mathematical formulation:

$$X = \frac{\sum_{i=1}^{n} V_i \cdot R_i \cdot X_i}{\sum_{i=1}^{n} V_i \cdot R_i} \qquad Y = \frac{\sum_{i=1}^{n} V_i \cdot R_i \cdot Y_i}{\sum_{i=1}^{n} V_i \cdot R_i} \qquad (1)$$

where

V_i: Transport flow from/to point i
R_i: Transport rate to send one unit of merchandise from/to point i
X_i, Y_i: Coordinates of point i
X, Y: Coordinates of the centre of gravity

As we can see, this method tends to be used for cases with the variables transport rates and transport flows (Weber 1909). The proposed methodology ignores transport rates ($R_i = 1$) and, instead of considering transport flow, uses this variable with weighted weights for each influential factor.

3.2.1 Decision-Making Phase

Having located more than one possible location option, the next step is multicriteria decision making being done by AHP, which Saaty (1980, 1990) developed to solve multicriteria decision-making problems by a hierarchisation process. Hurtado and Bruno (2005) define AHP as a process that requires whoever makes decisions to provide subjective evaluations about the relative importance of each criterion and to then specify his/her preference for each decision alternative and for each criterion. The outcome of AHP is hierarchisation with priorities that reveals the overall preference for each decision alternative. To run AHP, it is necessary to use the largest possible amount of quantitative data. However, this method also allows the use of qualitative data, which are difficult to measure and might prove essential to evaluate options. To evaluate the criteria and the alternatives to choose, we use a numerical scale that represents the verbal expressions by allowing the hierarchisation of the elements of the matrix shown in Table 1.

Table 1 Evaluating criteria (numerical-verbal)

Numerical scale	Verbal scale
1	Of equal importance
2	Between being equally and moderately preferable
3	Moderately preferable
4	Between being moderately and considerably preferable
5	Considerably preferable
6	Between being considerably and very considerably preferable
7	Very considerably preferable
8	Between being very considerably and extremely preferable
9	Extremely preferable

4 Case Study

To apply and validate the proposed decision model methodology in order to locate a fast-food restaurant, we selected the city of Alicante (east Spain). According to the 2016 census, this Mediterranean city has 330,525 inhabitants. Its main economic activities target general services, tourism, administrative services and real estate business. By selecting the city to study, the next stage is to choose the area where the location study is to take place. For this book chapter, we selected the city centre of the city of Alicante because the franchise to be located would be the first one here and would not start from any restrictions related to competition with the same brand. Moreover, this city centre comprises the districts with more commercial activity and receives more pedestrians than anywhere else in the city.

We considered a US fast-food franchisee that specialises in preparing baguettes and personalised salads. This chain of fast-food restaurants has more than 26,709 points of sale worldwide. It has 63 restaurants in Spain and estimates favourable growth there. This company has an ample human resources flow chart that allows its restaurants to operate in more than 112 countries. However, the company's structure does not include a department that evaluates the locations of its newly opened restaurants; instead of that, franchisors make the decision about where to locate restaurants at specific points in cities after obtaining approval from area directors.

The franchisee has no quantitative method to locate restaurants and bases its decisions on the franchisor's and area director's knowledge and qualitative criteria. PAVE is the name of the methodology that the company follows to approve locations. It consists in a population restriction that does not allow the locations of its restaurants in cities with fewer than 60,000 inhabitants, and it expects premises to meet PAVE: *people*, people stopping at premises; *access*, parking places and public transport stops near premises; *visibility*, making the restaurant visible from several points on main streets; *energy*, places with lots of people moving around and plenty of commercial activity.

Based on the location methodology that the franchise implements, it considers that there is a problem with dealing with both investors and the brand. Such an important strategic decision is made according to four qualitative factors and one quantitative one (minimum population). A mistaken point of sale location is one of the main catalysers of failure for fast-food franchises. Closing a restaurant not only affects the investor but also the brand image. So decisions about locating a restaurant of this franchise must be made using more quantitative tools that lower the percentage of failed points of sale.

Having selected the city and area (Alicante and the city centre) and, in turn, the fast-food restaurant, we apply the location and decision methodology proposed in Sect. 3 of this book chapter.

4.1 Data Collection Phase

The purpose of this phase is to find point X_i, Y_i, expressed in Eq. (1), on a geographical map of a city that allows to use the location centre of gravity method. To generate the possible locations, we must firstly sector the areas around the main streets in the city of Alicante. Then we have to define the influential values and assign them quantitative values. Finally, we have to do the location method calculations.

4.1.1 Selecting Streets or Avenues

Selecting streets and avenues is a complex process because no quantitative methods are used on this occasion. So it depends on the analyst's experience and knowledge to identify the busiest and most occupied streets in a city. Normally, knowing the area, visiting streets and avenues and observing how the local market performs at different times of the day suffice. It is essential to remember that, based on the work by Widaningrum et al. (2018), the population density of the districts in a city centre as an influential factor may be ignored. With the qualitative analysis of the streets in Alicante, we selected five alternatives (see Table 2). We can see that streets are presented by letters in alphabetical order. As these streets were no longer than 500 m, it was not necessary to divide them.

Table 2 Information about the selected thoroughfares

Nomenclature	Type	Traffic type	Length (m)
A	Parade	Pedestrian	350
B	Street	Pedestrian and traffic	300
C	Avenue	Pedestrian and traffic	500
D	Avenue	Pedestrian and traffic	350
E	Avenue	Pedestrian and traffic	450

- Option A: Parade A is the most visited street by tourists in Alicante. It overlooks the sea and sport harbour and is an area with restaurants and somewhere to walk through to reach the beach. It is pedestrian.
- Option B: This street has the peculiarity of dividing the two most popular festivity areas of the city, so many night visitors use it. In the daytime, it witnesses plenty of activity, thanks to the surrounding banks and government buildings. Vehicles use this street, and pedestrians walk on its footpaths.
- Option C: This avenue is with the most vehicle traffic and pedestrians in Alicante. Offices, residential buildings and shops surround it. It houses the main Alicante market, which is a popular tourist attraction and is well used by local inhabitants.
- Option D: The main importance of this avenue is that it opens out to the Alicante railway station. Its other end borders a square, and governmental institutions stand on either end of it.
- Option E: Avenue E is a fashion shopping area, and it houses two relevant shopping centres on both ends. Apart from shopping, there are also many offices and a large pedestrian area. It tends to be busier during working hours and quieter at nighttime.

Having selected and marked the selected streets on the geographical map, the area of influence must be demarcated with the 200 m-high rectangular area. We take street length as a basis (Fig. 2).

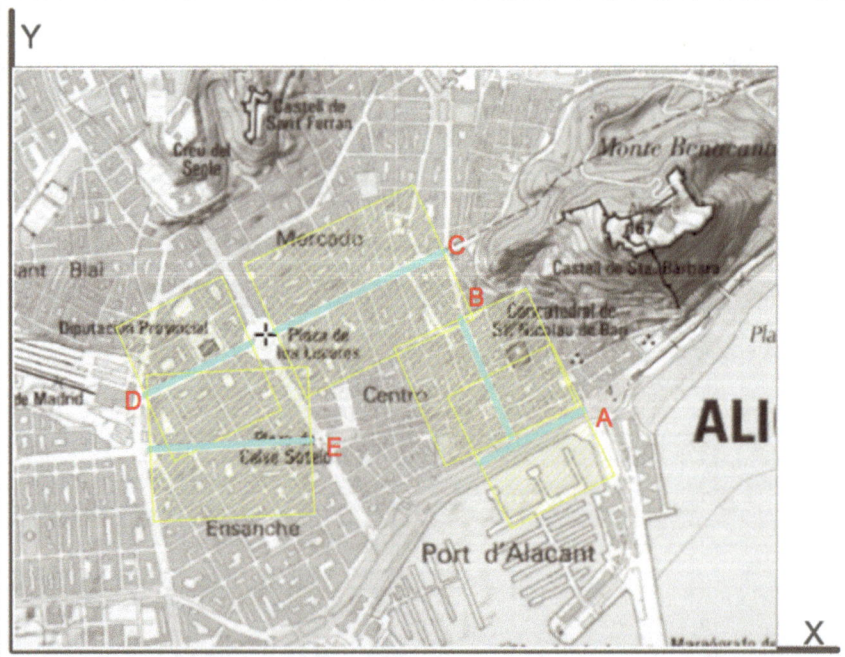

Fig. 2 The area of influence of each thoroughfare

As we can see, the areas of influence are marked out in yellow. Figure 2 shows that some areas intersect others, e.g., A intersects B and E intersects D. This initially indicates that they are potential thoroughfares because they are very close to another busy street.

4.1.2   Defining Influential Environmental Factors

Having demarcated the areas of influence for each street or avenue, we must use GIS to identify the influential environmental factors in the yellow zones on the geographical map (Fig. 2). To locate these factors, we firstly define and create a weighted matrix of each factor to assign them quantitative values to substitute them for variable V_i in Eq. (1) and, in this way, to calculate the centre of gravity for each thoroughfare.

As each type of fast-food restaurant has distinct characteristics, the demand of its products is affected by the variables that differ from other points of sale. Moreover, the demand of products is not the same for all places. Cities possess different personalities, and the public willing to purchase a product is not necessarily the same for all places. Hence, defining influential environmental factors is not considered the work of only one person. Indeed, quite the opposite is true because reaching a consensus of experts with different perspectives is recommended. In this case, in order to conduct this study and to define the factors, three people knowledgeable of the franchise and place participated. The first decision maker is a representative of the franchise from a Spanish autonomous community. The second decision maker is a worker in a restaurant of the franchise in a Mediterranean city close to Alicante. The third decision maker is a franchisee of the brand. These three participants reached a consensus about their criteria by defining the influential environmental factors and points of interest shown in Table 3. In order to assign them quantitative values, we created numerical sources: an evaluation one to address the factors and an intensity one that corresponds to the points of interest. The value corresponds to the quantitative weight that the experts assigned to each factor based on their own experiences. The higher the numerical value, the stronger the impact on the restaurant's demand. Table 3 presents the numerical-verbal scale for each factor.

Intensity is about a numerical value that expresses the amount or volume of people moving around a point of interest on a map. The higher the numerical value, the more people possibly visiting the point of interest. On this occasion, obtaining

Table 3 The numerical-verbal scale of the factors

Numerical scale	Verbal scale
1	Barely relevant for the restaurant's demand
2	Moderately relevant for the restaurant's demand
3	Very relevant for the restaurant's demand
4	Extremely relevant for the restaurant's demand

the average flow of people at each site would be the ideal process. However, it is a complex task to perform and one that requires long research times that investors are not willing to invest in. Therefore, we provide a quantitative value backed by experts' experience. Table 4 presents the corresponding numerical-verbal scale.

Having defined and evaluated the influential environmental factors and points of interest, we assign the numerical values to the aforementioned variables. To achieve this weight, the three above-cited experts participated. As a result, the experts came to the conclusion offered in Table 5, where we find the highly relevant factors for the restaurant's demand (4 points), namely, competitors and leisure. Another obtained result was that the barely relevant factor for the market's demand (1 point) is education. The evaluation made of the points of interest does not appear in Table 5 because these values depend on the intensity of each point of interest. For this reason, the evaluation is reflected when placing the points in the areas of influence of each street or avenue.

Table 4 The numerical-verbal scale of the points of interest

Numerical scale	Verbal scale
1	Not busy
2	Quite busy
3	Very busy

Table 5 Defining the influential environmental factors

Factor	Numerical evaluation	Point of interest	Colour on the map
Transport	3	Parking spaces	E
		Bus stops	A
		Metro stations	M
Competitors	4	Direct competitors (fast food restaurants)	C
		Local restaurants offering similar products	S
Commercial activities	2	Markets	M
		Shops	T
		Banks	B
Occupational activities	3	Offices	O
		Public Institutions	P
Leisure	4	Discos	D
		Hotels	H
		Public places and monuments	C
Health	2	Hospitals	H
		Clinics	C
		Dentists	D
Education	1	Schools	C
		University	U
		Nurseries	G

Fig. 3 Demarcation of the points of interest

4.1.3 Geographical Information System (GIS)

In this case study, we used the Google Maps database to collect points of interest and the AutoCAD software to demarcate the points on the map. Figure 3 offers the result of locating the points of interest on the axis (X, Y) on the geographical map of Alicante.

4.2 Data Analysis and Processing Phase

Having located the points of interest on the map, we calculated the centre of gravity for each area of influence separately. This gave five centres of gravity for thoroughfares A, B, C, D and E. By applying Eq. (1), and with the modification of $R_i = 1$, where V_i represents the multiplication of the numerical value of each factor by the intensity of each point of interest, we calculated the centre of gravity for each thoroughfare. As a result, we obtained the coordinates shown in Table 6.

Table 6 Coordinates of the
centres of gravity

Centre of gravity		
	Coordinates	
Alternative locations	X	Y
Alternative A	2892.53	789.34
Alternative B	2723.48	864.97
Alternative C	2166.01	1357.17
Alternative D	1438.89	1021.80
Alternative E	1476.46	646.04

Fig. 4 Location of the centres of gravity on the coordinate axis

Having established the centres of gravity for each section, we must locate them
on the coordinate axis (X, Y). Figure 4 graphically provides the results of calculating
the centre of gravity for each location (marked out in yellow).

4.2.1 Decision-Making Phase

To locate the fast-food restaurant, we used AHP as the quantitative tool to help
decision making. Saaty (1990) considers that AHP deals with breaking down the

problem and then combining all the solutions of the sub-problems in one conclusion. Hurtado and Bruno (2005) state that AHP efficiently and graphically organises information about the problem by decomposing it and analysing it in parts and by visualising the effects of changes to levels and then synthesising. The first step to perform AHP involves defining both alternatives and criteria. The centre of gravity method defines alternatives. In this way, we obtained five locations on the geographical map of Alicante (Alternatives A, B, C, D and E). The criteria correspond to the variables that positively affect the demand of the restaurant's product, namely, transport, competitors, commercial activity, occupational activity, leisure, health and education. Apart from these variables, we considered two more criteria that the experts believed were most relevant for the fast-food restaurant's economic performance: economic and pedestrian (Fig. 5).

Below we define the evaluation criteria:

- Transport: This criterion refers to the presence of parking places and public transport stops. Fast-food restaurants must be located at the points where many people pass by. So it is worth locating them in those places where citizens tend to go to catch buses, metros, etc. Likewise, having parking places around the restaurant is important as it allows passing drivers to leave their vehicles to eat and then continue their daily living activities.
- Competitors: Having competitors close by is an important factor because it helps attract the customers seeking similar food options to those that the restaurant pending to be located can offer. However, having competitors nearby means having to be more competitive in price and quality terms.

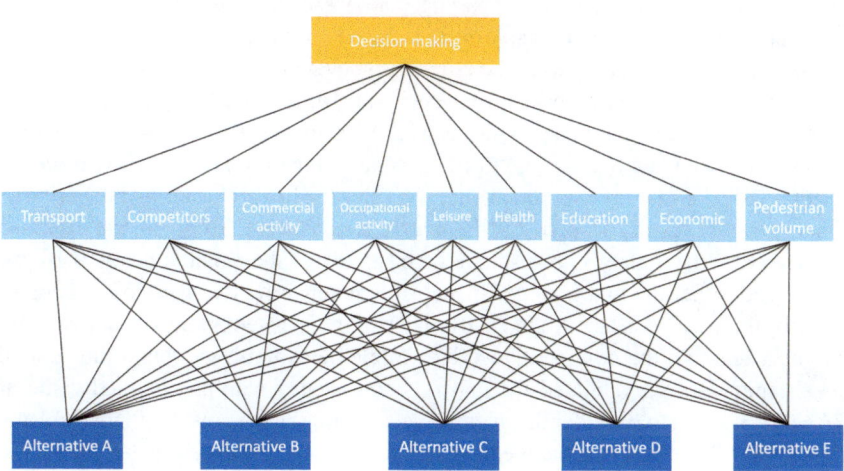

Fig. 5 Hierarchy tree

- Commercial activity: Premises like markets, shops and banks are appealing points for citizens. They are frequently used by populations in cities and generate constant repetitive pedestrian traffic that can grow accustomed to eat in the restaurant that stands close to these points of interest.
- Occupational activity: Such activity involves the premises where the tasks related to offices, public institutions and services are carried out. These customers play a key role for the restaurant because lots of them eat on premises close to their workplace on a daily basis. The proximity of the restaurant to these points of interest can help draw regular customers.
- Leisure: Based on the experts' experiences, we consider that places of leisure, like disco, cultural places and places of public interest, among others, are appealing for fast-food restaurants. Moreover, tourists are loyal franchise users as they are present in almost all countries worldwide.
- Health and education: Those premises that perform health and education tasks are good sources for customers as they involve many people.
- Economic: We propose the economic criterion as an indicator of the rented land value per square metre. It might not always be convenient to locate restaurants on the most expensive streets. The higher the company's fixed costs, the bigger the sales volume needed to strike a balance.
- Pedestrian volume: This criterion is crucial because it measures the quantity of pedestrians per hour who move around each location. The bigger the pedestrian volume on a street, the greater the visibility and the more probabilities of them sampling products.

Having defined the evaluation criteria, the comparison pairwise matrix is created by prioritising each alternative compared to another in terms of importance based on the experts' preference opinions. Weight is based on the numerical-verbal scale in Table 1. The result of comparing the criteria is shown in Table 7. Having created the pairwise weight matrix, we prioritise the criteria. To calculate this prioritisation, we must sum the matrix columns, divide each criterion by the sum of the corresponding column and calculate the average of the normalised matrix elements. The obtained result is called an average vector, and it represents the hierarchisation of the criteria. Finally, it is necessary to verify if the matrix is consistent. To do so, we establish the degree of the matrix's consistency with Eq. (4). If the result is below 0.10, we can consider that the matrix is consistent. It is noteworthy that the closer it comes to zero, the more consistent the matrix is. If the consistency ratio is above 0.10, we must reassign the comparative values to elements until we obtain the desired consistency. Having validated the matrix's consistency with an obtained value of $RC=0.033$, we then consider the average vector values as the result of hierarchising the criteria. Table 7 shows that the most relevant identifying criterion is closeness to

Table 7 Pairwise comparison matrix and the average vector

Criteria		Reorganised criteria									Average vector
		Health	Education	Commercial activity	Transport	Occupational activity	Pedestrian volume	Economic	Leisure	Competitors	
Criteria	Health	1	1/2	1/3	1/4	1/5	1/6	1/7	1/8	1/9	0.02
	Education	2	1	1/2	1/3	1/4	1/5	1/6	1/7	1/8	0.03
	Commercial activity	3	2	1	1/2	1/3	1/4	1/5	1/6	1/7	0.04
	Transport	4	3	2	1	1/2	1/3	1/4	1/5	1/6	0.05
	Occupational activity	5	4	3	2	1	1/2	1/3	1/4	1/5	0.08
	Pedestrian volume	6	5	4	3	2	1	1/2	1/3	1/4	0.11
	Economic	7	6	5	4	3	2	1	1/2	1/3	0.15
	Leisure	8	7	6	5	4	3	2	1	1/2	0.22
	Competitors	9	8	7	6	5	4	3	2	1	0.31
		45.00	36.50	28.83	22.08	16.28	11.45	7.59	4.72	2.83	

competitors, followed by places of leisure and finally followed by the premises that offer health-related practices.

$$IC = \frac{N_{\max} - n}{n - 1} \tag{2}$$

$$IA = \frac{1.98 \, (n - 2)}{n} \tag{3}$$

$$RC = \frac{IC}{IA} \tag{4}$$

where

IC: Consistency index
RC: Consistency ratio
IA: Random consistency index
n: Number of matrix elements

Having created the hierarchy matrices of the alternatives per criterion, we calculate the final weight of the alternatives by means of the weighted sum of each row of alternatives by the weight of the criteria (Table 8).

The end result indicates that the X,Y coordinate located on the thoroughfare dubbed B is the location with the highest hierarchical level, followed by Alternative A and finally by Alternative D. Therefore, thoroughfare B is the alternative that the proposed methodology selects. The location of this street in the centre of Alicante is strategic as it is the one that most tourists and Alicante citizens take to go down to the beach. There are also two nearby areas with bars, pubs and discos that receive many nighttime visitors. Another important factor is its closeness to public institutions like the Alicante City Hall. Thus, having analysed the results obtained with the applied methodology, it is essential that experts validate them from their business perspective. Indeed, the three consulted experts agreed with both the conducted study and the obtained results. Figure 6 graphically shows the location and hierarchy of the alternatives.

Table 8 Final hierarchy of alternatives

	Health	Education	Commercial activity	Transport	Occupational activity	Pedestrian volume	Economic	Leisure	Competitors	Hierarchy
Alternative A	0.04	0.05	0.05	0.04	0.68	0.07	0.13	1.00	0.87	**0.57**
Alternative B	0.19	0.08	0.14	0.09	0.71	0.68	0.30	0.78	1.06	**0.69**
Alternative C	0.50	0.63	0.35	0.56	0.13	0.22	0.46	0.30	0.21	**0.30**
Alternative D	0.08	0.12	0.07	0.35	0.25	0.07	0.68	0.11	0.07	**0.20**
Alternative E	0.19	0.33	0.62	0.19	0.52	0.60	0.05	0.06	0.12	**0.21**
Weight	**0.02**	**0.03**	**0.04**	**0.05**	**0.08**	**0.11**	**0.15**	**0.22**	**0.31**	

Fig. 6 Graphical representation of locations

5 Conclusions

The methodology proposed and developed in this book chapter was able to locate the possible locations for a fast-food restaurant in urban areas by the centre of gravity method and by taking the influential environmental factors that positively affect the demand of this restaurant's products as a reference, which we classified into these groups: health, education, commercial activity, transport, occupational activity, pedestrian volume, economic, leisure and competitors.

We considered selecting one of the location alternatives by using AHP with which to evaluate and weight the factors that disturbed business performance. We reached the following conclusions while developing the proposal and conducting this work: (1) using GIS allowed us to spatially analyse the factors that positively affected the demand of products at several points of sale; (2) the location centre of gravity method is capable of generating location alternatives on a geographical map by taking the points of interest that attract fast-food restaurant customers as inputs; and (3) it is possible to hierarchise the selection of the best location option from several alternatives by AHP. To do so, we must consider the opinions and weights of experts in this theme about the factors that affect a fast-food restaurant's economic performance and its sales volume.

We also identified the following future research lines: (1) develop a decision system that supports the proposed methodology; (2) consider a mathematical programming model capable of contemplating the location method as an alternative to the location centre of gravity method; (3) apply and validate the proposed methodology in other case studies; (4) check the result by contemplating the population density variable in the pairwise weight matrix; (5) develop techniques to measure the intensity of the most influential environmental factors according to the weight assigned by experts; (6) compare with other previous approaches such as Achabal et al. (1982), Ghosh and Craig (1986) and/or Baray and Cliquet (2007); (7) contemplate a dynamic environment (Ghosh and Craig 1983); (8) consider the location of other fast-food restaurants of the same chain in order to avoid any sales cannibalisation (Ghosh and Craig 1991); and, finally, (9) extend the proposed methodology to the analytic network process (ANP) using neural networks (Saaty 2013).

References

Achabal D, Gorr WL, Mahajan V (1982) MULTILOC: a multiple store location decision model. J Retail 58:5–25

Asakereh A, Soleymani M, Sheikhdavoodi MJ (2017) A GIS-based fuzzy-AHP method for the evaluation of solar farms locations: case study in Khuzestan province, Iran. Sol Energy 155:342–353

Baray J, Cliquet G (2007) Delineating and analyzing trade areas through morphological analysis. Eur J Oper Res 182(2):886–898

Carro-Paz R, Gómez-González D (2012) Localización de instalaciones. Universidad Nacional de Mar del Plata, Buenos Aires

Caves RE, Murphy WF (1976) Franchising: firms, markets and intangible assets. South Econ J 42:572–586

Chasco-Lafuente P (2000) Modelos de gravitación comercial: una aplicación al anuario comercial de España. Universidad Autónoma de Madrid, Madrid

Chauhan A, Singh A (2016) A hybrid multi-criteria decision making method approach for selecting a sustainable location of healthcare waste disposal facility. J Clean Prod 139:1001–1010

Chen LF, Tsai CT (2016) Data mining framework based on rough set theory to improve location selection decisions: a case study of a restaurant chain. Tour Manag 53:197–206

Cliquet G (2006) Geomarketing: methods and strategies in spatial marketing. ISTE, London

Ghosh A, Craig CS (1983) Formulating retail location strategy in a changing environment. J Mark 47(3):56–68

Ghosh A, Craig CS (1986) An approach to determining optimal locations for new services. J Mark Res 23:354–362

Ghosh A, Craig CS (1991) FRANSYS: a franchise distribution system location model. J Retail 67(4):466–495

Ghosh A, McLafferty SL (1987) Location strategies for retail and service firms. Lexington Books, Massachusetts

Ghosh A, Rushton G (1987) Spatial analysis and location-allocation models. Van Nostrand Reinhold, New York

Hong L, Xiaohua Z (2011) Study on location selection of multi-objective emergency logistics center based on AHP. Procedia Eng 15:2128–2132

Hotelling H (1929) Stability in competition. Econ J 39:41–57

Huff D (1963) A probabilistic analysis of shopping center trade areas. Land Econ 39:81–90

Hurtado T, Bruno G (2005) El proceso analítico jerárquico (AHP) como herramienta para la toma de decisiones en la selección de proveedores: aplicación en la selección de proveedores para la Empresa Grafica Comercial MyE S.R.L. Perú. Universidad Nacional Mayor de San Marcos. Facultad de Ciencias Matemáticas, Lima

Kaufmann PJ, Lafontaine F (1994) Costs of control: the source of economic rents for McDonald's franchisees. J Law Econ 37:417–453

Kaufmann PJ, Donthu N, Brooks CM (2000) Multi-unit retail site selection processes: incorporating opening delays and unidentified competition. J Retail 76(1):113–127

Kazazi S, Akbari A, Jabbari M, Asefi H (2018) Parking lot site selection using a fuzzy AHP-TOPSIS framework in Tuyserkan, Iran. J Urban Plan Dev 144(3):04018022

Lafontaine F, Shaw KL (1999) The dynamics of franchise contracting – evidence from panel data. J Polit Econ 107(5):1041–1080

Nakanishi M, Cooper LG (1974) Parameter estimation for a multiplicative competitive interaction model: least squares approach. J Mark Res 11(3):303–311

Reilly WJ (1931) The law of retail gravitation. Reilly Inc, New York

Rodríguez-Sirgado M (2011) El consumo de comida rápida. Situación en el mundo y acercamiento autonómico. EAE Business School, Barcelona

Saaty TL (1980) The analytic hierarchy process. McGraw-Hill, New York

Saaty TL (1990) How to make a decision: the analytic hierarchy process. Eur J Oper Res 48:9–26

Saaty TL (2013) The modern science of multicriteria decision making and its practical applications: the AHP/ANP Approach. Oper Res 61(5):1101–1118

Sevtsuk A (2014) Location and agglomeration: the distribution of retail and food businesses in dense urban environments. J Plan Educ Res 34(4):374–393

Thornton LE, Lamb KE, Ball K (2016) Fast food restaurant locations according to socioeconomic disadvantage, urban- regional locality, and schools within Victoria. SSM Popul Health 2:1–9

Tzeng GH, Teng MH, Chen JJ, Opricovic S (2002) Multicriteria selection for a restaurant location in Taipei. Int J Hosp Manag 21(2):171–187

Weber A (1909) Über den Standort der Industrie, Mohr, Tübingen, traduit par Freidrich C. J. (1929) The theory of the location of industry. University of Chicago Press, Chicago

Widaningrum DL (2015) A GIS-based approach for catchment area analysis of convenience store. Procedia Comput Sci 72:511–518

Widaningrum DL, Surjandari I, Arymurthy AM (2018) Visualization of fast food restaurant location using geographical information system. IOP Conf Ser Earth Environ Sci

Yıldız N, Tüysüz F (2018) A hybrid multi-criteria decision making approach for strategic retail location investment: application to Turkish food retailing. Socio Econ Plan Sci

Zhao L, Li H, Li M, Sun Y, Hu Q, Mao S, Li J, Xue J (2018) Location selection of intra-city distribution hubs in the metro-integrated logistics system. Tunn Undergr Space Technol 80:246–256

Part II
Cooperatives

Horizon and Portfolio Investment Constraints in Agricultural Cooperatives

Jason Franken and Michael Cook

Abstract Though horizon and portfolio problems are commonly thought to limit cooperatives' ability to capitalize on investment opportunities, empirical inquiry into the existence of these constraints is sparse, and recent conceptual arguments suggest that the horizon problem in particular may be less severe than commonly believed. Using surveys of members of three cooperatives, this study investigates the extent to which indicators of potential horizon and portfolio problems influence members' preferences for cooperative investment in value-added processing technology. The evidence points to the existence of three types of horizon problems and two types of portfolio problems influencing cooperative members' investment preferences.

1 Introduction

Scholars suggest that restrictions on transferability of residual claim rights and a lack of a liquid secondary market for them result in a disincentive for user-owners to invest in business growth opportunities (Condon 1990; Iliopoulos 1998; Nilsson 2001; Vitaliano 1985). For these reasons, traditional cooperatives seem particularly susceptible to investment horizon and portfolio problems and, in some cases, adopt

This research received funding from the USDA under Cooperative Research Agreement RBS-09-40. We also acknowledge the detailed and enthusiastic responses of survey participants and the helpful comments of an anonymous reviewer.

J. Franken (✉)
School of Agriculture, Western Illinois University, Macomb, IL, USA
e-mail: JR-Franken@wiu.edu

M. Cook (✉)
Department of Agricultural and Applied Economics, University of Missouri, Columbia, MO, USA
e-mail: CookML@missouri.edu

© Springer Nature Switzerland AG 2019
J. Windsperger et al. (eds.), *Design and Management of Interfirm Networks*,
Contributions to Management Science,
https://doi.org/10.1007/978-3-030-29245-4_10

179

nontraditional cooperative models (Chaddad and Cook 2002; Cook 1995; Cook and Iliopoulos 1998; Hendrikse and Veerman 2001; Nilsson 1999).

Conceptualization of horizon and portfolio investment constraints in agricultural cooperatives was first formalized in the 1980s and has been a subject of increasing concern by academics ever since (Porter and Scully 1987; Staatz 1987; Vitaliano 1985). King et al. (2010) summarize proposed investment constraints in a survey of agribusiness economics and management literature and promising research topics. Plunkett et al. (2010) provide an excellent description of investment constraints in Australian irrigation cooperatives. Bijman et al. (2012) review numerous cases of farmer cooperatives in Europe alluding to or explicitly identifying such investment constraints. Cadot et al. (2015) present a case study of the horizon problem in Bordeaux wine cooperatives. Cook and James (2016) conceptualize these investment constraints from increasingly important ethical and behavior economics viewpoints. Cook and Iliopoulos (2016) introduce measurable indicators for testing these investment constraints and describe increasingly sophisticated solutions being adopted to address the inefficiencies created by these constraints. In his 2012 Agricultural and Applied Economics Association presidential address, Robert King identifies this evolution of institutional and organizational dynamics in response to such investment constraints as a prime example of the innovative work being done on mechanism design (King 2012).

Horizon and portfolio investment constraints are two of the five vaguely defined property rights problems—horizon, portfolio, shirking, control (i.e., agency), and influence cost problems—considered limitations of the cooperative form (Cook 1995; Iliopoulos 1998; Peterson 1992; Porter and Scully 1987; Staatz 1987; Vitaliano 1985). In Cook's (2018) cooperative life cycle piece, he argues that these five problems stem from heterogeneity arising during periods of cooperative growth and identifies examples of cooperatives that he contends have succumbed to and others that have overcome some of these challenges in recent years. For instance, horizon and portfolio problems, respectively, indicate different time and risk preferences, which result in different investment preferences of the members. Höhler and Kühl (2018) review the literature on member heterogeneity in cooperatives and identify 15 dimensions of member heterogeneity and rate investment preferences, at roughly 8% of reviewed studies, as the third most investigated relationship to member heterogeneity after performance (20%) and governance structures (12%). As Höhler and Kühl (2018, p. 704) note, "(M)ost of the reviewed literature on cooperatives does not explicitly examine the impact of member heterogeneity on their dependent variables … Different dimensions of member heterogeneity are named but only few are included in economic models."

Despite conceptual and anecdotal support, empirical evidence of horizon and portfolio problems, in particular, is scarce and inconclusive. Iliopoulos (1998) finds evidence of both constraints using surveys of US cooperatives' CEOs and CFOs. Alho's (2016) finding that Finnish meat producers' willingness to invest in various hypothetical cooperative forms tends to increase with farm size and decrease with plans to exit may also be consistent with portfolio and horizon problems, respectively. Fahlbeck (2007) finds no evidence of horizon problems using surveys of Swedish cooperatives' members. Moreover, mathematical models by Olesen (2007) and Fulton and Giannakas (2012) imply that the horizon problem is less severe than typically argued. Olesen (2007, p. 252) concludes from his own findings that "horizon problems cannot explain underinvestment in cooperatives. Instead, underinvestment must be explained by other problems, e.g. free rider problems, portfolio problems, or limited access to capital." Still, Chaddad et al. (2005) find that US cooperatives are capital constrained, implying that one or both of these potential constraints are binding to some degree.

This study investigates the extent to which variants of the investment horizon and portfolio problems exist in a traditional multipurpose cooperative and a new generation cooperative in the US and a member-investor cooperative in New Zealand using responses to member surveys. The approach shows that members' characteristics impact their perceptions of cooperative investment in value-added processing technology across cooperative type and in both countries. Binary probit analysis of survey data informs whether members' attributes (e.g., nearness to retirement, commodity diversification, intentions to expand production) significantly impact their preferences for cooperative investments in value-added processing technologies.

Literature on the investment horizon problem has focused primarily on the *residual* horizon problem (Ellerman 1986; Gittinger 1972). This issue is also referred to as the *short-term* horizon problem, as active members nearing retirement may oppose investments from which they cannot extract the complete present value of future benefits during their membership horizon. In addition to this horizon problem, this study finds support for a *return of capital* or *wait-to-receive* horizon problem where, upon retirement age, members of traditional cooperatives and nontraditional ones with transferable shares, respectively, prefer accelerated redemption of equities and only those investment opportunities that are believed to lead to a higher share price (Furubotn and Pejovich 1972). Support is also found for a *current obligation* horizon problem, where members with high debt obligations and/or cash constraints may oppose additional investments, particularly if they have limited ability to borrow against their cooperative investment (i.e., lender places little value on cooperative shares as collateral).

The quintessential portfolio problem is believed to occur in cooperatives spanning many commodity divisions with increasingly specialized members (Plunkett 2005). Such lateral portfolio problems arise as members are unable to adjust their cooperative asset portfolios to reflect their degree of commodity specialization. In addition to this version of the portfolio problem, this study also finds evidence of a vertical dimension that arises as members are unable to adjust their cooperative asset portfolios to reflect their preference for degree of vertical integration and capital intensity within a specialized commodity.

The study proceeds with a summary of the relevant literature and resulting hypotheses. Then, the survey data and research context are discussed, followed by the empirical results. The study concludes with implications and direction for further research.

2 Literature and Hypotheses

Difficulties in acquiring and redeeming cooperative patrons' equity capital are considered major constraints to the growth and sustainability of these organizations (Bonin et al. 1993; Caves and Petersen 1986; Furubotn and Pejovich 1972; Murray 1983). Several explanations are offered for the inability of user-owned organizations to acquire sufficient risk capital to finance investment opportunities.

First, property rights allocations in traditional cooperatives do not offer strong incentives to invest (Cook 1995; Cook and Iliopoulos 2000; Knoeber and Baumer 1983; LeVay 1983; Vitaliano 1983). Residual claims in these organizations are non-appreciable, since they are nontransferable and are redeemable only at book value (Van Wassenaer 1989). As patrons therefore benefit mainly through usage via favorable prices and patronage refunds, their incentive to invest risk capital is limited. Furthermore, patrons may share in the cooperative's return on equity without investing, thereby giving rise to free riding and underfinancing of the cooperative (Knoeber and Baumer 1983).

Second, cooperatives traditionally have restricted residual claims since only active members provide equity capital. That is, traditional cooperatives can only source equity from active members. Thus, the acquisition of risk capital is limited by the number, wealth, and risk-bearing capacity of current members. The afore-mentioned inability to transfer residual claims prevents the functioning of secondary markets for cooperative stock and leads to portfolio and horizon problems. That is, members of traditional cooperatives tend to influence investment decisions since they cannot capture the future payoffs of the cooperatives' risky investments due to the horizon problem nor adjust their individual investment portfolios to match their risk preferences due to the portfolio problem (Jensen and Meckling 1979; Porter and Scully 1987).

Other arguments supporting the presence of capital constraints in cooperatives include that equity capital is tied to patronage, cooperative equity is not permanent, and cooperatives have limited access to external funding. Cooperatives depend mainly on internally generated capital or patronage to acquire risk capital. Internally generated capital is redeemable at the discretion of the board of directors. Since redeeming equity is a cash outlay, lenders may not consider allocated patronage refunds sufficiently permanent equity capital to support loans, thus limiting cooper-atives' access to debt capital (Parliament and Lerman 1993).

Each of these explanations for potential investment constraints in cooperatives stems from heterogeneity in cooperative membership. While cooperative member-ships have always included farmers of all ages and at all points in the life of their farm businesses, most farms in the Midwest USA (and likely elsewhere) were typically diversified family operations with grain, hogs, cattle, or perhaps dairy and similar production technologies up until the 1970s (Ginder 1999). However, over time, membership became more heterogeneous, placing greater emphasis on the time horizon issue. The degree of membership heterogeneity can be measured by variation in size, degree of specialization, financial position, and geographic dispersion of farm operations, farmers' age or time horizon, education level, and percentage of non-farm income (Ginder 1999; Iliopoulos and Cook 1999). Hence, the general hypothesis advanced here is that heterogeneity in cooperative members' characteristics leads to varying perceptions of the cooperative's proposed investments; or in other words, members' characteristics have a nonzero effect on their perceptions of these investments.

The literature on cooperative investment horizon problems has largely focused on the return on capital in the *residual* or *short-term* horizon problem, in which members who are near retirement prefer only short-term investments that may be recouped quickly.[1] This horizon problem occurs when a member's residual claim on the net income generated by a growth opportunity is shorter than the asset's productive life and ownership rights to the firm's assets are nontransferable (Ellerman 1986; Porter and Scully 1987). Traditional cooperatives tie formal claims on residual income to patronage (Staatz 1987). Thus, members benefit from investments until they cease to patronize the cooperative and surrender any future residual claims (Staatz 1987; Vitaliano 1983). That is, members do not directly realize the capitalized value of the cooperatives' future income streams beyond their expected membership horizons. Thus, active members nearing retirement might have time preferences skewed slightly toward the present. Since they have shorter membership horizons, these members discount associated income streams beyond their membership horizon to zero. These members prefer short-term investments with a quick payback since they cannot capture the future value of long-term investments during their membership horizon.

Hypothesis 1a (H1a) The number of years until retirement is positively associated with the preference for further investments in the cooperative.

The *return of capital* or Furubotn-Pejovich (1972) horizon problem is also known as the *wait-to-receive* horizon problem, because members wait to receive the book value of their residual claims until the board of directors chooses to redeem the equities (Cobia 1989). Inactive or retired members of traditional cooperatives might pressure the board to accelerate redemption of older equities, because they no longer benefit through patronage (Furubotn and Pejovich 1972, Ellerman 1986). Members of nontraditional cooperatives with transferable shares may, as they approach retirement, wish for a higher share value price. These members may pressure the board of directors to set the share price at a higher value, and while they may oppose certain investments, they may support those that they anticipate will be capitalized in a higher share price. Thus, we hypothesize:

Hypothesis 1b (H1b) The number of years until retirement is negatively associated with the preference for higher share value price.

---

[1] See Vitaliano (1985) for a conceptual framework depicting the residual horizon problem using a graphical analysis of a two-period investment and Ellerman (1986) for a framework covering the residual horizon problems while comparing ownership rights in investor-owned and labor-managed firms.

Following Krumpleman-Farmer (2005), other variants of the horizon problem may exist. Under the *current obligation* horizon problem, members with current cash flow constraints have time preferences skewed toward the present (Krumpleman-Farmer 2005). While such members benefit from residual claims, taxes on residual claims in combination with current obligations to service debt may outweigh those benefits. Therefore, these members pressure the cooperative to not retain all of the equity allocated as they generally prefer to receive higher cash in the year earned but may accept slightly lower amounts if they can borrow against the cooperative investment. However, if members are unable to secure such loans, then they will likely oppose any further investments. Thus, we hypothesize:

Hypothesis 2 (H2) The ability to borrow against the cooperative investment is positively associated with support of investment opportunities.

The *portfolio problem* constitutes another investment constraint in traditional cooperatives. The lack of transferability, liquidity, and appreciation mechanisms for residual claims prevents members from adjusting their cooperative asset portfolios to match personal risk preferences (Cook 1995). Since investment and patronage decisions are linked, some members find they hold suboptimal investment portfolios and pressure the cooperative to rearrange the portfolio to be more consistent with their preferences, even if it means lower expected returns. As noted earlier, most farms were historically diversified family operations producing several commodities with similar technologies (Ginder 1999); but more recently many operations have become more specialized, and traditional multipurpose cooperatives now serve the input procurement and marketing needs of a more heterogeneous mix of diversified and specialized patrons. Heterogeneity of membership, particularly in large, diversified cooperatives, presents difficulties in achieving consensus and establishing viable coalitions (Feng and Hendrikse 2012). Variation in diversification/specialization among cooperative memberships leads to the *classical (lateral) portfolio problem*. Accordingly, we hypothesize:

Hypothesis 3 (H3) Diversification in commodity production is negatively associated with support of investment into specialized value-added technology.

Plunkett (2005) introduces the possibility of a *vertical portfolio problem*, where support for cooperative investments that entail vertical integration, for instance, into value-added processing, may also vary with the size of members' farm operations. As opposed to the classical (lateral) portfolio problem that is common in cooperatives dealing with multiple commodities, the vertical portfolio problem may arise in single-commodity cooperatives that process the commodity into branded products. For example, some dairy cooperatives become more involved in the production of capital-intensive consumer-ready, branded products. Essentially, differences in farm size may underlie differences in cooperative members' support for such investments. However, as outlined below, sound arguments can be made for both positive and negative effects of farm size, and hence, empirical analysis may provide insights as to the overriding effect. For instance, research indicates that larger farmers tend to participate more in cooperatives (Wadsworth 1991) and, in general, larger farmers are more likely to adopt new technology (Barham et al. 2014; Just et al. 1980; Khanna 2001). Furthermore, smaller, diversified members may prefer less investment in cooperative assets that underpin further specialization in value-added processes relative to larger, expanding, specialized farmers. Hence, larger farmers may be relatively more supportive of cooperative investments and those in value-added processing technologies in particular.

Hypothesis 4a (H4a) Intentions to expand the farm operation are positively associated with support of investment into specialized value-added technology.

However, Plunkett (2005) also argues that patron-members with larger and expanding operations may be more interested in investment opportunities that support farm profitability and expansion, whereas members with smaller operations that face constraints in expansion will more likely support investment opportunities that add value to existing production. This conclusion is drawn based on the logic that large farmers should enjoy a greater on-farm return on investment (ROI) than smaller farmers due to economies of scale. Conceivably, the prospective ROI in cooperative processing technology, for instance, may be less than the on-farm ROI for large farmers and greater than that of small farmers. Hence, any prospective cooperative investment in investor assets (e.g., value-added processing technology) with an anticipated ROI between that of small and large farmers will be more likely to be supported by small farmers than by large farmers. Large and expanding farmers rather support investments in user assets (e.g., collection stations, warehousing, and agronomy services, like spraying) that further facilitate on-farm ROI. Hence, we may also hypothesize:

Hypothesis 4b (H4b) Intentions to expand the farm operation are negatively associated with support of investment into specialized value-added technology.

3 Methodology

3.1 Research Design and Data

This study analyzes data from mail surveys of three agricultural cooperatives conducted between December 2004 and May 2005. The data, though dated, provide insights into investment constraints faced by one cooperative still in operation, a second that serves its members through a merger to form a new cooperative, and a third that has transitioned to a limited-liability company. Fonterra Co-operative Group (Fonterra) is a member-investor cooperative that is a leading multinational dairy company accounting for the majority of New Zealand's milk. West Central Cooperative (WCC) was a grain marketing multipurpose cooperative that formed the Landus Cooperative through a "merger of equals" with Farmers Cooperative Company in 2016 to ensure local ownership in Iowa for generations to come (Landus Cooperative 2015). Northeast Missouri Grain Processors (NMGP) was a

Table 1 Ownership rights and response rates for surveyed cooperatives

Ownership rights	West Central	Northeast Missouri Grain Processors	Fonterra
Restricted to members	Yes	Yes	Yes
Redeemable from cooperative	C stock, 10–12-year revolving period; B stock, retire	Non-redeemable	Immediate
Benefits: user or investor	User	Investor/user	Investor
Proportional to member investment	No	Yes	Recently yes
Survey response rate	17.6% (160 of 910 sent)	31% (96 of 311 sent)	8.2% (997 of 12,144 sent)

new generation cooperative that provided the majority of equity for a corn ethanol plant in Macon, Missouri, and has since transitioned to a limited-liability company to facilitate further non-farmer investment but remains held largely by corn farmers (Retka Schill 2013).

Table 1 summarizes the ownership rights and survey response rates for each of the three cooperatives at the time of the survey. WCC is a multipurpose cooperative with passive investment where the cooperative allocates a portion of its net income to members in proportion to levels of patronage (i.e., user benefits). NMGP and Fonterra, as new generation and member-investor cooperatives, respectively, have proactive investment where members directly invest cash in the organizations and returns are distributed in proportion to investment (i.e., investor-oriented benefits). Considering different types of cooperatives with different characteristics allows examination of whether these differences affect the kinds of investment constraints faced.

Personal interviews with cooperative top management, the board of directors, and research from various branches of new institutional economics (Coase 1998) informed the general survey design. This draft was sent back to key individuals (e.g., general manager, chief financial officer, board chairperson) at each cooperative, and meetings were arranged to modify the survey to better fit the circumstances of each cooperative in order to enhance comprehension of the questions. Once approved by the respective cooperatives, finalized surveys were sent to the entire memberships of NMGP and Fonterra and subsamples of WCC's membership based on size and specialization. For the WCC, this choice was made to facilitate sufficient variety in size of farmer members in the sample to observe effects of heterogeneity in farm size. Specifically, all 122 of the large-grain members (over 1000 acres of grain), all 303 of the medium-grain members (500 and 1000 acres of grain), and a random sample of 500 small-grain members (less than 500 acres of grain) were surveyed. Surveys were sent to 910 members of WCC, and 160 completed surveys were returned for a 17.6% response rate or about 5% of the membership (Table

1). Surveys were sent to all 311 members of NMGP, and 96 completed surveys were returned for a 31% response rate. Surveys were sent to the entire Fonterra membership of 12,144 shareholders at that time, and 997 completed surveys were returned for an 8.2% response rate. Accounting for omitted responses yields slightly smaller samples for analysis with 155 observations for WCC, 91 for NMGP, and 902 for Fonterra.

3.2   Measures

Summary statistics are given in Table 2. The dependent variable is based on a seven-point scale item ranging from one indicating a strong preference for investment in "new" or "value-added" processing technology to seven indicating a strong preference for traditional investments likely to increase volumes marketed and another item indicating a desire for no further investments. Thus, *ValueAddedTech* is coded as a binary variable equal to one if the responding member reports a preference for cooperative investment in value-added processing technology (i.e.,

Table 2 Summary statistics

Cooperative/variable	Mean	Standard deviation	Min	Max
Fonterra (N = 902)				
ValueAddedTech	0.49	0.50	0.00	1.00
Relinquish in >5 years	0.65	0.48	0.00	1.00
Lender value >90%	0.77	0.42	0.00	1.00
Farm/HH income >50%	0.09	0.29	0.00	1.00
Commodities	2.15	1.07	1.00	6.00
Intend to expand	0.67	0.47	0.00	1.00
NMGP (N = 91)				
ValueAddedTech	0.59	0.49	0.00	1.00
Relinquish in >5 years	0.73	0.45	0.00	1.00
Lender value >90%	0.77	0.42	0.00	1.00
Farm/HH income >50%	0.22	0.42	0.00	1.00
Commodities	3.51	1.28	1.00	6.00
Intend to expand	0.58	0.50	0.00	1.00
West Central (N = 155)				
ValueAddedTech	0.57	0.50	0.00	1.00
Relinquish in >5 years	0.83	0.38	0.00	1.00
Lender value >90%	0.67	0.47	0.00	1.00
Farm/HH income >50%	0.14	0.34	0.00	1.00
Commodities	2.57	0.73	2.00	5.00
Intend to expand	0.53	0.50	0.00	1.00

Notes: NMGP denotes Northeast Missouri Grain Processors cooperative

less than four on the seven-point scale) and zero otherwise (i.e., if traditional investments or no further investment is preferred). The mean statistic indicates that the percentage of respondents who support (i.e., prefer) such investments in value-added processing technology varies between 49% for Fonterra and 59% for NMGP.

The only continuous explanatory variable is the number of *Commodities* that respondents produce, which ranges from one to six, as farmers may produce multiple commodities even if they are members of cooperatives that specialize in processing one commodity (e.g., corn-ethanol or milk). The average respondent produces about two or three commodities, depending on the cooperative sample.

The remaining explanatory variables are binary, with values of one and zero indicating affirmative and negative responses, respectively. Some underlying survey items allow selection of ranges in years or percentages and also an option for "I don't know" or "Not applicable." In order to retain the observations for which respondents are unsure or consider the issue not applicable, the following binary coding is adopted. *Relinquish in >5 years* equals one if the respondent is sure it will be more than 5 years before relinquishing control of the farm and zero if it will be sooner or the respondent is unsure. *Lender value >90%* equals one if the lender accepts cooperative equity (i.e., shares) as collateral at more than 90% of its market value and if the respondent doesn't know or doesn't have debt (i.e., it is not an issue) and zero otherwise. *Farm/HH income 50%* reflects whether the respondent relies primarily on the farm for income and equals one if over 50% of the household income is from the farm and zero otherwise. *Intend to expand* equals one if the respondent indicated intention to expand the farm operation over the next 5 years and zero if no expansion is planned.

Mean statistics (Table 2) indicate that, depending on the cooperative sample, about half or a little more of the respondents plan to wait at least 5 years before relinquishing control of the farm (*Relinquish in >5 years*). Between 67 and 77% have lenders who value cooperative equity as collateral at 90% or more of its market value or don't have debt and/or don't know what value a lender would place on cooperative equity (*Lender value >90%*). Between 9 and 22% have over half of their household income coming from the farm (*Farm/HH income >50%*). Over half of respondents intend to expand (*Intend to expand*).

4 Results

4.1 Correlations

Most of the correlations are fairly small (Table 3). The strongest correlations are 0.32 and 0.25 between *Intend to expand* and *Relinquish in >5 years* and *ValueAddedTech*, respectively, for WCC reflecting that at least some members of this cooperative who plan to hold onto the farm for a while also plan to expand

Table 3 Correlations

	(1)	(2)	(3)	(4)	(5)	(6)
Fonterra (N = 902)						
(1) ValueAddedTech	1.000					
(2) Relinquish in >5 years	0.058	1.000				
(3) Lender value >90%	0.043	0.006	1.000			
(4) Farm/HH income >50%	0.006	0.013	−0.016	1.000		
(5) Commodities	−0.083	0.030	0.039	−0.005	1.000	
(6) Intend to expand	0.062	0.105	−0.029	0.059	−0.001	1.000
NMGP (N = 91)						
(1) ValueAddedTech	1.000					
(2) Relinquish in >5 years	−0.209	1.000				
(3) Lender value >90%	0.184	0.014	1.000			
(4) Farm/HH income >50%	−0.047	−0.030	−0.024	1.000		
(5) Commodities	0.118	0.051	−0.028	−0.107	1.000	
(6) Intend to expand	0.161	0.078	0.012	−0.304	0.074	1.000
WCC (N = 155)						
(1) ValueAddedTech	1.000					
(2) Relinquish in >5 years	0.011	1.000				
(3) Lender value >90%	−0.084	−0.104	1.000			
(4) Farm/HH income >50%	−0.149	0.033	0.077	1.000		
(5) Commodities	−0.071	0.008	−0.133	−0.102	1.000	
(6) Intend to expand	0.246	0.316	−0.193	−0.080	0.079	1.000

Notes: NMGP denotes Northeast Missouri Grain Processors cooperative

and some who plan to expand have positive views of the cooperative investing in value-added processing technology. Some members who rely predominately on farm income prefer WCC not make such investments, as indicated by the −0.15 correlation between *ValueAddedTech* and *Farm/HH income >50%*.

The −0.19 correlation between *Intend to expand* and *Lender value >90%* for WCC means that some members who plan to expand have lenders who do not place full market value on their cooperative equity and these members may prefer accelerated redemption of equities if they otherwise had to borrow money to finance the expansion. Notable correlations with *ValueAddedTech* for the NMGP sample include −0.21 with *Relinquish in >5 years*, 0.18 with *Lender value >90%*, and 0.16 with *Intend to expand*. These correlations are consistent with some hypothesized relationships and also appear in regression results, as discussed in the next section. In the Fonterra sample, most correlations are around 0.10 or less, foreshadowing a relatively lower ability of the independent variables to explain the variability in members' investment preferences for this sample.

4.2 Regression Results

Results for probit regressions of the binary dependent variable, *ValueAddedTech*, are reported for each cooperative sample in Table 4. McFadden's (1974) R^2 is low for each sample, particularly for Fonterra. Hoetker (2007) emphasizes that no pseudo-R^2 has the same meaning as R^2 in ordinary least squares regressions (i.e., proportion of variance explained) and, hence, recommends considering the proportion of correct predictions. The model correctly classifies 57, 64, and 64% of the observations on *ValueAddedTech* for the Fonterra, NMGP, and WCC samples, respectively, which exceeds the power of naïve models (e.g., predicting a value of one for every observation) that, as indicated by means of *ValueAddedTech* (Table 1), predict 49, 59, and 57% of observations correctly. Even though the model identifies some significant relationships and outperforms naïve models, relatively low proportions of correct predictions likely reflect that other factors, which may be identified in the future, help to better explain cooperative member investment preferences.

As just noted, several statistically significant marginal effects are detected (Table 4). The marginal effect of 0.058 for *Relinquish in >5 years* indicates that Fonterra members who plan to retain control of their farms for at least the next 5 years are almost 6% more likely to support investment in value-added technology on average, which supports Hypothesis 1a (i.e., *residual* or *short-term* horizon problem). A stronger effect of the opposite sign (−0.27) is observed for NMGP, which is

Table 4 Results for binary probit regression of preference for cooperative investment in value-added technology

	Fonterra	NMGP	WCC
Relinquish in	0.0576_*	-0.2730_{***}	-0.0898
>5 years (binary)	(0.035)	(0.105)	(0.107)
Lender value	0.0571	0.2456_*	-0.0556
>90% (binary)	(0.040)	(0.127)	(0.089)
Farm/HH income	0.0030	0.0166	-0.2050_*
>50% (binary)	(0.058)	(0.136)	(0.118)
Commodities	$-0.0413_{***}(0.016)$	$0.0531(0.043)$	$-0.0818(0.057)$
Intend to expand (binary)	$0.0613_*(0.036)$	$0.1878_*(0.112)$	$0.2609_{***}(0.083)$
N	902	91	155
McFadden's R^2	0.012	0.100	0.071
Percentage correctly classified:			
$Y = 1$	50%	74%	73%
$Y = 0$	63%	49%	52%
Overall	57%	64%	64%

Notes: $_{***}$, $_{**}$, and $_*$ denote statistical significance at 1, 5, and 10% levels, respectively. Standard errors are in parentheses. NMGP denotes Northeast Missouri Grain Processors cooperative

consistent with Hypothesis 1b (i.e., the *return of capital or wait-to-receive* horizon problem).

Support for Hypothesis 2 (i.e., the *current obligation* horizon problem) is also obtained, as evidenced by the significant effect of *Lender value >90%* in the NMGP sample. Specifically, if a lender values cooperative equity at 90% of market value or more, then that member is 25% more likely to support the investment on average. In other words, a cooperative member is more likely to support further investment in the cooperative if the member can use that equity as collateral against a loan.

Evidence of portfolio problems is also apparent (Table 4). Hypothesis 3 (i.e., the *classical lateral* portfolio problem) is supported by the statistically significant effect of *Commodities* in the Fonterra sample, which indicates that producing an additional commodity decreases the probability of support for investments in value-added technology by 4% on average. That is, producers specializing in milk production are more likely than diversified farmers to support such investments by Fonterra, given that it would enhance the value of only milk production.

Hypothesis 4a (i.e., *vertical* portfolio problem) is supported by the significant effect of *Intend to expand* in all three samples, which indicates that anticipated expansion of production in the next 5 years increases the probability of supporting such investments by 6, 19, and 26% in Fonterra, NMGP, and WCC samples, respectively. This result is also consistent with the generally greater membership and patronage of cooperatives by larger producers (Wadsworth 1991). Though the vertical portfolio problem seems particularly likely to occur in specialized cooperatives, the effect is surprisingly strongest for the multipurpose WCC. Given these results, no support is found for the negative relationship proposed in Hypothesis 4b (i.e., the argument that divergent investment preferences could arise if cooperative-level ROI exceeds that of small but not large farmers). Perhaps the vertical portfolio problem overwhelms any differences in on-farm ROI stemming from scale economies, or the anticipated ROI of the proposed investments by these cooperatives exceeds ROI on both large and small farms. Of course, intentions to expand do not necessarily imply that the farm is currently small or large either, so this variable may be an imperfect indicator of the validity of Hypothesis 4b. *Farm/HH income >50%* is included to control for whether the household relies primarily on farm income, and its marginal effect indicates that households with primarily non-farm income are 21% more likely to support cooperative investments. This effect could be interpreted as support for Hypothesis 4b if small farms also have primarily non-farm income, or it may simply reflect that the farm is a small enough portion of household income that the cooperatives' investments are of little concern to the household.

5   Conclusions

Though horizon and portfolio problems are commonly thought to limit cooperatives' ability to capitalize on investment opportunities (Cook 1995; Iliopoulos 1998; Peterson 1992; Porter and Scully 1987; Staatz 1987; Vitaliano 1985), empirical inquiry into the existence of these constraints is sparse (Fahlbeck 2007; Iliopoulos 1998), and conceptual arguments suggest that the horizon problem in particular may be less severe than commonly believed (Olesen 2007). Using surveys of members of three cooperatives, this study investigates the extent to which indicators of potential horizon and portfolio problems influence member preferences for investment in value-added processing technology.

The evidence points to the existence of two types of portfolio problems and three types of horizon problems influencing cooperative members' investment preferences. All three cooperatives show evidence of the *vertical portfolio problem*, as members' support of investments in commodity-specific, value-added processing technology tends to increase if members plan to increase production of that commodity. Fonterra Co-op Group, a member-investor dairy cooperative in New Zealand, also shows strong evidence of the *classical (lateral) portfolio problem*, as its members' opposition to such investments increases with the number of commodities the member produces.

Some evidence of the *current obligation* horizon problem is found for Northeast Missouri Grain Processors, as members who have lenders who take cooperative equity at or near its market value as collateral against loans (i.e., current debt obligations) are more likely to support cooperative investments. There is also some evidence of the classic *residual* or *short-term* horizon problem for Fonterra Co-op Group, as members further from retirement are more likely than those nearing retirement to support cooperative investments in processing technology, since it may not be recovered before impending retirements. Strong support exists for the *return of capital* or *wait-to-receive* horizon problem for Northeast Missouri Grain Processors, a corn-ethanol new generation cooperative, as members near retirement are significantly more likely to support cooperative investments in processing technology, since it likely will increase the value of their tradable shares.

The divergent results regarding impacts of members' nearness to retirement may reflect differences in equity redemption policies for the two cooperatives at the time of our survey. Fonterra would buy back delivery right shares at book value from members scaling back production or ceasing to patronize the cooperative, and equity was redeemable from the cooperative immediately upon a member's exit. In contrast, since Northeast Missouri Grain Processors redeemed equities on a traditional revolving basis, the only way its members could extract the value of their tradable delivery right shares was through use (i.e., patronage) or sale to another corn producer. That is, the return of capital seems to have been higher for Fonterra than Northeast Missouri Grain Processors, even if the return on capital for these two cooperatives may have been similar. The nonzero effect of members' nearness to retirement in each cooperative is consistent with the general hypothesis that heterogeneity of members' characteristics influences their investment preferences. Changes at both businesses (e.g., Fonterra capping redemption at 5% of total equity and later adopting tradable shares and Northeast Missouri Grain Processors transitioning to a limited-liability company to facilitate outside investment) were responses to the frictions created by these horizon problems (Cook 2018).

Lastly, although the reported regression models provide statistically significant evidence of the above-described effects, they account for only small amounts of the variation in investment preferences, suggesting opportunities for future work to delve deeper into determinants of cooperative members' investment preferences.

References

Alho E (2016) Survey evidence of members' willingness to invest in agricultural hybrid cooperatives. J Chain Net Sci 16(1):41–58

Barham BL, Chavas J-P, Fitz D, Salas VR, Schechter L (2014) The roles of risk and ambiguity in technology adoption. J Econ Behav Organ 97:204–218

Bijman J, Pope KJ, Cook ML, Iliopoulos C (2012) Support for farmers' cooperatives; case study report Cebeco. Wageningen UR, Wageningen

Bonin JP, Jones DC, Putterman L (1993) Theoretical and empirical studies of producer cooperatives: will ever the twain meet? J Econ Lit 31:1290–1290

Cadot J, Ugaglia AA, Bonnefous B, Del'homme B (2015) The horizon problem in Bordeaux wine cooperatives. Int J Entrep Small Bus 29(4):651–668

Caves RE, Petersen BC (1986) Cooperatives' tax "advantages": Growth, retained earnings, and equity rotation. Am J Agric Econ 68:207–213

Chaddad FR, Cook ML (2002) An ownership rights typology of cooperative models. Department of Agricultural Economics working paper: 2002–2006

Chaddad FR, Cook ML, Heckelei T (2005) Testing for the presence of financial constraints in US agricultural cooperatives: an investment behaviour approach. J Agric Econ 56:385–397

Coase R (1998) The new institutional economics. Am Econ Rev 88(2):72–74

Cobia DW (1989) Cooperatives in agriculture. Prentice Hall, New Jersey

Condon AM (1990) Property rights and the investment behavior of US agricultural cooperatives. Virginia Polytechnic Institute and State University, Virginia

Cook ML (1995) The future of US agricultural cooperatives: a neo-institutional approach. Am J Agric Econ 77:1153–1159

Cook ML (2018) A life cycle explanation of cooperative longevity. Sustainability 10(5):1586

Cook ML, Iliopoulos C (1998) Solutions to property rights constraints in producer-owned and controlled organizations: prerequisite for agri-chain leadership? In: Ziggers G, Trienekens J, Zuurbier P (eds) Proceedings of the third international conference on chain management in agribusiness and the food industry held in Ede, The Netherlands, 28–29 May 1998, pp 541–553

Cook ML, Iliopoulos C (2000) Ill-defined property rights in collective action: the case of US agricultural cooperatives. In: Menard C (ed) Institutions, contracts and organizations. Edward Elgar, London, pp 335–348

Cook ML, Iliopoulos C (2016) Generic solutions to coordination and organizational costs: informing cooperative longevity. J Chain Net Sci 16(1):19–27

Cook ML, James H (2016) Cooperatives. In: Kolb RW (ed) Encyclopedia of business ethics and society, 2/e. Sage, Thousand Oaks, CA

Ellerman DP (1986) Horizon problems and property rights in labor-managed firms. J Comp Econ 10:62–78

Fahlbeck E (2007) The horizon problem in agricultural cooperatives–only in theory? In: Karantininis K, Nilsson J (eds) Vertical markets and cooperative hierarchies. Springer, Dordrecht, pp 255–274

Feng L, Hendrikse GWJ (2012) Chain interdependencies, measurement problems and efficient governance structure: cooperatives versus publicly listed firms. Eur Rev Agric Econ 39:241–255

Fulton M, Giannakas K (2012) The value of a norm: open membership and the horizon problem in cooperatives. Special issue: cooperative values in internationalized operations. J Rural Coop 40:145–161

Furubotn EG, Pejovich S (1972) Property rights and economic theory: a survey of recent literature. J Econ Lit 10:1137–1162

Ginder RG (1999) Who will retire member's equity? Working paper, Department of Economics. Iowa State University, Ames, IA

Gittinger JP (1972) Economic analysis of agricultural projects. John Hopkins University Press for the World Bank, Baltimore

Hendrikse GW, Veerman CP (2001) Marketing cooperatives and financial structure: a transaction costs economics analysis. Agric Econ 26:205–216

Hoetker G (2007) The use of logit and probit models in strategic management research: critical issues. Strateg Manag J 28:331–343

Höhler J, Kühl R (2018) Dimensions of member heterogeneity in cooperatives and their impact on organization – a literature review. Ann Publ Cooper Econ 89(4):697–712

Iliopoulos C (1998) A study of the property rights constraints in US agricultural cooperatives: theory and evidence. Dissertation, University of Missouri-Columbia

Iliopoulos C, Cook ML (1999) The efficiency of internal resource allocation decisions in customer-owned firms: the influence costs problem. In: 3rd annual conference of the International Society for New Institutional Economics. Citeseer, Washington, DC, pp 16–18

Jensen M, Meckling W (1979) Rights and production functions: an application to labor managed firms and codetermination. J Bus (4):496–506

Just RE, Zilberman D, Rausser GC, Yaron D, Tapiero C (1980) A putty-clay approach to the distributional effects of new technology under risk. In: Yaron D, Tapiero C (eds) Operations research in agriculture and water resources. North-Holland, Amsterdam, pp 97–121

Khanna M (2001) Sequential adoption of site-specific technologies and its implications for nitrogen productivity: a double selectivity model. Am J Agric Econ 83:35–51

King R (2012) The science of design. Am J Agric Econ 94(2):275–284

King R, Boehlje M, Cook ML, Sonka ST (2010) Agribusiness economics and management. Am J Agric Econ 92(2):554–570

Knoeber CR, Baumer DL (1983) Understanding retained patronage refunds in agricultural cooperatives. Am J Agric Econ 65:30–37

Krumpleman-Farmer EL (2005) The investment horizon issue in user-owned organizations. Dissertation, University of Missouri

Landus Cooperative (2015) Members approve merger of farmers cooperative company and west central cooperative. http://www.landuscooperative.com/news_release/members-approve-merger-of-farmers-cooperative-company-and-west-central-cooperative/. Accessed 29 May 2019

LeVay C (1983) Agricultural Co-operative theory: a review. J Agric Econ 34:1–44

McFadden D (1974) Conditional logit analysis of qualitative choice behavior. In: Zarembka P (ed) Frontiers in econometrics. Academic, New York, pp 105–142

Murray G (1983) Management strategies for corporate control in British agricultural co-operatives—Part 1. Agric Adm 14:51–63

Nilsson J (1999) Cooperative organizational models as reflections of the business environments. Finnish J Bus Econ 4:449–470

Nilsson J (2001) Organisational principles for co-operative firms. Scand J Manag 17:329–356

Olesen HB (2007) The horizon problem reconsidered. In: Karantininis K, Nilsson J (eds) Vertical markets and cooperative hierarchies. Springer, Dordrecht, The Netherlands, pp 245–253

Parliament C, Lerman Z (1993) Risk and equity in agricultural cooperatives. J Agric Coop 8:1–14

Peterson HC (1992) The economic role and limitations of cooperatives: an investment cash flow derivation. J Agric Coop 7:61–78

Plunkett B (2005) The portfolio problem in agricultural cooperatives: an integrated framework. Dissertation, University of Missouri

Plunkett B, Chaddad FR, Cook ML (2010) Ownership structure and incentives to invest: dual structured irrigation cooperatives in Australia. J Inst Econ 6(2):261–280

Porter PK, Scully GW (1987) Economic efficiency in cooperatives. J Law Econ 30:489–512

Retka Schill S (2013) Missouri's first ethanol plant has a rich history. Ethanol Producer Magazine July. www.ethanolproducer.com/issues. Accessed June 18, 2019.

Staatz JM (1987) The structural characteristics of farmer cooperatives and their behavioral consequences. In: Royer JS (ed) Cooperative theory: new approaches. USDA. Agricultural Cooperative Services, Washington, DC, pp 33–60

Van Wassenaer APW (1989) An optimal ownership structure for cooperatives. Thesis, Harvard University

Vitaliano P (1983) Cooperative enterprise: an alternative conceptual basis for analyzing a complex institution. Am J Agric Econ 65:1078–1083

Vitaliano PW (1985) Potential benefits and costs to agricultural cooperatives from assuring access to input and product markets. In: Farmer cooperatives for the future, proceedings of the workshop farmer cooperatives for the future, Saint Louis, Missouri, pp 64–74

Wadsworth JJ (1991) An analysis of major farm characteristics and farmers' use of cooperatives. J Agric Coop 6:45–53

Member Heterogeneity and Exit

Julia Höhler

Abstract Members of cooperatives are becoming increasingly diverse and hetero-geneous. Scholars have argued that this is problematic for cooperatives. Therefore, one might expect that many members leave the cooperative. However, this conclusion does not fit with the reality in which cooperatives continue to exist. Based on the work of Hirschman as well as different theories of collective action, fairness, and identity, a theoretical framework is developed to account for this observation. The identified factors provide starting points for cooperatives to retain their members even with increasing heterogeneity.

1 Member Heterogeneity in Practice and Theory

Cooperatives in many sectors around the world are growing and diversifying. This development is associated with an increasing heterogeneity and diversity within the membership in terms of, for example, firm, personal, or product characteristics of the members. Greater heterogeneity has often been described in the literature as a disadvantage for cooperatives, with researchers assuming that it may have negative effects on member commitment, willingness to invest, or decision-making processes (Hansmann 2000; Höhler and Kühl 2018; Iliopoulos and Valentinov 2018; Elliott et al. 2018). Most of this research assumes that members act in their own interest and, as homines economici, only have an interest in their own payoffs. If member heterogeneity really was such a disadvantage, would not most members leave their cooperatives sooner or later? But can this actually be observed in reality? Consider two cooperatives.

First, Deutsches Milchkontor (DMK) is Germany's largest dairy cooperative. It was created in 2010 by the merger of two dairy cooperatives and has 6900

J. Höhler (✉)
Institute of Farm and Agribusiness Management, Justus Liebig University Giessen, Giessen, Germany
e-mail: julia.hoehler@agrar.uni-giessen.de

© Springer Nature Switzerland AG 2019   197
J. Windsperger et al. (eds.), *Design and Management of Interfirm Networks*,
Contributions to Management Science,
https://doi.org/10.1007/978-3-030-29245-4_11

active members (DMK 2018). Group sales in 2017 amounted to 5.8 billion euros. Germany is the most important sales market, accounting for approximately 56.1% of sales. Further sales are generated in the EU and in third countries (DMK 2018). Member heterogeneity has increased in recent years. For example, in 2016, DMK merged with DOC Kaas, the second-largest cheese manufacturer in the Netherlands. Heterogeneity has increased due to this merger because the current membership consists of members of two countries, while there were only members from one country before the merger. It is also increasing because farm sizes differ more and more as a result of structural change. In addition, DMK (2017) has implemented a mandatory sustainability program. Depending on the measures implemented, individual members receive a bonus payment. Heterogeneity increases as members receive different payout prices. Second, Arla is the world's seventh-largest dairy company in terms of turnover (Rabobank 2018). Arla Foods was created in 2000 by the merger of Denmark's largest dairy cooperative (MD Foods) with the Swedish dairy Arla Mejeriförening (Arla 2019b). It has 11,319 members in seven countries (Arla 2019a). Group sales amounted to 10.3 million euros in 2017 (Arla 2019a). Europe accounts for 62% of the total sales (Arla 2019a). Arla (2018) emphasizes their concept of "ONE milk price," which includes that each farmer in their seven member countries receives the same milk price. However, the cooperative offers different milk varieties in different markets: conventional, non-GMO, pasture fed, and organic milk. These varieties are inevitably connected with different production systems and cost structures of the farmers.

Despite the increasing heterogeneity, most members remain in their cooperative. It could have been transaction or switching costs that kept the members from leaving the cooperative. Switching causes costs due to the search for information and the completion of a new contract. However, it could also be that the previous explanations do not suffice to describe the influence of member heterogeneity on the cooperative. The two most commonly mentioned dimensions of member heterogeneity according to the literature review by Höhler and Kühl (2018) are firm size and product type. But just because a new member enters the cooperative with a new product does not necessarily mean that anything changes for the existing members. Likewise, the growth of some large businesses does not necessarily mean that smaller businesses behave differently. Members could still have the same economic interests (Poteete and Ostrom 2004). Even if they had different economic interests, would that inevitably have an impact on the cooperative? The above examples illustrate that the answer is not as clear as previously assumed.

If something for the members changed with increasing heterogeneity, what would it be? Increases in decision-making, control, and influencing costs are often mentioned in the existing literature. It is also believed that less confidence, less commitment, less willingness to invest, and worse decisions result (Höhler and Kühl 2018). However, these developments cannot result directly from member heterogeneity: just because other members differ, the willingness to invest must not decrease; the trust must not decrease. The examples suggest that this may even be the case if one assumes that member heterogeneity occurs simultaneously with different payout prices for members. From the point of view of an individual member, there must be reasons why the additional heterogeneity, while possibly even leading to a deterioration of one's own position, nevertheless does not lead to changes in his or her behavior. In order to understand what these reasons might be and to explain the puzzling observations, factors influencing member behavior in general must be taken into account. The goal of this paper is to create a theoretical link between member heterogeneity and member exit.

Hirschman's well-known *Exit, Voice, and Loyalty* (1970) provides an important starting point for the investigation of member behavior, although member heterogeneity comes into his reflections only marginally. Hirschman claims that not every member speaks out when firm performance deteriorates. In addition, he assumes that the members differ in when they choose the "exit" option. In his review of Hirschman's work, Barry (1974) criticizes that the logic of collective action is not sufficiently taken into account. In particular, he means situations in which individual members use "voice" without the resulting costs being covered by their individual benefits. With member heterogeneity, however, it can also happen that the performance does not deteriorate for everyone equally. It remains unclear how this heterogeneity affects the members' behavior and the organization. Moreover, Barry (1974: 95) considers loyalty as an "equation filler" which Hirschman introduces to fit the facts retrospectively. Dowding et al. (2000) take up this statement and assume that group loyalty depends on the identification with a group. This identification makes the exit painful and costly. Similarly, Simon (1991) suggests that the identification with an organization can create additional utility and explain motivation beyond the usual neoclassical explanations.

The extension of Hirschman's approach to the aspects of member heterogeneity in cooperatives, possible performance differences for individual members, collective action, and identity seems promising to discuss the impact of heterogeneity on individual behavior and the organization. The central question is as follows: How does member heterogeneity affect exit of members? In order to contribute to answering this question, the second section illustrates the different theoretical concepts and connections with member heterogeneity in cooperatives. Various influencing factors that determine the relationship between member heterogeneity and exit are identified. In section three, the concepts get combined into a theoretical framework, which is subsequently associated with the two cases. Finally, the results are discussed and a research agenda for cooperative research is developed.

2 Hypotheses

This section describes different approaches to explaining member behavior. These approaches are used to derive hypotheses on the factors influencing the exit of members.

2.1 Exit, Voice, and Loyalty in Cooperatives

In *Exit, Voice, and Loyalty,* Hirschman describes the responses of consumers and members to deteriorating performance in organizations. Previous literature on member heterogeneity suggests that one might expect members to choose the "exit" option when heterogeneity increases and conditions deteriorate. Another possibility is to choose "voice," expressing complaints or requesting changes to achieve improvement. "Loyalty" affects how members behave in the face of these two options: it may cause members to postpone their exit and/or strengthen their voice (Hirschman 1970). In a similar vein, Fulton (1999) uses the concept of member commitment. He assumes that the members prefer to do business with their cooperative rather than with an IOF. The strength of their preferences determines how members behave in the event of deteriorating prices.

Hirschman (1970) discusses several determinants of the decision against "exit." One of them is the question of how efficient a member views the prospects for using his voice. Another important factor is the prospect that the company will recover. In addition, the feeling and the will to exert influence also play a role. Alternatively to the use of one's own voice, one can expect other members to use their "voice." The decision will also be linked to previous experience with the cost and effectiveness of "voice." The likelihood that members use their voice increases with loyalty. At the same time, loyalty opens up the possibility of threatening to exit. In addition, the switching costs and the availability of and the substitutability with alternatives are important determinants. With "unconscious" loyalist behavior, Hirschman (1970) describes the situation that a member does not notice the deterioration and accordingly does not use his voice.

In contrast, the decision to leave the company is linked to losses through the abandonment of loyalty discounts and search costs for information about substitutes. The exercise of "voice," however, also costs time and money. Hirschman (1970: 40) concludes that "in comparison to the exit option, voice is costly and conditioned on the influence and bargaining power [. . .] members can bring to bear within the firm." In the case of a public good, he describes that a member compares "disutility, discomfort, and shame of remaining a member" with "damage as a prospective non-member and the society at large" (Hirschman 1970: 103) by resigning.

Based on Hirschman's considerations, the following hypotheses are formulated:

H1 The higher the perceived deterioration in performance, the more likely is an exit.

H2 A decrease in the prospect of improving one's own conditions increases the likelihood of exit.

H3 The lower the possibility to use the voice, the more likely is an exit.

H4 The lower the willingness to use voice or the trust in other members using voice, the more likely is an exit.

H5 The higher the expected effectiveness of the use of voice, the less likely is an exit.

H6 The lower the loyalty, the more likely is an exit.

H7 The higher the number and quality of the alternatives for the members, the more likely is an exit.

2.2 Identity

As mentioned earlier, Hirschman's concept of loyalty is criticized as being rather arbitrary. One possible approach to depicting loyalty is the concept of identity. People identify with some groups and differentiate themselves from other groups. Different identities can explain differences in behavior (Simon 1991). Turner (1975: 8) refers to social identity as the membership in a group that is related to a "positive evaluation of its attributes in comparison with other groups." Akerlof and Kranton (2000, 2005) define identity as a person's sense of self as well as the person's social category. According to Shayo (2009), members identify with a group when they care about their status and want to be like members of the group. All these definitions indicate that identities could influence the behavior of members.

Akerlof and Kranton (2005) model the utility of a worker as a function of income *y*, effort *e*, social category *c*, utility from identity I_c, and disutility from diverging from the ideal effort level $e*(c)$ for her assigned category:

$$U\,(y, e; c) = \ln y - e + I_c - t_c \mid e^*(c) - e \mid \tag{1}$$

If a worker identifies with the firm, she is an insider and does the high-effort action. If she is an outsider she will lose utility if she deviates from the low-effort action. This equation takes into account the importance of social categories as well as norms and ideals.

In an earlier paper, Akerlof and Kranton (2000) assume that the utility also depends on other players' actions and their matching with the norms of their assigned social category. These norms relate to specific situations and can change over time. They also state that there exist many identities within the population and that different activities have different meanings for individuals. Depending on the situation, one of these identities determines the actions of a person (Shayo 2009). People will look for those individuals who have the same identity or who attribute the same meaning to certain actions. Members of a group are prepared to forego part of their payoff to improve group status (Shayo 2009). Moreover, identity is assumed to influence the way people process information (Baumeister and Leary 1995).

The concept of identity can also be applied to cooperatives. We assume that it is possible that members identify with the cooperative and gain additional utility through their membership. This utility can also compensate for a loss of performance. However, it is also conceivable that the members would rather identify themselves with another group (e.g., a professional association or a production method) and judge the behavior of the cooperative from their point of view. If one member identifies strongly with the cooperative, then she is less likely to join another cooperative. It is possible that there exist different groups and identities within the cooperative. This leads to the following identity-based hypotheses about member behavior:

H8 The lower the identification of a member with the cooperative and the higher the identification with other (sub-)groups, the more likely is an exit.

H9 The higher the identification of a member with the cooperative, the higher is her loyalty.

2.3   Fairness Perceptions

We assume that membership heterogeneity can also result in the fact that the performance does not change in the same way for individual members. An example would be a cooperative offering different products and investing specifically in the warehousing of one product. Another possibility would be the (majority-favored) investment in branding, which will only affect the payout prices in the future and will therefore not benefit every member. The approaches to identity give an indication that a member's reaction could depend on her own identity and the identity of the other members. Different types of members could, in Hirschman's sense, respond differently to inequality. Depending on the type of identity they have, they may have different answers as well as perceptions of this inequality. On the one hand, the comparison with the outcomes of the other members may be relevant for their behavior; on the other hand, the process of decision-making could play a role for their perception of fairness.

As Fehr and Schmidt (1999) point out, in addition to selfish subjects, there are subjects who "are willing to give up some material payoff to move in the direction of more equitable outcomes" (Fehr, Schmidt 1999: 819). Their reference group and the reference outcome for this kind of relative comparison depend on various contextual factors. With n players i ($i \in \{1, \ldots, n\}$) and payoffs $x = x_1, \ldots x_n$, the utility function for i is:

$$U_i(x) = x_i - \alpha_i \frac{1}{n-1} \sum_{j \neq i} \max\{x_j - x_i, 0\} - \beta_i \frac{1}{n-1} \sum_{j \neq i} \max\{x_i - x_j, 0\}$$

$$(2)$$

The coefficients α and β are weighting factors for disadvantageous and advantageous equality. Included in the utility function are thus also the respective advantages or disadvantages compared to other players. Figure 1 shows the utility curve for a given payoff x_i and different payouts for a member j. With increasing

Fig. 1 Preferences with inequity aversion according to Fehr and Schmidt (1999)

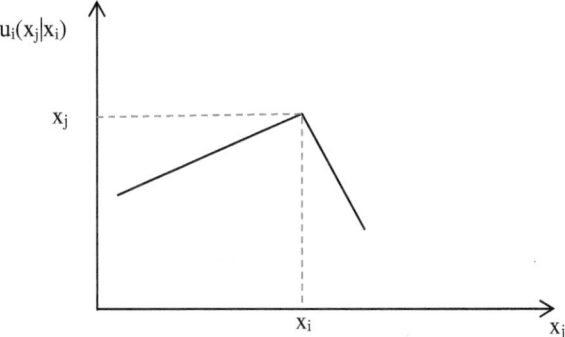

deviation from the own payoff, the utility decreases. This is more pronounced if the other member receives a higher payoff.

With an application to cooperation games, Fehr and Schmidt show how their approach can explain voluntary cooperation. If punishment is possible and certain players are sufficiently upset by inequality to their disadvantage, then they are willing to bear the cost of punishment. This may lead to a credible threat of punishment and can cause potential defectors to cooperate. Similarly, members could respond to inequalities in the distribution of benefits within the cooperative or inequalities compared to reference groups outside. Fehr and Schmidt (1999) show that there is an equilibrium outcome in this case. We assume that the heterogeneity of a cooperative's members may be reflected in different payoffs to the different members. As a result, they may benefit differently from the cooperative's invest-ments. Those members who perceive themselves as disadvantaged are therefore prepared to act to reduce inequality. At the same time, the model could explain why those who are better off might be willing to financially accommodate the worse off members.

What this theory suggests is that in addition to the level of the outcome itself, the perceived fairness of the outcome compared to the outcome of others plays an important role (see also Tyler and Blader 2000). Besides the outcomes, the inputs of the members can also be part of their fairness perception. In this case, fairness is assessed on the basis of the outcome-input relationship (Adams 1965). The equity theory states that individuals will compare their own outcome-input relationship with that of others, whether in a direct exchange between two persons or between two persons and a third party. In the following, no distinction between equity and equality is made. It is assumed that the overarching construct of distributive justice plays a role in the behavior of members:

H10 The lower the perceived distributive fairness, the more likely is an exit.

We further assume that members might accept the outcome of democratic decisions that are to their disadvantage simply because they see the decision-making process as fair. This behavior could be explained by the concept of procedural justice (Tyler and Blader 2000, 2003). It turns out that "voice" also plays a role here. The mere existence of the possibility of voice can help someone to perceive a procedure as fairer. The perception of procedural justice also depends on whether the person feels treated with respect (Tyler and Blader 2003). Tyler and Blader (2003) name four components of procedural justice in their group engagement model: formal quality (e.g., rules, statutes) and informal quality of decision-making processes as well as the formal and informal quality of treatment. We therefore assume that the following variable also influences the behavior of the members:

H11 The lower the perceived fairness of the decision-making procedure, the more likely is an exit.

2.4 Rational Egoists, Conditional Cooperators, and Willing Punishers

Barry (1974) criticizes Hirschman's (1970) approach for not appreciating the logic of collective action. To address this weakness, Ostrom's (2000) different types of players can be used. Her approach also provides a rationale for why members use the "voice" option.

Participants behave differently in public good experiments. Ostrom (2000) uses this result of various experiments to justify her theory of collective action. Since the assumption of the "rational egoist" alone cannot explain the results of this kind of experiments, she adds two more player types. The first type of player is the "conditional cooperator." Conditional cooperators are willing to cooperate, as long as they expect that enough other players cooperate. Their presence can also cause rational egoists to contribute more. Some of the conditional cooperators will be disappointed when other players start free riding. Then they spend less. Communication can counteract this. The second type of player is the "willing punisher." This kind of player is willing to punish free riders, even if it costs money. Willing punishers can also become willing rewarders, depending on the relationships. Through the interaction of both types of players, collective action becomes possible.

Although many cooperatives do not manage public goods or common-pool resources, as described by Ostrom and studied in the underlying experiments, the results may be transferable. If a cooperative has an open membership policy, it cannot deny access to any potential member (non-excludability). Similarly, members cannot be excluded from benefiting from certain investments. At the same time, not all members may equally contribute to an investment or benefit equally from an investment (rivalry). Thus, the situation is similar to the management of a common-pool resource. Leviten-Reid and Fairbairn (2011) argue that members are actors with different interests who work together and decide how to manage resources or assets for the group as a whole. Thus, it is also important for a cooperative with different types of players being present among the members. The relationship between the types of players and member behavior is described in the following hypothesis:

H12 The higher the expected proportion of rational egoists in the membership, the more likely is an exit.

Ostrom shows how different types of players contribute to achieving collective action. At the same time, however, she does not discuss the interactions of heterogeneity with member behavior as well as the possible reactions to deteriorating performance (exit, voice, and loyalty). Neither Hirschman nor Ostrom explicitly include these performance differences.[1] The different types of players of Ostrom (2000) are associated with different standards (or norms) of fairness and reciprocity. The role of the conditional cooperator may be linked to certain preferences for fairness and equal outcomes (see also Fischbacher et al. 2001). Likewise, the willing punisher may be motivated by wanting to create fair outcomes or punish unfair acts (Fehr and Fischbacher 2004).

So far, it has mainly been argued that heterogeneity is increasing with the addition of new members. However, members also leave the cooperative (Hendrikse 2011; Hakelius et al. 2013). What has received less attention is that the withdrawals also have an impact on heterogeneity. Therefore, it might be interesting to think about which members choose the different options mentioned by Hirschman and how this is related to heterogeneity and performance. From a production point of view, the firm size of the exiting members certainly plays a role in determining the impact on performance. For the long-term functioning of the cooperative in terms of member commitment, willingness to invest, and decision-making processes or, in short, collective action, it could be more crucial how different types of members behave. More specifically, it is of interest and importance to the cooperative how conditional cooperator, willing punisher, and rational egoist behave in terms of exit, voice, and loyalty. As the fairness theories show, this probably also depends on perceived fairness. In addition, identity could affect member behavior. In the following, the different approaches and the identified factors are connected with each other.

It can be assumed that the rational egoists, i.e., purely selfish players, will be the first type of player to leave the cooperative if performance deteriorates. However, rational egoists will not leave the cooperative if only the payoffs of other members change, not their own. Their utility function is neither affected by the payoffs to other members nor by identity. In addition, the purely selfish player is not interested in distributive or procedural justice. Compared to the other member types, their decision is likely to be less determined by the availability and design of the voice option as voice is costly. However, their behavior may depend on the alternatives available (see H7).

---

[1]Ostrom bases her ideas on observations from public good experiments. Although there are different levels of contributions from the members, the payoff is evenly divided among them.

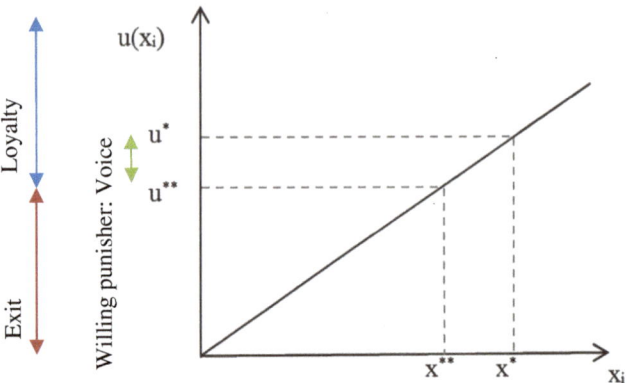

Fig. 2 Preferences for different payoffs

With deteriorating performance, it is assumed that the conditional cooperators and willing punishers stay longer in the cooperative compared to the rational egoists. They do so as long as deterioration is not too high and they do so taking into account the payoffs to other members (see H1 and H10).

Their utility can be represented through two different utility functions. Figure 2 shows different levels of utility depending on the payoff. For the sake of simplicity, we assume a linear utility function. The higher the payoff a member receives, the higher the utility level. If the utility level drops to a level between u^* and u^{**}, voice is used. If the level is above u^{**}, the members are loyal. If it falls below u^{**}, they exit the cooperative. The limits within the function also depend on how well voice is available and how the opportunities for improvement are assessed by the use of voice (see H2–H5). The level of the lower limit (u^{**}) also depends on the loyalty of the member (see H6) as well as on the outside options (see H7). The behavior of willing punishers will depend in particular on the availability and design of the voice option as well as on the perceived (un)fairness (see H10 and H11). A punishment is only possible if the willing punisher has the opportunity to exercise it. Voice is associated with costs that the willing punisher is willing to bear. In addition, the behavior of this group of players will depend on how they assess the proportion of rational egoists in the group (see H12).

In addition to the overall payoff, the performance differences also play a role for these players. If a player's payoff changes, then the distance to the other players may change as well. Figure 3 shows this second utility function for a given payoff x_i and different payoffs for member j (x_j). The more the own payoff differs from the payoff to member j, the lower the utility level. If member j receives á higher payoff than member i, the utility of i decreases more than in the opposite case. Again, we

Fig. 3 Preferences for
performance differences

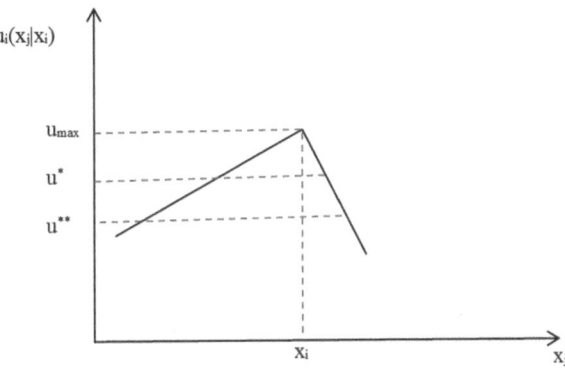

assume that certain utility thresholds exist. If the benefit lies between u^* and u^{**}, voice is used. If the value is below u^{**}, then the member exits.

We assume that identity is reflected in the assessment of fairness (see H6, H8, and H9). On the one hand, identity can influence who serves as a reference group—all the other members of the cooperative, parts of the other members, or possibly the members of another cooperative. On the other hand, an influence of identity on the utility curve's slope is conceivable. Depending on the strength of the identity, differences to other members are weighted more or less. As a result, identity also changes behavior (voice and exit). If an individual suffers a loss of utility due to identity, then it can cause him to encounter this either through voice or exit (see also Tajfel and Turner 2001).

Not only the avoidance of inequality but also the desire for conformity can cause a deviation from selfish behavior (Shayo 2009). If the member does not identify with the cooperative, then she behaves like a rational egoist. Identity also determines what alternatives members are considering as exit options. We can assume that members that identify less with the cooperative will be the first to leave. This would leave the cooperative less heterogeneous. Dowding et al. (2000) assume that the decision to exit also influences future identity. At the same time, the use of voice can increase someone's own identification with the organization.

Overall, we can distinguish four effects which determine the course and limits of the utility functions for this group of players: the pure payoff effect (Fig. 2), the fairness effect (Fig. 3), the voice effect, and an identity effect (Figs. 2 and 3). The payoff effect partly determines the utility of the members. The higher the payment, the higher their utility. Depending on their level of utility, they are loyal; they use their voice or exit. The fairness effect states that a member's utility also depends on the payoff to other members. The more different these payoffs are, the lower their utility. Here, too, the level of utility determines behavior. The voice effect describes how well voice is available and thus determines in which utility range members use voice. The identity effect determines with which members a member compares his payoffs when assessing fairness. Depending on how these effects turn out, individual members will show different behaviors.

How do the exit of rational egoists and the voice of willing punishers affect the cooperative? We can assume that the conditional cooperators and willing punishers know that the rational egoists and the members with a low identification at first step out. Therefore, they would now be more willing to cooperate and to use their voice. Their identity and the stability of the cooperative could be increased. Some research supports our framework. In their public good games, Chaudhuri and Paichayontvijit (2006) come to the same conclusions as previous studies: the majority of their participants (students) are conditional cooperators. By providing information about the presence of other conditional cooperators in the group, the participant's contributions increased. If the rational egoists really leave the cooperative first, it means that the other participants get more information about the presence of other conditional cooperators in the cooperative. Overall, a short-term worsening of conditions could in the long term lead to an improvement in collective action. The use of exit by some members may leave the remaining members better off (Barry 1974).

Orbell et al. (1984) allow the possibility of "exit" in a prisoner's dilemma game. They also quote Hirschman, but they do not take into account the concept of "loyalty" and different perceptions of fairness. This might be the reason why they assume that cooperators leave the group sooner than defectors. Furthermore, Hirschman's assumption that performance is declining is not fully reflected in the structure of the experiment. The payout schemes are the same for all participants. According to their diverging results, Orbell et al. (1984) revise their assumptions and add that cooperators might be more optimistic about the number of cooperators. In addition, they hypothesize that a concern for the welfare of the group motivates the cooperators' behavior.

2.5   Theoretical Framework

The presentation and discussion of the four approaches has shown various factors that can influence the behavior of the members and that can explain their motivation to stay or go. Figure 4 shows our hypotheses, the factors influencing the likelihood of exit, and the assignment of hypotheses to the sections concerning Hirschman, identity, Ostrom, and fairness perceptions. In the following we discuss several of the hypotheses using the example of the two cases from the introduction.

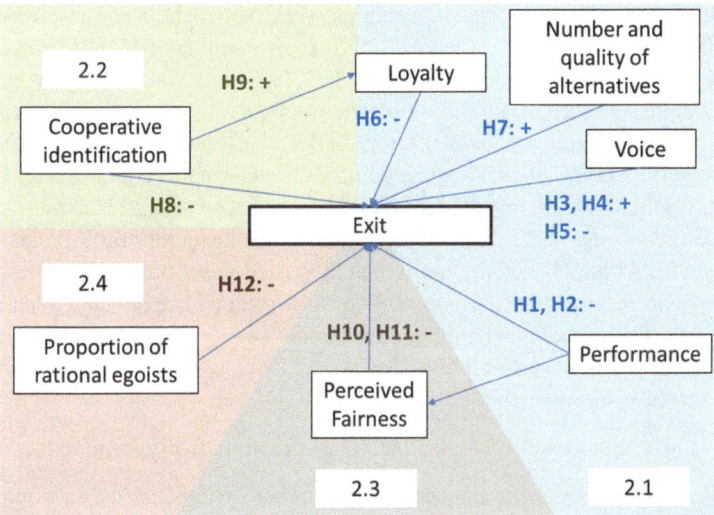

Fig. 4 Theoretical framework

3 DMK and Arla

The use of case studies can demonstrate the relevance of several of the hypotheses. Case studies are particularly suitable for answering questions of "how" and "why" about a contemporary set of events over which a researcher has little or no control (Yin 2018). The prerequisite for our cases is that data on the performance, heterogeneity, and exit behavior of the members is available. This is the case for the two selected cooperatives. We are interested in how these developments affect member behavior. As described in the two examples in the introduction, some members remained in their cooperative despite comparatively low prices and increasing heterogeneity. With the theoretical framework, a number of explanations for this behavior can be provided that go beyond the purely rational, selfish idea of the homo economicus. In addition to the hope for better prices in the future or the lack of better alternatives, voice, fairness, and identity can explain why members stay.

From the observation of deteriorated performance and the figures on exit behavior, conclusions can be drawn about the loyalty of the members. Information on heterogeneity can be found on the one hand in the product groups, qualities, and geographic positions of the members, on the other hand from annual reports. The formal possibility for voice can be found in reports about the bodies available for this purpose. Information on the informal possibility of using "voice" is not available and limits the applicability for outside researchers.

H1 The higher the perceived deterioration in performance, the more likely is an exit.

In 2016, the milk prices of both dairies were below the average payout price (LTO 2017). While Arla recorded a 5.5% loss of members, DMK reportedly lost up to 20%. The average price at DMK was 23.95 cents, well below Arla's price of 26.77 cents. The 2016 annual report claims that "[. . .] we feel that our dairy farmers' situation and the level of the milk price paid to them by DMK are unsatisfactory" (DMK 2017: 4). According to the German Federal Cartel Office's (2018) investigations, members' terminations could lead to a 20% reduction in the volume of processed milk. DMK (2017) blames unsatisfactory milk prices for this development. Although heterogeneity has increased and prices have declined, the members who supply the remaining 80% of the volume have decided to stay in the cooperative. Therefore, other influencing factors seem to be relevant for the exit. These factors provide starting points for cooperatives to retain their members even with increasing heterogeneity.

H3 The lower the possibility to use the voice, the more likely is an exit.

DMK tries to give a voice to different member groups through a young dairy farmers' working group, a committee for member relations and member loyalty as well as through regional assemblies. For its Annual Assembly elections in 2015, it reports an increase in the participation rate to 40% DMK 2016). Its merger with the Dutch DOC Kaas in 2016 necessitated a new application procedure in the election for the supervisory board. According to the annual report, this reflects the developments of increasing growth and internationalization. Due to the unsatisfactory milk prices, an extraordinary assembly took place in February 2016 (DMK 2017).

Arla (2018) states that they have regional district councils and that they have adopted a new governance structure to strengthen farmer participation. In both cases, the possibility of using the voice seems at least formally given. DMK seems to have more different ways of exercising voice. However, the informal aspects of voice are not visible to external observers.

H8 The lower the identification of a member with the cooperative and the higher the identification with other (sub-)groups, the more likely is an exit.

The impact of identities becomes visible in the behavior of some members during protests. In Germany, the farmers' association traditionally represented the interests of all farmers. With the Federal Association of German Dairy Farmers (BDM 2018), a new advocate for the dairy farmers has emerged in 1998. Both organizations have repeatedly represented different or even contrary positions on politics and the milk market. The BDM association organized various protest actions and demonstrations in front of the DMK plant during the "milk price crises." The BDM's umbrella organization—the European Milk Board (EMB)—reports protests from the subsidiaries across Europe (EMB 2015). Furthermore, this umbrella organization is critical of cooperatives (see EMB 2012). It complains that the cooperatives have become too big and that there is no difference for the member, whether they deliver their milk to the cooperative or to a private company.

A similar picture emerged in the UK in 2013, where the organization "Farmers for Action" attempted to block Arla's dairy supply chain. Arla Food UK's farmer board of directors has subsequently issued a statement: "*We question the motives of the farmers who are protesting against a farmer owned business*" (Astley 2013). The different identities of the members could explain both their protest behavior and recent terminations. The identity aspect appears to be relevant for both dairies. However, members with a stronger identification with another group seem to distinguish themselves first by more "voice" and not necessarily by exit.

H11 The lower the perceived distributive fairness, the more likely is an exit.

As mentioned above, both dairies offer different products and have members in different countries. This heterogeneity could also be the source for different payoffs. The annual report of DMK (2017) mentions its sustainability program with different bonus payments as well as GMO and transport allowances.

Arla (2018) emphasizes its concept of "ONE milk price," which includes that each farmer in the seven member countries receives the same milk price. The different payment prices for the different production branches (e.g., organic, conventional) are not mentioned. Whether the members perceive these differences as fair cannot be observed as an outsider. Their perception is likely to depend on the identity or identities of the members. If members see themselves as members of ONE cooperative, they may be more willing to tolerate differences in payoffs. However, if there is a strong subgroup identity, for example, as a conventional farmer, then higher payments to producers of organic milk could lead to a loss of utility.

4 Conclusion and Discussion

Member heterogeneity is often described in the literature as a disadvantage. However, in practice, one can observe an increase in heterogeneity. In this paper, this contradictory observation has been used as an opportunity to take up new explanations for the effect and meaning of member heterogeneity. Based on the model of Hirschman (1970), a theoretical framework was developed that contains the components of collective action, fairness, and identity. One of the findings is that the phenomenon of member heterogeneity is more complicated than previously thought. Although the dimensions discussed so far may play a role, several of the mentioned other factors seem to influence the behavior of the members. The frequently made assumption of the homo economicus cannot explain these factors. Future research should also include behavioral economic aspects to explain the behavior of members.

Hirschman's (1970) approach has some weaknesses in explaining member behavior. It is unclear why members should use their "voice," how members respond to performance differences, and why some members are loyal. Ostrom's (2000) player types fill one of these gaps by showing why some members use their voice, while others tend to leave the cooperative. Approaches to the perception of fairness provide indications as to how members could evaluate performance differences. In addition, identities can contribute to an understanding of member behavior. Identity determines who a member is comparing to, to what extent she accepts inequality, and how loyal she is. From the various theories and approaches, 12 different hypotheses have been derived that contribute to explaining how member heterogeneity and member behavior interact. These factors were used to construct a theoretical framework. The derived hypotheses provide an opportunity to test our understanding of member behavior and challenge previous explanatory patterns.

As shown in the theoretical framework, heterogeneity can also have a positive impact on the cooperative and its members. In the reaction of the remaining members, the availability and efficiency of voice, the perceived fairness, and the social identities of the members play crucial roles. The identified factors represent starting points for cooperatives to retain their members even with increasing heterogeneity and (temporarily) worse performance. By retaining those members who are willing to forego short-term profits in favor of long-term performance improvement, the continued existence and performance of cooperatives can also be secured. For example, the cooperative can invest in the development of brands. This investment only pays off in the long term. Possible measures to increase loyalty include the strengthening of identity, the formal and informal design of voice, and the design of price structures for different products.

We have discussed four hypotheses using the example of two dairies. It remains questionable to what extent the results can be transferred to other cooperatives and can be generalized. For testing all of the hypotheses, it would be necessary to supplement the case studies with other social science methods. For example, information on the informal possibility of using "voice" is not available and limits the applicability of case studies. Identity, the perception of fairness, and other social norms can also be observed to a limited extent from the outside. Further empirical work with the theoretical framework presented here is necessary.

Unlike exit, voice is a continuous variable (Dowding et al. 2000). The type and quality of the content may vary from member to member. The voice can be used more constructively or destructively. Of course, it also depends on how the cooperative reacts to "voice." This is also clear in the conditions described above: if "voice" is perceived as ineffective, then an "exit" is more likely. Group size and governance structures may have additional roles. Institutional design and heterogeneity are likely to interact over time (Poteete and Ostrom 2004). As mentioned above, identities can be changed. All members have different identities. It is also up to the cooperatives what identity their members have and whether they even identify with the cooperative. The question remains as to how the heterogeneity and the different identities affect the decision-making processes in the cooperative.

The assessment probably also depends on how one defines heterogeneity. Does one understand heterogeneity as a variance of different characteristics within the membership? Then, it is likely to increase in the course of the life cycle. Or does one assume that heterogeneity refers to the fact that there are simply different types of members? Then, a cooperative is heterogeneous from the beginning on and heterogeneity does not necessarily increase. This would suggest that heterogeneity is not detrimental per se. No matter how one defines the term, in the end, it will be less the heterogeneity itself than the impact on the behavior of the members that will be important for the cooperative. In this context, the question remains as to when and if increasing member heterogeneity is really a problem for a cooperative.

In addition to understanding member heterogeneity, there are a number of research fields for the future research agenda. It is not yet clear to what extent members identify with their cooperatives and what role different identities play in their behavior as members. In addition, playing public good games with members could provide insights into the distribution of Ostrom's roles in cooperatives. There is also a need for research in the area of fairness. It is unknown how members evaluate fairness and which dimensions of fairness they include in their decision-making. Although Hirschman's work appeared as early as 1970, it also provides further inspiration for cooperative research. Current cases of membership withdrawals could be used to validate Hirschman's statements and help cooperatives avoid or respond to future withdrawals. Knowledge from these research fields can contribute to a better understanding of members' behavior.

Acknowledgment The author thanks the German Research Foundation (DFG) for the financial support of her stay at the Center for the Study of Co-operatives (University of Saskatchewan, Saskatoon, Canada). In addition, she thanks the Center for the instructive and enjoyable stay.

References

Adams JS (1965) Inequity in social exchange. In: Berkowitz L (ed) Advances in experimental social psychology. Academic, New York, pp 267–299

Akerlof GE, Kranton RE (2000) Economics and identity. Q J Econ 115(3):715–753

Akerlof GE, Kranton RE (2005) Identity and the economics of organizations. J Econ Perspect 19(1):9–32

Arla (2018) Consolidated annual report 2017. Available at: https://www.arla.com/company/investor/annual-reports/

Arla (2019a) Consolidated annual report 2018. Available at: https://www.arla.com/company/investor/annual-reports/

Arla (2019b) History. Available at: https://www.arla.com/company/unser-unternehmen/history/

Astley M (2013) Farmers for action protests 'harming' milk supplier livelihoods, says Arla. Available at: https://www.dairyreporter.com/Article/2013/07/31/Farmers-for-Action-protests-harming-milk-supplier-livelihoods-Arla

Barry B (1974) Review article: Exit, voice, and loyalty. Br J Polit Sci 4(1):79–107

Baumeister RF, Leary MR (1995) The need to belong: desire for interpersonal attachments as a fundamental human motivation. Psychol Bull 117(3):497–529

BDM (2018) The history of the BDM – background of the founding of the BDM. Available at: http://bdm-verband.org/html/index.php?module=Content&func=view&cat=31&pid=2

Chaudhuri A, Paichayontvijit T (2006) Conditional cooperation and voluntary contributions to a public good. Econ Bull 3(8):1–14

Deutsches Milchkontor (2016) Combined annual report and sustainability report 2015. Available at: https://www.dmk.de/fileadmin/redaktion/presse/publikationen/dmk/DMK_combined_annual_report_2015_en.pdf

Deutsches Milchkontor (2017) Combined annual report and sustainability report 2016. Available at: http://www.dmk.de/fileadmin/redaktion/presse/publikationen/dmk/DMK_GROUP_Combined-annual-report-and-sustainability-report-2016.pdf

Deutsches Milchkontor (2018) Combined annual report and sustainability report 2017. Available at: https://www.dmk.de/en/dmk-group/annual-report/all/

Dowding K, John P, Mergoupis T, Van Vugt M (2000) Exit, voice and loyalty: analytic and empirical developments. Eur J Polit Res 37(4):469–495

Elliott M, Elliott L, Van der Sluis E (2018) A predictive analytics understanding of cooperative membership heterogeneity and sustainability. Sustainability 10(2048):1–31

EMB (2012) Cooperatives: between myth and reality. European Milk Board, Germany

EMB (2015) What is currently happening in Europe? Available at: http://www.europeanmilkboard.org/hr/special-content/news/news-details/browse/7/article/what-is-currently-happening-in-europe.html?tx_ttnews%5BbackPid%5D=78&cHash=afaf6870a35dd13a49b50d9896c61952

Fehr E, Fischbacher U (2004) Social norms and human cooperation. Trends Cogn Sci 8(4):185–190

Fehr E, Schmidt KM (1999) A theory of fairness, competition and cooperation. Q J Econ 114(3):817–868

Fischbacher U, Gächter S, Fehr E (2001) Are people conditionally cooperative? Evidence from a public goods experiment. Econ Lett 71(3):397–404

Fulton, M. 1999. Cooperatives and member commitment. LTA 4/99: 418-437.

German Federal Cartel Authority (2018) Press release – Proceeding against DMK dairy discontinued. Bonn, Germany

Hakelius K, Karantininis K, Feng L (2013) The resilience of the cooperative form: cooperative beehiving by Swedish cooperatives. In: Ehrman T, Windsperger J, Cliquet G, Hendrikse G (eds) Governance of alliances, cooperatives and franchise chains. Springer, Heidelberg

Hansmann H (2000) The ownership of enterprise. Belknap Press, Cambridge, MA

Hendrikse G (2011) Pooling, access, and countervailing power in channel governance. Manag Sci 57(9):1692–1702

Hirschman AO (1970) Exit, voice, and loyalty: responses to decline in firms, organizations, and states. Harvard University Press, Cambridge, MA

Höhler J, Kühl R (2018) Dimensions of member heterogeneity in cooperatives and their impact on organization – a literature review. Ann Public Cooper Econ 89(4):697–712

Iliopoulos C, Valentinov V (2018) Member heterogeneity in agricultural cooperatives: a systems-theoretic perspective. Sustainability 10(1271):1–22

Leviten-Reid C, Fairbairn B (2011) Multi-stakeholder governance in cooperative organizations: toward a new framework for research? Can J Nonprofit Soc Econ Res 2(2):25–36

LTO Netherland (2017) Standardized milk price calculations for November 2016 deliveries. Available at: http://www.milkprices.nl/Reviews/eng201611.pdf

Orbell JM, Schwartz-Shea P, Simmons RT (1984) Do cooperators exit more readily than defectors? Am Polit Sci Rev 78(1):147–162

Ostrom E (2000) Collective action and the evolution of social norms. J Econ Perspect 14(3):137–158

Poteete AR, Ostrom E (2004) Heterogeneity, group size and collective action: the role of institutions in forest management. Devel Change 35(3):435–461

Rabobank (2018) Global dairy top 20. RaboResearch, Utrecht

Shayo M (2009) A model of social identity with an application to political economy: nation, class, and redistribution. Am Polit Sci Rev 103(2):147–174

Simon H (1991) Organizations and markets. J Econ Perspect 5(2):25–44

Tajfel H, Turner J (2001) An integrative theory of intergroup conflict. In: Hogg MA, Abrams D (eds) Key readings in social psychology. Intergroup relations: essential readings. Psychology Press, New York, NY, pp 94–109

Turner JC (1975) Social comparison and social identity: some prospects for intergroup behavior. Eur J Soc Psychol 5(1):1–34

Tyler TR, Blader SL (2000) Cooperation in groups: procedural justice, social identity, and behavioral engagement. Psychology Press, Philadelphia

Tyler TR, Blader SL (2003) The group engagement model: procedural justice, social identity, and cooperative behavior. Pers Soc Psychol Rev 7(4):349–361

Yin RK (2018) Case study research: design and methods, 5th edn. Sage, Thousand Oaks

Cooperatives in Modern Food Supply Chains: A Case Study of the Malt Barley Sector in Ethiopia

Delelegne A. Tefera and Jos Bijman

Abstract Increases in food demand, product differentiation, and agribusiness growth provide new market opportunities for smallholders in Africa. Yet, smallholders face challenges of meeting quality, volume, and timing requirements to capture these opportunities. Cooperatives have been identified as a strategy to improve smallholder linkage to evolving food systems, by providing various supply chain services. However, empirical evidence is sparse on the performance of cooperatives in commercializing farm products and coordinating supply chain integration. In addition, a debate exists on which farmers are more likely to be member of a cooperative. In other words, do all smallholders have an equal chance of benefitting from the activities of cooperatives? Ethiopian malt barley cooperatives are used as an empirical case. Mixed methods were used to collect and analyze primary data. Our case study analysis shows that cooperatives provide diverse services, including contract brokerage, output marketing, input supply, and provision of technical assistance. Our empirical results also show that the members of these marketing cooperatives have larger landholdings, better farm resources, and better access to extension services compared to non-member farmers.

1 Introduction

Smallholder agriculture remains crucial for economic development and reduction of poverty in developing countries (World Bank 2008). A growing body of literature shows that food systems in Africa are undergoing fundamental changes

D. A. Tefera
Department of Agribusiness and Value Chain Management, Hawassa University, Hawassa, Ethiopia

J. Bijman (✉)
Business Management and Organisation Group, Wageningen University and Research, Wageningen, The Netherlands
e-mail: jos.bijman@wur.nl

© Springer Nature Switzerland AG 2019
J. Windsperger et al. (eds.), *Design and Management of Interfirm Networks*,
Contributions to Management Science,
https://doi.org/10.1007/978-3-030-29245-4_12

(Minten et al. 2016; Verhofstadt and Maertens 2013; Tefera et al. 2019). These changes are often characterized by increased supply chain coordination, higher quality and food safety requirements, and a shift to modern distribution systems (Reardon et al. 2009; Minten et al. 2016). Smallholders face numerous challenges in entering into these modern supply chains, including high costs associated with accessing information, negotiating, and complying with quality and volume requirements (Poulton et al. 2010). For addressing these challenges, three organizational innovations have been identified in the development literature (World Bank 2008; Royer et al. 2016): cooperatives, contract farming arrangements (CFAs), and partnerships. In this article, we focus on cooperatives.

There is a renewed interest from donors, governments, and academia in cooperatives as an institutional solution to enhance smallholder performance through adoption of technologies and accessing markets (Bernard and Spielman 2009; Fischer and Qaim 2012; Narrod et al. 2009; Shiferaw et al. 2011). Many African governments are promoting cooperatives, particularly because of their ability to reduce transaction costs in coordinated food chains (Latynskiy and Berger 2016). These policies have been supported by studies that show that cooperatives are able to improve smallholder market positions through strengthening bargaining power, facilitating access to modern inputs and market information, and reducing marketing risks (Bernard et al. 2008a; Kaganzi et al. 2009; Markelova et al. 2009; Shiferaw et al. 2011). Cooperatives are instrumental in improving farm income and agricultural performance (Chagwiza et al. 2016; Fischer and Qaim 2012). In addition, cooperatives help farmers to manage quality and meet the increasing quality requirements of evolving food systems (Faysse and Simon 2015; Francesconi and Ruben 2012).

However, in many Sub-Saharan African countries, cooperatives have primarily been set up to provide farming inputs, and they have difficulties in strengthening their marketing functions (Bernard et al. 2008b; Verhofstadt and Maertens 2014b). For instance, in Ethiopia the role of cooperatives in output marketing is estimated at only 10% (Abate 2018). In addition, cooperatives have internal governance problems (Hannan 2014), and they may not be as inclusive as many NGOs and policy stakeholders would like them to be (Bernard and Spielman 2009; Verhofstadt and Maertens 2014a). Studies are scarce on how good cooperatives perform their commercial functions, particularly their coordination role in supply chains. Our study attempts to fill this knowledge gap.

In Ethiopia, cooperatives have long been accepted as one of the policy instruments for enhancing smallholder commercialization and rural transformation. Over the last decade, both the number of cooperatives and the size of membership have rapidly grown (Tefera et al. 2016). According to 2016 data from the Federal Cooperative Agency, the number of cooperatives has grown to about 83,000 cooperatives with a total membership of about 18 million. Despite the significant policy attention given to cooperatives, they face a challenging trade-off between inclusiveness and competitiveness (Lutz and Tadesse 2017), a lack of trust among the members of the organization (Tadesse and Kassie 2017), a weak market orientation, and disruptive external interventions.

We used the Ethiopian malt barley industry for studying the supply chain functions of cooperatives. Driven by the fast growing brewery industry, malt barley supply chains are fundamentally changing (Rashid et al. 2015). The demand for malt barley is growing at an annual rate of 20%. Several multinational brewers, including Heineken, Diageo, Castel Group, and Bavaria, have been investing in the Ethiopian brewery industry and have started local sourcing of malt barley directly from smallholders (Tefera et al. 2019). This has resulted in the rise of modern supply chains, which are supply chains characterized by contracting arrangements, high-quality requirements, and few spot market transactions. The production of barley with good malting quality is of critical importance to the brewery industry. Cooperatives are the major suppliers of malt barley to the brewers and the malt factories. They play an important role in the distribution of modern inputs, in malt barley aggregation, in supply chain coordination, and in quality upgrading.

Our paper has two main objectives. First, we seek to understand the (changing) role of the cooperative in the emerging malt barley supply chains. Second, given the changing role of cooperatives in modern barley chains, we want to explore which farmers are more likely to be member of a cooperative and thus may benefit from the new role of the cooperatives. The Ethiopian barley sector is a suitable case for studying the above questions because it has a long tradition of producing (malt) barley. The investments by foreign brewers have introduced changes in malt barley supply chains, including a changing role for cooperatives. This allows us to study the impact of new supply arrangements on the functions as well as on the composition of the membership of those cooperatives.

The paper is structured as follows. Section 2 provides background information on Ethiopian cooperatives in evolving food systems. Section 3 presents the theoretical framework, focusing on cooperatives' role in rural transformation and determinants of membership. Section 4 describes data collection and research methods. Section 5 presents results. Section 6 discusses the findings, while Sect. 7 concludes with policy implications and further research.

2 Cooperatives in the Evolving Food Systems of Ethiopia

Minten et al. (2016) have shown that Ethiopia's food systems are rapidly changing due to dietary, agricultural, and supply chain transformations. The authors distinguish four major drivers for these changes: high population growth, rapid urbanization, infrastructure investments, and income growth. Smallholder agriculture is still the major source of food in the country, and smallholders are increasingly required to fulfil quality and volume requirements. Cooperatives can play a key role in supporting farmers in getting access to remunerative markets.

Over the past years, both the number of cooperatives and the size of overall membership have rapidly grown (Tefera et al. 2016). Despite this progress, most cooperatives are mainly supplying farmers with inputs and providing social services, with few output marketing activities (ATA 2016). Cognizant to this, the government has developed a plan to increase the effort of cooperatives in marketing farm products. By 2020, cooperatives should account for the marketing of 50% of all agricultural products (ATA 2016).

Agricultural cooperatives in Ethiopia can be divided into two main types: multi-purpose and single-purpose cooperatives (Tefera et al. 2016). Single-purpose cooperatives focus on a particular business activity and are prevalent in the coffee, fruit, vegetables, and dairy supply chains. Multi-purpose cooperatives are engaged in a wide range of activities and services such as distribution of fertilizers and seeds, and sometimes output marketing. The latter also organize agricultural training for members, provide market information, and facilitate credit provision. In this study, we focus on multi-purpose agricultural cooperatives that provide various services to rural communities in the Arsi Highlands. The rural cooperatives in this region are facilitating both the production and the commercialization of grains such as wheat and barley.

In the Arsi Highlands, large brewers such as Heineken and Diageo source malt barley directly from smallholders through various vertical coordination arrangements. As part of their contract packages, brewers introduce new varieties and strengthen coordination in the supply chain. In addition, brewers use cooperatives as their main agents to distribute modern inputs, arrange logistics, and aggregate malt barley from smallholders.

3   Literature Review

Our literature review consists of two parts. First, we explore existing knowledge on the diverse functions of cooperatives in facilitating supply chain coordination. Second, we review current insights on the determinants of membership of cooperatives, particularly on the different types of farmers that may be included or excluded from cooperatives.

Integration in modern food chains often requires innovations such as product upgrading and effective farm business management (Kaganzi et al. 2009). Quality requirements and product upgrading demand a new set of skills and resources, which African smallholders usually cannot attain by themselves. Smallholders also struggle to keep up with the demand for larger volumes and consistency of supply (Poulton 2010).

To meet market requirements and to access modern food chains, smallholders may benefit from membership in cooperatives, because these collective action organizations can reduce transaction costs, increase bargaining power, and provide a range of services (Barham and Chitemi 2009; Chagwiza et al. 2016; Verhofstadt and Maertens 2014b). However, not all cooperatives may provide those marketing services. A distinction has been made between community-oriented and market-oriented cooperatives (Bernard et al. 2008a). A community-oriented cooperative has multiple objectives and provides multiple services to the whole community. A market-oriented cooperative, on the other hand, focuses on generating economic benefits mainly for its members. Although most cooperatives in Sub-Saharan Africa are still community-oriented and have a focus on rural development, the number of agricultural marketing cooperatives is increasing (Lutz and Tadesse 2017). When integrating into modern food chains, these dedicated marketing cooperatives may become more selective in admitting members because competing in modern food chains requires higher investments, quality upgrading, and a business focus. Lutz and Tadesse (2017) discussed that for cooperatives to access modern food chains and achieve efficiency, the following would be important: (a) commitment of members to sell through the cooperative to realize the required scale, (b) active participation in the decision-making in the cooperative, (c) commitment to invest in the cooperative, and (d) clearly specified (i.e., narrow) objectives.

Rigorous empirical research on the functions of cooperatives in modern supply chains is rare. Most studies on the activities and performance of cooperatives focus on the impact of cooperative membership, without paying much attention to how cooperatives generate benefits for their members. Most impact studies have shown that cooperatives play a positive role in enhancing rural livelihoods through facilitating agricultural production and market access (Fischer and Qaim 2012; Ito et al. 2012; Verhofstadt and Maertens 2014b). For instance, agricultural cooperatives have a positive effect on the adoption of modern inputs (Abebaw and Haile 2013), on farm technical efficiency (Abate et al. 2014), and on farm product marketing (Barham and Chitemi 2009; Francesconi and Heerink 2010; Wollni and Zeller 2007). Details on the mechanisms of impact generation are often not disclosed.

The performance of cooperatives varies depending on the type of supply chain. For instance, in rural Africa the positive performance of cooperatives is often linked to traditional cash crops such as coffee (Mojo et al. 2017) and to emerging horticultural and dairy supply chains (Chagwiza et al. 2016; Fischer and Qaim 2014; Kaganzi et al. 2009; Verhofstadt and Maertens 2014b). Our paper provides empirical evidence on the role of cooperatives in one of the major grains supply chains of Ethiopia.

A key question, particularly for policy makers, is whether cooperatives provide benefits to the rural community at large or only to a specific group of farmers. In other words, which farmers are members of the cooperatives that engage in supply chain coordination? Various studies have shown that farmer membership of agricultural cooperatives is determined by demographic, economic, and institutional factors. Farmer characteristics such as the level of education and the age of the household head positively account for membership (Abebaw and Haile 2013; Chagwiza et al. 2016; Fischer and Qaim 2012; Verhofstadt and Maertens 2014a). Farm characteristics such as landholding and livestock holdings have a positive effect on the probability of cooperative membership (Abebaw and Haile 2013; Bernard and Spielman 2009; Fischer and Qaim 2012). However, other studies found that farm size has a significant negative effect on the probability of cooperative membership (Chagwiza et al. 2016; Verhofstadt and Maertens 2014a).

Several studies reported that the poor are excluded from membership (Francesconi and Heerink 2010; Verhofstadt and Maertens 2014a). Other studies showed that there is a "middle-class effect," indicating that both very small and very large farms are least likely to participate (Bernard and Spielman 2009; Fischer and Qaim 2012). Distance to a market (or to an asphalt road) has a nonlinear or an inverted U-shaped relationship with cooperative membership (Abebaw and Haile 2013; Fischer and Qaim 2012), which suggests that cooperatives are effective in reducing transaction costs for farmers at intermediate distance. In sum, the empirical evidence for determinants of farmer membership are inconclusive. Our study contributes to this academic debate by exploring factors affecting membership in a grains supply chain in Ethiopia.

4 Methods

This section describes the research design and the methods of data gathering. First, it presents the context of the study. Second, it provides a description of the data collection process. Finally, it explains the analytical framework.

4.1 Study Context

The study was conducted in the Arsi Highlands of Oromia, Ethiopia. The Arsi Highlands account for 85% of the national malt barley production (ATA 2016). In this region, barley is the second most important crop next to wheat (in volume terms). In 2016/2017, the total harvest of barley, produced on 95,265 hectares of land, was 268,573 tons (CSA 2017). More than 60% of all barley is used for household consumption. The Galema Farmers' Cooperative Union is one of the key aggregators of malt barley in the region. This union has about 90 primary cooperatives as its members.

Malt barley is the dominant cash crop in the region. Traditionally, local traders buy malt barley from farmers and sell to the Assela Malt Factory (AMF), the main malt factory in the country and located in this region. The AMF is responsible for 70% of total malt supply to the brewery industry. Traditionally, brewers did not interact with malt barley farmers, as they only transacted with AMF in buying malt. However, the foreign brewers that entered the Ethiopian market over the last decade wanted to upgrade the quality of malt barley and therefore started to source malt barley directly from smallholders using contract schemes. These brewery-directed malt barley supply chains are the modern chains; they are governed by contracts, have few brokers, and have high barley quality requirements. The conventional chains are characterized by spot-market transactions, a high number of brokers, and low product quality.

In the Arsi Highlands, participation in collective action institutions has a long tradition. Cooperatives support rural livelihoods through the provision of various inputs and services. For instance, agricultural cooperatives play a critical role in the supply of fertilizers to farmers (Agbahey et al. 2015). In addition, cooperatives are engaged in the supply of improved seeds, the provision of market information, and the supply of household consumables (e.g., edible oil and sugar). More recently, cooperatives have started to play a brokering role in linking farmers to the malt factory and to the (foreign) breweries.

4.2 Data Collection

The research employed a combination of qualitative and quantitative approaches. The qualitative research methods, for gaining information on the various functions of the cooperative, consisted of focus group discussions, key informant interviews (KII), observations, and document analysis. The quantitative part of the research consisted of a survey among member and non-member farmers. Combining a qualitative and quantitative approach has a merit of minimizing the weakness of each method and gathering more rich data. We used a multi-stage sampling procedure for selecting survey respondents. First, we purposively selected Lemu Bilbilo district in the Arsi region. Second, seven cases were purposefully selected based on cooperatives' participation in modern and conventional malt barley chains. In order to compare the role of cooperatives and the type of farmers in conventional and modern chains, we selected four cooperatives that operate in a modern chain and three cooperatives that are part of a conventional chain (Table 1). For each of these seven cooperatives, we explored its functions in the respective supply chain. The fieldwork was carried out in January–May 2015.

Semi-structured interview guides were developed for interviewing members and leaders of the cooperative, as well as the supply chain manager of a brewing company, NGOs experts, traders, and agricultural researchers (Table 1). Information gathered from these interviews covers the services provided by the cooperative, the management structure of the cooperative, the member-cooperative relationship, the cooperative's interaction with other supply chain actors (e.g., traders, AMF, brewers, research institutions), the organizational capacity of the cooperative, and the challenges the cooperative faces.

In addition to the qualitative research, a cross-section survey was conducted among member and non-member farmers. For this survey, three cooperatives were selected that operate in conventional chains. Table 2 presents the characteristics of these cooperatives. A total of 148 farm households were selected. The sample includes 78 cooperative members and 70 non-member farmers. Cooperative members were randomly selected from the members' list of the three cooperatives. Non-members were selected from the same district using a snowball sampling method. Finally, well-trained enumerators conducted the face-to-face interviews with the household head, using a structured questionnaire.

Table 1 Case cooperatives by type of supply chain and type of interviewees

Case cooperative	# of interviews (n = 30)	Type of interviewee	Type of supply chain	Secondary data sources and additional KIIs (n = 25)[a]
Bekoji Negesso [cooperative₁]	4	Three co-op leaders and one member	Modern chain	*Secondary data sources*: gov't documents, consultant reports, brewery project reports, Galema Union reports, and published articles
Lemu Dima [cooperative₂]	4	Three co-op leaders and one member	Modern chain	*Key informant interviews*: Kulumsa Agri. Research Center (2), co-op promotion office (2), NGOs (4), AMF (2), and brewers project experts (5)
Lemu Burkitu [cooperative₃]	5	Three co-op leaders and two members	Modern chain	
Chiba Michael [cooperative₄]	4	Three co-op leaders and one member	Modern chain	
Lemu Michael [cooperative₅]	4	Three co-op leaders and one member	Conventional chain	*Secondary data sources*: gov't documents, consultant reports, and published articles.
Ulule Hassa [cooperative₆]	6	Four co-op leaders and two member	Conventional chain	*Key informant interviews*: Kulumsa Agri. Research Center (2), co-op promotion office (2), NGOs (4), and AMF (2)
Koma Katerra [cooperative₇]	3	Three co-op leaders	Conventional chain	

[a] *KII* Key Informant Interview

Table 2 Characteristics of surveyed cooperatives

Villages	Cooperatives	Membership			Sample size	Distance to market (km)
		Male	Female	Total		
Lemu Micheal	Cooperative$_5$	359	8	367	25	8.1
Ulule Hassa	Cooperative$_6$	181	8	189	26	12.3
Koma Katerra	Cooperative$_7$	158	6	164	27	16.2
Total	3	698	22	720	78	–

Source: Survey data 2015

4.3 Analytical Framework

The study employs a binary logit model to analyze determinants of smallholder participation in cooperatives. The model is used to estimate the factors that influence a given farmer's decision to join a cooperative. Considering the discrete nature of a farmer's decision of whether or not to join cooperatives, binary choice models such as the probit and logit models are most suitable.

Following Abebaw and Haile (2013), Fischer and Qaim (2012), and Wollni and Zeller (2007), a farmer's decision to join a cooperative can be determined using a random utility framework. This framework states that a farmer chooses being a member of a cooperative if the utility gained from membership is larger than the utility from non-membership. The utility gain from membership can be expressed as a function of observed covariates (X) in a latent variable model as follows:

$$D_i^* = \beta X_i + \varepsilon_i \text{ with } D_i = \begin{cases} 1 \text{ if } D_i^* > 0 \\ 0 \text{ otherwise} \end{cases} \tag{1}$$

where D_i^* is an indicator of latent cooperative membership, β is a vector of parameters to be estimated, and ε_i is the error term. The observed dependent variable, membership status (D_i), where $D_i = 1$ for cooperative members and $D_i = 0$ for non-members, is also related to the latent variable as shown in Eq. (1). The choice of explanatory variables included in X is guided by theory and previous studies. A farmer's decision to participate in a cooperative is conditioned by various baseline farm and farmer characteristics (Abate et al. 2014; Abebaw and Haile 2013), such as demographic characteristics, resource endowment, and access to services. In our study, we also used these farm household characteristics to model the likelihood of cooperative membership (see Table 4). The logistic regression model is specified as follows:

$$D_i = \beta_0 + \sum_{i=1}^{n} \beta_i X_i + \varepsilon_i \text{ where, } i = 1, \ldots, n \tag{2}$$

where D_i is the dependent variable (a farmer's decision of whether or not to join in a cooperative), X_i is the vector of control variables that influence a farmer's decision of whether or not to participate in the cooperative, $\beta_i's$ are the coefficients of the control variables, and ε_i is the error term capturing all immeasurable effects that influence a farmer's participation decision.

5   Empirical Results

We present the findings of the study in three parts. First, qualitative results are presented regarding the services of the cooperative, distinguished by the type of supply chain. Second, we present a comparison between members and non-members based on socioeconomic characteristics, as well as a comparison of farm performance in terms of total production, product quality, price, gross income, and food crops income. Third, we provide econometric results on the determinants of membership.

5.1   Services Provided by the Cooperatives

The results of our case study analysis show that cooperatives provide diverse services to support quality upgrading and chain coordination. These services provide economic benefits for the member and their rural communities. Particularly, the benefits in terms of access to fertilizers and improved seeds were well acknowledged in the focus group discussions (FGDs). We learned from the FGDs that cooperatives organize farm management trainings, which has a positive impact on yield as well as on malt barley quality.

Within the modernizing malt barley supply chains, cooperatives provide services such as collecting and distributing market information, bargaining with buyers, and aggregating, transporting, and storing grains (Source: FGDs). Figure 1 shows the input supply function (solid arrows) and the output marketing function (dashed arrows) of cooperatives in the malt barley chains. Primary cooperatives distribute to their members the inputs they receive from the cooperative union (which is a federation of primary cooperatives). Cooperatives also facilitate, on behalf of the brewers, the technical trainings regarding productivity and quality improvement. Cooperatives are also involved in facilitating quality grading of malt barley, together with experts from the brewery company. Consequently, member farmers are engaged in product upgrading and receive price premiums of up to 20%, which has a direct positive effect on farm income.

In the FGDs, participants from cooperatives that are not linked to brewers and malt factories indicated that their involvement in upgrading and value-adding activities is limited. We also learned from the case study that low performance of the cooperative in marketing services was mainly attributed to weak organizational

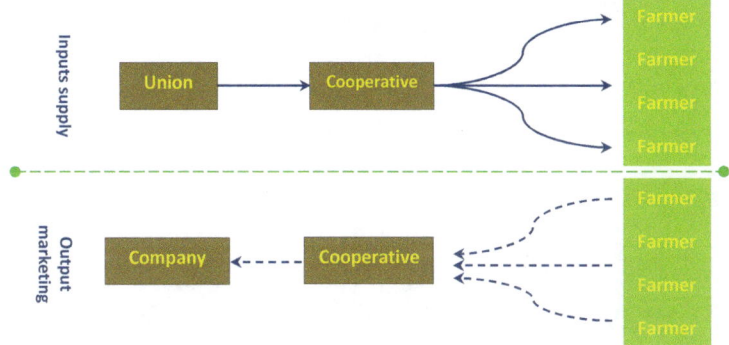

Fig. 1 Inputs supply and marketing functions of cooperatives in malt barley chains

capacities, low educated leaders, limited financial means, and a difficult relationship with the union.

5.2 Integration of Cooperatives into Malt Barley Chains

Local sourcing from a large number of small farmers is often done by brokering organization; a cooperative, an NGO, or even a large-scale farmer may serve as a link between the company and the small farmers. The case study analysis shows that cooperatives are actively engaged in the distribution of modern inputs and the aggregation of malt barley. Capacity building and management trainings provided by brewery companies enhance the management of malt barley cooperatives, which in turn improve their market orientation and performance.

Before the appearance of foreign brewers, the role of cooperatives in the malt barley chain was often limited to distribution of inputs (Source: interview at AMF). This economic function required only low organizational effort. The foreign brewers that entered the Ethiopian beer industry encouraged cooperatives to engage in output marketing. Figure 2 shows the increasing number of cooperatives in malt barley marketing for the period 2013–2017.

Our interview respondents indicated that the Galema Union is the only cooperative union engaged in malt barley marketing in the Arsi region. It is a multi-purpose cooperative union established in 2000. The Union has a high level of political influence and is playing a crucial role in the aggregation of malt barley from its member primary cooperatives. Specifically, it performs marketing functions through signing sales agreements, and it delivers inputs to primary cooperatives (Source: interviews). The union also facilitates transport of the aggregated malt barley to its warehouse. In addition, it is involved in the selection of primary cooperatives for the local sourcing of malt barley by brewery companies.

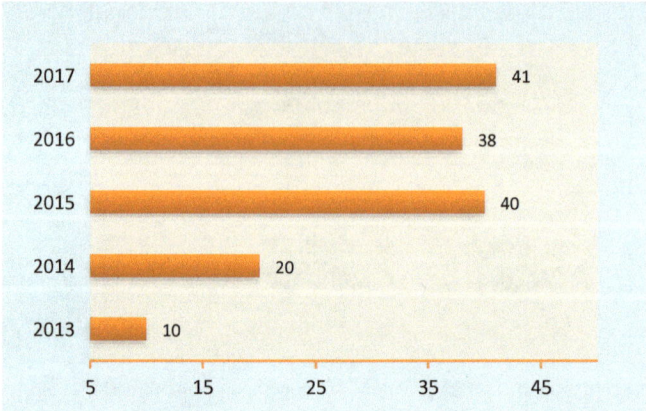

Fig. 2 Number of primary cooperatives engaged in malt barley marketing. Source: Data received from Galema Farmer Cooperative Union

Table 3 Summary of cooperatives constraints as identified in the FGDs

Constraints	# of groups	Suggested solutions
• Weak interaction and functional linkages with the Union	7	• Enhance relationships with the Union via effective communication
• Storage, grading equipment, and logistic problems	7	• Facilitate availability of logistics and storage
• Poor in timing for input provision due to delay by the Union	7	• Facilitate timely delivery of inputs by the Union
• Provision of inadequate technical assistance	6	• Improve provision of technical assistance
• Low members motivation and participation in decision-making	6	• Provision of training on co-op business for members
• Low financial incentives for co-op leaders	5	• Arrange incentives for leaders during product aggregation
• Limited market access	4	• Support for market linkages

Source: Field study 2015

Despite the crucial role of cooperatives in enhancing malt barley chain development, their performance is weak, particularly in the creation of robust competitive advantage for smallholder farmers. Our qualitative results from the FGDs and interviews reveal that malt barley cooperatives are still suffering from governance and leadership challenges. Table 3 presents a summary of the key challenges that the cooperatives in the malt barley chain face and the suggestions by the respondents to remedy these problems.

5.3   Comparative Analysis

5.3.1   Characterization of Members and Non-members

We used an independent t-test for the comparative analysis between members and non-members. Results are presented in Table 4. We found that cooperative members differ from non-members in terms of socioeconomic characteristics, productive asset ownership, and access to institutions and services. On average, cooperative members have a larger-sized family and have more family labor available. Cooperative members have a significantly more entrepreneurial attitude and show more innovativeness as compared to non-members.

Table 4 Characteristics of farmers, according to cooperative membership

Variables	Total sample	Member	Non-member	Diff.	Statistical sig.
Socioeconomic characteristics					
Age (year)	44.16 (0.97)	45.45(1.27)	42.73(1.48)	2.72	
Gender (0 = female,1 = male)	0.986 (0.01)	0.987(0.01)	0.985(0.01)	0.001	
Family size (#)	6.46 (0.22)	7.37(0.27)	5.44(0.29)	1.93	***
Available family labor (#)	3.92 (0.16)	4.49(0.23)	3.28(0.19)	1.2	***
Education (year)	4.54 (0.28)	4.03(0.38)	5.11(0.42)	−1.08	*
Innovativeness[a]	2.73 (0.07)	2.89 (0.09)	2.54 (0.08)	0.35	***
Entrepreneurial attitude[b]	2.66 (0.07)	2.79 (0.09)	2.51 (0.08)	0.28	**
Livelihood and resource endowment					
Farm size (ha)	2.79 (0.21)	3.73 (0.34)	1.76(0.17)	1.96	***
Malt barley area (ha)	0.69 (0.06)	0.94 (0.10)	0.44(0.03)	0.5	***
Off-farm activity (0–1)	0.22 (0.03)	0.19 (0.04)	0.27(0.05)	−0.079	
Total livestock holding (TLU)[c]	8.60 (0.79)	11.47 (1.38)	5.39(0.47)	6.08	***
Access to institutions					
Access to saving (0–1)	0.48 (0.04)	0.61 (0.05)	0.34(0.06)	0.27	***
Access to mobile (0–1)	0.62 (0.04)	0.67 (0.05)	0.57(0.06)	0.09	
Extension contact (0–1)	0.43 (0.04)	0.62 (0.05)	0.21(0.05)	0.41	***
Distance to market (km)	9.68 (0.36)	12.29 (0.52)	6.76(0.17)	5.54	***
Iddir membership (year)	19.05 (0.92)	19.05 (1.18)	19.04(1.45)	0.007	
N	148	78	70	148	

Note: Standard errors in parentheses; $***p < 0.01$, $**p < 0.05$, $*p < 0.10$

[a]The variable "Innovativeness" was measured, using a Likert scale (ranging from 1 to 5), by asking farmers their extent of agreement with the following statements: "I am enjoying trying out new things;" "I am among the first to try new activities;" "I am actively seeking new markets"

[b]The variable "Entrepreneurial attitude" was measured, using a Likert scale (ranging from 1 to 5), by asking farmers their extent of agreement with the following statements: "I consider myself as an entrepreneur;" "My neighbors consider me as an entrepreneur;" "I see and recognize good chances"

[c]*TLU* Tropical Livestock Unit, to describe livestock numbers of various species as a single unit; *ha* hectare; *km* kilometer

In terms of resource endowment, cooperative members have larger livestock holdings, farm size, and malt barley area as compared to non-member farmers. With respect to access to services, cooperative members (62%) have significantly more contact with extension services than non-members (21%). On average, 61% of cooperative members have savings, which is significantly higher compared to non-members (34%). The mean distance to markets is higher for cooperative members at the 1% level of significance. The number of years of membership of an Iddir, which is an informal association for funerals and social events, is the same for both groups of farmers.

5.3.2 Production, Quality, and Income

In Table 5, we present the results on malt barley production, prices, product quality, malt barley income, production costs, food crops income, and total household income. We observe important differences in total production, prices, product quality, production costs, and total farm income between cooperative members and non-members. The results indicate that membership has a positive and significant effect on malt barley production and product quality and hence on malt barley prices. Members also make more costs than non-members, which might be linked to improving quality. Moreover, cooperative membership has a positive and significant impact on food crop income and total farm income.

Table 5 Comparison in the mean performance of member and non-member farmers

Performance indicators	Unit	Mean outcomes			Diff.	Statistical sig.
		Total sample	Member	Non-member		
MB total production	100 kg	12 (0.85)	15.39 (1.46)	8.20 (0.49)	7.19	***
MB selling price	Birr per 100 kg	829 (8.33)	871(10.40)	782 (10.80)	89.56	***
MB variable cost	Birr per ha	237(10.29)	246(11.77)	196(16.88)	50.27	*
MB gross income	Birr per ha	15,576 (47)	15,813 (738)	15,312 (567)	500.6	
MB stated quality[a]	Scale of 1–3	2.08 (0.04)	2.21(0.06)	1.96 (0.06)	0.25	***
Food crops income	Birr per ha	7202 (82)	7710 (1138)	6635 (1200)	1075	
Total farm income	Percent	94.5 (0.92)	96.2 (0.99)	92.64(1.57)	3.51	*

Note: Standard errors in parentheses   ·
***$p < 0.01$, **$p < 0.05$, *$p < 0.10$; *ha* hectare
[a]Farmers ranked quality of their malt barley (MB), 1 low quality through 3 high quality

6 Regression Results

This section presents the results of the logistic regression model on the determinants of farmers' decision to join a cooperative. It also provides the results on the association between member characteristics and cooperative performance.

6.1 Determinants of Farmer Membership

The likelihood of being a member of a cooperative is modelled as a function of selected observed characteristics. In the analysis, we include ten covariates, seven of which explain membership. These include farm size, access to mobile, livestock holding, extension contact, saving, social network (Iddir), and distance to market.

We also conducted a correlation analysis among covariates to detect potential multicollinearity. We present the correlation matrix in the Appendix, Table 8. The results indicate that the correlation coefficients for all covariates are less than 0.7 (0.006–0.486), which suggests that multicollinearity is not a major problem. Second, an OLS model was fitted and the model was tested for multicollinearity using the variance inflation factor (VIF). The VIF for all covariates are less than 10 (1.03–1.68), which indicates that multicollinearity is not a serious problem in this model. The mean uncensored VIF test results (1.32) also show no concern of multicollinearity in the model.

The results of the logistic regression analysis (Table 6) show a highly significant association of membership with the covariates. The model's chi-square value

Table 6 Determinants of smallholders' participation in malt barley cooperative

Membership	Coef.	Std. error	p-value	dy/dx
Family active labor	0.485	0.281	0.084*	0.070
Access to mobile	−2.155	0.902	0.017**	−0.276
Savings	1.730	0.770	0.025**	0.249
Innovativeness	0.314	0.490	0.522	0.045
Extension contact	1.991	0.731	0.006***	0.271
Farm size	0.517	0.293	0.078*	0.075
Livestock holding	0.208	0.088	0.019**	0.030
Distance to market	0.745	0.178	0.000***	0.108
Iddir membership	−0.189	0.051	0.000***	0.027
Constant	−8.524	2.284	0.000***	
Model diagnostics:				
Observation = 144	Pseudo R^2 = 0.681			
Model χ^2 = 135.71***	Log likelihood = −31.74			
Percentage of correct prediction = 91%	*$p < 0.10$; **$p < 0.05$; ***$p < 0.01$			

Source: field survey 2015

indicates a high significance level. Moreover, the pseudo R^2 (0.68) also shows a good model fit. Finally, the model indicates that 92% of sample observations are correctly predicted. Cooperative membership is positively related to farm size, saving, livestock holding, extension contact, and distance to market, but negatively associated with access to mobile and social network (Iddir membership). We found that livestock ownership has a positive and significant effect on the probability of membership. In general, these results show that cooperative membership is biased toward farmers who have more productive resources. The latter is an indication that the cooperatives are not inclusive of the poorest farmers.

The distance from the farm to the district market has a positive effect on membership. This is plausible because farms in remote areas face higher transaction costs of accessing markets and hence turn to a cooperative for access to inputs, market information, and technical assistance. In addition, we found that access to a mobile phone and having a social network (Iddir membership) have a negative effect on farmers' interest to join a cooperative. Farmers who own a mobile phone are more likely to contact traders and wholesalers in the zonal and regional markets.

6.2   Is Cooperative Performance Related to Member Characteristics?

We examine whether there is a relationship between the performance of the cooperative and several characteristics of the members. We focused on member attributes that could directly affect cooperative performance: innovativeness, entrepreneurial attitude, loyalty, leadership, and participation. We employed a non-parametric Kruskal-Wallis test on the selected member attributes. The attributes are measured on a five-point scale, ranging from strongly disagree to strongly agree. We used Cronbach's alpha for testing the validity. As the results are higher than 0.7 for all attributes, there is sufficient internal consistency. The volume of malt barley produced, the stated quality, and the selling price are used as performance indicators.

The results (Table 7) show that cooperatives differ in member attributes and that these attributes correlate with business performance. For instance, cooperative$_6$ performs better in all selected performance indicators and has members with a higher level of innovativeness, entrepreneurship, and commitment.

Table 7 Member attributes and performance of malt barley cooperatives

Characteristics	Mean values			p-value
	Cooperative$_5$	Cooperative$_6$	Cooperative$_7$	
Member attributes				
Innovativeness	2.80	3.26	2.63	0.091*
Entrepreneurial attitude	2.68	3.08	2.63	0.125
Loyalty/commitment	3.57	3.68	3.52	0.640
Active participation	3.19	3.22	3.11	0.151
Leadership assessment	3.45	3.65	3.34	0.798
Performance indicators				
MB total production	9.4	24.4	12.3	0.000***
MB selling price	798	933	880	0.000***
MB stated quality	1.9	2.4	2.3	0.003***
Number of observation	25	26	27	

Source: field survey 2015

$*p < 0.10; ***p < 0.01$

7 Discussion

The main aim of this paper was to analyze cooperatives' role in leveraging supply chain relations in the African food systems context. We also explored marketing functions and internal governance issues of cooperatives in emerging Ethiopian malt barley supply chains. A combination of qualitative and quantitative approaches was used to gather primary data. Our qualitative results show that malt barley cooperatives provide diverse services including modern inputs distribution. Our findings are in line with other studies about cooperatives that provide services to improve farm productivity (Latynskiy and Berger 2016; Shiferaw et al. 2011). In the modern chains, cooperatives facilitate contract negotiation, product aggregation, sharing of market information, and integration of farmers into company supply chains. Similar results are reported by Trebbin (2014), showing that cooperatives in India play an important role in linking farmers to modern supply chains; by Fischer and Qaim (2012), showing similar results for banana farmers in Kenya; and by Moustier et al. (2010), showing that cooperatives in Vietnam help farmers to access high-value markets.

We find that capacity building and business trainings provided by brewing companies enhance the management and governance of malt barley cooperatives, which in turn improve their market orientation and performance. This result is consistent with Hannan (2014), who showed that good governance of a cooperative essentially concerns good management and leadership which ultimately determines the market performance of a cooperative. Bijman et al. (2016) argued that effective participation in supply chains and linkages to demanding markets require good leadership, increased member commitment, and active participation. In sum, to link farmers to demanding markets, the provision of business-oriented services, the adherence to good governance, and having committed members and effective leaders are all necessary.

Our findings, consistent with Abate et al. (2014), Bernard and Spielman (2009), and Fischer and Qaim (2012), show that larger farms have a higher probability of being members of a cooperative. Contrary to this, Verhofstadt and Maertens (2014a) and Chagwiza et al. (2016) show that membership declines with an increase in landholding size for farmers in Rwanda and Ethiopia, respectively. Distance to the district market has a positive effect on membership. Similar results have been reported by Abebaw and Haile (2013). Consistent with Fischer and Qaim (2012) and Abebaw and Haile (2013), we found that the distance to the market has a positive and significant effect on the probability of cooperative membership. However, Chagwiza et al. (2016) and Verhofstadt and Maertens (2014a, b) have found that distance to markets has a negative and significant effect on the likelihood of cooperative membership.

We find that cooperative membership is biased toward those farmers who have more productive resources. Put differently, farmers with low resource endowments are less likely to be a member of a cooperative. Similar results have been reported for smallholder farmers by Bernard and Spielman (2009) in Ethiopia, and Fischer and Qaim (2012) in Kenya. Both studies indicated that the very poor are excluded from membership. Contrary to these studies, a more recent study by Chagwiza et al. (2016) has indicated that dairy cooperatives in Ethiopia are inclusive of poorer smallholders. The latter authors claim that resource-limited small farmers benefit from cooperative services through intensification effects.

8 Conclusion

Due to changes in markets, technology, and government policies, the institutional environment of rural cooperatives in Sub-Saharan African countries is rapidly changing. Cooperatives need to adjust their organizational structures and their strategies in order link smallholders to modern supply chains. Cooperatives are becoming more business-oriented (Bijman et al. 2016; Penrose-Buckley 2007). In this paper, we examine the emerging role of cooperatives in facilitating supply chain relations in the African food system context. We used malt barley cooperatives in Ethiopia as empirical case. The paper had two main objectives. First is to understand the changing role of cooperatives in the emerging (modern) malt barley supply chains. Second is to explore which farmers are more likely to be member of a cooperative and thus may benefit from the new role of the cooperative. A combination of qualitative and quantitative methods was used to generate data.

Our descriptive analysis shows that cooperatives engage in agribusiness activities and perform a brokering role, which supports their participation in the emerging malt barley supply chains. This has a positive impact on farmers' income and livelihoods. Our findings also show that cooperatives enhance supply chain relations through facilitating contract negotiation, communication, product aggregation, and storage. In addition, our results show that there is a correlation between the performance of a cooperative and the entrepreneurial attitude of the members. The latter finding could indicate that cooperatives are likely to exclude less entrepreneurial farmers when they become more integrated in the modern barley chain. Our regression results show that the motivation to join a cooperative is determined by demographic, economic, and institutional factors.

Our study has important implications for public policies in Ethiopia. Strengthening the role of cooperative in modern supply chains seems an appropriate goal of public policies. This can be done through various types of support, such as enhancing access to finance, providing management training, providing facilities for quality grading and storage, improving the relationship between primary cooperatives and their union, and using appropriate incentives for increasing members output.

Clearly, our work is limited by the cross-sectional nature of our data and the small sample size. These do not allow us to rigorously analyze the impacts of cooperatives at the micro level nor to fully check for potential reverse causality. This could be overcome in future research by a larger sample and panel data. The results of our study encourage further research regarding the following issues. First, the issue of inclusiveness of cooperatives needs more study, because policy makers and NGOs often assume cooperatives to include the poor. However, from a business perspective, there are reasons to expect that cooperatives become less inclusive when they further integrate in modern supply chains. Second, to explore whether cooperatives are truly participatory organizations, research is needed on the internal governance of cooperatives, particularly regarding the influence of the common members on the strategies and policies of the cooperative. Finally, cooperatives still face a number of internal governance and capacity challenges. Research on these challenges and their solutions would be very useful for developing effective support programs.

Appendix

Table 8 Correlation matrix

	Variables	1	2	3	4	5	6	7	8	9
1	Family active labor	1.000								
2	Access to mobile	−0.152	1.000							
3	Saving	−0.017	0.249	1.000						
4	Innovativeness	−0.088	0.422	0.314	1.000					
5	Extension contact	0.148	0.081	0.188	0.259	1.000				
6	Farm size	0.535	−0.063	0.006	0.016	0.167	1.000			
7	Livestock holding	0.013	0.081	−0.036	0.131	0.093	0.048	1.000		
8	Distance market	0.176	−0.100	−0.052	−0.255	0.006	0.196	−0.039	1.000	
9	Iddir membership	0.486	−0.404	−0.018	−0.234	0.089	0.483	−0.031	0.062	1.000

References

Abate G (2018) Drivers of agricultural cooperative formation and farmers' membership and patronage decisions in Ethiopia. J Cooper Org Manage 8(2):53–63

Abate GT, Francesconi GN, Getnet K (2014) Impact of agricultural cooperatives on smallholders' technical efficiency: empirical evidence from Ethiopia. Ann Publ Cooper Econ 85:257–286

Abebaw D, Haile MG (2013) The impact of cooperatives on agricultural technology adoption: empirical evidence from Ethiopia. Food Policy 38:82–91

Agbahey JU, Grethe H, Negatu W (2015) Fertilizer supply chain in Ethiopia: structure, performance and policy analysis. Afrika Focus 28:81–101

ATA (2016) Agricultural transformation agenda annual report (2015–2016). Agriculture Transformation Agency, Addis Ababa

Barham J, Chitemi C (2009) Collective action initiatives to improve marketing performance: lessons from farmer groups in Tanzania. Food Policy 34:53–59

Bernard T, Spielman DJ (2009) Reaching the rural poor through rural producer organizations? A~study of agricultural marketing cooperatives in Ethiopia. Food Policy 34:60–69

Bernard T, Collion M-H, De Janvry A, Rondot P, Sadoulet E (2008a) Do village organizations make a difference in African rural development? A study for Senegal and Burkina Faso. World Dev 36:2188–2204

Bernard T, Taffesse AS, Gabre-Madhin E (2008b) Impact of cooperatives on smallholders' commercialization behavior: evidence from Ethiopia. Agric Econ 39:147–161

Bijman J, Muradian R, Schuurman J (2016) Cooperatives, economic democratization and rural development. Edward Elgar, Cheltenham

Chagwiza C, Muradian R, Ruben R (2016) Cooperative membership and dairy performance among smallholders in Ethiopia. Food Policy 59:165–173

CSA (Central Statistical Agency of Ethiopia) (2017) Agricultural sample survey (Vol I). Report of area and production of major crops. Addis Ababa

Faysse N, Simon C (2015) Holding all the cards? Quality management by cooperatives in a Moroccan dairy value chain. Eur J Dev Res 27:140–155

Fischer E, Qaim M (2012) Linking smallholders to markets: determinants and impacts of farmer collective action in Kenya. World Dev 40:1255–1268

Fischer E, Qaim M (2014) Smallholder farmers and collective action: what determines the intensity of participation? J Agric Econ 65:683–702

Francesconi GN, Heerink N (2010) Ethiopian agricultural cooperatives in an era of global commodity exchange: does organisational form matter? J Afr Econ 20:153–177

Francesconi GN, Ruben R (2012) The hidden impact of cooperative membership on quality management: a case study from the dairy belt of Addis Ababa. J Entrep Org Divers 1:85–103

Hannan R (2014) Good co-operative governance: the elephant in the room with rural poverty reduction. J Int Dev 26:701–712

Ito J, Bao Z, Su Q (2012) Distributional effects of agricultural cooperatives in China: exclusion of smallholders and potential gains on participation. Food Policy 37:700–709

Kaganzi E, Ferris S, Barham J, Abenakyo A, Sanginga P, Njuki J (2009) Sustaining linkages to high value markets through collective action in Uganda. Food Policy 34:23–30

Latynskiy E, Berger T (2016) Networks of rural producer organizations in Uganda: what can be done to make them work better? World Dev 78:572–586

Lutz C, Tadesse G (2017) African farmers' market organizations and global value chains: competitiveness versus inclusiveness. Rev Soc Econ:1–21

Markelova H, Meinzen-Dick R, Hellin J, Dohrn S (2009) Collective action for smallholder market access. Food Policy 34:1–7

Minten B, Tamru S, Engida E, Kuma T (2016) Transforming staple food value chains in Africa: the case of teff in Ethiopia. J Dev Stud 52:627–645

Mojo D, Fischer C, Degefa T (2017) The determinants and economic impacts of membership in coffee farmer cooperatives: recent evidence from rural Ethiopia. J Rural Stud 50:84–94

Moustier P, Tam PTG, Anh DT, Binh VT, Loc NTT (2010) The role of farmer organizations in supplying supermarkets with quality food in Vietnam. Food Policy 35:69–78

Narrod C, Roy D, Okello J, Avendaño B, Rich K, Thorat A (2009) Public–private partnerships and collective action in high value fruit and vegetable supply chains. Food Policy 34:8–15

Penrose-Buckley C (2007) Producer organisations, a guide to developing collective rural enterprises. Oxfam, Oxford

Poulton C, Dorward A, Kydd J (2010) The future of small farms: new directions for services, institutions, and intermediation. World Dev 38:1413–1428

Rashid S, Gashaw TA, Solomon L, Nicholas M (2015) The barley value chain in Ethiopia. International Food Policy Research Institute (IFPRI), Addis Ababa

Reardon T, Barrett CB, Berdegué JA, Swinnen JF (2009) Agrifood industry transformation and small farmers in developing countries. World Dev 37(11):1717–1727

Royer A, Bijman J, Bitzer V (2016) Linking smallholder farmers to high quality food chains: appraising institutional arrangements. In: Bijman J, Bitzer V (eds) Quality and innovation in food chains. Lessons and insights from Africa. Wageningen Academic Publishers, Wageningen, pp 33–62

Shiferaw B, Hellin J, Muricho G (2011) Improving market access and agricultural productivity growth in Africa: what role for producer organizations and collective action institutions? Food Security 3:475–489

Tadesse G, Kassie GT (2017) Measuring trust and commitment in collective actions: evidence from farmers' marketing organizations in rural Ethiopia. Int J Soc Econ 44:980–996

Tefera DA, Bijman J, Slingerland MA (2016) Agricultural co-operatives in Ethiopia: evolution, functions and impact. J Int Dev. https://doi.org/10.1002/jid.3240

Tefera DA, Bijman J, Slingerland MA (2019) Multinationals and modernisation of domestic value chains in Africa: case studies from Ethiopia. J Dev Stud:1–17. https://doi.org/10.1080/00220388.2019.1590551

Trebbin A (2014) Linking small farmers to modern retail through producer organizations – experiences with producer companies in India. Food Policy 45:35–44

Verhofstadt E, Maertens M (2013) Processes of modernization in horticulture food value chains in Rwanda. Outlook Agric 42:273–283

Verhofstadt E, Maertens M (2014a) Can agricultural cooperatives reduce poverty? Heterogeneous impact of cooperative membership on farmers' welfare in Rwanda. Appl Econ Perspect Policy 37:86–106

Verhofstadt E, Maertens M (2014b) Smallholder cooperatives and agricultural performance in Rwanda: do organizational differences matter? Agric Econ 45:39–52

Wollni M, Zeller M (2007) Do farmers benefit from participating in specialty markets and cooperatives? The case of coffee marketing in Costa Rica. Agric Econ 37:243–248

World Bank (2008) Agriculture for development, world development report. World Bank, Washington, DC

Hybrids in the French Apple Industry: Opportunistic and Cognitive Differences Between a Cooperative and an Investor-Owned Group

Louis-Antoine Saïsset and Jean-Marie Codron

Abstract The rising concern of European consumers for pesticides residues left on fruit and of some far distant countries in Asia and Americas for quarantine organisms has turned compliance with SPS requirements into one of the main challenges of the French apple industry. Using transaction cost and cognitive governance theories, we investigate how differences in property rights structures, inter-firm arrangements, and mechanisms of firm governance may impact the modalities of SPS risk management. Our case study of two leading groups of the French fresh apple industry with different property rights structures (cooperative vs. private) and different marketing strategies (customers with more or less stringent SPS requirements) highlight the role of cognitive governance mechanisms (knowledge sharing) in the management of SPS risks. This paved the way for integrating governance structures, cognitive resources, and transaction attributes into a single model.

1 Introduction

Over the last two decades, French apple companies have been faced with twin challenges: to become "bigger and safer," "bigger" to remain competitive in a world market where globalization and supplier competition have increased drastically, and "safer" because of the huge increase in sanitary and phytosanitary (SPS[1])

---

[1] The acronym SPS (sanitary and phytosanitary) is used by the WTC for SPS agreements. It includes both regulations on pesticide residues in fruit (S: sanitary) and regulations on the presence of harmful organisms (PS: phytosanitary).

L.-A. Saïsset (✉) · J.-M. Codron
INRA, UMR MOISA, CIRAD, Montpellier SupAgro, Montpellier University, Montpellier, France
e-mail: louis-antoine.saisset@supagro.fr; jean-marie.codron@supagro.fr

© Springer Nature Switzerland AG 2019
J. Windsperger et al. (eds.), *Design and Management of Interfirm Networks*,
Contributions to Management Science,
https://doi.org/10.1007/978-3-030-29245-4_13

requirements. The higher sanitary requirements come from European consumers and citizens who are more and more demanding in terms of pesticides residues and eco-friendly agricultural practices. This has led to the European Union and national governments raising levels of public standards and strengthening controls. Moreover, most retailers, who are faced with increasing pressure from NGOs and the media, tend to impose on their supplier's private standards that are more restrictive than public ones, in particular concerning maximum pesticide residue limits (MRL), authorized molecules, and agroecological indicators (Codron et al. 2005; Scandella and Vernin 2018). As regards to the phytosanitary requirements, they are quite new for French companies. They are issued by new destination countries (mostly in Asia and North and South America) which raise increasing barriers to avoid importing and disseminating quarantine organisms (in particular pests) and limit the economic effects of regulated non-quarantine organisms.

Meeting such a double challenge requires significant changes in strategies, structures, and governance. "Growing bigger" is obtained by concentrating volumes, diversifying products (new varieties), and changing sourcing (from regional to national and international) and destinations (most of them with phytosanitary constraints).[2] It is also obtained by significant concentration movements (mergers-acquisitions, alliances, subsidiaries, holdings, etc.) leading to complex corporate structures and governance. "Growing safer" requires close coordination between the different operators along the supply chain. This coordination must be all the closer, especially between farmers and shippers, when the aim is to export to destinations with demanding sanitary and phytosanitary requirements. To comply with SPS requirements, product inspection at the packing level is in no way sufficient. It has to be complemented by process inspection, pesticide residue analysis being costly, time-consuming, and only affordable for a small percentage of total shipped volume. A first step for process inspection is to require a certificate of good agricultural practices (GAP) from the farmer. Global GAP—launched in the late 1990s by Northern European retailers—has progressively turned into a universal standard and tends to perform this function (Codron et al. 2005). A further step when SPS requirements become more stringent is strong involvement of the shipper in the production process with a delegation of control/decision rights to the shipper by the farmer for SPS management: elaboration of the phytosanitary program, pest and disease monitoring, decisions to apply chemical or biological treatments, control of parameters influencing the decisions for treatment, etc. (Codron et al. 2017).

In such a complex and challenging environment, governance issues matter: firms need a high level of flexibility and skills, appropriate governance mechanisms, and inter-firm relationships. Notwithstanding this deep-set trend, we may observe a diversity of patterns of governance. Many factors may cause variations in modalities of governance: property right structures, marketing or sourcing strategies, cognitive aspects.

---

[2]The ten top structures represent 35% of total turnover (Crédit Agricole SA, agrifood businesses financial observatory).

Transaction cost economics provides valuable insights in understanding how, in a context of uncertainty and complexity, the governance of a transaction may be linked to investments in specific assets, the organization of knowledge skills, as well as the existence of good relationships between partners. While TCE focused mostly in the 1970s and 1980s on opportunism and transaction cost savings, it has significantly evolved since the 1990s in two complementary directions. Some scholars (Williamson 1985; Ménard 2013) have stressed the role of relationships between partners to explain how incomplete contracts can be efficient (Williamson 1985), or how the relational contract correlates with the level of pooled strategic resources and the degree of centralization control (Ménard 2013). Other scholars working on organizations have dug more deeply into the bounded rationality behavioral assumption, either by focusing on information asymmetries and risks of manipulation by the party with more expertise (Barzel 1982, 2005) or by putting forward the organization of knowledge skills with the objective of creating more value added than saving costs (Nooteboom 2000; Madhok 2002). To that purpose, Nooteboom (2000) and Madhok (2002) draw on knowledge-based approaches to better qualify the nature of knowledge (Winter 1987) and explain how differences in the organization of knowledge skills may result in different governance structures even though the transactions have the same characteristics (specific assets, frequency, uncertainty).

Our case study on SPS risk management illustrates the advances made in both directions. Using the first way of thinking, we show that two types of hybrid forms governing almost the same transaction may be differentiated: a strategic center and a system of information sharing. From the second, we describe and analyze the cognitive mechanisms managing the complexity of transactions (nature of knowledge and system of skills, good flow of information and knowledge, convergence of values and objectives). Drawing on Madhok (2002), we formulate insights into the organization of these knowledge sets and show how this organization aligns transaction attributes with governance structures.

The aim of our paper is to compare the organizational design of two large-scale French business entities aimed at marketing apples worldwide and faced with high SPS requirements. Drawing on our two-sided theoretical framework, we assume that there is some alignment between transaction attributes, governance attributes, and knowledge resources, in particular regarding the management of SPS risk. Our key research question is how differences in property rights structures, inter-firm arrangements, and mechanisms of governance impact the modalities of SPS risk management.

In this paper, we design our conceptual framework drawing on two theoretical advances of TCE dealing with differences in decision-making processes and cognitive aspects to explain the choice of a governance structure. We then describe our qualitative methodology, analyze the main features, and finally draw our conclusions from the data collected in the two case studies.

2   Theoretical Framework

Due to bounded rationality, transaction complexity characterizing SPS risk management raises questions of knowledge production and circulation. It was taken into account by TCE literature in different ways. It may be considered as another transaction attribute, which adds to asset specificity, frequency, and uncertainty or also as the source of some specificity of human resources, which influence, as any specific asset, the choice of a governance structure (Williamson 1985). The theoretical prediction is henceforth that an increased level of complexity or of specific human resources leads to more integration. There are possible variations of governance for the same transaction. This depends on the quality of the relational contract, which is a mechanism to help manage contractual incompleteness (Ménard 2013).

Another approach, exploring the black box of the knowledge production and circulation processes, has enriched the previous approach. Similar transaction attributes may lead to different modalities of governance depending on how capabilities are organized within a firm or within an alliance of firms. Such an approach focuses on the interactive processes implemented in hybrid forms in order to organize capabilities or available human resources. Let us delineate these two approaches.

2.1   Transaction Complexity and Governance

Transaction costs economics (TCE) is a theoretical framework which considers the transaction as the unit of analysis and defines it as a transfer of decision and or control rights. Organizations are the structures entitled to rights and acting transactions and governance the modalities to allocate and monitor assets and rights (Ménard 2018). Our analysis deals with "the comparative costs of organizing rights to use resources and to transfer these rights through different arrangements" (Ménard 2018, p. 7). It aims at choosing between different arrangements going from market to hierarchy as the most efficient one in terms of cost savings. Hybrid forms are intermediate arrangements combining the advantages of market (incentives) and hierarchy (administrative control). Their governance is a mix of incentives and decision rules and can be characterized by its level of decentralization or delegation of decision rights (Williamson 1985).

Until the late 1980s, technology was held constant for the purposes of analysis, and little attention was put on knowledge which was expected/assumed to be equally transmitted between parties transacting on the market and those transacting internally (Lukasz 2009). Hence, little emphasis was put on bounded rationality and complexity. The main behavioral assumption was opportunism, and the main transaction attributes under scrutiny were asset specificity, frequency, and uncertainty. Although specific assets also include human-capital investments, whose illustrations are notably specialized training and learning-by-doing economies in production operations (Williamson 1979), the analysis of knowledge organization remains limited.

It is only since the 1990s, with the emergence of the post-industrial society built on knowledge rather than things, that more emphasis has been placed on bounded rationality and complexity. The increase in complexity calls for a more integrated arrangement such as hybrids (i.e., strategic alliances, groups, cooperatives, supply chains) or hierarchies (Ménard and Klein 2004). Another consequence of complexity is the increasing share of "non-contractibilities" that cannot be enforced through formal contractual mechanisms but require non-contractual mechanisms such as trust and reputation.

Macaulay (1963) and Macneil (1974, 1978) introduced relational contracts into the management and economic literature to emphasize the mix of contractible and non-contractible elements and the importance of the latter. According to Goldberg (1980) and also to Baker et al. (2002), parties establish tightly meshed relationships to limit the impact of: (a) imperfect and costly information, (b) opportunistic behavior, and (c) difficulties for outsiders to enforce agreements plagued with non-verifiable elements. "'Relational governance'" is understood to be social processes emerging from repeated interaction and which facilitate adaptation. Ménard (2013) positions the different arrangements along two axes: the level of control decentralization and the level of strategic resources, including knowledge skills. This scheme allows for a differentiation of hybrids. Two forms of governance are useful for our case study: information networks and strategic centers.

On the left of the spectrum, close to spot markets, information-based networks rely essentially on information platforms to coordinate activity, while ownership over assets and decision rights remains distinct. In this way payoffs are closely linked to the actions of separate parties. In all cases, information devices/platforms are intended to make partnerships sustainable by reducing risks of opportunism, facilitating mutual control, and lowering transaction costs. Shared information can help reaching these goals through: (a) modularity and replicability of know-how, allowing for implementing joint routines; (b) open standards, making communication easier while increasing the transparency of transactions; (c) implementation of devices that allow conversion and translation of protocols and interfaces at low cost; and (d) the development of "intuitive" interfaces (Langlois 2002; Clemons and Row 1992; Paché and Paraponaris 1993; Anderson and Gatignon 2005). From this perspective, the role of flexible two-tier organizations such as federations of cooperatives, economic interest groups, or some investor-owned groups with decentralized coordination is important: they facilitate the development of very flexible and adaptive inter-firm networks where informal coordination prevails.

At the other end of the spectrum, partners rely on tight coordination by strategic centers empowered with formal authority: contractual clauses constraining members, who pool significant rights and appropriation of residual gains, become a key issue. Strategic centers exert authority on a limited subset of rights. They can constrain partners by: (a) adjusting collective action or joint decision rights, (b) designing enforcement mechanisms to discipline parties, (c) framing bargaining

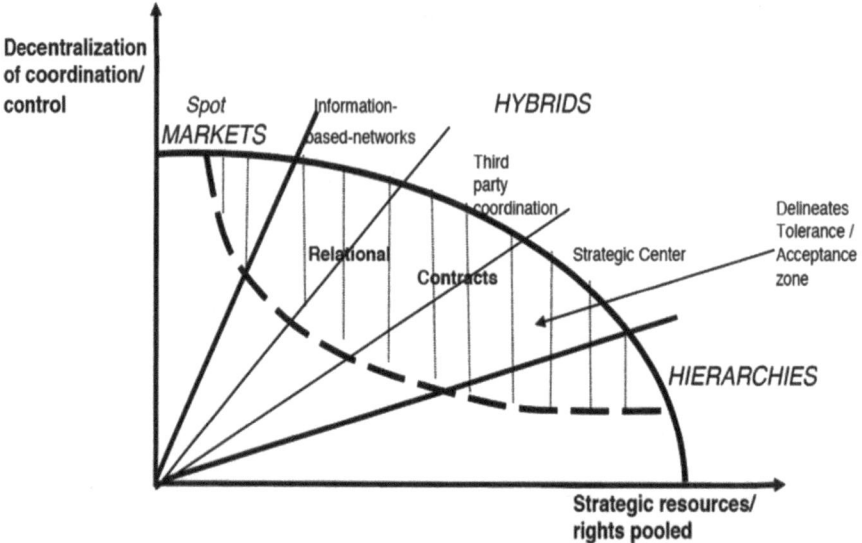

Fig. 1 Transaction cost economics, hybrid forms, and relational contracts. Source: Ménard (2013)

processes over quasi-rents, and (d) deciding dispute resolution procedures. On that basis, a lot of cooperatives, some associations with quite strict rules, but also investor-owned firms or groups with centralization can be seen as such hybrids. Indeed, in these complex organizations, one of the main points is to harness stakeholders and more particularly members or shareholders so that bargaining between different coalitions does not involve inertia. Coordination, internal communication, and, for cooperatives, collective decision rules are key points.

Variations in organization modalities are made possible by the quality of existing relationships (relational contract) and their capacity to informally manage "non-contractibilities." The lens-shaped area (Fig. 1) captures the idea of a tolerance/acceptance zone that allows adjustment and adaptation among partners. The lower bound delineates the inferior limit of what is acceptable to parties. Hence, the shaded area is where modes of governance operate most of the time.

Another strand of transaction cost literature that has been useful when examining the notion of complexity is the branch of measurement cost headed by Barzel (1982, 2005). He brings to the fore bounded rationality and measurement cost, which he considers as important as opportunism and asset specificity for governance analysis.[3] He starts from the asymmetries of expertise or perception of the value of the partners of a transaction and then considers the measurement costs that are

---

[3]In the same vein as Barzel (2005), Garicano and Rayo (2016) consider bounded rationality problems as important as incentive problems to explain failures in an organization. The lack of talent of those giving directions and code incompatibility are among the examples given by the authors.

necessary to find an agreement in a transaction. Given those asymmetries, there is a risk of manipulation by the party with more expertise and consequently the need for spending time and resources to avoid it. To Barzel (2005), the main solution to reduce those transaction costs is to transfer/allocate part of the decision or control rights to the party with more expertise, together with the provision of monetary guarantees to the party less informed. Such a solution is aligned with the proposition by Ménard (2013) linking the level of decentralization of the decision to the level of pooled resources.

In the three versions of the theory, the role of knowledge skills is identified but superficially and in a static way without entering into the "black box" of the interactive processes which create and develop capabilities. The focus is still on the cost saving transactional objective. Learning or value-added creation aiming at a better knowledge organization is almost always ignored.

2.2   Governance of Knowledge

Cognitive approaches that are used in organization studies and management sciences have a vision of firms or firm alliances as processes of production and circulation of information. In such approaches, knowledge is no longer considered as a given or easy to access on the market but, most often, tacit[4] and costly to transfer within the firm or between firms. The focus is on learning and knowledge complementarity when firms need skills they cannot develop on their own (Teece et al. 1997). An application of this view can be found in the economic model of the Japanese firm by Aoki (1986, 1990).

Knowledge complexity that could be considered as another transaction attribute justifies—as in TCE—the reliance on hybrid firms. However, while in TCE the questions are "make or buy?" or "if I buy, what kind of contract do I need?" (putting forward cost saving criteria), in cognitive governance the key questions are "how to make" and "does the firm own the adequate resources to do so competitively?" In a nutshell, the question is one of cognitive governance.

The analysis focuses on the key role of learning and capabilities and deals with the performance and competitive advantage that can be obtained through an adequate organization of knowledge skills producing a higher value added than organizational costs. Providing, transferring, and managing necessary knowledge skills through well-delineated processes become the key issue.

---

[4] Winter (1987) considers that there are four important dimensions of knowledge transactions: tacitness versus explicitness, system quality versus stand-alone, teachability versus non-teachability, and complexity versus simplicity.

Most firms, large or small, private or cooperative, are concerned with cognitive governance issues such as cognitive cost or cognitive alignment as stated by several scholars. Cognitive costs, which rely on knowledge asymmetry and higher informal practices, have been assessed in relation to the size of the firm. For Wirtz (2006, 2011), cognitive costs increase as the size of the firm increases. Similarly, Nooteboom (2009) emphasizes how coordination is easier in smaller firms, whereas larger businesses need to codify their functioning.

Cognitive alignment is another important issue. Alignment first concerns values and norms of conduct. It is considered a hot topic for governance and cooperation in different types of capitalistic firms: large firms (Nooteboom 2009), fast-growing firms (Wirtz 2011), firms with takeovers (Cadot 2017). It is also crucial when collective action is at stake, such as in agricultural cooperatives. A growing body of literature has emerged to deal with this topic. Among the pioneers, Huse et al. (2005) have stressed, using the case study of a milk cooperative group, how important the process and board diversity are to reach this cognitive alignment. More recently, Bijman et al. (2013) have shown the complexity in analyzing board models and the role of managers, while Saïsset et al. (2017) have designed a specific model concerning the manner of governing cooperative mergers and highlighted the relevancy of a cognitive approach in such a complex process. Alignment is also very important for strategy in hybrids. The ability to work together—in a few words to manage—is dependent on shared challenges (Noteboom 2009) and on a shared strategic vision (Forbes and Milliken 1999), that is to say on important cognitive aspects. In the cooperative sector, cognitive convergence among decision makers appears crucial in terms of governance (Saïsset 2016) and has an impact on operational management.

Finally, alignment of cognitive aspects concerns perceptions and cognitive biases. As pointed out by the work of Amos Tversky and Daniel Kahneman, individuals tend to make systematic errors in risk assessments. However, when put together within the framework of a firm, they start to estimate risk in more objective ways thanks to different individual experiences. Thus, by employing a specific organizational form (the firm), the negative effects of biases caused by the heuristic availability can be reduced. The firm has come to be seen as an important device for extending cognitive capacity of individual economic agents as well (Lukasz 2009).

Given the complexity and tacitness of most knowledge concerned by SPS risk management, there is a clear link of such management with the cognitive dimension of governance. This is confirmed by one of the few studies dealing with such a risk. Indeed, Breukers et al. (2009) examined the relationships between actual risk, risk perception, and decision-making with respect to phytosanitary risks in order to develop a conceptual framework that provides a qualitative understanding of the main determinants of phytosanitary risk management.

Their reasoning is grounded in different approaches to risk perception. Cognitive aspects of risk perception are often pointed out in this field and consequently in risk management. More precisely, Loewenstein et al. (2001) proposed the "risk-as-feelings" framework in which feelings/perception and cognitive evaluation interact and are considered as risk behavior drivers and certainly influence risk management.

Breukers et al. (2009) also studied external variables affecting risk behavior such as characteristics of the manager and his firm, as well as the socioeconomic and spatial environment. From this perspective, they confirmed Botteril and Mazur's (2004) research which shows that a lack of knowledge increases risk perception and can lead to bad management decisions. In a similar way, Breukers et al. (2009) dealt with the way education may influence the level of understanding of a risk, which affects risk perception. Other governance factors influencing risk—especially SPS risk—management are the level of cognition among stakeholders, and especially decision makers, (understanding, education, shared knowledge), together with the conditions of transfer of decision rights.

The cognitive governance issue aims at giving more insights into the governance structure issue tackled by TCE. It is complementary as well to the TCE approach since it deals with the cost of organizing knowledge not only from a production point of view but also from a transactional point of view due to bounded rationality and opportunism of individuals or groups. That is the reason why cognitive approaches of the "resource-based view"[5] type can easily share ideas with the classical transactional approaches.[6] Madhok (2002) takes it a step further by proposing a model integrating both theories. Based on his observation that there are variations in organizational forms under similar transaction characteristics, he explains that it is not just transaction particulars that matter but also firm particulars. To Madhok (2002), most competitive firms or alliances of firms are obtained through an alignment of transaction attributes, firm resources, and governance structures (Fig. 2).

To summarize, our twofold theoretical framework gives us deeper insights into both dimensions that had been neglected early by TCE, namely, complexity and bounded rationality on the one hand and learning and capabilities on the other, and provides us with useful material to guide our case study. The TCE extended framework gives a pathway to differentiate hybrids along two axes (level of pooled strategic resources and level of centralization of the decision) and substantiates the two contrasted hybrids that show up in our case study: information sharing networks and strategic centers. It also stresses the role of informal mechanisms in private ordering given the incompleteness of contracts in hybrids, in particular, the role of relational contract, and inter-firm or inter-individual trust. Cognitive theory applied to business gives us criteria to describe, qualify, and contrast cognitive governance of different types of firms (private vs. cooperative, small vs. large, etc.).

---

[5]Boiled down to its core, the resource-based view explains networks and other hybrids as ways to deal with uncertainties and change by sharing essential inputs, particularly competencies (Wernerfelt 1984; Nooteboom 1999).

[6]Nooteboom (2000) considers that in the case of hybrids, seen as complex networks, the theory of knowledge and the vision of the cognitive firm are close to governance problems (Nooteboom 2000), especially considering that efficiency of collaboration and agreement increases when interactions increase and cognitive distance decreases.

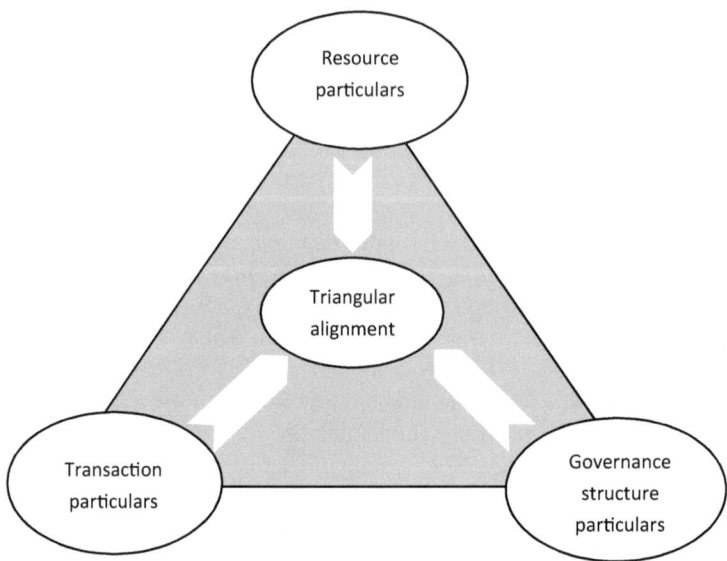

Fig. 2 The triangular alignment hypothesis. Source: Madhok (2002)

3 Methodology

Building on a theoretical framework mixing transaction cost economics and cognitive governance theories, our survey is first and foremost exploratory. Its objective is to analyze governance structures and processes that can explain ways of managing SPS risks and their potential efficiency. Given the complexity of SPS risk management, the tacitness of most knowledge, and the need for hybrids, our case study enables us to analyze the cognitive governance aspects for each of the two groups (see Box 1 for more details). It also gives consistent information to check the alignment or misalignment of transaction attributes, governance structures, and cognitive governance with a main application to SPS risk management, as proposed by Madhok (2002).

Our methodology first followed Yin's research (2013): iterative process and data triangulation were carried out, leading to a kind of hard form of research. It relies on case studies with in-depth analysis of ownership, governance, and cognitive processes regarding farmers and SPS constraints. In line with Yin's approach (2013), we investigated a contemporary phenomenon—agrifood group governance and SPS issues—in its specific context (viz., economic, geographic, and social). In particular, we tended to focus on large-sized apple groups, which in the last 10–15 years have become among the most competitive economic actors in the international market.

A description of the two groups is provided in Box 1. We carried out 10 semi-structured interviews (lasting from1 to 2½ h, most of them being recorded and transcribed) with 14 top executive managers, general managers, technicians, and chairmen of firms composing each group, from 2014 to 2019 (see Appendix 1 for further information). We also collected internal data (reports, accountings, statutes, etc.) as well as external information (newspapers articles, websites pages). All these qualitative and eclectic data led us to an in-depth analysis and a better understanding of the complex reality concerning the dynamics and cognitive processes linked to governance practices.

Box 1 Groups Description

Co-op Group A

- Foundation in 1969 as a "GIE" (Economic Interest Group)
- Active external growth with other co-ops in the last 5 years
- Global structure: a single holding with 3 main types of shareholders and 4 main subsidiaries
- 300 farmers-members spread out over a very large area (South West, Southeast, West)
- Different fruits production: apple, plum, pear, kiwi, grape
- Average apple output: 220,000 t (92% of total fruit output)
- Average turnover: € 250,000,000
- More than 2000 employees

Capitalistic Group B

- Foundation in 1960
- 4 businesses have joined the group since 2014
- Global structure: a single holding with one main shareholder and 10 subsidiaries gathered in 5 subgroups
- Apple specialization
- Average apple output: 120,000 tons
- Average turnover: € 100,000,000
- 330 employees

Sources: Websites of each Group and interviews

We adopt a blend of a narrative and synthetic strategy (Langley 1999). A narrative strategy underlines key points and important events for each group, and a synthetic strategy builds an emerging model of governance practices enabling good SPS risk management.

From this perspective, we studied two main actors of the French apple industry that presented some similarities (supplying at the national level, with strong and ambitious strategies) and differences (capital structure and legal status, i.e., capitalistic organization vs. cooperative). Considering the complexity of these case studies and the newness of observations in this sector, we preferred to concentrate our research on the two largest groups, encouraging in-depth analysis more than repetition of cases. This last point is motivated by their dissimilarities, which made it likely to show us the factors which could explain their differences in governance as well as their differences in managing SPS risks and efficiency.

4 Results and Analysis

4.1 Two Apple Groups as Two Hybrid Forms

4.1.1 Co-op Group A

Co-op Group A is a very big firm in the fruits and vegetables industry in France, compared to the average turnover of French co-ops in the same sector (€ 30,000,000, source: FELCOOP) or to the one of the producer's organizations (€ 120,000,000, source: Crédit Agricole). Since its foundation in the late 1960s in the southwest of France, firstly as an informal economic group, decisions have always been made in the interest of the farmers, and they have been collectively governed. Being one of the most famous spearheads of the French apple industry, it has progressively become the real leader of this sector, particularly with regard to export sales, thanks to its evolution toward a co-op federation.

As a part of its DNA, collective action and decisions have thus always been one of the most important specificities of Group A. It has been based on a very close relationship between sales managers, packing house managers, and farmers (members of the co-op stations). Intangible matters (brands, labels, and certificates) have always been decided on a day to day basis including strategic concerns: Group A was mainly focused on exports when it was founded, and the brand BW still exists today. It was launched at the same time as the group was established. Moreover, a highly sophisticated quality management system has been built over the past decades (ISO 9002, Agri-Confiance), along with the development of production specifications to comply with distribution requirements.

Since 2006, the group has achieved strategic alliances with upstream businesses and another co-op federation (Co-op Federation Y), leading to external growth and an increase in its area of production. Today, as shown by Fig. 3, it is made up of 11 co-ops (Co-op 1 to Co-op 11), members of 2 co-op federations (X and Y), a marketing subsidiary at the head of the group (SAS Z), and 4 other subsidiaries of SAS Z (Z1 to Z4). Far from a single firm and a hierarchy form, Group A is composed of a structured network of firms and co-ops that makes it an original, four-tier complex hybrid.

Group A is collectively owned by farmers gathered into several co-ops (6 in the Federation X, based in the southwest, and 5 in the Federation Y, based in the Loire Valley) which jointly own the trade office (a simplified joint-stock company, SAS Z). The latter holds interests in 4 other companies which are service providers or have additional activities (e.g., communication). So, this group is shaped by

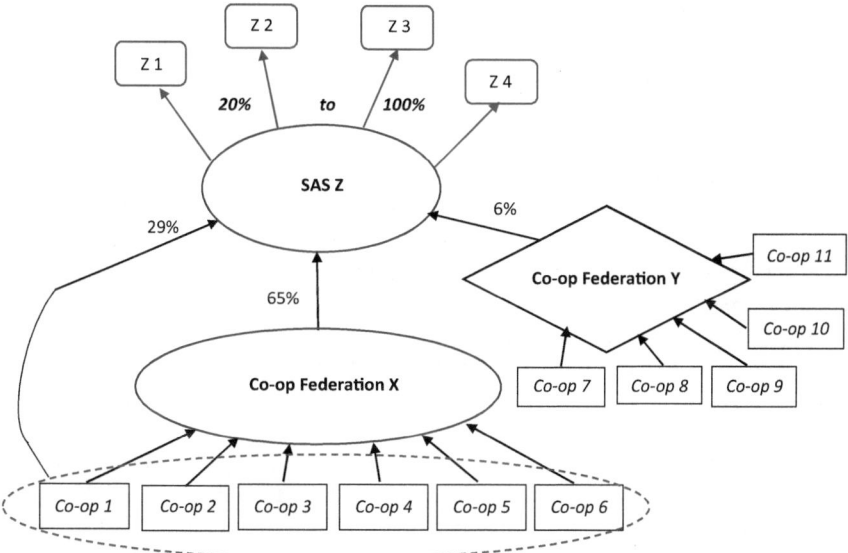

Fig. 3 Composition and share ownership of co-op Group A. Sources: Diane data base and co-op Group A

the collective action of apple farmers through co-ops and present, for this reason, a widely dispersed ownership structure (because of the great number of farmer-members), leading to very vaguely defined property rights. This could be a source of governance issues, particularly in the decision-making process.

Going further in our analysis, it appears that Group A is really centralized concerning its governance and strategy, although its complexity and collective governance system may lead us to think otherwise at first glance. Indeed, with such a strong brand and identity to its credit, Co-op Group A has very important and increasingly centralized functions. We can observe at its third level SAS Z: global or strategic governance, marketing strategy, and technical/production strategy. These crucial points concern the whole value chain and strategic resources. In this context, SAS Z, at the head of the group, is market-oriented and brings together all the sales forces of the 9 co-ops making up Group A. As an executive officer says, "There is a centralized sales department." All these characteristics confer strength and cohesion to the group: "The governance is very strong, being attentive to customers' needs." (Manager of a co-op) In particular, it relies on a delegation of power from the BoD of SAS Z to top executive management. The CEO is recognized as leader by producers and directors. Because he has their confidence, "he can operate freely" (manager of a co-op)—leading to an easier and faster decision-making process.

So, Group A can be considered as being in the hybrid category according to Fig. 1, with a high level of strategic resources that have been pooled and a high level of centralization of decision rights over the use of these strategic resources, i.e., a hybrid with a strategic center, quite close to hierarchy.

4.1.2   Capitalistic Group B

The capitalistic Group B is closely linked to families of western France (Val de Loire). It is the most important private firm in the French apple industry, with an average turnover of € 100,000,000. It was launched in the 1950s to market fruit from family orchards. The first packing house was created in 1960 and paved the way for growth and progressive build-up of the group. Like Group A, Group B is highly specialized in apple production, collection, and marketing. Since its beginnings, the group has developed exports and invested in high-level, unique, and innovative facilities (maturity laboratory, new pre-graders, etc.) and may be considered as a real pioneer in apple industry innovations.

Over the past 15 years, Group B has been very dynamic with very rapid external growth: 4 firms entered the group on both sides of the value chain, upstream as well as downstream. Those firms are focused almost exclusively on apple production and distribution and have a wide range of activities (production, trading, and marketing). All of them have developed standards and certificates at all levels of the chain: *Vergers Eco-Responsables* ("Eco-Responsible Orchards"), a French label related to integrated fruit production, Global Gap at the farming level, and BRC as well as IFS at the packing level.

So, since its creation, Group B has moved from the position of a single production company to the one of a capitalistic four-tier fruit group. As is shown in Fig. 4, the SAS Holding B, owned by two families, has 7 subsidiaries (B1–B7) with 6

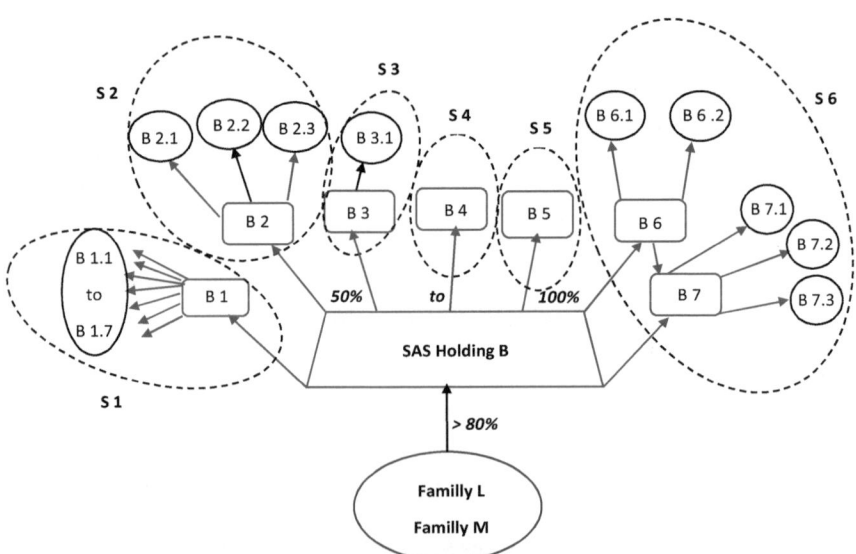

Fig. 4 Composition and share ownership of capitalistic Group B. Sources: Diane data base and capitalistic Group B

subgroups (S1–S6), themselves with 16 subsidiaries (B1.1–B1.7 for S1, B2.1–B2.3 for S2, B3.1 for S3, B6.1, B6.2 and B7.1–B7.3 for S6).

Group B is controlled financially by two families with close links—a western apple-producing family and a wholesaler one—and one man who holds many directorships or chairman mandates, inside or outside the group. The holding company, owned by these families (SAS Holding B, a simplified joint-stock company, as in Group A), is at the head of a wide range of subgroups and subsidiaries—a sort of patchwork of firms—involved in apple production (orchards or packing houses), domestic markets, and exportations. So, in this group, the ownership structure is highly concentrated, which seems to foster group cohesion. These aggregated property rights suggest that governance and strategy are centralized and clearly defined.

In this context, this capital structure could lead us to characterize Group B as a kind of centralized hybrid. But, looking deeper into its "heart," we can say that appearances are deceiving. This group is in fact quite decentralized considering its global internal functioning. Indeed, it appears that the concentration of family shareholding does not mean centralization of decision rights over the use of strategic resources that are owned by both families. In fact, the group is quite loose and disparate because of the autonomy of its different components. This situation comes from the progressive growth of the group and the related successive companies' acquisitions. These components (6 subgroups) are "managed as autonomous business units" (statement made by the manager of a large firm of the group), with varying profit centers' strategies and without real global strategic coordination (strategic aims and particularly marketing ones are not clearly defined). In this case, centralization is weak, and a real identity based on consistency and strong strategic vision is difficult to achieve. That is why Group B recently changed its name (before it was very regionally oriented) and adopted the slogan: "Fruit grown with dedication." These aspects of communication notwithstanding, the aim of this group appear to be first and foremost financial (as it is controlled by a small number of people from the same family) and quite active politically in order to speak with one voice to professional organizations and public institutions.

So, according to Ménard (2013), Group B appears to belong to the category of hybrids which present a quite low level of centralization and resource pooling, that is to say, a hybrid of the information-sharing type, more distant from hierarchy than Group A.

4.2 Two Hybrid Forms with Different Knowledge Asymmetry and Cognitive Governance Processes

Here we will deal with the degree of centralization or decentralization of coordination, inside the "black box" of each group, and its impact on governance bodies and process, including their very contrasted knowledge sharing to make decisions. Bounded rationality and knowledge asymmetry will be at the center of our study.

First and foremost, the two groups are dissimilar in nature: Group A is rooted in democratic control and collective action, whereas Group B is based on capitalistic objectives benefitting a smaller number of shareholders. This situation affects both governance systems, as underlined by the CEO of a large co-op, member of Co-op Group A: "The cooperative system [Group A] is a pyramidal bottom-up system" whereas Group B is based on a "top-down system." In other words, Group A is characterized by vertical integration and farmers' shareholding from upstream to downstream of the value chain, whose center is SAS Z, with strong economic objectives. For its part, Group B is mainly driven by financial aims, with a holding (SAS B) which owns the different businesses, themselves frequently orchard owners.

Moreover, each of the two groups is a specific hybrid form, as we characterized them from a general point of view in the former subsection. So, thanks to the numerous interviews we ran, we can now analyze them from an in-depth approach, mixing their global nature and hybrid type, their centralized/decentralized aspects, and their consequence for knowledge sharing, as shown in Table 1 (main knowledge sharing location in bold type).

This table leads us to clarify strategic resources and knowledge sharing among the components of each group. It also gives us a more precise idea about the balance in decision-making inside both groups:

– Group A is strongly centralized in terms of strategic governance, marketing strategy, and technical/production strategy, but with a certain balance between co-ops (first tier) and SAS Z (third tier), namely, concerning marketing matters, and a rather centralized circulation of knowledge.
– Group B is quite decentralized (marketing strategy, technical and production strategy, SPS risk management are decided within each subgroup), with a partial centralization of strategic governance (a recent trend) and much autonomy of subgroups with very low level of knowledge sharing.

To illustrate the specific equilibrium in Group A, it is interesting to deal with the informal arrangement that managers call "commercial arbitration." Indeed, marketing aspects are well-balanced between strategic orientations at the SAS Z level and operational choices at the individual co-op level. The marketing department develops an unrestrained market strategy, sets market needs, and informs co-ops about them. They then "choose destinations which suit them best," declared the CEO of the Group. Another manager said, "Packing houses have the power to agree or disagree. [. . .] It brings them to maturity." This point is somewhat surprising for such a big-sized group, with crucial financial objectives for its members. However, it is in fact realistic because of the necessity of keeping close to apple farmers' requirements, thanks to each cooperative packing house. This specific system is well-managed and enables each co-op to optimize its SPS risks by choosing markets adapted to its technical capacities. Thanks to this ascending and descending information and decision system, issues are shared, cognition can be improved, and flexibility becomes a keyword for the group.

Table 1 Group typology, centralization/decentralization, and knowledge sharing location in the hybrid apple groups studied

Group/Global nature/Hybrid type	Centralization	Decentralization	Knowledge sharing location
Co-op Group A	Strategic governance	Investment strategy	**Head of the Group** Co-op
Democratic-Pyramidal Bottom-up System	Marketing strategy	Marketing operational choices	**Head of the Group** Co-op
Centralized with Strategic Center Hybrid	Technical and production strategy	Operational risk management	**Head of the Group** Co-op
	Financial and partly strategic governance	Partly strategic governance	**Head of the Group Subgroups**
Capitalistic Group B			
Top-down System	Political lobbying		Head of the Group
Decentralized and Information-Sharing Network	Partial Pooling (information, varietal distribution, packaging purchase)		Head of the Group Subgroups
		Marketing strategy	**Subgroups**
		Technical and production strategy	**Subgroups**
		Operational risk management	**Subgroups**

Sources: websites and interviews

At the top of Group B, sharing information, as well as some technical aspects, is crucial: coordination concerning "club varieties" (production, internal sales, and mutual aid) and regional varietal distribution, after discussions between the different subgroups in relation to orchard issues. On the other hand, these functions are not the most strategic ones, and there is in fact a great deal of decentralization: for example, in foreign markets, competition between different firms of the group is a striking reality, as pointed out by Peng et al. (2018). One manager said, "It is everyone for himself and God for everyone." Intra-group marketing relationships are scarce and lead to operational decisions within each subgroup, with bounded cognition and so without any real coordination. In this context, this group can be seen as a company network where autonomy prevails, relying on a complex and dispersed decision-making process. However, things are slowly moving in a more centralized direction by the recent setting of an adaptive and flexible strategic board (informal governance body, see Table 2). It is certainly a first step toward more strategic coordination, leading to reduce bounded rationality through circulation of knowledge.

We can see that centralization or a balance between centralization and decentralization in these hybrid forms creates a need for a higher knowledge sharing, which reduces knowledge asymmetry. This phenomenon is synthesized in Table 2, dealing with arrangements that influence better cognition as far as governance and management are concerned.

As far as informal governance bodies are concerned (non-statutory and non-mandatory bodies with proper governance mechanisms), Group A has been developing them for a few years. They appear to be good channels for conveying useful information and knowledge to and from the farmers, the managers, and their co-ops.

In this context, an official "managers committee" (made up of a CEO from each co-op) is now functioning to "work on shared language" and to "enable productive exchanges," that is to say to reinforce a common culture and vision. The top manager states: "We must give a Group A culture to new co-op managers."

Using a knowledge-based approach to technical aspects, the Technical Commission—composed of a farmer called the "technical delegate" and a technician from each packing house—has important functions at the group level: long run varietal orientations, technical arrangements analysis, and visits. Thanks to the "technical delegate," this commission can be seen as "the transmission belt between Group A, its strategy, its orientations and the packing house" (CEO of Group A). This Technical Commission keeps close links from upstream to downstream of the group, helping to develop interaction and better cohesion, crucial in this complex hybrid form of organization. A CEO said, "There is a permanent connection between upstream and downstream, enabling orchards and their production to cope with markets. There is no confrontation between upstream and downstream, but a real complementarity among them." Consequently, SPS risk management, essentially relying on tacit knowledge (customers' specific and changing requirements), can be more easily coordinated and is more secure. Market requirements—in terms of varieties and pesticide residues—are explained to apple producers through the Technical Commission but also through other

Table 2 Formal and informal arrangements influencing cognitive governance and management process

Group	Informal governance bodies *Head of the group*	Formal relationships with farmers *Base of the group*	Informal relationships with farmers *Base of the group*
Co-op Group A	Managers committee Technical commission	Cooperative contract Quality management "Agri-Trust"	Farmers implication in many processes *Solidarity, information, and knowledge sharing*
Capitalistic Group B	Strategic board	Business relationship Quality management "eco-responsible orchards" Toward an upstream integration approach Work in progress	Moral contracts, farmers as performers *Personal relationships, habits, opportunism*

Sources: Interviews

information/knowledge networks existing at each co-op level (members' meetings, periodic training sessions, local commissions). In fact, the development of varietal strategy, related to marketing strategy and markets' requirements, with specific SPS constraints, is discussed and decided at the SAS level. So there is an informal and centralized decision-making process, not only due to its nature as a co-op but also because of its specific hybrid form.

Concerning Group B, the decision-making process is mostly delegated to each homogeneous part of it. However, there is now a crucial informal governance body at the level of the SAS Holding B called the "Strategic Board." It is composed of some members of the managing board, the quality manager of the group, and some other executive managers, depending on necessity. Meetings take place every three months in Paris, and their aim is to design and coordinate implementation of group strategy. Its way of functioning is not hierarchical and is very flexible. It is a kind of committee for strengthening the identity of the group and the quality management. The CEO insists, "The governance of the Group is mostly horizontal. It is very important for us to be adaptable and agile." It is a good way, but a limited one, to reduce knowledge asymmetry in the group and to improve rationality in the decision-making process, even in global aspects of SPS risk management. So, in this investor-owned group, SPS risk management is very decentralized, due to the decentralization of the production and marketing strategy and also to the standard nature of the SPS requirements of the targeted markets. This form of SPS risk governance is mainly due to the hybrid form and not to the capitalistic nature of the group.

As for formal relationships with farmers, they are very different in co-op groups from capitalistic ones. In Group A, farmers are suppliers and shareholders at the same time and are to be considered as internal stakeholders. A cooperative contract, relying on this double commitment (economic and financial), is a foundation of farmers' relationships. Linked with the duty for members to supply their apple production to the packing house (duration and quantity) and their voting rights, each co-op has a moral obligation to inform its members of and provide them with training in technical aspects, especially SPS ones. In this group, technical management is very important and leads to close monitoring of producers. The manager of SAS Z states: "We are working to move all packing houses and farmers to the same level of know-how." With that in mind, Group A has emphasized the development of quality management and more particularly the "Agri-Confiance" ("Agri-Trust") approach, which is an AFNOR[7] norm. It deals with environmental and quality management systems of agricultural production: alternative technics, floral fallow land, and energy diagnostics among other things. Nearly 100% of Group A farmer members are following this normative system, which is exceptional. It includes phytosanitary requirements from customers' specifications and enables close links between staff and apple farmers. "Agri-Trust" leads to a mutual understanding between technicians and farmers and strengthens upstream linkage,

---

[7] AFNOR: French Association of Normalization.

allowing a better understanding among members about SPS constraints. It reduces asymmetry of tacit knowledge in order to create value. So, in this group, the ambitious and diversified broader marketing strategy, characterized by the high level of SPS constraints imposed by countries (like Germany, UK, USA, China, Taiwan, etc.), is a strong driver of its upstream requirements and the development of such an involving quality management system as "Agri-Trust." There are strong links with apple farmer members, but not just due to the cooperative nature of the group.

Regarding Group B, farmers' relationships are formally those prevailing in on-going business relationships. No written purchase contract exists. Law of supply and demand applies, and farmers are completely free, as well as firms of Group B, to stop their businesses from 1 year to another. Economic opportunism is a usual behavior: "Dissatisfied producer this year goes away next year and it is not a problem; the grass always looks greener on the other side of the fence!" But it still remains that some firms of this group own orchards and are traditionally apple producers, even if it represents a limited part of the total production. In this context, Group B has developed and generalized the French label "Vergers Eco-Responsables," following a specific charter of integrated fruit production: fostering biodiversity, giving preference to biological control methods, and controlling production methods. It is a more flexible approach than "Agri-Trust." It enables SPS risk management in a more standardized manner than in Group A, due to targeted markets not having excessive requirements. Nevertheless, formal relationships are changing: the group wants to develop an upstream integration approach in the long run with orchard financing, technical advice, and market commitments for apple farmers. In the future, Group B will hire several agronomists for these reasons to carry this out. The CEO said, "I believe in skills, human capital, so I want to invest in them."

To go further in our analysis, informal relationships appear as important as formal ones. They place importance on trusting human relationships. In Group A, volunteers-members have the possibility of being involved in operational thinking and the decision-making process by taking part in work groups, quality groups, or technical commissions. The different informal bodies exist from the basic level of the group (co-ops) to the top level (SAS Z) and are a good way to achieve mature decisions about SPS and share a common vision in order to achieve a high level of coordination. Farmers seem to be increasingly open to new ways of producing apples including the development of organic production. "Things are changing a lot, it is going forward all the time, and it demonstrates our vitality!" said one manager. From this perspective, every co-op must have quality relays to implement decisions but also to explain to farmers what to do and why. "Group A is not a watertight organization closed to outside projects." A cognitive process is at work and farmers can be active stakeholders, taking part in SPS risk management and the expansion of good practices. Solidarity also exists and enables smaller farmers with less technical and financial means to follow the changes coming, thanks to the technicians' assistance.

In Group B, 25% of the supply comes from the wholly owned orchards and another significant part is based on club varieties. This specific sourcing, like Juliette organic variety, is used for complex markets with high level of SPS requirements.

In this context, cognitive governance and knowledge sharing with apple producers is not always useful. So, farmers are frequently considered as simple suppliers and often can be seen behaving as "price-takers" or opportunists depending on apple payments and technical constraints. They are totally free. In this group, "supplies are varied." In fact, top executive staff point out that the "relationship is loyal, without any contract," "suppliers' relationships are based on moral commitment." So, business relationships rely on mutual trust. Furthermore, technical links seem to be one-sided. Some managers see farmers as people who just implement the firm's decisions: "Farmers are given orders as to what is required from them." However, top executives recognize that mastering the value chain requires information flow upstream and downstream. It's still true that farmers' interactions with each firm of the group often rely on personal relationships and work habits. Proving this state of mind, a manager said, "I have been in business for 45 years, I have a lot of relationships [. . .] Concerning Saudi Arabia, my company has been working with almost the same farmers for 44 years." It can be an advantage because of close links, but it could also be a disadvantage in terms of SPS risk management if no other contractual relationship is established.

5 Conclusion

Until the late 1980s, the analysis of corporate governance within the TCE framework was made from a cost savings point of view, with opportunism as the main behavioral assumption. Bounded rationality and learning were mentioned but not really implemented in the analysis. From this perspective, the recurrent question was whether it was less costly to make or to buy or what was the optimal contract (Williamson 1985). Later on, more focus was put on bounded rationality and the role of relational contracts in providing hybrids with flexibility to manage complexity and "non-contractibilities." Ménard (2013) predicts the type of hybrid governance from the level of centralization of the decision-making process and the level of strategic resources, the latter including knowledge resources. Drawing on this model, we identified in our case study two contrasted hybrid forms: one with a strategic center and one with an information-sharing network.

Additional analysis of these two hybrid forms used cognitive governance approaches (Nooteboom 2009; Wirtz 2011), where knowledge is no longer considered as a given or easy to access on the market. Knowledge is most often tacit and costly to transfer within the firm or between firms. Given the complexity and tacitness of most knowledge concerned by SPS risk management, there is a clear link of such management with the cognitive dimension of governance. In such approaches, knowledge asymmetries, learning, and capabilities are at the center of the theory, and the key question is "how to make (or buy)" and "does the firm (or the alliance of firms) own the adequate resources to do so competitively."

The cognitive governance approach, which gives more insights into the governance structure issue tackled by TCE, is complementary to the TCE approach. It deals with the cost of organizing knowledge not only from a production point of view but also from a transactional point of view due to the bounded rationality and opportunism of individuals or groups. By integrating these two theoretical frameworks, Madhok (2002) suggested that variations in organizational forms exist under similar transaction characteristics. He pointed out that firm particulars are as important as transaction particulars. Capabilities and knowledge are crucial for competitiveness, particularly when they lead to an alignment of transaction attributes, firm resources, and governance structures.

We used these two complementary governance approaches to describe and qualify the two apple groups.

– Co-op Group A, which we classify as a "democratic centralized hybrid with strategic center," enables circulation of knowledge and cognition thanks to informal governance structures and practices. It thus makes tacit and complex knowledge, related to SPS management, progressively more explicit and clearer for internal stakeholders, and creates the conditions to improve risk management and to create value on SPS-stringent and high-quality export markets.

– Capitalistic Group B, which we can call a "decentralized and information-sharing network," provides subgroups with a high level of autonomy and consequently a low level of coordination and knowledge sharing between subgroups. Such governance leads to opportunistic behaviors, standard SPS risk management, and little value creation since most affordable markets have few SPS requirements and do not offer high prices for apples. The only possibility for such a capitalistic group to target more demanding markets is to have their own production or to capture club varieties to gain some monopoly over their marketing.

Our study underlines the complexity of hybrid governance and particularly the importance of processes and mechanisms compared to structural features, in as far as SPS risk management relying on tacit knowledge is concerned. It also points out the key role played by the informal aspects of governance in the two case studies. Finally, it illustrates the existence of some triangular alignment between the transaction, resource, and governance attributes, which could suggest, according to Madhok (2002), some efficiency for each of the two groups. We must emphasize however that the two groups feature contrasting characteristics, work with different markets, and are not faced with the same SPS constraints. The two groups do not therefore produce the same value added. Neither bears the same production and transaction costs, which can explain that they may be both efficient. From this perspective, it appears that bounded rationality and cognition levels are different from one hybrid to another, leading to contrasted effectiveness in terms of SPS risk management and, as a result, to differential access to markets, in particular to high value SPS demanding markets.

Centralized hybrids adopting both strong and participatory governance which promote collective action with strong coordination and a marked cognitive dimension (in particular through sharing strategic and operational objectives and the involvement of producers in the decision-making process) appear to be better equipped to implementing a more specific, interactive management of SPS risks and enabling access to complex and value-oriented markets. With regard to decentralized hybrids adopting a more "shareholder-oriented" form of governance, more rigid, less participatory, and rarely defined by contract, operational governance appears to be weaker and more fragmented. Against this backdrop, asymmetries between upstream and downstream knowledge, as well as between managers and producers, are more significant, while management of SPS risks is less interactive and less optimal for value-oriented markets.

This qualitative survey, though limited, constitutes directions for further research. In order to verify that property rights and strategic resources are crucial in the model we designed, a qualitative study over a larger sample of apple firms would strengthen the validity of our analysis. Such a survey could be carried out in other sectors or other countries to improve the external validity of our results.

Acknowledgments The research leading to this paper has received funding from the French National Research Agency (ANR) under the project Sustain'Apple (2014–2018). We are grateful for the comments received for presentation at the eighth international conference on Economics and Management of Networks that was held in cooperation with the Universidad de la Habana (La Habana, Cuba, November 15–17, 2018). We are grateful to Xavier Vernin (CTIFL, Paris) and Zouhair Bouhsina (INRA, Montpellier) for their participation in data collection and comments. We are also grateful to George Hendrikse and an anonymous reviewer whose comments and criticisms helped us further refine our paper.

Appendix 1 Semi-Structured Interviews

Co-op Group A

Interviews characteristics

Interview number	Year	Interviewees	Type of firm Position in the group
1	2014	Technical manager and quality/technical executive	Shareholder of the group Head of a subgroup
2	2016	CEO	Shareholder of the group Head of a subgroup
3	2016	CEO and technical manager	Head of the group
4	2018	CEO	Shareholder of a subgroup Packing house

Interviews guidelines: some examples

Interview no 3
• Historical aspects—general presentation
• Group dynamics: coordination, production and marketing arbitrations, varietal innovation, farm structures
• Evolution at the head of the group: roles played by co-op federations, by the holding
• Group governance and strategy: global aspects and mechanisms, BoD, technical commission, managers committee
• Management of the group: importance of the general manager (CEO), sales managers' management, financial and sales reporting, relationships with suppliers, with farmers members, SPS risk management
• Packing houses (co-ops) situation: size, investments, main evolutions
Interview no 4
• Historical aspects—general presentation—main stages
• Farmer members' characteristics: size, specialization, varieties, dynamics
• Production and marketing: links, production orientation considering market trends
• Varieties choices and SPS management in relation to markets (viz., exportation)
• Production specifications, quality management: description, evolution, members' involvement, benefit for the packing house
• Members' payment: cost calculations, payment scales, evolution

Capitalistic Group B

Interviews characteristics

Interview number	Year	Interviewees	Type of firm Position in the group
1	2014	Quality manager and head of cultivation	Subsidiary of a subgroup Packing house
2	2016	CEO	Subsidiary of the group Appel trader
3	2016	CEO	Subsidiary of the group Head of a subgroup
4	2017	Export manager and quality manager	Subsidiary of the group Head of a subgroup
5	2019	CEO	Head of the group

Interviews guidelines: some examples

Interview no 3

• Group internal relationships/functioning: formal/informal relationships, type of coordination, centralization/decentralization of decision and management

• Markets specificities: varieties, SPS constraints linked to markets, farmers' understanding

• Apple farmers' relationships: formal/informal contracts, confidence, habits, duration, price mechanisms

• Production specifications: types, constraints level, evolutions, farmers' involvement

• Technical advice for apple farmers: reasons, importance/level, evolution

• Relationships with professional organizations: nature, frequency, importance

Interview no 5

• Historical aspects—general presentation

• Group dynamics: coordination, tangible and intangible investments, varieties (innovations)

• Group governance and strategy: roles played by the holding and by each subgroup, global aspects and mechanisms, governance structures/bodies, centralization/decentralization of decision and management, evolutions

• Management of the group: importance of the general manager (CEO), financial and sales coordination, relationships with apple farmers' suppliers

• Quality and SPS risk management: decision-making process, coordination, roles played by each subgroup, main evolutions

• Packing houses situation: size, investments, main evolutions

References

Anderson E, Gatignon H (2005) Firms and the creation of new markets. In: Ménard C, Shirley M (eds) Handbook of new institutional economics. Springer, Berlin, pp 401–431

Aoki M (1986) Horizontal vs vertical information structure of the firm. Am Econ Rev 76:971–983

Aoki M (1990) Toward an economic model of the Japanese firm. J Econ Lit 28:1–27

Baker G, Gibbons R, Murphy KJ (2002) Relational contracts and the theory of the firm. Q J Econ 117:39–84

Barzel Y (1982) Measurement cost and the organization of markets. J Law Econ 25:27–48

Barzel Y (2005) Organizational forms and measurement costs. J Inst Theor Econ 161:357–373

Bijman J, Hendrikse GWJ, Oijen A (2013) Accommodating two worlds in one organisation: changing board models in agricultural cooperatives. Manag Decis Econ 34:204–217

Botteril L, Mazur NA (2004) Risk and risk perception: a literature review. Australian Government, Rural Industries Research and Development Corporation, Kingston

Breukers MLH, Bremmer J, Dijkxhoorn Y, Janssens SRM (2009) Phytosanitary risk perception and management. Development of a conceptual framework. Wageningen University, Wageningen

Cadot J (2017) Neutraliser les mécanismes de gouvernance... et s'en mordre les doigts. Un cas de reprise d'entreprise qui tourne mal. Revue de l'Entrepreneuriat 16:177–196

Clemons EK, Row MC (1992) Information technology and industrial cooperation: the changing economics of coordination and ownership. J Manag Inf Syst 9:9–28

Codron J-M, Giraud Heraud E, Soler LG (2005) Minimum quality standards, premium private labels, and European meat and fresh produce retailing. Food Policy 30:270–283

Codron J-M, Engler A, Adasme C, Bonnaud L, Bouhsina Z, Cofre-Bravo G (2017) Food safety management through the lens of hybrids: the case of fresh fruit and vegetable shippers. In: Hendrikse GWJ, Cliquet G, Ehrmann T, Windsperger J (eds) Management and governance of networks: franchising, cooperatives, and strategic alliances. Springer, Cham, pp 295–322

Forbes DP, Milliken FJ (1999) Cognition and corporate governance: understanding boards of directors as strategic decision-making groups. Acad Manag Rev 24:489–505

Garicano L, Rayo L (2016) Why organizations fail. J Econ Lit 54:137–192

Goldberg VP (1980) Relational exchange: economics and complex contracts. Am Behav Sci 23:337–352

Huse M, Minichilli A, Schøning M (2005) Corporate boards as assets for operating in the new Europe: the value of process-oriented boardroom dynamics. Organ Dyn 34:285–297

Langley A (1999) Strategies for theorizing from process data. Acad Manag Rev 24:691–710

Langlois RN (2002) Modularity in technology and organization. J Econ Behav Organ 49:19–37

Loewenstein GF, Weber EU, Hsee CK, Welch N (2001) Risk as feelings. Psychol Bull 127:67–286

Lukasz H (2009) The history of transaction cost economics and its recent development. Erasmus J Philos Econ 2:29–51

Macaulay S (1963) Non contractual relations in business: a preliminary study. Am Sociol Rev 28:55–67

Macneil IR (1974) The many future of contracts. South Calif Law Rev 47:691–816

Macneil IR (1978) Contracts: adjustments of a long term economic relation under classical, neoclassical, and relational contract law. Northwest Univ Law Rev 72:854–906

Madhok A (2002) Reassessing the fundamentals and beyond: Ronald Coase, the transaction cost and resource-based theories of the firm and the institutional structure of production. Strateg Manag J 23:535–550

Ménard C (2013) Hybrid modes of organization: alliances, joint ventures, networks, and other 'strange' animals. In: Gibbons R, Roberts J (eds) The handbook of organizational economics. Princeton University Press, Princeton, pp 1066–1108

Ménard C (2018) Organization and governance in the agrifood sector: how can we capture their variety? Agribusiness 34:142–160

Ménard C, Klein PG (2004) Organizational issues in the Agri-food sector: toward a comparative approach. Am J Agric Econ 86:746–751

Nooteboom B (1999) Inter-firms alliances: analysis and design. Routledge, London

Nooteboom B (2000) Learning by interaction: absorptive capacity, cognitive distance and governance. J Manag Gov 4:69–92

Nooteboom B (2009) A cognitive theory of the firm: learning, governance and dynamic capabilities. Edward Elgar Publishing, Cheltenham

Paché G, Paraponaris C (1993) L'entreprise en réseau. Presses Universitaires de France, Paris

Peng X, Hendrikse GWJ, Deng W (2018) Communication and innovation in cooperatives. J Knowl Econ 9:1184–1209

Saïsset L-A (2016) Les trois dimensions de la gouvernance coopérative agricole: le cas des coopératives vinicoles du Languedoc-Roussillon. Revue Internationale de l'Economie Sociale 339:19–36

Saïsset L-A, Chériet F, Couderc J-P (2017) Cognitive and partnership dimensions in merger processes in agricultural cooperatives: the case of winery cooperatives in Languedoc-Roussillon. Int J Entrep Small Bus 32:181–207

Scandella D, Vernin X (2018) Les stratégies de gestion des risques SPS par la distribution française. In: Gérer durablement les risques sanitaires et phytosanitaires dans la filière pomme. Synthèse des résultats du projet Sustain'Apple INRA, Montpellier, pp 28–29

Teece DJ, Pisano G, Shuen A (1997) Dynamic capabilities and strategic management. Strateg Manag J 18:509–533

Wernerfelt B (1984) A resource-based view of the firm. Strateg Manag J 5:171–180

Williamson OE (1979) The governance of contractual relations. J Law Econ 22:233–261

Williamson OE (1985) The economic institutions of capitalism. Free Press, New York

Winter SG (1987) Knowledge and competence as strategic assets. In: Teece DJ (ed) The competitive challenge: strategies of industrial innovation and renewal. Ballinger Publishing Co, Cambridge, MA

Wirtz P (2006) Compétences, conflits et création de valeur: vers Une approche intégrée de la gouvernance. Finance Contrôle Stratégie 9:187–201

Wirtz P (2011) The cognitive dimension of corporate governance in fast growing entrepreneurial firms. Eur Manag J 29:431–447

Yin RK (2013) Case study research: design and methods. Sage, Thousand Oaks

Part III
Alliances

Collocation for Supplier–Client Knowledge-Based Coordination: Niche Positioning, Task Complexity, and Comparative Costs

Douglas J. Miller and Carmen Weigelt

Abstract We examine how clients and suppliers govern vertical relationships for knowledge work. Collocation—having supplier personnel interact with the client's personnel and systems at the client's site—is a contractual mechanism that facilitates coordination for knowledge co-creation. Using a sample of 1609 credit unions' relationships with 50 IT suppliers during the rise of Internet-based banking from 2000 to 2004, we examine the initial development of arrangements for online share account and loan processing. Results show that client positioning and task complexity partially determined the choice of collocation vis-a-vis a supplier delivering standard services from a remote location. However, as broadband communications reduced the costs of remote service, clients moved away from collocation.

1   Introduction

In knowledge-based services (KBS), professional service firms (e.g., IT, law, consulting, or auditing), as suppliers, specialize in distinct knowledge areas and achieve economies of scale by repeating similar tasks for multiple clients (Jacobides and Winter 2005; Mayer et al. 2012). Due to these supplier economies and domain expertise, client firms, especially small clients, rarely fully integrate the respective function. For example, even if a firm employs in-house attorneys to conduct the most sensitive or firm-specific tasks, the same firm also usually relies on outside providers for generic legal services (to save money) or for highly specialized services (that the client needs infrequently). Client firms often develop long-term

D. J. Miller (✉)
Rutgers Business School-Newark and New Brunswick, Piscataway, NJ, USA
e-mail: doug.miller@rutgers.edu

C. Weigelt
A.B. Freeman School of Business, Tulane University, New Orleans, LA, USA
e-mail: cweigelt@tulane.edu

© Springer Nature Switzerland AG 2019
J. Windsperger et al. (eds.), *Design and Management of Interfirm Networks*,
Contributions to Management Science,
https://doi.org/10.1007/978-3-030-29245-4_14

relationships with service providers, such that for new tasks the "buyer" may keep the same "supplier" (Baker and Faulkner 1991) and continue aspects of the same contract design (Mayer and Bercovitz 2008). Thus, vertical inter-organizational relationships (Lumineau and Oliveira 2016; Parmigiani and Rivera-Santos 2011) are the norm in KBS, providing a setting for not only provision of standardized services but also customized solutions and even co-creation of knowledge and co-production of services (Barras 1990; Larsson and Bowen 1989; Mahr et al. 2013; Santos and Spring 2015). A client firm can learn about software engineering or process management from the professional services supplier to better conduct operations or better contract with the supplier (Clark et al. 2013; Ethiraj et al. 2005; Mayer and Salomon 2006). Client and supplier may develop the ability to co-solve problems through relationship learning (Kohtamaki and Partanen 2016), and customer knowledge and relationships are vital to supplier firm learning and growth (Zander and Zander 2005). Organizational forms such as *equity alliances* or *joint ventures* can provide appropriate incentives and monitoring to govern joint knowledge production (Gulati et al. 2005; Heide et al. 2014; Puranam et al. 2013).

However, another governance mechanism that facilitates knowledge co-creation, but has not been adequately studied, is *collocation* of the supplier and buyer. By collocation, we do not mean geographic proximity, such as a supplier and client being located in the same city (e.g., Knoben and Oerlemans 2006). Rather, in collocation, suppliers place personnel at the buyer's site, working within the client organization and using the client's assets to complete tasks. These in-person contacts can range from periodic visits (Dyer and Hatch 2006) to a supplier embedding an "intense live-in" employee at the client site, as in JIT-II systems (Wilson 2000). Collocation is a long-term arrangement that can be specified in service contracts and enforced by the location of physical assets, making it a stable arrangement to organize the relationship.

Advances in communication technology have made it possible to have rich information exchanges even when people are in different physical locations. Yet face-to-face interaction remains the richest communication medium for information processing and business decision-making (Ambrose et al. 2008; Daft and Lengel 1984). Even in the most digital of environments—Google—with employees linked to each other through always-on video portals, "no one considers them as good as being co-located," and initial face-to-face conversations are recommended as a foundation for ongoing collaboration (Karis et al. 2016: 50). Therefore, the choice to collocate depends on the costs and benefits for a set of tasks.

In our empirical context, IT suppliers provided credit unions (CUs) with technology solutions and IT platforms. Internet banking emerged in the 1990s, with adoption rates among CUs surpassing 50% around 2000. Few CUs fully developed in-house activities such as system design, loan origination and service, or the operation of information-gathering systems for faster decision-making. As of 2005, over 95% of the USA's CUs had IT supplier relationships (Ono and Stango 2005). This time period was also a time of strategic positioning by CUs, as legislation in 1998 opened the doors to the "multiple common bond" charter, which could rapidly change a CU's size and customer profile. The decision to collocate the supplier's knowledge work in this setting meant the CU retained control of computer hardware hosting the software, required supplier personnel to work frequently at the client's site, and typically worked with the supplier to create customized IT solutions. Security and reliability are paramount in financial services, and CUs serving local customers were cautious about ceding control and databases to external providers. For instance, large IT vendor Jack Henry and associates purchased both Symitar and CU Solutions in 2002. Each provider had only offered programs meant to run on the client's own systems. After each acquisition, the vendor invested in upgrades to its systems and offered the same solutions via remote service bureaus, yet few clients switched to the new format.

Based on theory about governance of inter-organizational relationships, we develop hypotheses about how client niche positioning and task complexity affect the likelihood of collocation, as well as the role of declining costs of remote service that occurred with broadband penetration during the emerging period of Internet banking. We demonstrate that collocation is a means for clients and suppliers to work together on knowledge-based tasks. The sample consists of 1609 CUs' sourcing relationships with a total of 50 information technology (IT) suppliers for technology solutions from 2000 to 2004.

2 Theory and Hypotheses

The knowledge-based view (KBV) of the firm emphasizes the importance of knowledge in firm strategy and structure. Firm hierarchy tends to hold advantages over the market in the coordination of knowledge-based tasks (Argote and Ingram 2000; Grant 1996; Kogut and Zander 1992) due to firms' internal communication channels and a common language among employees that facilitate knowledge transfer. These firm advantages tend to outweigh the costs of bureaucracy inside the firm as contractual hazards increase. However, sometimes knowledge creation may require the combination of the prior knowledge of more than one firm. An extensive literature on R&D alliances describes governance of knowledge exchange and co-development under these circumstances (e.g., Oxley and Sampson 2004). Some knowledge-based capabilities may never be fully housed in a single firm but are inherently relational capabilities (Dyer and Singh 1998). Firms in long-term relationships may learn from each other as well as about each other (Davenport et al. 1996; Inkpen and Tsang 2007) and jointly generate new knowledge (Den Hertog 2000; Lavie 2006) by sharing their technical knowledge and their "interfirm expertise" (Parmigiani and Mitchell 2009). For example, one reason for concurrent sourcing—making and buying some of the same input—is to facilitate joint learning in buyer–supplier relationships (Parmigiani 2007).

Knowledge-based tasks—where the value of knowledge outweighs the value of physical assets deployed (Bajari and Tadelis 2001)—have become an important part of business activities (Grant 1996; Kogut and Zander 1992). The market for outsourced knowledge work has expanded in recent decades where specialized firms perform knowledge-based tasks in areas such as IT, legal work, consulting, or accounting (Mayer et al. 2012). These firms develop deep capabilities in domains such as data handling or software applications. Therefore, due to specialization, client firms can access an array of expertise in the market (Dyer and Singh 1998; Schilling and Steensma 2002). For example, Jacobides and Winter (2005) discuss how specialization in financial services led to the rise of data handling and software specialists such as IBM and EDS that leveraged knowledge from outside the industry to solve issues in financial services. Such specialization results in heterogeneous capabilities across firms, as firms focus on areas of strength while contracting for specialized skills related to a profession or field of knowledge such as software engineering or law (Jacobides and Winter 2005; Mayer et al. 2012). In this paper, we emphasize that clients also have specialized knowledge and requirements, which affects governance of inter-organizational relationships.

The architecture of alliance governance depends on coordination costs and appropriation concerns (Gulati and Singh 1998), with the primary driver of coordination costs being task interdependence and the resulting need for extensive information exchange. Collocation reduces coordination costs for team production within an organization (Rafii 1995). Likewise, regarding new product development alliances in manufacturing industries, "Co-location tends to be used more frequently when the technical complexity of the purchased part is high, the supplier is involved in a higher level of assembly (e.g., system versus subsystem level), the purchased part is of strategic importance, and when electronically linked information systems are limited" (Ragatz et al. 1997: 197). We expect firms to consider multiple factors like these for team production in vertical inter-organizational relationships for service industries (Larsson and Bowen 1989; Mayer and Nickerson 2005).

In information technology (IT), tremendous economies of scale and scope are possible through remote provision of standardized services, solutions, and software packages. An IT service company may benefit greatly by learning from key clients during the product development process, but once the product is being sold to the mass market, the supplier may try to reduce its costs of client training and customization through such strategies as a centralized data storage facility or help desk. From the perspective of the supplier, working with clients that set industry standards or present convincing use-cases helps the supplier develop a quality, marketable product. For the client, off-the-shelf software will often suffice, so there needs to be a compelling reason to invite a closer relationship with any service provider. Two key processes—learning with (from) a client and ongoing customization of a service—both require extensive interface between supplier and client personnel. The balance of knowledge development and knowledge application may vary across clients. When this interface takes place via the placement of supplier personnel at the client's site, operating software on the client's hardware, and with the client owning ancillary assets (such as storage), the interface is a form of collocation.

When supply of a particular service is dominated by large, independent suppliers, such as IT vendors, a common choice is between collocation and use of a remote service bureau (e.g., design center or call center). Remote service bureaus can create multiple efficiencies. First, the primary cost driver in KBS is economies of scope in human resources. Suppliers develop competitive advantages through economies of scale (Mayer et al. 2012; Poppo and Zenger 1998) and specialization of knowledge (Jacobides and Winter 2005). Overall, suppliers may have lower production costs than buyers, on average (e.g., Ang and Straub 1998; Tiwana and Bush 2007). With dozens of accountants, attorneys, or programmers, the supplier can allocate skilled personnel's time efficiently across tasks for various clients. If enough demand exists for a knowledge specialty, a large supplier can employ one or more professionals with that focus. Furthermore, the problems that arise at various clients are likely to repeat, such that supplier personnel can share and implement common solutions, enabling the supplier firm's learning-by-doing (Ethiraj et al. 2005; Hatch and Dyer 2004; Jacobides and Hitt 2005). For software, particularly, creating an "off-the-shelf" application that handles most functions for any client allows the supplier to amortize the cost of product development across many buyers. Second, suppliers who serve many clients benefit from economies of scale in physical assets at the supplier's location. For Internet-based services, collocation adds to the cost of implementation because the client creates relatively small computing infrastructure (e.g., servers) compared to the typical supplier. In other KBS contexts, scale can save costs at suppliers in terms of records storage, copying, mailing, or other processes. Third, remote service eliminates costs of transportation, time spent in transit, and the cost of scheduling travel. IT suppliers may still visit a client's site periodically to support a standard product, but primarily during sales talks and for initial training. Therefore, if collocation is to be adopted as part of a long-term contract, it must reduce costs of coordination more than it increases these other costs.

A client wants the supplier's product to align with the client's specific strategy, structure, and culture. Thus, in IT-based KBS, the client wants the supplier's personnel to understand the client firm's business processes and operations including who knows what, the codes for sharing information, and the rules of coordination (Clark et al. 2013; Kogut and Zander 1992). Suppliers may be reluctant to make such client-specific investments in learning as those investments take time to develop and are not easily applicable to its other clients (Kim and Mahoney 2006; Mayer et al. 2012; Mesquita et al. 2008). The supplier may instead offer more generic, "best-practice" solutions (Ethiraj et al. 2012; Mayer 2006). However, coordination—including adaptation over time—is more efficient when knowledge workers make firm-specific investments. If the supplier wishes to invest in client-specific capabilities (Dyer and Singh 1998; Ethiraj et al. 2005), embedding their personnel in the client's operations is likely to achieve results more quickly and thoroughly than occasional visits to the client's site. For example, Elfenbein and Zenger (2013) find that physical proximity increases relational capital between a buyer and supplier; arguing proximity reduces costs of repeated in-person contact.

Suppliers also want to learn from clients (e.g., Bettencourt et al. 2002; Gronroos and Voima 2012). A supplier may offer preferential scheduling, its most experienced personnel, or discounted pricing to a client whose knowledge is valuable for developing the software-based service (Den Hertog 2000; Mahr et al. 2013). The supplier recognizes that some relationships have high transactional value (Zajac and Olsen 1993). Further, a supplier with sufficient experience serving a diversity of clients will be better able to convince new clients to adopt its innovations (Weigelt and Sarkar 2009). In some cases, the supplier may even need to convince the client to share its knowledge. Recommended inducements are that the supplier educate the client, prevent problems (if possible), and rapidly solve problems that would detract from the client's motivation (Santos and Spring 2015). These inducements can be enhanced through placing supplier personnel at the client's site.

Therefore, client and supplier interests align to support collocation when the client has unusual knowledge about its operations that can combine with the supplier's knowledge of software and systems. We propose that two broad categories of clients fit this description. First, clients with niche market positions—offering unique products or services to their customers—require extensive initial learning for co-creation of new supplier-provided knowledge services. Second, clients whose diversity of products or services to their customers creates a complex, interrelated set of tasks therefore require suppliers to continuously customize and adapt the system as different bottlenecks and interdependencies emerge. In their seminal theory paper on the design and coordination of services, Larsson and Bowen (1989) employ the term "diversity of demand" to convey "both the uniqueness of the customer's [or client's] supply of goods and/or self that is to be serviced and the uniqueness of the desired outcome . . . The wider the range of unique customer demands, the greater the specific information not possessed by the [supplier] organization before the actual service encounter . . ." (Larsson and Bowen 1989: 218). They predict high diversity of demand will correspond to either "sequential customized" service design (e.g., appliance repair) or "reciprocal" service design (e.g., psychotherapy), which we contend are both enhanced by collocation.

2.1 Client Niche Positioning

A client's knowledge about how to best serve its end customers is particularly important for clients that pursue niche market positions (Cooper et al. 1986; Phillips et al. 1983; Porter 1980). A niche strategy may entail distinctive customer knowledge (Adams et al. 2015), requiring the client to develop unique routines and language, and offer different products or services to its customers than are prevalent in the industry. Knowing customers' preferences is crucial to effectively design a product. Therefore, a niche player would not be able to use "off-the-shelf" software or solutions from suppliers but require customization (Nickerson et al. 2001). Niche players often prefer to vertically integrate (Argyres and Bigelow 2010), but when supplier efficiencies and scale differences obviate vertical integration, client personnel can help to specify unique needs to the supplier (Fichman and Kemerer 1997) through extensive face-to-face interaction.

Niches can be created by various barriers. In our research context, the niche aspect that drives customization is the type of customer. A CU is chartered on the basis that it serves a particular customer base: employees of a certain firm, affiliates of a university, or citizens of a community. In the USA, there are few CUs that specialize in serving members of non-profit associations, the military, or other "single common bond" customers. For example, in the early 2000s, there were only about 50 US CUs chartered to explicitly serve military personnel. These CUs provided an array of unusual services, such as online payment in foreign currencies, overseas customer service numbers, home monitoring for deployed personnel, and tax preparation assistance. For loan processing, communication may have been by phone and email, some CUs offered small unsecured installment loans to military personnel, and financial planning tools were a common service to help military customers manage debt. Post-1998, most CUs became community-based or "multiple common bond" which means multiple employers and associations within the same geographic location banded together (Emmons and Schmid 2000). Those CUs that remain as single common bond serve customers with distinctive needs.

Niche positioning in other industries could be based on other barriers. From the design of retail websites, to maintenance of healthcare records, to specialized accounting for firms with operations in emerging economies, clients with niche positioning have valuable knowledge about their customers that needs to be incorporated into the systems and solutions purchased from an IT supplier. The supplier may benefit from access to that knowledge to streamline the development process, to avoid costly revisions if the beta version does not work, and to extend the limits of its software or service. Thus, not only do the client and supplier create knowledge together, but the supplier's learning sometimes enables it to develop new services for other clients. Collocation ensures the client's rare customer knowledge can be fully incorporated into the knowledge-based service through IT customization.

Hypothesis 1 Client niche positioning is positively related to collocation of supplier-provided knowledge work.

2.2   Client Task Complexity

Task complexity increases when there are more knowledge dimensions involved in a task and those dimensions are more interrelated (Kauffman 1995). A larger set of interdependent decisions or steps increases coordination costs and may involve ill-structured problem-solving processes including ad-hoc adaptations during task execution (Gulati et al. 2005; Macher 2006; Macher and Boerner 2012; Nickerson and Zenger 2004). Interdependencies between knowledge sets may be difficult to discern prior to engaging in the task, such that more customization and adaptation during task execution is required, what Thompson (1967) terms "reciprocal" interdependence (Larsson and Bowen 1989). These interdependencies often become tacit knowledge, embedded in routines that even client employees find difficult to explain (MacDuffie 1997; Ethiraj et al. 2012). The initial development of routines and codification of knowledge may be better realized through collocation (Daft and

Lengel 1986), because the important supplier personnel have more interaction with multiple contacts in the client firm, rather than just a few managers.

Firm-specific knowledge that spans interrelated tasks or components—what Parmigiani and Mitchell (2009) call "within-firm shared experience"—also aids ongoing adaptation, as the partners solve problems that arise during implementation. For IT, each product has an architecture, which is typically modular, combining various software and hardware components. Developers create "interim modularity" (Chuma 2006) to facilitate collective sensemaking. Over time, incidental interactions emerge between modules, requiring system fine-tuning. This is essentially an architectural or integrative task, not one that can be completed by people who are separated by organizational boundaries or other dimensions of distance.

In their intensive study of innovations in protocol analyzer software requested by clients of a major measurement firm, Ethiraj et al. (2012) find that the supplier is less likely to agree to customization when the requirement request is more complex. They state, "Customer feature requests that were complex to fulfill (i.e., those that spanned multiple modules) also demanded high labor input" (Ethiraj et al. 2012: 155). Therefore, the client may need to take on a greater share of the innovation process to develop such features, which may be accomplished through collocation. Further, task complexity may arise from a client having a broader product line or serving multiple markets, compared to the standard competitor. For instance, in Internet banking, banks varied in the number of services offered online, and in how much each service required synchronization between the Internet platform and its core processing services and human resources (Weigelt and Miller 2013). More diversified clients are more likely to continue to enter new markets than are less diversified clients, requiring ongoing adaptation. For these reasons, we propose:

Hypothesis 2 Client task complexity is positively related to collocation of supplier-provided knowledge work.

2.3   Improved Communication Technology

The benefits of collocation arise from the superiority of face-to-face interactions vis-a-vis other media of communication (Daft and Lengel 1984, 1986), since face-to-face communication conveys information with greater quantity and richness. The low cost and immediacy of e-mail, long-distance telephone service, and computer conferencing in the 1990s enhanced the frequency and richness of communication at a distance, and the advent of videoconferencing offered a new way for virtual teams to communicate "face-to-face." Although physical presence continued to outperform videoconferencing in terms of productivity and process satisfaction (e.g., in software development; Andres 2002), the advent of broadband technology improved the quality and reliability of connections. The public good of the Internet infrastructure reduced coordination costs relative to dedicated telecom systems. To be a close substitute for face-to-face meetings, an alternative medium needs to enable rich communication between multiple people. Such a medium is then sufficient to build relational capital: "the level of mutual trust, respect, and friendship that arises out of close interaction at the individual level" (Kale et al. 2000: 218). Similarly, Dyer and Singh (1998) propose that sub-processes that facilitate relational rents include partner-specific absorptive capacity, the ability to identify and evaluate potential complementarities, and self-enforcing, informal controls that encourage transparency and reciprocity. The benefits of rich, effective communication are shared by the client and supplier (Vickery et al. 2004).

Improved communication technology can lead to lower measurement costs between buyers and suppliers and hence less need for vertical integration (Barzel 1982). Likewise, information sharing for the purpose of knowledge co-creation is affected by communication media that becomes more effective over time. Collaboration between employees of the client and software designers at a remote supplier location became more effective, relative to collocation, in the late 1990s and early 2000s. As in higher education, online communication has not fully replicated the face-to-face experience in business services (Ambrose et al. 2008; Karis et al. 2016). However, over the time period of our study, we expect that clients and suppliers chose collocation less often as broadband Internet service reached their area.

Hypothesis 3 The use of improved communication technology is negatively related to collocation of supplier-provided knowledge work.

3   Methods

Similar to banks, credit unions are depository institutions that take deposits, make loans, and offer additional financial services such as trust accounts, investment services, insurance, and securities brokerage. They are dissimilar to banks in that they are non-profit, cooperative financial institutions that are owned by their members who share a common bond such as community, occupation, or association (US Department of the Treasury 2001). Following deregulation under the Credit Union Membership Act of 1998, CUs have evolved into full-service depository institutions that are often in direct competition with banks (Emmons and Schmid 2000).

This empirical setting is suitable for this study for several reasons. First, the financial services industry has experienced disintegration along the value chain over the past few decades. Specialized firms such as EDS and IBM have become providers of information technology services, software, and systems (Jacobides and Winter 2005) to support CUs' loan management systems. Over 95% of CUs partner with a technology supplier for their information systems. Second, a CU changes IT suppliers only rarely. The typical contract between IT suppliers and CU clients is for a period of 5–7 years (ABA Banking Journal 2013; Stewart 2013). Our data show that only 2% of CUs switch suppliers during each six-month time period.

The observed continuity in relationships may be due to CU processes becoming intertwined with supplier applications, resulting in supplier switching costs as well as client switching costs. Third, suppliers to CUs provide information systems and platforms for loan servicing processes that vary in task interdependence based on the CU's loan portfolio, consisting of different types of loan offerings.

3.1 Data and Sample

We use archival data from Call Reports that US CUs file semi-annually with the National Credit Union Administration (NCUA). The Call Reports contain information on a CU's financials and information on each CU's primary share and loan information processing supplier (e.g., EDS, CUSA, Fiserv). We collected data for all CUs with at least $50 million in assets covering eight semi-annual time periods from June 2001 to December 2004. We selected a period of years in which CUs were actively developing online portals and Internet-based services and products were still evolving. The advent of online loan processing followed the earlier, related trend toward customer-facing Internet services. The percent of CUs (with $\geq$$50 M in assets) offering Internet banking increased from close to 50% in June 2000 to 84% by December 2002, with small increases after that to 91% by mid-2004.

The use of IT suppliers is widespread in the CU industry with 98% of CUs contracting with a supplier for their loan and share systems. We used the Call Reports to identify each CU's primary IT supplier by name and manually coded each CU's supplier history. Although CUs may source from multiple suppliers, they are only required to report their primary supplier by name as those suppliers tend to be responsible for the majority of the client's IT services: "over 80% of the IT budget is almost always provided by one supplier, either the internal staff or one external supplier" (Lacity and Willcocks 1998: 370). There are 50 technology suppliers in the sample, each with at least five clients. In the Call Report, CUs add the name of their IT supplier, which we coded, correcting for slightly different spellings. Entries listed fewer than five times were typically not usable responses (e.g., "a local provider"). From June 2001 to June 2004, the unbalanced panel with all variables has 12,929 observations for 1609 CUs. For panel estimations, the average CU has over six observations with the maximum number of observations per firm being seven.

Dependent Variable *Collocation* of supplier-provided knowledge work is binary where 1 reflects a vendor-supplied in-house system and 0 indicates use of a remote service bureau. About 75% of CUs in our sample collocate, where the technology supplier provides, installs, and maintains IT platforms and technology solutions at the CU, while 25% conduct loan processing via software, IT platforms, and systems that reside at the supplier's site (a remote service bureau), using standard PC hardware to access and transmit information to the supplier (Lacity and Willcocks 1998; Levina and Ross 2003).

Independent Variables Taking deposits and making loans is a CU's core business with loans comprising over 62% of CU assets, indicating that how a CU organizes for its loan management and servicing matters. We thus focus on a CU's market positioning and complexity of the tasks that the CU conducts for its loan portfolio, as well as Internet-based indicators of the cost of organizing those services through a remote service bureau.

Client niche market position is the inverse of the number of CUs of the same type in the focal period. For example, at the midpoint of the sample window, December 2002, over half the CUs (with $\geq$$50 M in assets) are either community-based (251) or other multiple-common-bond (814) institutions. The remaining types have membership by association (e.g., a fraternal group) (21), military (65), educational institution (119), government agency (150), manufacturing employees (159), service employees (144), or "other single common bond" (63). The counts total to more than the number of CUs in the regression analysis because of missing data on variables for some CUs. As a robustness check, we code a variable *single common bond* that equals 1 if the charter is single common bond, else 0.

Client task complexity is based on the diversity of the CU's income base. The percentage of income obtained from noninterest sources (noninterest income divided by total revenues) captures a CU's reliance on non-traditional income sources, such as account fees, real estate closing costs, and debit and credit card transaction processing. Greater diversity underlying a CU's income base may require more applications and specialized staff to handle the different activities and interdependencies among them (Ono and Stango 2005). For instance, there is a fundamental difference in regulation between banks and CUs when it comes to issuing credit cards or other unsecured loans. Bank-issued credit cards are not protected by any specific collateral. Default on a bank-issued credit card leads to collection efforts requiring extensive legal steps. A bank may only be able to penalize the delinquent borrower through a bad report to the credit bureaus, not having the authority to repossess property or garnish wages without going to court. In comparison, CUs are owned by the depositors; thus, the main account is considered a "share" account, and checking, loans, or other accounts are tied to this share account. CUs are allowed to deduct from the share account items such as delinquent payment on a loan or a fee for over-drafting a checking account. If a borrower does not make a minimum payment on a credit card issued by a CU, the CU may extract the payment from any of the borrower's other accounts. This "cross-collateralization" may not be apparent to most borrowers but comes into play any time there is default on CU credit cards. CUs post statements clarifying cross-collateralization on their websites, as well as in loan documentation (Tampa Bay Times 2011). Therefore, managing unsecured loans is a much more complicated process for CUs than managing other kinds of loans, requiring more firm-specific customization of information processing services pertaining to the loan portfolio.

Broadband penetration relates to the costs to conduct loan processing and software development over the Internet. Statistics on historical broadband usage by households is from the Pew Research Center, which began tracking Internet usage in 2000. (The Pew Research Center Internet/Broadband Fact Sheet is accessible at http://www.pewinternet.org/fact-sheet/internet-broadband/. See "Who has home broadband" sorted by "Community" and click on "Data.") Pew reports broadband penetration for urban, suburban, and rural locations in each period of observation, sometimes multiple reports in a month, from 3/31/2000 to 11/22/2004 (and beyond). We connect these statistics to each CU by zip code, using the rurality measures provided by the Data Sharing for Demographic Research Knowledge Base curated at the University of Michigan Population Studies Center, following definitions provided by the US Department of Agriculture. We also include dummy variables to control for *suburban location* and *rural location*, with urban location the excluded category. We consider that the focal client's adoption of Internet banking may be endogenous to its choice of collocation, with both depending on broadband penetration. *Client offers Internet banking* is taken from item 892A on the Call Reports and is coded as a "1" if the CU's website is "transactional" rather than just "informational" or "interactive." In alternative specifications, we create a variable *Percent of clients offering Internet banking* in the sample as of the focal year. This measure correlates highly with broadband penetration.

Control Variables *Client firm size* is the log of a CU's total loans in US $B. Resource availability and scale economies may affect the choice to collocate supplier-provided knowledge work (DosSantos and Pfeffers 1995). We measure *Client firm age* as the log of the number of years since a CU was established. Resource availability increases as firms age and advance through their life cycle (Combs and Ketchen 1999). *Client liquidity* is total loans divided by total shares, a proxy for a CU's financial health and asset/liability management. Client liquidity may impact slack resources and resources available for hosting work in-house (Teece 1986).

CUs also report their total professional and outside services expenses. We divide this by the sum of (a) employee compensation and benefits and (b) professional and outside services to create *Client outside service expenses*, to control for a client firm's past reliance on external knowledge work (e.g., legal and audit fees or accounting services). Higher values indicate more familiarity with managing external providers and thus a possible tendency not to collocate.

Client loan risk is the weighted average of the risk of default for all secured loans in the CU's portfolio. CUs offer mortgage, vehicle, commercial, and agricultural loans to differing degrees based on local demand. Most CUs increase the size and scope of their loan portfolio over time. In their evaluation of the industry from 1994 to 2011, Malikov et al. (2018: 1104) report, "the majority of credit unions falls into the following three categories: (1) those that provide consumer loans and investments ... (2) those that provide real estate and consumer loans as well as investments ... and (3) those that provide all types of outputs: real estate, business and consumer loans, and investments." Different loan categories vary regarding their risk level, default rates, maturity, and lending limits and therefore vary in their transaction risk (Jacobides and Hitt 2005). National rates of default in each period come from the Federal Reserve Bank's quarterly reports on bank loans (www.federalreserve.gove/releases/chargeoff/). We exclude unsecured loans from this measure as credit cards and other unsecured loans see default rates over 5%, compared to less than 1% for secured loans. Thus, offering credit cards takes CUs to a different level of risk.

Client operational efficiency is the amount of loans processed divided by loan servicing expenses. Loan servicing expenses are recording fees, credit reports, processing expenses (e.g., tracking payments or refinancing), and collection expenses. We use a natural log transformation to reduce skewness. During the sample period, large CUs improved their cost-efficiency more than small CUs, but "the Credit Union Membership Act of 1998 ... did not substantially affect long-run patterns of productivity or efficiency change" (Wheelock and Wilson 2013: 84).

Credit Union Service Organizations (CUSOs) are non-profit entities owned by single or multiple CUs to provide back-office services, such as managing property, HR benefits, and IT. A client that uses a CUSO for other computer services may have a tendency to also use it for online loan processing. In the Call Reports, CUs report on their CUSO relationships in two ways. First, they must list the set of services for which they use a CUSO (items 834A–J). Second, they may list the CUSO as the primary service provider for specific activities, such as maintaining the client's website. If the focal CU reports either that a CUSO is its primary service provider for online share and loan processing, or it lists "Electronic Data Processing" among the services it receives from its CUSO, we impute a value of 1 for a dummy variable *Client uses CUSO*, which has a value of zero otherwise. In effect, opting to rely on the CUSO as a remote service bureau is different from relying on an independent vendor, because the CUSO is probably located nearby and is partially or wholly owned by its client(s). Thus, collocation is not as necessary to facilitate joint learning between a CUSO and client CU.

3.2   Statistical Analysis

Since collocation of supplier-provided knowledge work and whether the client offers Internet banking are binary dependent variables, we estimate a bivariate probit model with endogenous regressor, applying the "eprobit" command in STATA. This system of equations is appropriate if some of the same factors influence when a client chooses to offer Internet banking and the governance mode (i.e., collocation) it will employ to implement its services. Results reported in tables are from pooled cross-sectional models, including dummy variables for each time period and each supplier that appears in at least 40 observations across the full sample. In robustness checks, we estimate pooled cross-sectional models with time dummies and clustering of standard errors by client and panel probit models with random effects by supplier. Results are consistent across all specifications. The preferred specification allows us to handle two potential sources of endogeneity: the simultaneity of choosing a governance mechanism and choosing a supplier and the fact that both the services a client offers its customers and the services it receives from its suppliers depend on some common factors.

In negotiating for a new task to be completed by a supplier, a client not only selects a preferred governance mode or mechanism but also a supplier that is more or less familiar with that governance mode or mechanism. As already described, supplier relationships in KBS tend to be long-lasting, and clients tend to work with an existing supplier on a new task. However, the negotiation may proceed differently if the existing supplier has a strong preference for one governance mode over another for the new task, and since the client is free to select a new supplier for all its tasks periodically (subject to contract length and other terms), the choice of supplier is linked with the choice to collocate or not. However, just as clients may pursue niche positioning, suppliers of KBS may specialize in a method of working with clients. For this reason, we control for supplier in models explaining collocation. Reported models include dummy variables for each supplier that has at least 40 client observations in the sample. There are 24 supplier dummies, and three suppliers drop from the sample because all their clients use collocation. Including more supplier dummies causes models not to converge.

It is important to distinguish between a client (CU) receiving service from a supplier via the Internet and the same client offering services to its customers (account holders) via the Internet. A CU could use collocation or a remote service bureau even before the "World Wide Web" became widely popularized. Financial institutions, even small ones, used dedicated telecom lines to transfer data, including to government agencies and clearinghouses. CUs were likely to move to the more open and universal Internet platform before most of their customers. Thus, even CUs that accessed remote service bureaus over the Internet might wait months or years before offering Internet services to their customers. Nevertheless, the option to move operations, including IT supplier services, to the Internet would have occurred about the same time as customers would have been "going online" themselves. As US financial institutions updated their systems around "Y2K" concerns, they realized that offering service over the Internet could be a major point of differentiation (Sheshunoff 2000) and save them money (e.g., by needing fewer tellers and locations). Thus, both the cost of using a remote service bureau and the benefit of offering Internet banking to customers depended on the availability of broadband, which varied by overall demand in the client's area, based on population density, and the cost to install fiber optics, based on physical characteristics of the geography.

We could test the third hypothesis by directly estimating the relationship between broadband penetration and collocation, while controlling for whether the client offers Internet banking to its customers. However, the customer offerings would be simultaneously determined with collocation, since both depend on broadband. Thus, in the bivariate probit, we use broadband penetration for similar areas across the country (urban, suburban, or rural) to explain whether the client offers Internet banking in its location, which is a more precise indicator that Internet

Service Providers (ISPs) are active in the specific location. The coefficient on *Client offers Internet banking* in the side of the bivariate probit model explaining collocation therefore incorporates the information about broadband penetration while considering the entirety of the covariance matrix. To identify the set of equations, we include two instrumental variables alongside broadband penetration. *Client market growth* is a CU's growth in deposits over the prior time period, hence its demonstrated ability to expand and grow market share. A second measure reflects potential future growth. The *Unserved % of current customers* is the percentage of potential members under the CU's current charter that are not currently members of the CU. For example, a multiple common bond CU approved to offer accounts to "anyone who lives, works, or worships" in a given county reports their estimate of potential members in those categories and their count of current members. The unserved percentage is {1-(current members/potential members)} using Call Report items 083 and 084. Many CUs changed to multiple common bond after the 1998 ruling, so the time period of our study saw them courting new types of customers. These instrumental variables (which have no explanatory power for collocation) reflect the incentive of a CU to differentiate itself by offering new, Internet-based services.

4   Results

Table 1 presents the means, standard deviations, and correlations. The mean CU is over 50 years old, has over \$95 million in loans outstanding, and is in an urban location. Client niche positioning negatively correlates with liquidity.

Table 2 presents bivariate probit estimates predicting collocation of supplier-provided knowledge work and adoption of Internet banking. Model 1 has the control variables and time dummies without supplier dummies. Model 2 adds the supplier dummies. For collocation, client firm size and client loan risk have positive and significant effects; clients having more extensive experience with external service providers (captured as client outside service expenses) are more likely to use remote services. Most of the supplier dummies are significant, indicating that suppliers have preferred modes for delivering their services. Models 3 and 4 add the independent variables. We draw conclusions from Model 4, which includes all variables.

Hypothesis 1 states that client niche market positioning positively relates to collocation. The coefficient for niche positioning is positive and significant ($\beta = 14.79$; $p < 0.001$). Results for the alternate measure (single common bond dummy) are consistent. A change in niche positioning from the minimum (not quite one s.d. below the mean) to one s.d. above the mean increases the predicted probability of collocation by 3.3%, an economically substantial influence. Another implication would be that a CU serving an educational institution, like a single university, is 2% more likely to use collocation than a CU serving the same community under a multiple-common-bond charter.

Table 1 Descriptive statistics and correlation matrix ($N = 12{,}929$)

	Variable	Mean	StDev	Min	Max	1	2	3	4	5	6	7	8	9	10	11	12	13	14	15
1	Collocation	0.766	0.423	0	1	1.00														
2	Client firm size	−2.347	0.904	−4.69	1.30	0.28	1.00													
3	Client firm age	3.924	0.344	1.10	4.55	0.03	0.07	1.00												
4	Client liquidity	0.728	0.169	0.08	2.24	0.07	0.33	−0.05	1.00											
5	Client loan risk	0.775	0.250	0.13	1.84	0.05	−0.13	−0.04	0.02	1.00										
6	Client outside service expenses	0.129	0.095	0.00	0.79	−0.40	−0.18	−0.04	−0.07	0.03	1.00									
7	Client oper. efficiency	−0.040	0.833	−2.77	7.96	−0.04	0.08	0.00	0.07	−0.06	0.01	1.00								
8	Suburban location	0.065	0.247	0	1	−0.05	−0.09	−0.01	0.03	0.00	−0.02	0.04	1.00							
9	Rural location	0.402	0.490	0	1	0.07	0.10	−0.05	0.07	0.02	−0.04	0.04	−0.22	1.00						
10	Client uses CUSO	0.106	0.308	0	1	−0.11	0.01	−0.01	0.03	0.02	0.05	−0.01	0.02	−0.01	1.00					
11	Client niche positioning	0.005	0.005	0.00	0.05	0.05	−0.01	−0.09	−0.09	−0.04	−0.02	−0.00	−0.03	−0.01	−0.00	1.00				
12	Client task complexity	0.149	0.081	−1.86	0.69	0.16	0.16	−0.05	0.19	0.21	0.01	−0.22	−0.07	0.01	0.03	−0.08	1.00			
13	Client offers Internet banking	0.791	0.406	0	1	0.14	0.26	0.02	0.09	0.01	−0.03	−0.10	−0.05	−0.06	0.01	−0.07	0.26	1.00		
14	Broadband penetration (%)	10.448	8.157	0	27	−0.03	−0.02	0.08	−0.15	−0.10	0.03	−0.08	0.16	−0.62	0.01	−0.06	0.23	0.22	1.00	
15	Market growth	0.051	0.667	−0.18	2.87	0.04	0.08	−0.02	−0.02	0.01	−0.02	0.03	0.01	−0.01	−0.01	0.02	−0.03	0.04	−0.07	1.00
16	Unserved % of current customer	0.594	0.266	0	1.00	0.05	0.06	0.01	0.16	0.06	−0.06	−0.06	0.04	−0.03	0.01	−0.17	0.23	0.16	0.13	0.01

Correlations of $|\rho| \geq 0.023$ are significant at $p < 0.001$

Table 2 Bivariate probit regression models with endogenous regressor

	1	2	3	4
Y1 = Collocation				
Client firm size (ln)	0.517***	0.576***	0.571***	0.577***
	(0.023)	(0.025)	(0.026)	(0.023)
Client firm age (ln)	−0.045	0.015	0.029	0.056
	(0.039)	(0.042)	(0.042)	(0.041)
Client liquidity	−0.533***	−0.450***	−0.429***	−0.582***
	(0.087)	(0.099)	(0.099)	(0.098)
Client loan risk	0.662***	0.585***	0.611***	0.432***
	(0.055)	(0.062)	(0.063)	(0.064)
Client outside service expenses	−5.640***	−4.389***	−4.411***	−4.290***
	(0.151)	(0.183)	(0.182)	(0.200)
Client operational efficiency	−0.093***	−0.093***	−0.091***	−0.059**
	(0.017)	(0.019)	(0.019)	(0.019)
Suburban location	−0.182***	−0.284***	−0.271***	−0.244***
	(0.055)	(0.064)	(0.064)	(0.062)
Rural location	0.070*	0.110**	0.118***	0.080*
	(0.031)	(0.035)	(0.035)	(0.034)
Client uses CUSO	−0.471***	−0.356***	−0.355***	−0.378***
	(0.041)	(0.061)	(0.062)	(0.060)
Client niche positioning (H1)			15.930***	14.786***
			(3.616)	(3.537)
Client task complexity (H2)				2.762***
				(0.217)
Client offers Internet banking (H3)	−0.057	−0.430**	−0.348*	−0.902***
	(0.120)	(0.132)	(0.137)	(0.141)
Supplier dummies		20 of 24*	20 of 24*	20 of 24*
Constant	2.978***	3.433***	3.192***	3.348***
	(0.224)	(0.251)	(0.262)	(0.243)
Y2 = Client offers Internet banking				
Client firm size (ln)	0.107***	0.100***	0.100***	0.095***
	(0.004)	(0.004)	(0.004)	(0.004)
Client firm age (ln)	−0.011	−0.012	−0.015	−0.006
	(0.010)	(0.009)	(0.010)	(0.009)
Client liquidity	0.141***	0.147***	0.141***	0.088***
	(0.021)	(0.021)	(0.021)	(0.022)
Client loan risk	−0.004	−0.022	−0.023	−0.067***
	(0.015)	(0.015)	(0.015)	(0.015)
Client outside service expenses	0.063	0.150***	0.145***	0.119**
	(0.035)	(0.037)	(0.037)	(0.037)

(continued)

Table 2 (continued)

	1	2	3	4
Client operational efficiency	−0.047***	−0.044***	−0.044***	−0.034***
	(0.004)	(0.004)	(0.004)	(0.004)
Suburban location	−0.092***	−0.077***	−0.078***	−0.065***
	(0.014)	(0.014)	(0.014)	(0.014)
Rural location	0.145***	0.147***	0.146***	0.133***
	(0.012)	(0.011)	(0.011)	(0.011)
Client uses CUSO	0.010	−0.004	−0.004	−0.007
	(0.011)	(0.013)	(0.013)	(0.013)
Broadband penetration	0.018***	0.018***	0.018***	0.017***
	(0.001)	(0.001)	(0.001)	(0.001)
Market growth	0.188***	0.155**	0.159**	0.158**
	(0.054)	(0.053)	(0.053)	(0.052)
Unserved % of current customers	0.140***	0.132***	0.125***	0.104***
	(0.013)	(0.013)	(0.013)	(0.012)
Client niche positioning			−2.342***	−2.290***
			(0.668)	(0.664)
Client task complexity				0.580***
				(0.047)
Supplier dummies		17 of 24*	20 of 24*	20 of 24*
Time dummies	7 of 7***	7 of 7***	7 of 7***	7 of 7***
Constant	0.519***	0.422***	0.459***	0.447***
	(0.049)	(0.052)	(0.053)	(0.053)
var(e.Y2)	0.137***	0.133***	0.132***	0.131***
	(0.002)	(0.002)	(0.002)	(0.002)
corr(e.Y2,e.Y1)	0.131**	0.223***	0.197***	0.379***
	(0.046)	(0.050)	(0.052)	(0.052)

Two-tailed statistical significance *$p < 0.05$; **$p < 0.01$; ***$p < 0.001$. $N = 12,929$

Hypothesis 2 proposes that client task complexity increases the likelihood of collocation. From Model 4, client task complexity has a positive and significant effect on collocation, ($\beta = 2.76$; $p < 0.001$). A change in task complexity from one s.d. below the mean to one s.d. above the mean increases the predicted probability of collocation by 6.9%.

Hypothesis 3 predicts a negative relationship between the use of broadband Internet service and collocation. In Table 2, we employ broadband penetration and two instrumental variables to predict whether the client offers Internet banking, which should likewise be enabled by broadband. The bivariate probit model is appropriate, as the correlation between the error terms of the two dependent variables is 0.395 ($p < 0.001$). In this specification, we test the final hypothesis through the coefficient on *Client offers Internet banking*. The coefficient is strongly negative ($\beta = -0.902$; $p < 0.001$). The change from a client that does not offer Internet banking to one that does offer it increases the probability of collocation by 2.9%.

Table 3 Robustness checks

Model	Pooled cross-sectional probit, clustering by client		Panel probit with supplier random effects	
	5	6	7	8
Client firm size (ln)	0.540***	0.541***	0.546***	0.547***
	(0.064)	(0.064)	(0.024)	(0.024)
Client firm age (ln)	0.067	0.070	0.080	0.083
	(0.108)	(0.108)	(0.044)	(0.044)
Client liquidity	−0.725**	−0.739**	−0.760***	−0.775***
	(0.243)	(0.244)	(0.108)	(0.108)
Client loan risk	0.572***	0.576***	0.613***	0.617***
	(0.169)	(0.169)	(0.075)	(0.075)
Client outside service expenses	−4.736***	−4.738***	−4.762***	−4.762***
	(0.417)	(0.417)	(0.176)	(0.177)
Client operational efficiency	−0.031	−0.029	−0.034	−0.032
	(0.045)	(0.045)	(0.020)	(0.020)
Suburban location	−0.199	−0.210	−0.167*	−0.177**
	(0.151)	(0.151)	(0.068)	(0.068)
Rural location	−0.111	0.064	−0.088	0.084*
	(0.112)	(0.085)	(0.057)	(0.038)
Client uses CUSO	−0.413**	−0.413**	−0.211**	−0.212**
	(0.149)	(0.148)	(0.068)	(0.069)
Client niche positioning (H1)	19.061*	18.763*	17.867***	17.573***
	(8.204)	(8.175)	(3.682)	(3.679)
Client task complexity (H2)	2.372***	2.429***	2.563***	2.627***
	(0.543)	(0.554)	(0.242)	(0.244)
Broadband penetration (H3)	−0.023***		−0.022***	
	(0.005)		(0.004)	
% of clients offering Internet banking (H3)		−1.139***		−1.146***
		(0.238)		(0.197)
Supplier dummies	10 of 24*	16 of 24*		
Time dummies	7 of 7*	1 of 7*	5 of 7*	1 of 7*
Constant	3.235***	3.682***	3.052***	3.504***
	(0.592)	(0.620)	(0.372)	(0.397)

Two-tailed statistical significance *$p < 0.05$; **$p < 0.01$; ***$p < 0.001$. $N = 12{,}929$

We chose the panel bivariate probit model with time dummies to control for endogeneity. However, this specification may exaggerate statistical significance because of the large sample size, without appropriately adjusting for the fact that there are repeated observations of the same clients or suppliers. Therefore, in robustness checks, we estimate simpler models of two types. In Table 3, models 5 and 6 report pooled cross-sectional probit models with clustering of observations by client, while models 7 and 8 report panel probit models with random effects by supplier. Results are consistent for the relationship of client niche positioning (H1) and client task complexity (H2) with collocation. To test H3, we employ broadband penetration as an exogenous variable, in models 5 and 7, and the percent of all clients that offer Internet banking in the focal year, in models 6 and 8. In all cases, negative coefficients ($p < 0.001$) confirm our results for H3. Clustering by supplier instead (dropping the supplier dummy variables) yields similar results.

As a further robustness check, we attempted to model a conditional fixed-effects logit model but encountered a significant loss in data observations. If a firm collocates (or not) in each of the seven time periods of observation, a fixed-effect estimator drops the firm from the analysis, only retaining firms that change their sourcing mode. Recall that we selected a sample period to cover the emergence of Internet-based loan processing, such that the entire history for each client in our sample is likely to be covered by its first IT contract for these services, which typically last 5–7 years. Therefore, sourcing mode switches occur rarely in our dataset, and using a fixed-effects logit model results in a loss of over 90% of the observations. The remaining firms would not be a representative sample.

5 Conclusion

We studied the impact of client niche market position and task complexity on the governance of supplier-provided knowledge work. Besides client firm size and location, the decision to collocate knowledge-based tasks depends on whether the focal client firm and its supplier need to work together closely, either so the supplier can incorporate the client's specialized knowledge about its internal operations and customers, or for ongoing customization of the service to support complex operations. However, collocation of services involving software is less likely when remote service is facilitated by broadband Internet infrastructure.

This study demonstrates that client positioning in the product market affects the services it receives from suppliers. Niche positioning requires specific client knowledge, such that collocation is the more efficient way to customize the supplier's product. Our findings also affirm the relationship between client task complexity and tighter governance of supplier-provided knowledge work, consistent with prior work on alliance design (Gulati et al. 2005; Gulati and Singh 1998) and firm boundary decisions (Hoetker 2006; Macher 2006; Nickerson and Zenger 2004; Walker and Weber 1984; Williamson 1991). We show that greater task complexity leads to collocation of supplier-provided knowledge work.

Likewise, this study points managers to consider how their firm's position in the market and task complexity work together in determining contractual terms for inter-organizational relationships. Managers need to not only consider why they would want the supplier to work closely with them on customization but why the supplier might see their firm as a valuable client with whom to co-produce innovations to their software. Even a smaller client can have distinct knowledge because of its differentiated position or strategy. In general, a firm with a tightly defined target market pursuing a complex, integrated set of activities in an inimitable manner likely has competitive advantage over some competitors. If so, it should be careful to invest in supplier relationships, offering to share knowledge with a trusted supplier, even at the cost of some spillovers, to ensure that the supplier's knowledge-based service is customized appropriately. Bringing the supplier "on-site," even if not conducting the entire task "in-house," may be necessary.

We examined collocation during the emergence of a communication medium, videoconferencing. No doubt today's knowledge workers are accumulating experience with communication at a distance and developing the knowledge, skills, and abilities to contribute to virtual teams (Schulze and Krumm 2017). Does collocation still matter? Videoconferencing and shared development tools (from Google docs to advanced CAD software) have not fully replaced face-to-face collaboration. In software design (Jolak et al. 2018), videoconferencing teams have extensive conversation, but less creative conflict and active discussion than collocated teams, detracting from the quality of their collaboration. Similarly, as more university courses move online, many interactive, discussion-based courses still work best in a classroom setting, and online students are often brought together for intensive time together at the beginning or end of a course, to facilitate co-learning. Therefore, physical proximity is still employed for knowledge co-creation, but the length of the on-site engagement has been shortened. Further, distributed services, such as servers or archives in "the cloud," mean businesses own less of the hardware required to run applications in-house. We studied collocation that was reported to government regulators during a period of uncertainty about security of Internet-based information exchange. This historical context provided a large sample of client–supplier relationships, but further research could investigate the extent to which clients continue to require a supplier representative on-site, and how that is scheduled. Future research may delve into contractual details such as required on-site visits or periodic personnel exchange. There may be not only a continuum of arrangements for a knowledge worker contributing to a team, from independent consultant to temporary employee to permanent employee, but also a progression toward more or less face time depending on the nature of the work. Our research highlights that in KBS, particularly, entire teams may be placed at the client's location for a period of time, especially at the start of an engagement or when a new project begins.

Limitations of this paper present future research opportunities. First, we did not explicitly consider firm performance, such as measuring the effect of governance (mis)alignment on performance. Second, while this paper investigated industry-wide changes over time due to broadband penetration, we did not consider other industry-wide evolutionary effects implied by Jacobides and Winter (2005). Future work may study how market convergence on sets of tasks of a certain complexity affects trends in alliance governance, e.g., whether firms lose skills and the market improves its skills as outsourcing becomes more prevalent. Future research could explore the role of organizational politics and bureaucracy in procurement (Simester and Knez 2002) and temporal changes in capability distribution caused by alliance design decisions (Mayer et al. 2012). Our research context did not include clear indicators of changes in the transaction environment beyond technological advances, so we were unable to test hypotheses about collocation and adaptability to regulatory policies, market demand, or other changes.

References

ABA Banking Journal (2013) Negotiating tech contracts. http://www.ababj.com/community-banking/item/1994-workbook-negotiating-tech-contracts 13 November, 2018. Published March 8, 2013

Adams P, Fontana R, Malerba F (2015) User-industry spinouts: downstream industry knowledge as a source of new firm entry and survival. Organ Sci 27:18–35

Ambrose E, Marshall D, Fynes B, Lynch D (2008) Communication media selection in buyer-supplier relationships. Int J Oper Prod Man 28:360–379

Andres HP (2002) A comparison of face-to-face and virtual software development teams. Team Perform Manag 8(1/2):39–48

Ang S, Straub DW (1998) Production and transaction economies and IS outsourcing: a study of the U.S. banking industry. MIS Quart 22:535–552

Argote L, Ingram P (2000) Knowledge transfer in organizations: a basis for competitive advantage in firms. Organ Behav Hum Dec 82:150–169

Argyres N, Bigelow L (2010) Innovation, modularity, and vertical deintegration: evidence from the early US auto industry. Organ Sci 21:842–853

Bajari P, Tadelis S (2001) Incentives versus transaction costs: a theory of procurement contracts. Rand J Econ 32:387–407

Baker WE, Faulkner RR (1991) Strategies for managing suppliers of professional services. Calif Manag Rev 33:33–45

Barras R (1990) Interactive innovation in financial and business services: the vanguard of the service revolution. Res Policy 19:215–237

Barzel Y (1982) Measurement cost and the organization of markets. J Law Econ 25:27–48

Bettencourt LA, Ostrom AL, Brown SW, Roundtree RI (2002) Client co-production in knowledge-intensive business services. Calif Manag Rev 44:100–128

Chuma H (2006) Increasing complexity and limits of organization in the microlithography industry: implications for science-based industries. Res Policy 35:394–411

Clark JR, Huckman RS, Staats BR (2013) Learning from customers: individual and organizational effects in outsourced radiological services. Organ Sci 24:1539–1557

Combs JG, Ketchen DJ (1999) Explaining interfirm cooperation and performance: toward a reconciliation of predictions from the resource-based view and organizational economics. Strateg Manage J 20:867–888

Cooper AC, Willard GE, Woo CY (1986) Strategies of high performing new and small firms: a reexamination of the niche concept. J Bus Venturing 1:247–260

Daft RL, Lengel RH (1984) Information richness: a new approach to manage information processing and organizational design. Res Org Behav 6:191–233

Daft RL, Lengel RH (1986) Organizational information requirements, media richness and structural design. Manag Sci 32:554–571

Davenport TH, Jarvenpaa SL, Beers MC (1996) Improving knowledge work processes. Sloan Manag Rev 37:52–65

Den Hertog P (2000) Knowledge-intensive business services as co-producers of innovation. Intl J Innov Manag 4:491–528

DosSantos BL, Pfeffers K (1995) Rewards to investors in innovative information technology applications: first movers and early followers in ATMs. Organ Sci 6:214–259

Dyer JH, Hatch NW (2006) Relationship-specific capabilities and barriers to knowledge transfers: creating advantage through network relationships. Strateg Manage J 27:701–719

Dyer JH, Singh H (1998) The relational view: cooperative strategy and sources of inter-organizational competitive advantage. Acad Manag Rev 23:660–679

Elfenbein DW, Zenger TR (2013) What is a relationship worth? Repeated exchange and the development and deployment of relational capital. Organ Sci 25:222–244

Emmons W, Schmid FA (2000) Bank competition and concentration: do credit unions matter? Econ Rev Fed Reserve Bank St Louis 82:29–42

Ethiraj SK, Kale P, Krishnan MS, Singh JV (2005) Where do capabilities come from and how do they matter? A study in the software services industry. Strateg Manage J 26:25–45

Ethiraj SK, Ramasubbu N, Krishnan MS (2012) Does complexity deter customer-focus? Strateg Manage J 33:137–161

Fichman RG, Kemerer CF (1997) The assimilation of software process innovations: an organizational learning perspective. Manag Sci 43:1345–1363

Grant RM (1996) Toward a knowledge-based theory of the firm. Strateg Manage J 17:109–122

Gronroos C, Voima P (2012) Critical service logic: making sense of value creation and co-creation. J Acad Market Sci 41:133–150

Gulati R, Singh H (1998) The architecture of cooperation: managing coordination costs and appropriation concerns in strategic alliances. Admin Sci Quart 43:781–814

Gulati R, Lawrence PR, Puranam P (2005) Adaptation in vertical relationships: beyond incentive conflict. Strateg Manage J 26:415–440

Hatch NW, Dyer JH (2004) Human capital and learning as a source of sustainable competitive advantage. Strateg Manage J 25:1155–1178

Heide JB, Kumar A, Wathne KH (2014) Concurrent sourcing, governance mechanisms, and performance outcomes in industrial value chains. Strateg Manage J 35:1165–1185

Hoetker G (2006) Do modular products lead to modular architecture? Strateg Manage J 27:501–518

Inkpen AC, Tsang EW (2007) Learning and strategic alliances. The Acad Manag Ann 1:479–511

Jacobides MG, Hitt LM (2005) Losing sight of the forest for the trees? Productive capabilities and gains from trade as drivers of vertical scope. Strateg Manage J 26:1209–1227

Jacobides MG, Winter SG (2005) The co-evolution of capabilities and transaction costs: explaining the institutional structure of production. Strateg Manage J 26:395–413

Jolak R, Wortmann A, Chaudron M, Rumpe B (2018) Does distance still matter: insights from revisiting collaborative distributed software design. IEEE Softw 35:40–47

Kale P, Singh H, Perlmutter H (2000) Learning and protection of proprietary assets in strategic alliances: building relational capital. Strateg Manage J 21:217–237

Karis D, Wildman D, Mané A (2016) Improving remote collaboration with video conferencing and video portals. Hum Comput Interact 31:1–58

Kauffman SA (1995) At home in the universe: the search for the laws of self-organization and complexity. Oxford University Press, New York

Kim SM, Mahoney JT (2006) Mutual commitment to support exchange: relation-specific IT system as a substitute for managerial hierarchy. Strateg Manage J 27:401–423

Knoben J, Oerlemans LAG (2006) Proximity and inter-organizational collaboration: a literature review. Int J Manage Rev 8:71–89

Kogut B, Zander U (1992) Knowledge of the firm, combinative capabilities, and the replication of technology. Organ Sci 3:383–397

Kohtamaki M, Partanen J (2016) Co-creating value from knowledge-intensive business services in manufacturing firms: the moderating role of relationship learning in supplier-customer interactions. J Bus Res 69:2498–2506

Lacity MC, Willcocks LP (1998) An empirical investigation of information technology sourcing practices: lessons from experience. MIS Q 22:363–408

Larsson R, Bowen DE (1989) Organization and customer: managing design and coordination of services. Acad Manag Rev 14:213–233

Lavie D (2006) The competitive advantage of interconnected firms: an extension of the resource-based view. Acad Manag Rev 31:638–658

Levina N, Ross JW (2003) From the supplier's perspective: exploring the value proposition in information technology outsourcing. MIS Q 27:331–364

Lumineau F, Oliveira N (2016) A pluralistic perspective to overcome major blind spots in research on inter-organizational relationships. Acad Manag Ann 12:440–465

MacDuffie JP (1997) The road to 'root cause': shop floor problem-solving at three auto assembly plants. Manag Sci 43:479–502

Macher JT (2006) Technological development and the boundaries of the firm: a knowledge-based examination of semiconductor manufacturing. Manag Sci 52:826–843

Macher JT, Boerner C (2012) Technological development at the boundaries of the firm: a knowledge-based examination in drug development. Strateg Manage J 33:1016–1036

Mahr D, Lievens A, Blazevic V (2013) The value of customer cocreated knowledge during the innovation process. J Prod Innovat Manag 31:599–615

Malikov E, Restrepo-Tobón DA, Kumbhakar SC (2018) Heterogeneous credit union production technologies with endogenous switching and correlated effects. Economet Rev 37:1095–1119

Mayer KJ (2006) Spillovers and governance: an analysis of knowledge and reputational spillovers in information technology. Acad Manag J 49:69–84

Mayer KJ, Bercovitz J (2008) The influence of inertia on contract design: contingency planning in information technology service contracts. Manag Decis Econ 29:149–163

Mayer KJ, Nickerson JA (2005) Antecedents and performance consequences of contracting for knowledge workers: evidence from information technology services. Organ Sci 16:225–242

Mayer KJ, Salomon RM (2006) Capabilities, contractual hazards, and governance: integrating resource-based and transaction cost perspectives. Acad Manag J 49:942–959

Mayer KJ, Somaya D, Williamson IO (2012) Firm-specific, industry-specific, and occupational human capital and the sourcing of knowledge work. Organ Sci 23(5):1311–1329

Mesquita LF, Anand J, Brush TH (2008) Comparing the resource-based and relational views: knowledge transfer and spillovers in vertical inter-organizational relationships. Strateg Manage J 29:913–941

Nickerson JA, Zenger TR (2004) A knowledge-based theory of the firm – the problem solving perspective. Organ Sci 15:617–632

Nickerson JA, Hamilton BH, Wada T (2001) Market position, resource profile, and governance: linking Porter and Williamson in the context of international courier and small package services in Japan. Strateg Manage J 22:251–273

Ono Y, Stango V (2005) Outsourcing, firm size, and product complexity: evidence from credit unions. Econ Perspect 29:2–11

Oxley JE, Sampson RC (2004) The scope and governance of international R&D alliances. Strateg Manage J 25:723–749

Parmigiani A (2007) Why do firms both make and buy? An investigation of concurrent sourcing. Strateg Manage J 28:285–311

Parmigiani A, Mitchell W (2009) Interdependence, capabilities, and the boundaries of the firm: the impact of within-firm and interfirm expertise on concurrent sourcing of complementary components. Strateg Manage J 30:1065–1091

Parmigiani A, Rivera-Santos M (2011) Clearing a path through the forest: a meta-review of interorganizational relationships. J Manage 37:1108–1136

Phillips LW, Chang DR, Buzzell RD (1983) Product quality, cost position, and business performance: a test of some key hypotheses. J Marketing April:26–43

Poppo L, Zenger TR (1998) Testing alternative theories of the firm: transaction cost, knowledge-based, and measurement explanations or make-or-buy decisions in information services. Strateg Manage J 19:853–877

Porter ME (1980) Competitive strategy. Free Press, New York

Puranam P, Gulati R, Bhattacharya S (2013) How much to make and how much to buy? An analysis of optimal plural sourcing strategies. Strateg Manage J 34:1145–1161

Rafii F (1995) How important is physical collocation to product development success? Bus Horiz 38:78–84

Ragatz GL, Handfield RB, Scannell TV (1997) Success factors for integrating suppliers into new product development. J Prod Innovat Manag 14:190–202

Santos JB, Spring M (2015) Are knowledge intensive business services really co-produced? Overcoming lack of customer participation in KIBS. Ind Market Manag 50:85–96

Schilling MA, Steensma HK (2002) Disentangling the theories of firm boundaries: a path model and empirical test. Organ Sci 13:387–401

Schulze J, Krumm S (2017) The 'virtual team player': a review and initial model of knowledge, skills, abilities, and other characteristics for virtual collaboration. Organ Psychol Rev 7:66–95

Sheshunoff A (2000) Internet banking—an update from the front lines. ABA Bank J:51–53

Simester D, Knez M (2002) Direct and indirect bargaining costs and the scope of the firm. J Bus 75:283–304

Stewart J (2013) Bankers hiring hagglers to negotiate IT contracts. American Banker. http://www.americanbanker.com/issues/178_99/bankers-hiring-hagglers-to-negotiate-it-contracts-1059329-1.html. Accessed 29 May 2019

Tampa Bay Times (2011) Surprise: credit unions can take car, boat, RV if you walk out on unsecured loans. Accessed at http://www.tampabay.com 13 November 2018. Published 10 December 2011

Teece DJ (1986) Profiting from technological innovation: implications for integration, collaboration, licensing, and public policy. Res Policy 15:285–306

Thompson J (1967) Organizations in action: social science bases of administrative theory. McGraw-Hill, New York

Tiwana A, Bush AA (2007) A comparison of transaction cost, agency, and knowledge-based predictors of IT outsourcing decisions: a U.S.-Japan cross-cultural field study. J Manage Inform Syst 24:259–300

US Department of the Treasury (2001) Comparing credit unions with other depository institutions, Washington DC

Vickery SK, Droge C, Stank TP, Goldsby TJ, Markland RE (2004) The performance implications of media richness in a business-to-business service environment: direct versus indirect effects. Manag Sci 50:1106–1119

Walker G, Weber D (1984) A transaction cost approach to make-or-buy decisions. Admin Sci Quart 29:373–391

Weigelt C, Miller DJ (2013) Implications of internal organization structure for firm boundaries. Strateg Manage J 34:1411–1434

Weigelt C, Sarkar MB (2009) Learning from supply-side agents: the impact of technology solution providers' experiential diversity on clients' innovation adoption. Acad Manag J 52:37–60

Wheelock DC, Wilson PW (2013) The evolution of cost-productivity and efficiency among US credit unions. J Bank Financ 37:75–88

Williamson OE (1991) Comparative economic organization: the analysis of discrete structural alternatives. Admin Sci Quart 36:269–296

Wilson DT (2000) Deep relationships: the case of the vanishing salesperson. J Pers Sell Sales Manag 20:53–61

Zajac EG, Olsen CP (1993) From transaction cost to transactional value analysis: implications for the study of inter-organizational strategies. J Manage Stud 30:131–145

Zander I, Zander U (2005) The inside track: on the important (but neglected) role of customers in the resource-based view of strategy and firm growth. J Manage Stud 42:1519–1548

Dealing with the Post-Honeymoon Blues: Tensions and Governance in Industry-University Alliances

Eveline Corine ten Hoor and Isabel Estrada Vaquero

Abstract Industry-university (IU) alliances are often subject to tensions caused by the dissimilarities between industry and university partners. Interestingly, due to a honeymoon effect, these tensions may not necessarily emerge immediately. However, shortly after the alliance is initiated, the likelihood of tension seems to increase rapidly. Thus, early detection of potential tensions seems crucial to the success of IU alliances. This paper explores how these tensions emerge and can be effectively managed through an exploratory study of two IU alliances in the energy sector. Based on our cases, we identified four types of dissimilarities (i.e., orientation-based, routine-based, administrative, and personal) that may lead to different types of tensions (i.e., orientation, routine, transaction, and distinctive), which in turn may be addressed through different governance mechanisms (i.e., communication, flexibility, contracts, and hierarchy). Beyond contributing to the literature on IU alliances, our exploratory study may help managers of these alliances in identifying potential tensions and effective governance practices.

1 Introduction

Industry-university (IU) alliances are an important phenomenon. IU alliances can have an enormous positive impact on innovation, as firms and universities have much to offer one another (e.g., Bishop et al. 2011; Du et al. 2014). Universities can generate high-quality research output and are aware of the latest developments in their field. Moreover, compared to other partners, universities are less likely to engage in competitive and opportunistic behavior (Breschi and Lissoni 2001; Du et al. 2014). At the same time, firms can provide funding and valuable research opportunities to universities (Bruneel et al. 2010).

E. C. ten Hoor (✉) · I. Estrada Vaquero
University of Groningen, Groningen, The Netherlands
e-mail: i.estrada.vaquero@rug.nl

© Springer Nature Switzerland AG 2019   295
J. Windsperger et al. (eds.), *Design and Management of Interfirm Networks*,
Contributions to Management Science,
https://doi.org/10.1007/978-3-030-29245-4_15

Despite the potential benefits, existing research on IU alliances emphasizes the tensions or barriers firms and universities face in their collaboration. For instance, Bruneel et al. (2010) argue that the different nature of university and industry partners may lead to orientation-related and transaction-related barriers. The former may occur, because universities and industry partners tend to have differing ideas about the way knowledge should be created and appropriated (Bruneel et al. 2010). Furthermore, their attitude towards the alliance goal, reciprocal objectives, and the alliance scope might differ (e.g., Estrada et al. 2016). On the other hand, transaction-related barriers appear when it is unclear to whom intellectual property belongs or when university administration challenges the collaboration (Bruneel et al. 2010). Additionally, other aspects such as routine-based dissimilarities (e.g., different communication and decision-making behavior) may challenge IU alliances (Estrada et al. 2016).

Interestingly, prior studies concluded that during early stages of IU alliances, the partners might not necessarily encounter these barriers, even when dissimilarities do exist at that point (Estrada et al. 2016). This phenomenon is described as the honeymoon effect (Fichman and Levinthal 1991). Over time, however, dissimilarities become noticeable and are more likely to provoke tension. Thus, early detection of potential tensions and barriers seems key to the governance and outcome of IU alliances (Bruneel et al. 2010; Lavie et al. 2012).

While extant research acknowledges the relevance of this phenomenon and provides valuable insights into the topics of dissimilarities, tensions, and governance, an in-depth examination of the connections between these issues in IU alliance formation is yet to be carried out. Therefore, this study seeks to explore how different types of dissimilarities and tensions emerge and can be managed through different governance mechanisms in the formation phase of IU alliances. We conducted an exploratory case study of two IU alliances in the energy industry. For theory, our study seeks to contribute to a richer understanding of the dynamics of IU alliance formation and governance. For managers, we expect to provide some recommendations for the effective design and governance of IU alliances. Overall, we expect that our study helps identifying tensions and barriers in IU alliances and potential strategies to overcome them.

2 Theoretical Framework

Scientific research has become a key knowledge source for commercial innovation (Du et al. 2014; Bruneel et al. 2010). Nonetheless, partners within IU alliances are known for having dissimilar perspectives and priorities in what concerns knowledge value and management (e.g., Carayol 2003). Industry players often engage in an alliance with strategic intentions: they strive to obtain a dominant competitive position through the integration, construction, and reconfiguration of internal and external competences (Teece et al. 1997). In order to withhold the competition, knowledge is traditionally regarded as a key resource that should be appropriated and protected (Wernerfelt 1984). Contrarily, scientific research is generally aimed at the creation of reliable and public knowledge (Bruneel et al. 2010). Therefore, universities are regarded as independent institutions providing access to scientific knowledge (Du et al. 2014). This conflicts with the industry's perspective to protect knowledge. Because of this fundamentally different perception towards knowledge, collaboration between industry and universities is often regarded as challenging (e.g., Carayol 2003; Dasgupta and David 1994).

2.1 Formation of IU Alliances

Although collaboration between industry and university partners has been regarded as challenging (Carayol 2003), scholars and practitioners have become more open towards this type of collaboration (Bishop et al. 2011; Chesbrough 2003). The open perspective towards innovation regards the firm as the center of a network, which uses external actors—such as universities—as a source of innovation (Chesbrough 2003). Findings from several studies such as George et al. (2002) demonstrate that IU alliances can positively influence the firm's innovation and economic performance, because the required R&D expenses are relatively low, while the levels of innovative output are high.

Eisenhardt and Schoonhoven (1996) argue that alliance formation is stimulated by strategic and social needs. They propose that from a strategic perspective, firms engage in an alliance when the benefits of forming the alliance exceed the benefits of proceeding alone. From a social perspective, they argue that firms form an alliance when they know that the potential partner is a trustworthy and valuable companion. Similarly, prior experience with IU collaboration increases the likelihood that a firm or university will engage in a collaboration with that partner again (D'Este and Patel 2007; D'Este et al. 2013; Gulati 1995). In IU alliances, both strategic and social needs are visible at the industry side. Strategically, universities can provide low-priced access to high-quality knowledge (Du et al. 2014). Socially, universities are regarded as trustworthy partners, because they are not in a competing position (Bruneel et al. 2010). Although IU alliances are viewed as a win-win game, less attention has been paid to the university's rationale of forming these alliances (Bishop et al. 2011; D'Este and Patel 2007). Thus, Du et al. (2014) have requested for a more detailed analysis of the interaction and contributions of both types of partners.

According to Doz et al. (2000), the process of alliance formation can be emergent or engineered, depending on the environmental interdependence between partners. In the emergent path, environmental interdependence is high, and partners are driven by similar interests (Doz et al. 2000). This situation often involves a market event by which all partners are affected. By joining forces, technological components can be combined to generate new innovation, or a shared standard can be created to stimulate a certain technology. In the engineered path, environmental interdependence is low, but alliance formation is driven by a triggering entity (Doz et al. 2000). In this case, an external institution or individual plays a substantial role in connecting the alliance partners. This triggering entity often has the lead in defining the alliance goals, partner contributions, and alliance governance. In IU alliances, however, the process of alliance formation can be more complex. On the one hand, pooling diverse entities can be a valuable source for new ideas, and it can ease the process of commercializing them (Chesbrough 2003; Deng and Hendrikse 2017). On the other hand, environmental interdependence is generally low, because partners do not necessarily depend on the success of the alliance (Carayol 2003; Gulati 1995). Because of this complexity, further research on the collaborative dynamics during the formation stage of IU alliances is needed.

2.2 Dissimilarities in IU Alliances

Scholars seem to have reached a consensus on the essence and risks of dissimilarities between industry and university, each forming their own tensions and barriers[1] (Bruneel et al. 2010; Carayol 2003; Cyert and Goodman 1997). First of all, orientation-based dissimilarities form a barrier in IU collaboration (Bruneel et al. 2010; Estrada et al. 2016). These involve dissimilar goals, such as the contrasting incentives for university and industry partners to engage in an alliance, as the products they deliver are substantially different (Cyert and Goodman 1997; Dasgupta and David 1994). Universities aim to generate state-of-the-art knowledge, to find proof for theoretical concepts, and to publish their findings (Carayol 2003). Conversely, companies aim to access new knowledge to stimulate innovation and to eventually increase their profits. Furthermore, expectations can differ, for instance, in what concerns reciprocal obligations, alliance scope, and alliance horizon (Estrada et al. 2016). Orientation-based dissimilarities increase the probability that tensions arise in an IU alliance and increase the likelihood for an IU alliance to fail shortly after the alliance has been initiated (Bruneel et al. 2010; Estrada et al. 2016). Despite these findings, scholars call for further research on the topic (Estrada et al. 2016).

Routine-based dissimilarities originate from the proposition that universities and firms fundamentally differ in culture and working behavior (Cyert and Goodman 1997; Estrada et al. 2016). These cultural differences become apparent in terms of language, learning, time perception, and behavior. Language and learning differences are regarded as a result of cognitive distance (Muscio and Pozzali 2012). An example of this is when a specialized professor uses jargon to explain a studied phenomenon to a less specialized company representative. Furthermore, time perception differs, because companies are often oriented at short-term deadlines, whereas university research is commonly based on long-term investigations (Du et

---

[1] In this study, we do not make an explicit distinction between "tension" and "barrier." We use both terms interchangeably to refer to challenges or situations of conflict in the context of IU alliances.

al. 2014; Muscio and Pozzali 2012). Estrada et al. (2016) point to other examples of routine-based dissimilarities, such as differences in decision-making or task execution. These authors suggest that, assuming that no other dissimilarities are present, these dissimilarities can lead to tension when the alliance partners put no coordination efforts to mitigate them.

Transaction barriers or tensions are partly related to orientation barriers, because they are often a result of the different orientations of universities and industry partners (Bruneel et al. 2010). However, transaction barriers are more related to patent filing or other time-consuming, administrative procedures that are required in IU alliances. An illustrative example of a transaction barrier is the conflict concerning intellectual property (Bruneel et al. 2010). As the provider of knowledge, universities may expect that the property rights belong to them. At the same time, companies claim their part of the property rights based on their financial contribution to the project. In some cases, this barrier is so strong that the IU alliance cannot be established (Hall et al. 2001). Further, whereas universities aim to publish new findings, firms tend to protect it from leaking to the competition (Dasgupta and David 1994). To prevent these conflicts, contracts are often developed by universities and technology transfer offices, which can lead to an amount of administration that in turn forms a new transaction barrier (Bruneel et al. 2010). Nonetheless, Bruneel et al. (2010) highlight that the relationship between university coordination and transaction barriers should be further explored.

2.3   Governance of IU Alliances

The way in which IU alliances and the accompanied tensions are managed can be explained by the governance structures that are applied. Alliance governance literature has been clearly divided into two theoretical perspectives: the structural and the relational perspective (Madhok 1995; Barney and Hansen 1994; Faems et al. 2008). The structural perspective is characterized by a single transaction focus, in which alliance partners are assumed to act opportunistically (Faems et al. 2008). Under the assumption of opportunism, firms are inclined to use control mechanisms to protect their private interest (Parkhe 1993). The relational perspective is characterized by an interfirm relational focus in which partners are assumed to act in a way that is trustworthy (Barney and Hansen 1994; Faems et al. 2008). This perspective is based on the social exchange theory (Blau 1964), which builds on the assumption that a person's actions in a relationship are based on the expected rewarding reactions from their partner (i.e., reciprocity). Trust is a vital aspect of the relational perspective, because it can provide alliance partners with assurance about their partners' competence and their intentions to collaborate (Dyer and Singh 1998). Therefore, these two perspectives tend to suggest different governance mechanisms, both structural and relational (Faems et al. 2008).

Following the structural perspective, contractual safeguards are commonly used to enforce control in an alliance (Parkhe 1993). Contracts can be particularly beneficial when transaction barriers are present in the IU alliance (Bruneel et al. 2010). For example, to prevent universities from publishing essential information, legal clauses are added into the collaboration agreement. Besides reducing alliance risk, contracts can be used as a coordination mechanism by which tasks are divided and decision-making is simplified (Madhok 1995; Reuer and Ariño 2007). This can be helpful in the presence of routine barriers, which can be mitigated through close coordination (Estrada et al. 2016). Contracts, formal coordination, and planning are specifically important in the formation phase of IU alliances in order to align expectations (Morandi 2013).

Another structural mechanism stressed in literature is hierarchy (Williamson 1975). Hierarchical control can be manifested through the formal design of the alliance (Das and Teng 1998). For instance, there is an obvious line of authority from the specific project teams to the board of management. Due to their obvious dissimilarities, this type of controls can be more complex in IU alliances: all partners report to different supervisors with different goals and expectations. That is why coordination is an important aspect in mitigating barriers (Estrada et al. 2016). Coordination can be achieved through the assignment of a project manager or knowledge transfer staff in the IU alliance (DiGregorio and Shane 2003; Lockett and Wright 2005). These managers have the authority to enforce control through formal policies and procedures (Das and Teng 1998).

Other authors highlight that, particularly in IU alliances, a relational approach can be effective (Deng and Hendrikse 2017; Du et al. 2014). Du et al. (2014) explain that close control is not fully necessary, because universities are not regarded as direct competition. Furthermore, strict management can decrease alliance performance, because it leaves little room for experimentation in the innovation process. Therefore, a way to exhibit trust in the alliance is through contractual flexibility (Das and Teng 1998). In this case, contracts are used, but there is room to adapt them to changing market conditions and partner preferences. Moreover, willingness to adapt according to the needs of the alliance rather than individual needs reinforces trust in the alliance (Das and Teng 1998).

Another relational mechanism that is argued to build trust is communication (Das and Teng 1998). Communication is necessary to develop a relationship and to make sure that frictions are dealt with in a productive manner. Moreover, communication mitigates information asymmetry. When partners openly share information, this can be perceived as an indication of trust (Creed and Miles 1996). Also, Mohr and Spekman (1994) define joint problem-solving as an effective mechanism to solve conflicts in alliances. They argue that this is an example of a constructive conflict resolution technique in which the outcome of the conflict is mutually satisfactory. In the process of joint problem-solving, communication is essential (Ariño and Doz 2000).

Table 1 The Wave Energy and Power Network alliances

	Wave Energy	Power Network
Goal of the project	Developing a new technology to generate sustainable energy	Developing a new technology to measure energy quality
Initiator	University	Industry
Phase	Pre-formation	Post-formation
Duration	At least 4 years	At least 4 years
Partners	Few contracts signed, looking for investors	Consortium of 8 partners

3   Methodology

To explore the emergence and governance of dissimilarities and tensions in IU alliances, we conducted an exploratory case study[2] (Yin 1984). This research design is suitable given the novelty of our focal topic (Eisenhardt 1989). Prior research emphasizes the relevance of dissimilarities, tensions, and governance in IU alliances. However, an in-depth examination of the connections between these issues has not yet been performed in the context of IU alliance formation.

We studied two cases selected for theoretical reasons (Eisenhardt 1989). To guarantee confidentiality, we use pseudonyms for both cases: "Wave Energy" and "Power Network" (see Table 1). While both cases are representative of the focal phenomenon (i.e., recently initiated IU alliances), they represented different alliance developmental stages. For simplicity, we refer to these stages as pre-formation stage (Wave Energy) and post-formation stage (Power Network). Analyzing these two cases together allowed us to map the full phase of IU alliance formation and to provide richer insight on the collaboration dynamics in recently initiated IU alliances.

We conducted two types of interviews in two phases: expert interviews and case interviews. In the first phase, before selecting the cases, we conducted five semi-structured interviews with experts in the energy industry. These interviews were used to find and select suitable cases for this study. Furthermore, we used insights from these interviews, combined with insights from extant research, to design the case interviews. In the second phase, ten semi-structured interviews were conducted (five in each case). In order to collect richer data, we asked interviewees to provide examples and we asked follow-up and "why" questions. Furthermore, similar questions were asked to different interviewees to identify similarities (or differences). The use of multiple sources and informants helped us enhance validity (Eisenhardt 1989). The results from the interviews were triangulated with available documents, which also helped us mitigate retrospective data collection biases (Yin 1984). Thirteen of the interviews were conducted in Dutch: the native language

---

[2]This study is based on the first author's master thesis project (MSc BA SIM, University of Groningen, 2018). We acknowledge the contributions of Pedro de Faria to this project.

of the interviewees. As Dutch was not the native language of all interviewees, two interviews were conducted in English. An overview of the data sources can be found in Appendix 1.

To analyze the data, we transcribed and coded the interviews and looked for initial links with relevant concepts from the literature review (Miles and Huberman 1984). First, the expert interviews were coded and linked to quotes from academic articles. Based on this, an initial codebook was developed, which was used to assign codes to the cases. As the analysis followed an iterative process, complementary, "open" codes were assigned to the interview transcripts and the supplementary documents. Thereafter, codes were assigned to all interview transcripts. Similar codes were combined and the least relevant codes were erased. Additional case-specific codes were again connected with the literature. The coding process was structured around three themes: dissimilarities, tensions, and governance. After the coding process, we examined the connections between the three themes, relying on interview data and insights from extant research. Eventually, four types of tension were identified, caused by four types of dissimilarities, and leading to four types of decisions.

4 Findings

4.1 Wave Energy Alliance

Wave Energy was initiated in 2013 by a university researcher. The project aimed to conduct research on wave energy and trigger the commercial interest of industry in the near future. To do so, a spin-off company would be founded. When this study started, this process had already been set in motion. The alliance structure had been set and a business plan had been developed. However, additional activities, such as establishing a physical knowledge infrastructure, developing agreements for intellectual property, and perfecting the marketing strategy, were still under construction. Upon completion of these processes, the company would officially recruit financial and supply partners that could contribute to the development of a prototype and the eventual commercialization of the product. At the time of our study, a few partners had been approached, but no official contracts were signed yet.

4.1.1 Dissimilarities and Tensions

Most of the partners at Wave Energy were connected with the university. A few industry partners had been involved to develop the first prototype, which could put them in an advantageous position when the product would be produced on a large scale. However, since there was still a long way to go until production, industry partners needed to be willing to invest in an uncertain project. This could challenge the collaboration. Additionally, university partners needed to be able to trust investors not to take advantage of their position. For example, when a large energy conglomerate invests in the project, it is important that they invest in the idea and the technology, rather than "buying the competition." Thus, trust was essential in the Wave Energy alliance:

> [Trust is important,] because we are in the development stage, in which we need to showcase that the principle will work. If a partner cannot be trusted, that means that either they cannot deliver what they are promising, or they probably sell the technology to other parties. (University partner)

Another barrier resided in the conflicting work ethic of entrepreneurs and employees of the university. One of the advisors at Wave Energy described the existence of a fundamental cultural difference between entrepreneurs and university researchers:

> Scientists are used to work from nine to five with regular breaks. As an entrepreneur, you have to be willing to start at seven in the morning and go home at ten in the evening, so to speak. It is an entirely different game. Therefore, I always advise to bring someone in from outside the company. (Industry partner)

In order to bridge the gap between the working styles of the university and the startup, an external CEO was hired. The CEO had experience in both academia and business and thus was able to bridge both worlds. According to the CEO, the complex knowledge structure at the university forms a large barrier to IU collaboration. He mentioned that the knowledge and information required to found a new startup is available at the university. However, this knowledge is widely dispersed, and it is challenging to find the right person to obtain a certain piece of information. Therefore, the process of founding the spin-off company remains time-consuming and inefficient. Furthermore, the way work is prioritized at the university may not align with the strict planning that is desirable at the startup:

> The entire institution is built around research and education, but now you are basically doing something else. [. . .] You just notice that the spin-off company does not have the highest priority and therefore you need to adjust your activities to the pace of the university. (CEO)

Because the spin-off company was involved in both research and business activities, patenting and publishing could form a conflict of interest. Two patents had been filed, which were owned by the university. The patents were made accessible to Wave Energy through licenses. This system was favored because it could prevent the patents from dissipating if the spin-off company runs into financial problems. In case the company succeeded, the spin-off company would eventually acquire the patents. However, the university would stay closely connected to Wave Energy, as fundamental research would be required to improve the product and to test its propositions. Furthermore, the project offered research opportunities for students. Nonetheless, since the publication of research might intervene with the patents, the partners regarded this as a large barrier:

> Half a year ago, we had an idea about energy storage. We did not have a patent, so we had to stay quiet. If we published it, we could never apply for a patent, because the idea would

already be out in the open. So, you have to be careful and make sure that certain pieces of technology are not published by academics. (University partner)

In order to found the spin-off company, investors were needed. However, as Wave Energy had been operated solely by university researchers in the past years, there was a lot of knowledge, but little entrepreneurial experience. When looking for financial partners, this could put Wave Energy in a disadvantageous position, relative to more experienced entrepreneurs. Furthermore, the university's knowledge base was highly dissimilar to that of potential industry partners. Many investors had extensive entrepreneurial experience, and they were trained in selecting high-potential projects. Therefore, creating partnerships could be challenging:

> It is like an adventure. I do not have experience with [founding a company], so I do not know the best way to run it. I just think that, as a team, we all have to agree on the decisions we make and the direction we take. (University partner)

> As an investor, I always look at the management team first: what do they do, what is their attitude, how do they talk, et cetera. I have done this for 20 years and within five minutes I have an impression. So, I hope that with the entrance of [the CEO], more experience is added to the management team. (Business Developer and Investor)

4.1.2   Tensions and Governance Decisions

In the formation of the spin-off company, recruitment of new partners was primarily based on mutual trust. In order to achieve this, the interviewees indicated that they attended networking events to establish relationships with potential partners. An important criterion for investment partners was that they were prepared to take a risk. Furthermore, the interviewees highlighted that a personal connection with the potential partner was essential, since the collaboration was meant to be long term. Once partners became involved in the spin-off, the relationship would become more formal:

> At this stage, it is especially important that there is mutual trust and simply a connection with a potential partner. (University partner)

> If the company is looking for a low risk activity or it is not open towards innovation, it is already a clear indication that they are not really a good match. (University partner)

Furthermore, interviewees stated that there was a conflicting work ethic between the university and the industry. Therefore, flexibility was an important aspect in managing the alliance. Differences in time perception were managed by adapting the planning of the spin-off to the speed of the university. As long as no industry partners were actively involved, there would still be time to do this:

> [The timing difference] is not a big problem, but you just have to know that your project does not have the highest priority, so the throughput time of the project will be adapted to the speed of the university. [. . .] For now, there is time to do so. (CEO)

However, when industry partners would become more involved in the spin-off, profitability would become more important. In order to achieve this, flexibility was essential. The long-term goals of the project were clear, but the steps in between could still change. In order to increase the chances of success, it was still possible to put some parts of the product aside if that would increase profitability prospects. Furthermore, the partners were positive towards the creation of a joint venture if that appeared necessary to continue developing the product:

> It is a modular product, so eventually, we look at the parts that generate the most value for the company. Whether that is the storage part or an entirely different technology, that does not matter. Either way, there will be enough research opportunities for the university. (CEO)

In order to prevent unintended knowledge spillovers due to the publication of competitive research, research and business would become two separate entities. The research entity would stay connected to the university and would provide research and development for the spin-off. Furthermore, the university would still arrange research projects for students, but it would not publish information that could harm the competitive position of the spin-off. The spin-off company itself would focus on the commercialization of the concept. This separation would prevent conflicting stakes and interests from entangling. Further conflicts between patenting and publishing would be formally prevented through contracts:

> To become less dependent on the university, we keep research at the university, but try to separate it from the company. This has some advantages for the company: you can apply for different types of funding and attract different types of investors. [. . .] Furthermore, it allows the company to grow in value. So, you can keep all intellectual property within the firm. (University partner)

Lastly, in order to compensate for the lack of entrepreneurial experience at Wave Energy, an external CEO was hired. Accordingly, the management team would become more convincing when they needed to pitch the concept in front of potential investors. The interviewees highlighted the importance of having someone in a leading position at the company. To illustrate, all knowledge about founding a company was available at the university, but accessing this knowledge was a demanding process. Hiring a CEO should ease the process of founding a company. Furthermore, the CEO could make sure that deadlines were met, agreements were followed, and responsibilities were clear. Nonetheless, the CEO stressed the need for formal guidelines at the university, in order to ease the processes of alliance formation and setting up a company:

> I think the entire process would have lasted much longer if I were not involved. You have to find a balance between your speed and the velocity of the university. [. . .] However, it would be useful if there was a general guideline for university startups or a first draft that explains how you would organize it and share information. (CEO)

4.2 Power Network Alliance

Power Network was initiated in 2017 as one of the pilots within a larger project that examined the commercial application of the 5G mobile network. This network was expected to be deployed for a wide range of novel products and services. Power Network was established as a consortium consisting of eight partners, with the objective to develop a digital platform that measures energy quality. This objective and the accompanied responsibilities were clearly laid out in a project plan. Although the consortium was formed, the project was in an early stage of development, as the platform had not yet been developed.

4.2.1 Dissimilarities and Tensions

At Power Network, the university had a supporting role, providing one of their university buildings as an experimentation hub. In turn, the project offered an opportunity for education, as graduation projects had been established for students. At the same time, industry partners were mainly motivated by exploration opportunities to improve their business. When 5G would be launched, the industry partners of Power Network would be among the first to have a commercial application for it:

> First, we want to discover the market potential of these new network applications. [. . .] Second, we can test our new services. [. . .] Third, it improves our brand and image to work on innovation projects. (Industry partner)

> We have many outdated medium voltage stations that all need to be supplied with communication. Currently, we use 4G to achieve this. With this project, we want to see if 5G is an option to supply the stations with communication. (Industry partner)

The different motives of the university and industry partners had provoked some tension in the Power Network alliance. One of the industry partners described an example in which university students worked on a project. The students were involved for a brief period, which limited their knowledge about the alliance. Therefore, their input turned out to have little value for Power Network:

> I think it is good to involve students in innovation projects. However, I wonder how reliable the results of the students are. [. . .] I saw the presentation of the students, but decided not to use the results, because the data was unreliable and the students had not completely understood the line of questioning. (Industry partner)

In the project plan, the objectives of the alliance were carefully projected. The project had four successive objectives, dividing the project into four phases. Within this structure, some tension emerged: industry partners focused on short-term goals, whereas the university had a long-term orientation. Before finalizing the first phase, the university had started preparing for the second phase. However, one of the industry partners indicated that it would have been more effective to focus on the first phase of the project before continuing with the next phase:

> What I find difficult in this type of innovation projects is that some partners focus mainly on pursuing their own interest. [. . .] The scope is clear for now, so we need to focus on that first, before we continue with the next phase. (Industry partner)

Because the consortium consisted of eight partners, various interests and stakes had to be managed. Interestingly, some tension emerged because of the lengthy administrative procedures of subsidy application. For the university and smaller industry partners, funding was essential. They did not have the budgets to invest in this type of projects. Therefore, they were willing to go through the long procedures of subsidy application:

> Currently, I have the time to work with students on these projects. If I had to arrange budgets within the university, this would not have been possible. (University partner)

Conversely, one of the larger industry partners highlighted that he did not want to be involved in the process of subsidy application. In the beginning of the project, this partner had a leading position as formal owner of the project. However, according to him, the time and effort needed for the application process outweighed the benefits of receiving the funding:

> I have plenty experience with subsidy projects, and I told my co-worker that [subsidy application] is something you should not want. It costs way too much time and effort, especially in a consortium with eight parties. (Industry partner)

> We noticed that during the formation, [a large industry partner] started to distance itself from the collective goals and focus on their own goals. [. . .] Eventually, we discovered that they did not like the extra responsibilities of being a project owner. (Project leader)

Shortly after the consortium was formed, each partner had established a role in the project. According to the interviewees, this had naturally emerged. However, the partners worked in a chain of activities, in which each activity depended on the progress of the precedent activity in the chain. Therefore, the partners did not all contribute to the project at the same time. As a result, some showed less commitment than other partners, which frustrated one of the partners:

> There are several parties who do not actually contribute to the project. [. . .] I think we could have achieved the same with four partners, we do not need all eight of them. (Industry partner)

> At this stage, some partners show little commitment, because they do not have a clear role yet. But once we have finished the first stage, they will have a larger role in the project and we will step down. (Industry partner)

The project leader at Power Network explained that dissimilar commitment was also caused by the partners' dependency on the outcome of the project. For university partners, the project served as an opportunity for research and education. It would have been in their interest if the project succeeded, but they did not financially or strategically depend on its continuity. Contrarily, the industry partners did depend on each other. They had a practical problem to solve, whereupon they were involved in the alliance. Whether the alliance succeeded or failed, it would have affected their position in the market:

> In the technical infrastructure, all partners are structured in a certain order. One partner has knowledge about the hardware, the other about the connections, and another about the physical energy infrastructure. These are complementary skills and knowledge. [. . .] Eventually, we are all working towards the same goal. (Project leader)

> From the perspective of the university, they just say: "We have to work on this type of projects, but whether it is this project or another, that doesn't really matter." It is more

about finding the right people who enjoy working on a project and who can make it happen. (University partner)

4.2.2 Tensions and Governance Decisions

In the Power Network alliance, there had been tension between university and industry partners, because their motivation to collaborate differed. For instance, because university students were involved for a brief period, their contribution had little value to the overall project. According to an industry partner, this could have been solved through communication and supervision of the students:

> There had been a miscommunication between what was asked and what the students had understood. I think the communication between the students and their supervisor could have been improved. The supervisor could have said: "These are the questions being asked and this is what you have to answer." (Industry partner)

Furthermore, one of the university partners described the importance of the human aspect of collaboration. He characterized collaboration as a social process in which the overall atmosphere is centralized:

> You have to keep the human factor in mind. It starts with the individual enjoying working on such a project and collaborating with other people. [. . .] In a project such as this one, we work on clear, tangible goals, which contributes to the group atmosphere. Many people look at collaboration in a systematic way, but all in all, it is the people who are doing it. (University partner)

Another issue that resulted from the interviews is a distinction in work ethic. University partners tended to take on a long-term approach, whereas the larger industry partners preferred focusing on short-term deadlines. This had frustrated one of the industry partners. In order to solve the problem and ease his frustration, he decided that an informal approach was the best solution:

> I made clear that we have defined the scope of the project and that it is important for me that we stick with that for now. The other plans are nice, but I want to focus on the first phase first. So right now, the others will take that into account and we will see how it turns out. (Industry partner)

Additionally, the project leader highlighted that the involved parties were not used to this type of collaboration. Therefore, they had to familiarize with the different cultures and routines they encountered. In managing these differences, he highlighted the importance of flexibility in addressing the needs of each partner:

> An important aspect is to bring matters to the surface. When there is friction between parties, and sometimes this can be invisible, I make sure we talk about it by asking questions such as: "What is actually going on?", "Why is this so important to you?" and "How does this intervene with the goals of the project?" And in general, the answers to these questions are already half of your solution. (Project leader)

As the above quotation indicates, governance was highly informal at Power Network. Nonetheless, most of the interviewees indicated that having clear agreements beforehand is important. For that purpose, a clear project plan had been developed and an additional clause defined how patents were handled in case they were filed. Nonetheless, the project leader mentioned that formally, the project plan had not been signed. Furthermore, the interviewees indicated that the project plan served as a guideline, but the content was flexible. Since the start of the project, the project plan had been adapted three times, and depending on the outcome of the first phase, it could still change:

> Well, formally there is a project agreement, but it is not even signed yet. So actually, it is inferior to the informal process. (Project leader)

> We were not satisfied with the plan, so [the project leader] has completely rewritten the plan. [. . .] I do believe that if we would have understood each other from the beginning, it was not necessary to rewrite it three times. (Industry partner)

Regarding the application of funding, some tension did arise. In the beginning of the project, one of the industry partners had a leading position as formal owner of the project. To him however, the efforts required for the application process outweighed the benefits of receiving the funding. Therefore, he decided to become a regular partner instead. Consequently, one of the smaller industry partners formally became the project owner. Thus, a structural change in the alliance solved the problem:

> [As a project owner], you have to apply for funding, there are all kinds of agreements and things you have to do. So, we decided that the project plan was rewritten with [our company] as a regular partner instead of a project owner. (Industry partner)

> We noticed that [the project owner] became distant from the collective goal and started to focus on their own goals. First, we tried to convince them to stay, up until the board level and through conversations with deputies from the province. That did not work. Therefore, we chose to involve another industry partner as project owner. This way, the problem was solved quickly and [the former project owner] found a suitable role in the project. (Project leader)

To conclude, in the Power Network alliance, partners were not equally committed at the same time, which led to tension in the alliance. The interviewees indicated that the project leader and the project coordinator played a large role in restoring commitment. The project leader organized all the meetings and paperwork. Additionally, the project coordinator served as an external expert. He was involved to advise and support the project leader when necessary:

> Having someone in a managing position is important. [. . .] People collaborating in the project normally do not work together, that relationship needs a little glue. (Project leader)

4.3   Summary of Findings

In Table 2, the findings are summarized. From left to right, the columns of the table represent (1) the different types of dissimilarities between industry and university

Table 2 Summary of findings

	Dissimilarities Industry	University	Tension	Decision
Wave Energy *Motivation*	Strategic intent	Personal interest	Lack of trust	Carefully choose partners
Power Network *Motivation*	Focus on strategic outcome	Focus on education	Misalignment of individual goals	Supervision, focus on "human aspect"
Wave Energy *Work ethic*	Strict deadlines	No driver to be quick	Different working styles	Flexibility
Power Network *Timing*	Focus on short-term goals	Focus on long-term goals	Different time perspective	Adaptable contracts
Wave Energy *Patenting*	Protect innovation	Publish findings	Conflict over IP	Split research and business
Power Network *Funding*	Avoid unnecessary procedures	Funding is essential	Conflict over administration	Formal agreements
Wave Energy *Experience*	Highly experienced	Little experience	Lack of experience	Hire new CEO
Power Network *Dependence*	High dependence on alliance success	Low dependence on alliance success	Lack of commitment	Project management

partners that were more salient in our cases,[3] (2) the different types of barriers or tensions that were caused by these dissimilarities, and (3) how these tensions were managed in the two alliances we studied.

First, in both our cases, tensions emerged due to the different motivation of industry and university partners. The motivation of the industry partners is clearly strategic (business-related), whereas the motivation of the university seems to be driven by personal factors. Second, tension arose because of different work ethic and time perspectives of both partner types. Whereas industry partners tend to have a more short-term focus with strict deadlines, university partners tend to have a more long-term perspective. Third, partners' different attitudes towards funding and administration became evident in our cases. For industry partners, applying for funding seems time-consuming and knowledge should be protected with patents. For university partners, on the contrary, it is vital to apply for funding and publish research papers. Fourth and last, two case-specific sources of tension became apparent. At Wave Energy, the knowledge base and level of experience differed between industry and university partners. At Power Network, commitment was an

---

[3] Besides orientation-based and routine-based dissimilarities, two key types of dissimilarities identified in prior studies (Estrada et al. 2016), we identified administrative and personal dissimilarities. We did so to fully describe the realities of the two alliances we analyzed in this study.

issue. In the next section, these findings will be discussed in connection to the topic of alliance governance.

5 Discussion

Extant research has widely stressed the role of interpartner dissimilarities in IU alliances (Bruneel et al. 2010; DiGregorio and Shane 2003; Estrada et al. 2016; Lockett and Wright 2005). While these dissimilarities do not necessarily cause tension immediately, due to a honeymoon effect (Estrada et al. 2016; Fichman and Levinthal 1991), early detection of potential barriers may be key to the effective governance of the alliance (Bruneel et al. 2010). In this paper, we have focused on this phenomenon and explored the connections between dissimilarities, tensions, and governance mechanisms in IU alliances. The resulting theoretical propositions are discussed below.

5.1 Orientation-Based Dissimilarities

In both alliances, we found dissimilarities regarding the partners' motivation to collaborate. From the industry perspective, the interviewees indicated that they were in the alliance for strategic reasons: being part of the alliance provided commercial opportunities when the eventual products would be launched. This is in line with the literature, stating that alliance formation is stimulated by strategic needs from the industry (Eisenhardt and Schoonhoven 1996). Conversely, university interviewees indicated that they were involved because of their personal interest in the topic. Therefore, university partners at Wave Energy aimed to find industry partners that could be trusted not to take advantage of their position as investor. This is in line with literature about social needs, stating that firms are more likely to form alliances with trustworthy partners (Eisenhardt and Schoonhoven 1996). At Power Network, these different motives have led to tension in the alignment of goals that were not included in the project plan. The fact that tension emerged because of different goals and motivations of partners is in line with theory about orientation-based dissimilarities (Bruneel et al. 2010).

At Wave Energy, these different goals and expectations have led to a situation where recruitment of industry partners was predominantly based on trust. In order to do so, they join network events and try to establish a personal connection with potential partners. At Power Network, differing goals and expectations have actually led to tension. More specifically, misalignment of the goals that were not specified in the project plan has led to misunderstanding. In governing this barrier, interviewees at both alliances stated that close communication and informal management were the right approach. In the literature, equally, communication is seen as a method to prevent tensions caused by information asymmetry (Das and Teng 1998). Moreover, communication is a vital element in joint problem-solving (Ariño and Doz 2000; Mohr and Spekman 1994). Our results build on these propositions and extend it with the context in which communication is an appropriate mechanism in IU alliances:

Proposition 1 Communication may be an effective governance mechanism in IU alliances in a situation in which orientation barriers are apparent.

5.2   *Routine-Based Dissimilarities*

Interviewees at both alliances experienced differences in the time orientation of the university and the industry. Whereas industry partners had the tendency to focus on strict deadlines and short-term goals, university partners had a more long-term perspective. Moreover, university partners were focused on long-term goals. This is in line with the literature, stating that universities consider the short-term orientation of firms a disadvantage of collaboration (Carayol 2003). Furthermore, one of the interviewees emphasized the difference in work ethic between the university and an entrepreneur. According to him, university employees often work from nine to five with regular breaks, whereas the entrepreneurial mindset is more flexible, timewise. Similarly, Estrada et al. (2016) describe that routine barriers occur because of differences in behavior, such as communication, decision-making, and flexibility of tasks.

To overcome these barriers, several decisions were made. At Wave Energy, the interviewees indicated that flexibility was essential. Partners were willing to adapt their planning when this would benefit the collective outcome of the alliance, even though the business plan was already operative. This aligns with theory about trust-building through contractual flexibility (Das and Teng 1998). At Power Network, routine barriers were mitigated by bringing tension to the surface in order to find a solution. Within this solution, the interviewees indicated that they were flexible in changing their planning. Furthermore, the project plan had been developed, but when the interviews were conducted, it was not formally signed. This allowed for contractual flexibility, which may indicate interpartner trust (Das and Teng 1998). This is in line with theory about relational governance (e.g., Barney and Hansen 1994), stating that trust is a vital aspect of collaboration. In this case, flexibility was used as a mechanism to constitute trust in the alliance (Das and Teng 1998). Combined with the case results on routine barriers, this leads to the following proposition:

Proposition 2 Flexibility may be an effective governance mechanism in IU alliances in a situation in which routine barriers are apparent.

5.3   Administrative Dissimilarities

All interviewees mentioned the disconnection between the university's objective of publishing new insights and the industry's tendency to protect new technologies. This issue is regularly mentioned by scholars as well (Dasgupta and David 1994; Carayol 2003) and aligns with literature on transaction barriers: barriers related to conflicts over intellectual property and university administration (Bruneel et al. 2010). However, in neither of the alliances, an actual conflict had arisen because of this phenomenon. In fact, one of the interviewed experts described that this disconnection is often an imaginary problem. At Power Network, no patents had been filed when the interviews took place. At Wave Energy, patents were filed, but this had not led to tension. Therefore, one could argue that the main barrier lies in the partners' perception of possible conflict regarding intellectual property, rather than it actually being a source of conflict.

Nevertheless, in both alliances, formal clauses and contractual safeguards were used to prevent tension. This aligns with the structural perspective on governance, in which scholars argue that conflicts should be prevented through formal contracts (Parkhe 1993; Morandi 2013). Furthermore, the development of formal structures is considered as an effective mechanism to create a successful alliance (Doz et al. 2000). At Wave Energy, the formal structure was used to prevent the publication of scientific articles from conflicting with the patents. The spin-off company would formally be divided into two separate entities: one focusing on the research side and one focusing on the business aspect. This division would be formalized in a contract, which could prevent unwanted knowledge leakages, even internally. These examples provide a context for IU alliances in which contracts are an effective governance mechanism, leading us to the following proposition:

Proposition 3 Contracts may be an effective governance mechanism in IU alliances in a situation in which transaction barriers are apparent.

5.4   Personal Dissimilarities

Lastly, we observed dissimilarities that were specific to the individual cases. At Wave Energy, university partners clearly had less entrepreneurial experience than the industry partners. Therefore, Wave Energy's main activities were aimed at gaining experience and preparing for the establishment of the startup. This aligns with theory about alliance formation, stating that experience increases the probability of alliance success (e.g., D'Este and Patel 2007). Moreover, at Power Network, lack of commitment formed a large barrier. Interviewees explained that dependence on the alliance was low for some of the partners, and therefore they had less incentive to be committed to the alliance. This aligns with alliance formation literature, stating that when interdependence is low, the alliance follows an engineered path (Doz et al. 2000). Because these dissimilarities were not found in either of the alliances, they can be considered case-specific. Therefore, we created a fourth barrier: distinctive barriers. These can be defined as the barriers that (1) are related to dissimilarities between industry and university partners in the alliance, but (2) are not specifically apparent in IU alliances in general.

We found a similarity between the approaches to managing this type of dis-similarities. At Wave Energy, lack of experience was compensated by hiring a CEO externally. This person had experience in both the business and academia, making him a suitable partner at Wave Energy. At Power Network, interviewees highlight that in order to increase commitment, the role of the project leader was essential. This "objective outsider" would have the ability to connect the alliance partners and motivate partners to stay involved in the projects. The appearance of an external party is also known in literature about alliance formation, stating that when interdependence is low, a triggering entity is necessary to connect partners (Doz et al. 2000). Furthermore, Das and Teng (1998) describe that hierarchical control can be an effective governance mechanism in alliances. We found that hierarchy is used to handle more unusual, case-specific barriers. This way, control can be enforced while having a pragmatic approach to governance. This leads to the following proposition:

Proposition 4 Hierarchy may be an effective governance mechanism in IU alliances in a situation in which distinctive barriers are apparent.

6 Concluding Remarks

6.1 Tension and Governance in IU Alliance Formation

In this study, we have explored two key questions in the context of IU alliance formation: *How do interpartner dissimilarities lead to tension? How does tension caused by interpartner dissimilarities connect to alliance governance decisions?* Regarding the first question, based on our cases, we identified different types of dis-similarities and observed that each can lead to different types of barriers or tensions: (1) orientation-based dissimilarities lead to orientation barriers; (2) routine-based dissimilarities lead to routine barriers; (3) administrative dissimilarities lead to transaction barriers; and (4) personal dissimilarities lead to what we refer to as distinctive barriers. In turn, and connecting to the second question, observations in the cases under study suggested different governance solutions that can be deployed to address each type of tension: (1) orientation barriers may be mitigated through communication; (2) routine barriers may be mitigated through flexibility; (3) transaction barriers may be mitigated through contracts; and (4) distinctive barriers may be mitigated through hierarchy. These findings are summarized in Table 3, where we proposed an exploratory framework to describe the emergence and governance of tension in IU alliance formation.

Our exploratory framework provides initial insight into the connections between interpartner dissimilarities, tension, and governance in the formation phase of IU

Table 3 Tension and governance in IU alliance formation: an exploratory framework

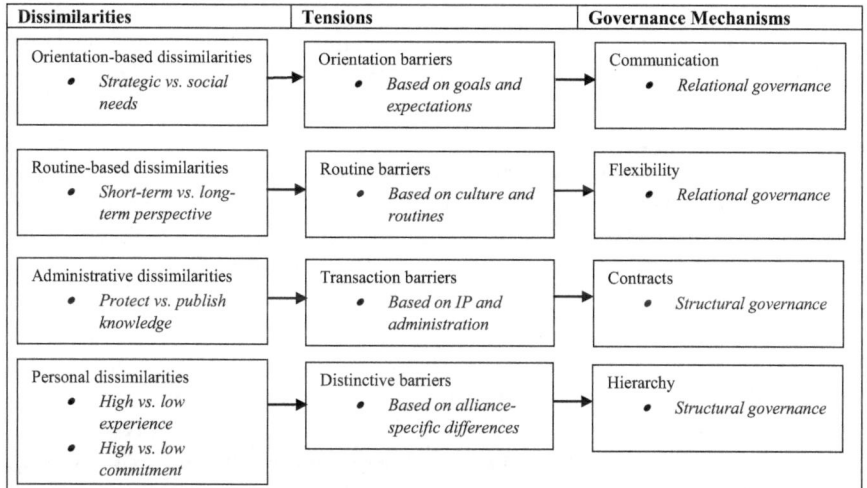

alliances. This way, our study adds to earlier work on IU alliance barriers and dissimilarities (Bruneel et al. 2010; Estrada et al. 2016) by extending the integrative perspective on alliance governance (Faems et al. 2008) to the context of IU alliances. By focusing on the formation phase, we were able to provide a detailed analysis of dissimilarities and tensions that may specifically affect the initial phases of these alliances. Moreover, we were able to indicate some ways in which governance design can be used to promptly mitigate tension or prevent it from escalating beyond the initial phases. For example, we identified the presence of what we refer to as distinctive barriers, barriers that (1) are related to dissimilarities between industry and university partners in the alliance, but (2) do not seem to be specifically apparent in all IU alliances. We have argued that this barrier can be managed through hierarchy, because it seems to require a pragmatic, yet controlled approach to governance. Overall, we hope that future studies in the field can build upon and extend our framework to further explore the links between dissimilarities, tension, and governance in IU alliances. At the same time, we hope that managers involved in the formation of these alliances can make use of our framework to timely detect problematic dissimilarities that can lead to tension in the alliance and, thus, anticipate to tension in the process of alliance design. Insights from our case studies may also assist managers in responding adequately when tensions do emerge in the IU alliance.

6.2 Limitations and Future Research

In this chapter, we have presented insights from an exploratory study of two IU alliances in the energy industry. These insights are primarily based on the

15 interviews we conducted with different informants. While our study offers initial insight on the connections between dissimilarities, tension, and governance in IU alliances, we need to acknowledge the limitations of our results in terms of generalizability. Further research on the topic would benefit from larger-scale research endeavors (e.g., a multiple case study based on large amounts of interview data). Moreover, future studies should explore tensions and governance in IU alliances in settings beyond the energy industry. It is also important to note that, since we studied two alliances in the formation phase, key aspects remained beyond the scope of our study. For instance, we did not formally assess the success of the governance mechanisms on the medium term. Therefore, future studies may build upon and extend our framework by conducting longitudinal analyses that cover the entire IU alliance lifecycle. Another interesting avenue concerns the fact that, in our cases, transaction barriers did not seem to lead to tension, whereas other barriers did. We pointed to contracts as a sort of preventive governance mechanism to address this type of tensions. However, in alliances where transaction barriers actually arise and lead to tension, contracts might not be effective. Exploring differences between types of barriers and between preventive and reactive governance mechanisms are, thus, promising research opportunities in the context of IU alliances.

Appendix 1 Overview of Data Sources

Interview	Type of interview	Role of interviewee	Interview details
1	Expert interview	University professor	Face to face, 01h22
2	Expert interview	Valorization expert	Face to face, 00h54
3	Expert interview	University advisor	Face to face, 01h02
4	Expert interview	University professor	Face to face, 01h02
5	Expert interview	University professor	Face to face, 01h19
6	Case interview: Wave Energy	Project leader & CTO	Face to face, 00h58
7	Case interview: Wave Energy	Assistant professor	Face to face, 00h49
8	Case interview: Wave Energy	Associate professor	Face to face, 00h29
9	Case interview: Wave Energy	Investor	Face to face, 00h57
10	Case interview: Wave Energy	CEO	Face to face, 01h09
11	Case interview: Power Network	University professor	Face to face, 00h50
12	Case interview: Power Network	Business developer	Face to face, 00h47
13	Case interview: Power Network	Project manager	Skype call, 00h52
14	Case interview: Power Network	Technical specialist	Telephone call, 00h45
15	Case interview: Power Network	Project coordinator	Face to face, 00h51

Document	Case	Type of document	Document details
1	Wave Energy	Private	Business plan
2	Power Network	Private	Project plan

Appendix 2 Overview of Coded Concepts

Dissimilarities	
Strategic position	Extent to which being part of the alliance enables a firm to access financial resources and other resources (Eisenhardt and Schoonhoven 1996)
Social position	Extent to which extensive personal relationships and trust create an awareness of alliance opportunities (Eisenhardt and Schoonhoven 1996)
Short-term vs. long-term orientation	Extent to which partners are accustomed to applying a long-term vs. short-term orientation research and innovation
Protect knowledge	Extent to which knowledge remains hidden within the firm or disclosed in a limited way through patents (Bruneel et al. 2010)
Publish knowledge	Extent to which research aims to create public knowledge (Bruneel et al. 2010)
Experience	Extent to which an organization is experienced with alliancing
Low vs. high interdependence	Extent to which an organization financially depends on the alliance outcome (Doz et al. 2000)
Tensions	
Orientation barriers	Partners have different ideas about the alliance rationale, their reciprocal obligations, and the alliance horizon and scope (Estrada et al. 2016)
Routine barriers	Partners behave differently towards communication, joint work and decision-making, and alliance task execution and flexibility (Estrada et al. 2016)
Transaction barriers	Partners have conflicting views on IP; also, barriers related with dealing with university administration (Bruneel et al. 2010)
Governance	
Trust	Extent to which partners rely on trust to address issues of safeguarding and coordination (Faems et al. 2008)
Flexibility	Extent to which partners are willing to accommodate deviations from the contract when necessary (Das and Teng 1998)
Contracts	Extent to which contractual rigidity is used to make sure that contingencies are dealt with and opportunism is mitigated (Das and Teng 1998)
Hierarchy	Extent to which partners rely on control based on authority and giving orders to subordinates and then evaluating their performance (Das and Teng 1998)

References

Ariño A, Doz Y (2000) Rescuing troubled alliances... before it's too late. Eur Manag J 18:173–182

Barney JB, Hansen MH (1994) Trustworthiness as a source of competitive advantage. Strateg Manag J 15:175–190

Bishop K, D'Este P, Neely A (2011) Gaining from interactions with universities: multiple methods for nurturing absorptive capacity. Res Policy 40:30–40

Blau PM (1964) Exchange and power in social life. Wiley, New York

Breschi S, Lissoni F (2001) Knowledge spillovers and local innovation systems: a critical survey. Ind Corp Chang 10:975–1005

Bruneel J, D'Este P, Salter A (2010) Investigating the factors that diminish the barriers to university-industry collaboration. Res Policy 39:858–868

Carayol N (2003) Objectives, agreements and matching in science-industry collaborations: reassembling the pieces of the puzzle. Res Policy 32:887–908

Chesbrough HW (2003) The era of open innovation. MIT Sloan Manag Rev 44:35–41

Creed WED, Miles RE (1996) Trust in organizations: a conceptual framework linking organizational forms, managerial philosophies, and the opportunity costs of controls. In: Kramer RM, Tyler TR (eds) Trust in organizations: frontiers of theory and research. Sage, Thousand Oaks, CA, pp 16–38

Cyert RM, Goodman PS (1997) Creating effective university-industry alliances: an organizational learning perspective. Organ Dyn 25:45–57

D'Este P, Patel P (2007) University-industry linkages in the UK: what are the factors underlying the variety of interactions with industry? Res Policy 36:1295–1313

D'Este P, Guy F, Iammarino S (2013) Shaping the formation of university-industry research collaborations: what type of proximity does really matter? J Econ Geogr 13:537–558

Das TK, Teng BS (1998) Between trust and control: developing confidence in partner cooperation in alliances. Acad Manag Rev 23:491–512

Dasgupta P, David PA (1994) Toward a new economics of science. Res Policy 23:487–521

Deng W, Hendrikse G (2017) Social interactions and product quality: the value of pooling in cooperative entrepreneurial networks. Small Bus Econ 50:749–761

DiGregorio D, Shane S (2003) Why do some universities generate more start-ups than others? Res Policy 32:209–227

Doz YL, Olk PM, Ring PS (2000) Formation processes of R&D consortia: which path to take? Where does it lead? Strateg Manag J 21:239–266

Du J, Leten B, Vanhaverbeke W (2014) Managing open innovation projects with science-based and market-based partners. Res Policy 43:828–840

Dyer JH, Singh H (1998) The relational view: cooperative strategy and sources of interorganizational competitive advantage. Acad Manag Rev 23:660–679

Eisenhardt KM (1989) Building theories from case study research. Acad Manag Rev 14:532–550

Eisenhardt KM, Schoonhoven CB (1996) Resource-based view of strategic alliance formation: strategic and social effects in entrepreneurial firms. Organ Sci 7:136–150

Estrada I, Faems D, Martin Cruz N, Perez Santana MP (2016) The role of interpartner dissimilarities in industry-university alliances: insights from a comparative case study. Res Policy 45:2008–2022

Faems D, Janssens M, Madhok A, Van Looy B (2008) Toward an integrative perspective on alliance governance: Connecting contract design, trust dynamics, and contract application. Acad Manag J 51:1053–1076

Fichman M, Levinthal DA (1991) Honeymoons and the liability of adolescence: a new perspective on duration dependence in social and organizational relationships. Acad Manag Rev 16:442–468

George G, Zahra SA, Wood DR (2002) The effects of business-university alliances on innovative output and financial performance: a study of publicly traded biotechnology companies. J Bus Ventur 17:577–609

Gulati R (1995) Social structure and alliance formation patterns: a longitudinal analysis. Adm Sci Q 40:619–652

Hall B, Link A, Scott J (2001) Barriers inhibiting industry from partnering with universities: evidence from the advanced technology program. J Technol Transfer 26:87–98

Lavie D, Haunschild PR, Khanna P (2012) Organizational differences, relational mechanisms, and alliance performance. Strateg Manag J 33:1453–1479

Lockett A, Wright M (2005) Resources, capabilities, risk capital and the creation of university spin-out companies. Res Policy 34:1043–1057

Madhok A (1995) Opportunism and trust in joint venture relationships: an exploratory study and a model. Scand J Manag 11:55–74

Miles MB, Huberman AM (1984) Qualitative data analysis. Sage Publications, Beverly Hills, CA

Mohr J, Spekman R (1994) Characteristics of partnership success: partnership attributes, communication behavior, and conflict resolution techniques. Strateg Manag J 15:135–152

Morandi V (2013) The management of industry-university joint research projects: how do partners coordinate and control R&D activities? J Technol Transfer 38:69–92

Muscio A, Pozzali A (2012) The effects of cognitive distance in university-industry collaborations: some evidence from Italian universities. J Technol Transfer 38:486–508

Parkhe A (1993) Strategic alliance structuring: a game theoretic and transaction cost examination of interfirm cooperation. Acad Manag J 36:794–829

Reuer JJ, Ariño AA (2007) Strategic alliance contracts: dimensions and determinants of contractual complexity. Strateg Manag J 28:313–330

Teece DJ, Pisano G, Shuen A (1997) Dynamic capabilities and strategic management. Strateg Manag J 18:509–533

Wernerfelt B (1984) A resource-based view of the firm. Strateg Manag J 5:171–180

Williamson OE (1975) Markets and hierarchies: analysis and antitrust implications. Free Press, New York

Yin RK (1984) Case study research: design and methods. Sage, Thousand Oaks, CA

The Co-evolution of Clusters and the Role of Trans-local Linkages

Francesca Mariotti, Muhammad Zafar Yaqub, and Sajjad Haider

Abstract In this paper, we explore trans-local relationships and their changing dynamics over time, particularly emphasizing their knowledge flows. The under-lying proposition is that the clusters are not isolated entities and that inter-cluster ties are as significant as local ties in sustaining the co-evolution of clusters. We use historical and retrospective analyses to study the inter-linkages between the NASCAR cluster and the UK motorsport industry. Our findings highlight that the structure of the inter-firm ties between the two clusters has evolved over time with a marked increase in the number of linkages established and the transfer of more sophisticated knowledge and components. At the same time, the research highlights some impediments that have delayed the transition of the NASCAR cluster to a more open entity. The authors propound that co-location and proximity are poor indicators of the structure of clusters and that the inter-cluster linkages play an important role in their co-evolution.

1 Introduction

Last decade has witnessed a revived interest in the analysis of clusters from a variety of perspectives ranging from economic geography, regional economics, industrial economics, sociology and organizational theory (e.g. Frenken et al. 2015; Bell and Zaheer 2007; Giuliani and Matta 2013; Balland et al. 2013; Storper 1992; Powell 1990; Powell et al. 1996; Porter 1998; Amin 2000). While these perspectives differ in terms of the arguments put forward, they all seem to agree that clusters are characterized by geographic concentrations of interconnected companies, where proximity ensures certain forms of commonality and increases the frequency and impact of interactions. Some recent studies have begun to emphasize the social

F. Mariotti · M. Z. Yaqub (✉) · S. Haider
Faculty of Economics and Administration, Department of Business Administration, King Abdulaziz University, Jeddah, Kingdom of Saudi Arabia
e-mail: fmariotti@kau.edu.sa; mzyaqoub@kau.edu.sa; ehaidar3@kau.edu.sa

© Springer Nature Switzerland AG 2019
J. Windsperger et al. (eds.), *Design and Management of Interfirm Networks*,
Contributions to Management Science,
https://doi.org/10.1007/978-3-030-29245-4_16

dimension of cluster formation and the importance of local social networks for the production and flow of information and knowledge within clusters (Balland 2012; Balland et al. 2015; Cohen and Fields 1999; Pinch and Henry 1999; Breschi and Lissoni 2001). According to this line of research, learning through networking is the crucial force pulling firms together into clusters. The ways firms learn in a cluster involve formal and informal collaborations, inter-firm mobility of skilled workers, spin-off of new firms from existing firms and links with universities and research centres. By continuously interacting and sharing knowledge with other actors, firms become embedded in a thick network of local relationships based on trust-inspired commitment stemming largely from the norms of reciprocation co-shared in the knowledge creation and sharing episodes through formal and informal interactions and collaborations.

Undoubtedly this literature has contributed to our understanding of why firms cluster together and the benefits associated to such clustering activity (Hervas-Oliver and Albors-Garrigos 2007; Perry 2007; Brown and Bell 2001), albeit too much importance is placed on 'proximity' and analyses are often conducted in a cross-sectional and static manner. Moreover, there has been a strong tendency to abstract clusters from the rest of the economic landscape and to ignore interdependencies of the firms with those outside these clusters. In other words, research to date has paid scant attention to the co-evolution of clusters and the changing nature of the linkages which underpin them. Notwithstanding several studies have attempted to unravel the pattern of inter-organizational relationship formation, the co-evolution dynamics among different clusters demand additional work (Ahuja et al. 2012; Chen et al. 2014). The aim of this research is to explore these issues in detail and to provide some insights into the processes and mechanisms through which inter-cluster connections develop and coevolve over time. Understanding, describing and approximating the inter-cluster performance through knowledge creation and sharing could, on one hand, facilitate such structural arrangement in devising highly efficacious structural and social permutations and, on the other hand, could facilitate an identification of the right cluster policy instruments to help these clusters coevolve strongly and effectively. The chosen empirical settings for this study are the NASCAR cluster and the UK motorsport industry. The long history of the NASCAR cluster and the changing nature of the linkages supporting it constitute a unique opportunity to assess the impact of inter-cluster connections upon its co-evolution with the UK motorsport industry.

Methodologically, the research has been carried out using a retrospective and processual mode of inquiry (Bizzi and Langley 2012). In adopting this approach, we were particularly interested in analysing the life history of the NASCAR cluster in terms of how and why linkages, choices and roles changed over time in the cluster. The data were collected using both primary and secondary methods. In total 24 interviews were conducted with industry specialists to trace the linkages among NASCAR and the UK motorsport industry.

The paper is structured as follows. First, we present an overview of the literature and discuss the current limitations with respect to the co-evolution of cluster linkages. This is followed by the methodology and a brief description of the

NASCAR cluster and the UK motorsport industry. We then outline the empirical findings and discuss the results. Finally, we provide concluding remarks and implication for future research.

2 Theoretical Background

Ever since Marshall and Marshall (1920) proposed the idea of industrial districts, researchers, while making an appeal to a variety of theoretical perspectives, have vigorously sought to explain the dynamics of clusters' performance. Whereas some have strongly argued for the benefits that firms in such structural arrangements might gain by virtue of the agglomerating effects of economic externalities, such as supply pools, vertical disintegration of production, specialized labour, better interactions among the parties in exchange, surrounding resources and knowledge spillovers (Asheim and Clark 2001; McCann and Folta 2008), others have maintained that having companies from the same industry in just one place is not enough to realize all these benefits (Malmberg and Maskell 2002).

The past decade has witnessed a revived interest in the analysis of clusters both by academics and policymakers. Central to this body of work is the notion of clusters as spatially contained agglomerations of firms (Huber and Fitjar 2016; Becattini 1989; Maillat 1991; Storper 1997; Porter 1998; Amin 2000; Miller et al. 2001). This notion seems to suggest that clusters develop and thrive through various forms of local interactions and spillover effects. Specifically, the literature identifies three drivers of agglomeration: (1) knowledge flows and learning, (2) economic efficiencies and increased specialization and (3) social capital.

Several scholars focus upon the dynamics of knowledge sharing and learning among co-located firms and how these dynamics affect the performance of clusters (Molina_Morales 2014; Balland et al. 2015; Giuliani and Matta 2013; Maskell and Lorenzen 2004; Powell et al. 1996; Cohen and Fields 1999; Pinch and Henry 1999; Tallman et al. 2004). Specifically, they maintain that co-location increases the ease and speed through which firms can find, access and transfer complex and tacit knowledge. Firms geographically proximate can engage in frequent interpersonal contacts and thus make knowledge exchange more effective. Moreover, co-located firms tend to exhibit higher levels of absorptive capacity and potential for learning (Grandinetti 2016; Lawson and Lorenz 1999; Breschi and Lissoni 2001). Hence, the possibility for individual firms to tap into a body of localized knowledge and capabilities depends in a fundamental way on the ability to establish and maintain effective social links and lines of communications.

A second strand of literature suggests that spatial proximity offers firms several economic benefits in terms of increased specialization (Ingstrup and Christensen 2017; Piore and Sabel 1984), reduced transaction costs (Branzanti 2015; Felton et al. 2010; Krugman 1991) and enhanced firm productivity (Ganau and Rodríguez-Pose 2018; Puga 2010; Cainelli et al. 2016; Romer 1987). While economic aspects are important, a third body of literature suggests that clusters may well benefit from social capital and firms' embeddedness in a dense network of local relationships (Martínez-Pérez et al. 2016). The most notable studies are those on the Italian industrial districts (Piore and Sabel 1984; Storper 1989) and Silicon Valley (Saxenian 1994). Informal interaction among proximate firms helps the building of strong ties, facilitates the exchange of information and generates trust and norms of reciprocation. For example, Liebeskind et al. (1995) show how biotechnology firms seem to be not worried about opportunism because of the development of shared norms of trustworthy behaviour.

Even though economists and geographers have undoubtedly contributed to our understanding of why firms cluster together and the benefits associated to such clustering activity, their approach takes 'proximity' as the only defining feature of clusters. Albeit there is a great deal of evidence supporting this assertion, it is not clear at all how proximate firms should be in a cluster. For example, Porter (1998, p. 204) speaks about clusters in the following way 'they are present in large and small economies, in rural and urban areas, and several geographical levels'. Porter's definition is representative of the vagueness with which clusters' boundaries are defined. More recently scholars have started to question the validity of notions narrowly based on spatial and geographical boundaries (Ingstrup and Christensen 2017; Balland et al. 2015; Huber and Fitjar 2016; Audretsch 1998; Oerlemans et al. 2001; Martin and Sunley 2003). Spatial proximity to organizations in the same or related industries affects the flows of knowledge and limits the possibility of engaging in extra-local interactions (Amin and Cohendet 1999). For example, Stenberg and Arndt (2001) have found that clusters often have widespread global connections and that firms with trans-local interactions tend to outperform those firms in the cluster which only deal locally. Capello and Faggian (2005) also maintain that knowledge creation and sharing should not be restricted only to the local areas, i.e. knowledge spillovers and exchange within a cluster might not be that beneficial in that the members have generally overlapping opportunities and orientations. On the contrary, firms with bridging (inter-cluster) ties could be quite instrumental in realizing new market opportunities (Burt 1997).

A second problem with the current literature is that it focuses on static and one-dimensional analyses. In other words, it tends to assume that the drivers of cluster performance (knowledge sharing, specialization, social capital) remain the same over time. This view is not necessarily accurate. Martin and Sunley (2003: 26) draw attention to the fact that 'economic landscapes are littered with local areas of industrial specialization that were once prosperous and dynamic but have since gone into relative or absolute decline'. Similarly, work on 'hot spots' has shown how clusters develop over time increasing levels of homogeneity and inertia which lead to their demise (Pouder and St. John 1996). Too much reliance on local knowledge and proximate relationships generates 'lock-in' effects such as those experienced by the Swiss watch industry (Glasmeier 1991) and the coal and steel industry in the Ruhr area (Grabher 1993). These studies along with more recent ones (Fornahl et al. 2015; Trippl et al. 2015; Franken el al. 2014) raise important questions in relation to clusters' performance over time and the mechanisms that may affect their performance. However, they do not offer any explanation of how clusters losing competitiveness can reverse this situation.

It is therefore important to analyse clusters not as isolated entities, but consider the evolutionary and co-evolutionary trajectories of firms inside clusters as well as outside clusters. This means that any study which attempts to research clusters and their development should incorporate 'time' and 'history' and should explore the mechanisms which are responsible for change (Haider and Mariotti 2016). This, in turn, can help to better understand how firms learn, share and exchange information. It can also explain why sometimes clusters decline and how this situation can be reversed.

This paper aims to bring some light into the above issues and explore in depth the changing nature and type of inter-cluster connections which underpin them and how these connections and knowledge flows coevolve. Such an examination can provide a better picture of the actual structure of clusters in terms of their linkages and can help to better understand their evolutionary patterns. These questions are explored through an historical and retrospective analysis of the linkages between the NASCAR cluster in North Carolina and the UK motorsport industry.

3 Methodology

3.1 Research Setting

The empirical settings chosen for this analysis are the NASCAR cluster and the UK motorsport industry. NASCAR racing has become over the years a major national sport in the USA crossing several States and cities. While racing venues are widespread in the country, most of the teams, suppliers and racing drivers are located in the surroundings of Charlotte in North Carolina. This area has been the home of NASCAR racing for over 80 years, and it is now best known as the 'NASCAR Valley' for its concentration of motorsport-related knowledge and the high profile of its skilled workforce. Research to date has focused mainly on the cultural aspects affecting the sport (see Pillsbury 1974; Howell 1997; Alderman et al. 2003), the economic impact of NASCAR racing in the Charlotte region (Hartgen et al. 1996) and the nature of the cluster (Hurt 2002). However, new trends seem to emerge, with NASCAR companies developing links with companies located outside the cluster (and in particular with companies located in the UK motorsport industry). The emergence of these inter-cluster connections signals the changing nature of the cluster and its knowledge flows (Figs. 1 and 2).

The UK is recognized as a leading centre of activity in motorsport engineering and technology involving about 4200 businesses and worth £4.6 billion to the national economy (MIA 2001). Most businesses are clustered in an area that spans the East of England, the Southeast and the East and West Midlands. The sector is continuously evolving and generating new knowledge and capabilities with a

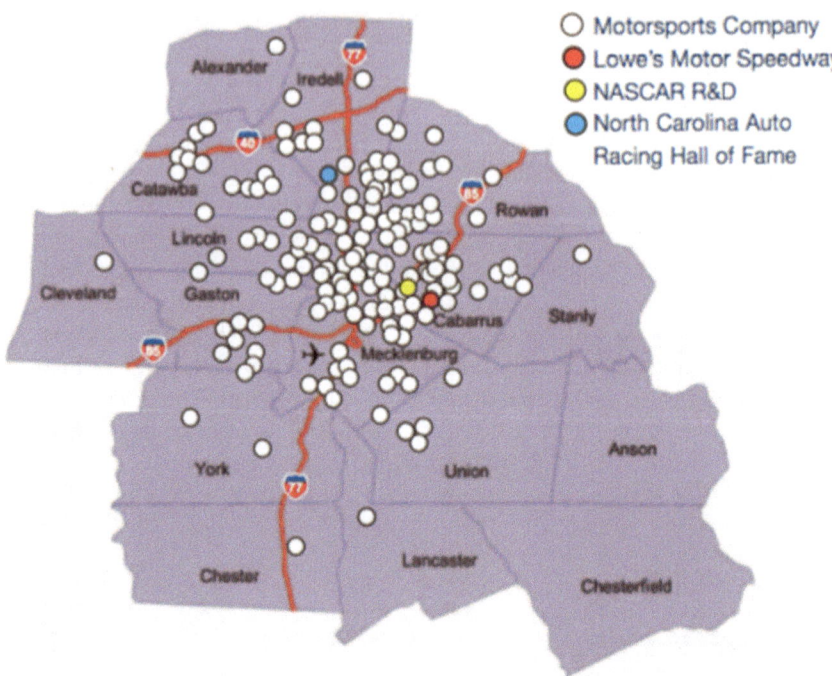

Fig. 1 The NASCAR cluster

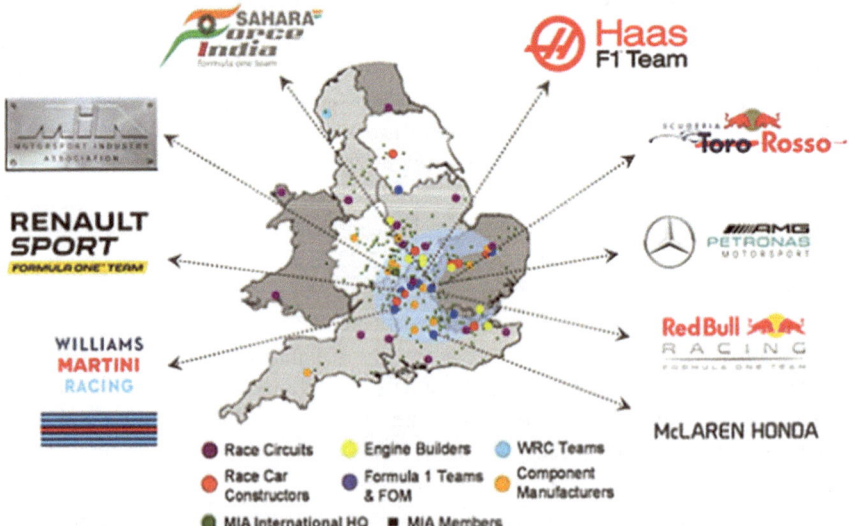

Fig. 2 UK motorsport industry

high number of businesses being world leaders in technology development and manufacturing. More recently, UK companies have started to develop significant linkages with the NASCAR cluster as a means to transfer technology, expand business opportunities and spur growth. For example, Evernham, Roush and Menard, three leading names in US oval racing, have recently established links with UK motorsport companies.

3.2 Data Collection

Consistent with a theory-building research design, the study is qualitative in nature, based on data from in-depth semi-structured interviews. The unit of analysis in this research is the network of inter-firm linkages within the NASCAR cluster and the connections established with companies operating in the UK motorsport industry. In addition, historical and archival data have been collected to identify the different phases of development of the NASCAR cluster. The need to collect primary and secondary data about the two industries is justified by the shortage of work in the area. A review of existing datasets has highlighted the fact that research on the NASCAR cluster focuses mainly on the cultural and marketing aspects of the business and its economic impact; there is, instead, not much work which systematically explores the evolution of the NASCAR cluster and its inter-connections with the UK motorsport industry.

Methodologically, the research has been carried out using a retrospective and processual mode of inquiry in the descriptive-inductive tradition of Bower (1970), Mintzberg (1978), Pettigrew (1990, 1997, 2012), Burgelman (1983) and other process researchers (Haider and Mariotti 2016; Haider 2014; Bizzi and Langley 2012; Dawson 2014; Langley and Tsoukas 2010). Moreover, it incorporates co-evolutionary analysis techniques (McKelvey 1997). This has ensured the collection of rich and multifaceted data for exploring inter-organizational relationship dynamics, knowledge flows and their impact on the development of clusters as a whole. Specifically, the research has focused on the NASCAR cluster and the emergence of linkages with companies in the UK motorsport industry through the analysis of multiple case studies.

Multiple sources of evidence have been used to analyse phenomena and cluster participants. These include 24 in-depth semi-structured interviews, both in the USA and the UK (13 in the UK and 11 in the USA), with chief executive officers, managers, engineers and industry experts to understand phenomena as expressed and observed by them. The data gathered through interviews have been supplemented with the analysis of archival data and industry publications. These helped in avoiding 'elite bias' (talking only to high-status respondents) (Sieber 1973) as well as to validate and corroborate findings.

4   Findings

4.1   The Evolution of the NASCAR Cluster: Building of Inter-cluster Relationships

NASCAR has traditionally been a technically conservative series. In the last 15 years, that attitude has slowly changed. European firms have gradually entered the market with more advanced equipment than their US counterparts. One reason for this is the increasing amount of money available in NASCAR. As NASCAR grew from a regional series to a national series, the sponsors changed from a Southern base to more national, Fortune 500 type, companies. A top-line Sprint Cup car will now cost approximately $20 m a year to run, four times more than 15 years ago. This increase in finance has led to a F1-style trickle-up of resources as teams increase in professionalism to match their funding.

The older, technically conservative, way of going racing is slowly giving way to a more open attitude towards the way in which new technology can lead to competitive advantage. This change in attitude should not, however, be overestimated. Entrenched regulatory standards, organized by NASCAR's technical committees, and the strength of existing suppliers' marketing relationships mean change is slow.

A further way in which NASCAR is changing is the increased concentration on safety. A number of high-profile accidents, particularly Dale Earnhardt's death at Daytona in 2001, have focused NASCAR on the safety aspects of their sport. NASCAR vehicles are technologically simple in many ways to European eyes, and advanced technology is one way in which safety in stock car racing might be improved.

There are many examples of the way technology might help the safety issues present in stock car racing. First is the use of advanced materials and construction to help the structure of the car survive a high-impact situation. Second, the increasing role of technology in safety matters is shown using advanced data acquisition in understanding the dynamics of the accident during and after it has occurred. Third is the use of aerodynamic research to further understand the way these large, heavy vehicles interact on the racetrack at extremely high speed. Fourth is the attempt to develop a barrier system for racetracks to minimize the impact of forces when these heavy, fast moving cars hit the concrete retaining walls of an oval. Within the lower levels of stock car racing, trends are fairly static. There is a slow trickle-down of technical innovation from the professional series as lower-ranking teams buy equipment from higher-ranking teams.

4.2   Building Trans-local Linkages with UK Suppliers

Domestic US firms supply the vast majority of stock car racing, from professional to amateur. At the amateur level, there is virtually no market share from overseas firms. In the middle-level series, there are some overseas component suppliers, while at the top level of professional stock car racing, there is the most impact from non-US firms. British firms already have a strong presence, compared to other overseas firms, as non-indigenous suppliers to professional stock car racing. It seems that professional stock car racing is opening up to trans-local relationships and British firms are one of the primary targets due to their expertise and technology. This will allow US teams to increase their professionalism and improve car technology.

The areas in which British firms have managed to penetrate are very much dependent on the tight regulatory nature of the US stock car series and the existing strengths of domestic US-based suppliers. One example is the supply of specialist components within the slightly less restrictive regulatory environments of NASCAR that currently allow some small leeway of technical innovation.

The establishment of working relationships with US teams lies not just in the supply of the components but also in the supply of extensive technical support for those components. The relationships being built up between the US end user and the British supplier mean that the better quality component includes a high level of technical feedback that cannot be at arms' length. This requires British firms to station personnel in the USA as part of the service required to stay ahead of the competition.

British firms are beginning to establish relationships also for the supply of technical equipment and services to improve the existing regulatory package. This is an important area of improvement for US teams and one that provides technical equipment and services to measure the small incremental changes allowed within the regulations by highly technical research and simulation models. This equipment and services is more likely to be found in Britain than domestically, due to the generally more advanced and better funded high-tech motorsport companies to be found in the UK. The areas of research and testing are twofold. One is in the area of Mechanical Engineering Development, for example, with test and motion simulation (e.g. seven-post rigs) and modelling software (e.g. CAD, FEA, CAE). Another area is aerodynamics research, particularly utilizing advanced wind tunnels and computational fluid dynamics (CFD).

Finally, British firms have also begun to test the market for the supply of safety equipment and services. This is to satisfy the increasing concerns over safety when racing heavy, high-speed vehicles on ovals lined with concrete walls. In this respect, British firms can offer their expertise in the supply of data acquisition equipment to measure/record the dynamics of the accident while at the same time helping US teams with the supply of engineering services to increase the safety aspects of the vehicles.

At the level of the basic, technologically simple components like spaceframes, wheels and body panels, the sheer size and experience of the US race industry means that British firms are unlikely to be able to match their pricing structure. British firms must be able to offer an innovative product, but not be too expensive or too advanced to scare the end user away.

4.3 The Persistence of Indigenous Relationships over Trans-local Ones

Due to the shared language and culture, the USA is one of the easier overseas markets to access for UK motorsport companies. For example, our interview respondents mentioned that buyers are open and easy to get along with. However, the interviews also revealed many impediments in the establishment of stronger and long-lasting relationships with US teams. This seems to suggest that there is a tendency for the NASCAR cluster to rely more on indigenous relationships and limit the number of trans-local ones. There are many reasons for this.

First, US manufacturers, who are likely to be in competition with UK companies, have a much closer relationship with US organizing bodies. This is very much important in technically restrictive formulae like NASCAR. In this instance, a UK firm bringing a more technically advanced product to the market will not only have to persuade the teams to accept that product but also the rule makers that the product should be allowed in. Obviously, the closer the relationship the manufacturer has with the organizing body, the easier it will be to conduct negotiations over acceptability. Second, contractual negotiations take up a long time and can be more protracted than in Europe due to the extra complications of US legal requirements. Interviewees suggested that in general terms the extra costs incurred were more in setting up contracts rather than actual legal claims after the fact.

Finally, UK-based suppliers have to work hard to establish a new US reputation to be accepted into the NASCAR motorsport community. Some interviewees suggested that setting up a US subsidiary rather than dealing solely through a distributor was one way of proving your worth to the US buyer. Setting up in the USA was seen to be a way of showing serious intent of staying in the market rather than being a 'fly-by-night' operator. Another way of doing this is to buy in US marketing expertise, with a knowledge and level of contacts in the market, that can help overcome the cultural difference. In this environment, the European method of a UK manufacturer advertising 'Formula 1 success' might be counterproductive. US end users, unaccustomed to F1, may see this form of involvement as of little relevance to their own formulae and even culturally arrogant in assuming that F1 success could translate across to US formulae.

5   Discussion and Conclusion

The evolution of clusters has received increasing consideration during the last decade, but theoretical and empirical research on the development of inter-cluster linkages and the underlying processes of knowledge exchange remain largely underdeveloped (Giuliani 2013). This paper explores this issue and contributes to a better understanding of how trans-local relationships develop and evolve in clusters and how these exchanges can lead to their co-evolution. Using primary and secondary data from the NASCAR and the UK motorsport industries, this study shows how and why companies from different clusters interact and what challenges they face including issues of status, proximity and strength of indigenous relationships. Our research shows that the NASCAR cluster has slowly transitioned from a local entity to a more open-ended cluster with trans-local relationships with European and UK-based motorsport companies. A plausible explanation for this change is that NASCAR motorsport companies have realized the need for more sophisticated tools and components not available in the local market as well as they became more concerned about safety issues. This has led the cluster firms to build trans-local relationships with specialized supplier companies in the UK and, in some cases, to establish a deep working relationship including support, dedicated development and knowledge sharing. While some research in the telecom and biotechnology industries has shown evidence of similar patterns (Niosi and Zhegu 2010; Romero 2011; Turkina and Van Assche 2018), more research is needed to better understand this phenomenon.

Our analysis has also revealed a number of impediments that have implication for the evolution of clusters. While we found that the NASCAR cluster expanded its connections with firms located in other clusters, we also observed that a number of aspects acted as barriers to knowledge exchange and ultimately delayed the cluster transition to a more open entity. For example, our research highlighted that the restrictive regulatory environment and the strength of existing local suppliers limited the extent to which companies belonging to different clusters were able to establish connections, even when there was a clear case for collaboration and knowledge sharing. The empirical evidence has indicated that in many occasions there was a case for inter-cluster exchange, but given the regulatory requirements, companies could not take advantage of knowledge and expertise which was available in another cluster. Our research, therefore, suggests that in order to build inter-cluster ties, companies need to instil change into their cluster existing social and structural dynamics, place more trust in trans-local companies and contribute to ease regulations.

The study also identified the startling differences between the clusters in relation to technological advancements, availability of diverse but relevant knowledge, different set of cluster and industry-based rules and regulations and differences in cultural norms. In contrast to existing studies on clusters, empirical evidence underscored the scope for business knowledge collaborations rather than technical knowledge reciprocity. The lack of technical knowledge reciprocity is due to the fact that trans-local connections are more sophisticated and high-tech making it difficult for NASCAR companies to understand their role and value. This is reflected by the tendency of NASCAR companies to rely on their existing set of indigenous suppliers. In this respect, our evidence is in line with recent empirical studies on the knowledge dynamics in clusters, which show that social ties are important drivers of knowledge diffusion (Giuliani 2013; Giuliani and Matta 2013).

Our paper has some limitations that suggest directions for future research. First, our sample included only formal linkages between NASCAR and UK-based companies. We, therefore, excluded the role of informal ties and the knowledge spillovers which may derive (Giuliani 2007). Second, we concentrated only on the linkages with UK-based companies, excluding the analysis of other trans-local relationships across Europe and beyond. These limitations suggest that future studies could benefit from the inclusion and analysis of both informal ties and trans-local ties located beyond UK. This could prompt researchers to better understand the structure and dynamics of inter-cluster linkages as well as validate the generalizability of our findings. Finally, it would be interesting to explore cluster inter-linkages from the point of view of knowledge exploitation and exploration. The current literature on clusters has mainly focused on the persistence of internal relations and trust to promote knowledge exploitation. This view, however, tends to underplay the role of over-embeddedness (Uzzi 1996) as well as does not take much into consideration the reduced motivation and blindness of companies when it comes to explore external ties. Future research could investigate the role of increasing competition in the motorsport sector in altering the knowledge exchange propensity from knowledge exploitation to knowledge exploration. This could highlight important insights about the nature and competitive advantage offered by trans-local ties.

References

Ahuja G, Soda G, Zaheer A (2012) The genesis and dynamics of organizational networks. Organ Sci 23(2):434–448

Alderman DH, Mitchell PW, Webb JT, Hanak D (2003) Carolina thunder revisited: toward a transcultural view of Winston cup racing. Prof Geogr 55(2):238–249

Amin A, Cohendet P (1999) Learning and adaptation in decentralised business networks. Environ Plann D Soc Space 17(1):87–104

Amin A (2000) Industrial districts. In: Sheppard E, Barnes TJ (eds) A companion to economic geography. Blackwell, Oxford, pp 149–168

Asheim BR, Clark E (2001) Creativity and cost in urban and regional development in the new economy. Eur Plan Stud 9(7):805–811

Audretsch D (1998) Agglomeration and the location of innovative activity. Oxf Rev Econ Policy 14(2):18–29

Balland PA (2012) Proximity and the evolution of collaboration networks: evidence from research and development projects within the global navigation satellite system (GNSS) industry. Reg Stud 46(6):741–756

Balland PA, Suire R, Vicente J (2013) Structural and geographical patterns of knowledge networks in emerging technological standards: evidence from the European GNSS industry. Econ Innov New Technol 22(1):47–72

Balland PA, Boschma R, Frenken K (2015) Proximity and innovation: from statics to dynamics. Reg Stud 49(6):907–920

Becattini G (1989) Modelli locali di sviluppo. Il Mulino, Bologna

Bell GG, Zaheer A (2007) Geography, networks, and knowledge flow. Organ Sci 18(6):955–972

Bizzi L, Langley A (2012) Studying processes in and around networks. Ind Mark Manag 41(2):224–234

Bower JL (1970) Managing the resource allocation process. Harvard Business School Press, Boston, MA

Branzanti C (2015) Creative clusters and district economies: towards a taxonomy to interpret the phenomenon. Eur Plann Stud 23(7):1401–1418

Breschi S, Lissoni F (2001) Localized knowledge spill overs versus innovative milieux: knowledge 'tacit-ness' reconsidered. Pap Reg Sci 80:255–273

Brown P, Bell J (2001) Industrial clusters and small firm internationalisation. In: Taggart J, Berry M, McDermott M (eds) Multinationals in a new era. Palgrave, New York, NY, pp 10–26

Burgelman RA (1983) Corporate entrepreneurship and strategic management: insights from a process study. Manag Sci 29(12):1349–1364

Burt RS (1997) The contingent value of social capital. Adm Sci Q:339–365

Cainelli G, Ganau R, Iacobucci D (2016) Do geographic concentration and vertically related variety foster firm productivity? Micro-evidence from Italy. Growth Change 47(2):197–217

Capello R, Faggian A (2005) Collective learning and relational capital in local innovation processes. Reg Stud 39(1):75–87

Chen VZ, Li J, Shapiro DM, Zhang X (2014) Ownership structure and innovation: an emerging market perspective. Asia Pac J Manag 31(1):1–24

Cohen S, Fields G (1999) Social capital and capital gains in Silicon Valley. Calif Manag Rev 41(2):108–130

Dawson JF (2014) Moderation in management research: what, why, when, and how. J Bus Psychol 29(1):1–19

Fornahl D, Hassink R, Menzel M-P (2015) Broadening our knowledge on cluster evolution. Eur Plann Stud 23(10):1921–1931

Frenken K, Cefis E, Stam E (2015) Industrial dynamics and clusters: a survey. Reg Stud 49(1):10–27

Ganau R, Rodríguez-Pose A (2018) Industrial clusters, organized crime, and productivity growth in Italian SMEs. J Reg Sci 58(2):363–385

Giuliani E (2007) The wine industry: persistence of tacit knowledge or increased codification? Some implications for catching-up countries. Int J Technol Global 3(2–3):138–154

Giuliani E (2013) Network dynamics in regional clusters: evidence from Chile. Res Policy 42(8):1406–1419

Giuliani E, Matta A (2013) Explaining path-dependence in the evolution of networks. The case of an electronics cluster in Argentina. In: 35th DRUID Conference 2013

Glasmeier A (1991) Technological discontinuities and flexible production: the case of Switzerland and the world watch industry. Res Policy 20:469–485

Grabher G (1993) The weakness of strong ties: the lock-in of regional development in the Ruhr area. In: Grabher G (ed) The embedded firm: on the socio-economics of industrial networks. Routledge, London, pp 255–277

Grandinetti R (2016) Absorptive capacity and knowledge management in small and medium enterprises. Knowl Manag Res Practice 14(2):159–168

Haider S (2014) Identification, emergence and filling of organizational knowledge gaps: a retrospective processual analysis. J Knowl Manag 18(2):411–429

Haider S, Mariotti F (2016) The orchestration of alliance portfolios: the role of alliance portfolio capability. Scand J Manag 32(3):127–141

Hartgen DT, Lord DJ, Campbell HS, Stuart AW, Spawn DL (1996) Survey of the motorsports industry. Publication no. 145. Centre of Interdisciplinary Transportation Studies, University of North Carolina, Charlotte

Hervas-Oliver JL, Albors J (2007) Does the cluster's resources and capabilities matter? An application of resource-based view in clusters. Entrep Reg Dev 19(2):113–136

Howell MD (1997) From moonshine to Madison avenue: a cultural history of the NASCAR Winston cup series. Bowling Green State University Popular Press, Bowling Green, OH

Huber F, Fitjar RD (2016) Beyond networks in clusters. In: Handbook on the geographies of innovation. Edward Elgar, Cheltenham

Hurt DA (2002) Dialed in? The geographic expansion and spiritual decline of NASCAR. In abstracts, the association of American geographers, 98th annual meeting, Washington, DC

Ingstrup MB, Christensen PR (2017) Transformation of cluster specialization in the wake of globalization. Entrep Reg Dev 29(5–6):500–516

Krugman PR (1991) Geography and trade. MIT, Cambridge, MA

Langley A, Tsoukas H (2010) Introducing perspectives on process organization studies. Process Sensemak Org 1(9):1–27

Lawson C, Lorenz E (1999) Collective learning, tacit knowledge and regional innovative capacity. Reg Stud 33:305–317

Liebeskind JP, Oliver AL, Zucker LG, Brewer MB (1995) *Social networks, learning, and flexibility: sourcing scientific knowledge in new biotechnology firms*. Working paper No. 5320. National Bureau of Economic Research, Cambridge, MA

Maillat D (1991) The innovation process and the role of the milieu. In: Bergman EM, Maier G, Tödtling F (eds) Regions reconsidered: economic networks, innovation, and local development in industrialized countries. Mansell, London, pp 103–118

Malmberg A, Maskell P (2002) The elusive concept of localization economies: towards a knowledge-based theory of spatial clustering. *Environ Plan* 34(3):429–449

Marshall A, Marshall MP (1920) The economics of industry. Macmillan and Company

Martin R, Sunley P (2003) Deconstructing clusters: chaotic concept or policy panacea? J Econ Geogr 3:5–35

Martínez-Pérez Á, García-Villaverde PM, Elche D (2016) The mediating effect of ambidextrous knowledge strategy between social capital and innovation of cultural tourism clusters firms. Int J Contemp Hospit Manag 28(7):1484–1507

Maskell P, Lorenzen M (2004) The cluster as market organisation. Urban Stud 41(5/6):991–1009

McCann BT, Folta TB (2008) Location matters: where we have been and where we might go in agglomeration research. *J Manag* 34:532–565

McKelvey B (1997) Quasi-natural organization science. Organ Sci 8:352–380

MIA (2001) The national survey of motorsport engineering and services 2000: executive summary report. Motorsport Industry Association, Federation House, Stoneleigh Park

Miller P, Botham R, Martin RL, Moore B (2001) Business clusters in the UK: a first assessment. Department of Trade and Industry, London

Mintzberg H (1978) Patterns in strategy formation. Manag Sci 24(9):934–948

Niosi J, Zhegu M (2010) Anchor tenants and regional innovation systems: the aircraft industry. Int J Technol Manag 50:263–284

Oerlemans LAG, Meeus MTH, Boekema FWM (2001) Firm clustering and innovation: determinants and effects. Pap Reg Sci 80(3):337–356

Perry M (2007) Business environments and cluster attractiveness to managers. *Entrep Reg Dev* 19(1):1–24

Pettigrew AM (1990) Longitudinal field research on change: theory and practice. Organ Sci 1(3):267–292

Pettigrew AM (1997) What is a processual analysis? Scand J Manag 13(4):337–348

Pettigrew AM (2012) Context and action in the transformation of the firm: a reprise. J Manag Stud 49(7):1304–1328

Pillsbury R (1974) Carolina thunder: a geography of southern stock car racing. J Geogr 73(1):39–47

Pinch S, Henry N (1999) Paul Krugman's geographical economics, industrial clustering and the British motor sport industry. *Reg Stud* 33(9):815–827

Piore MJ, Sabel CF (1984) The second industrial divide. Basic Books, New York

Porter ME (1998) On competition. Harvard Business School Press, Boston, MA

Pouder R, St. John C (1996) Hot spots and blind spots: geographical clusters of firms and innovation. Acad Manag Rev 21:1192–1225

Powell WW (1990) Neither market nor hierarchy: network forms of organization. In: Staw BM, Cummings LL (eds) Research in organizational behaviour, vol 12. JAI Press, Greenwich, CT, pp 295–336

Powell WW, Koput KW, Smith-Doerr L (1996) Interorganizational collaboration and the locus of innovation: networks of learning in biotechnology. Adm Sci Q 41:116–145

Puga D (2010) The magnitude and causes of agglomeration economies. J Reg Sci 50(1):203–219

Romer PM (1987) Growth based on increasing returns due to specialization. Am Econ Rev 77:56–72

Romero J (2011) Centripetal forces in aerospace clusters in Mexico. Innov Dev 1:303–318

Saxenian A (1994) Regional advantage. Harvard University Press, Cambridge, MA

Sieber SD (1973) The integration of fieldwork and survey methods. Am J Sociol 78:1335–1359

Sternberg R, Arndt O (2001) The firm or the region: what determines the innovation behaviour of European firms? Econ Geogr 77(4):364–382

Storper M (1989) The transition to flexible specialization in the U.S. film industry: external economics, the division of labour, and the crossing of industrial divides. Camb J Econ 13:273–305

Storper M (1992) The limits to globalization: technology districts and international trade. Econ Geogr 68(1):60–93

Storper M (1997) The regional world: territorial development in a global economy. Guilford Press, New York

Tallman S, Jenkins M, Henry N, Pinch S (2004) Knowledge, clusters, and competitive advantage. Acad Manag Rev 29:258–271

Trippl M, Sinozic T, Lawton Smith H (2015) The role of universities in regional development: conceptual models and policy institutions in the UK, Sweden and Austria. Eur Plann Stud 23(9):1722–1740

Turkina E, Van Assche A (2018) Global connectedness and local innovation in industrial clusters. J Int Bus Stud 49:706–728

Uzzi B (1996) The sources and consequences of embeddedness for the economic performance of organizations: the network effect. Am Sociol Rev:674–698

The Effects of Cluster Cooperation as a Source of Company Value Creation

Joanna Kuczewska ⓘ, Sylwia Morawska ⓘ, and Tomasz Tomaszewski ⓘ

Abstract The objective of the study is to investigate the effects of cluster cooperation which might affect company value creation. The study has been developed among companies cooperating and competing within two Polish business clusters: aviation and fish products. Due to the fact that the data used was from the questionnaire in which the authors attempted to measure latent variables, such as competitiveness or cluster awareness, the results of the survey were subject to the partial least squares (PLS) analysis. In conclusion, cooperation between specialised and geographically concentrated entities shows benefits affecting the increase in productivity. However, the enterprises' awareness of them benefiting from cluster cooperation and the formalisation of a cluster are not essential factors in the process of achieving additional benefits affecting company value creation.

1 Introduction

The global world economy and a turbulent and unstable business environment affect the need for sophisticated strategic actions aimed at generating business value and sustaining a long-term competitive position. A company that builds value is obliged to provide its customers with higher value added for the same price. However, building this value cannot take place at the expense of shareholders who expect a specific rate of return. It is important to correctly identify and use competitive advantages that are revealed not only in the effectiveness of managing the company's potential but also in the use of opportunities and threats from the competitive and macroeconomic environment.

J. Kuczewska (✉) · T. Tomaszewski
Faculty of Economics, University of Gdansk, Gdansk, Poland
e-mail: joanna.kuczewska@ug.edu.pl; tomasz.tomaszewski@ug.edu.pl

S. Morawska
Collegium of Business Administration, Warsaw School of Economics, Warszawa, Poland
e-mail: smoraw@sgh.waw.pl

© Springer Nature Switzerland AG 2019
J. Windsperger et al. (eds.), *Design and Management of Interfirm Networks*,
Contributions to Management Science,
https://doi.org/10.1007/978-3-030-29245-4_17

Value creates a competitive company. All possibilities of cooperation are used, ways to reach new markets and to use competitive advantages. One of the most popular methods increasingly used by companies is organising cluster groups. Geo-concentrated entities operating in a specialised sector, competing with each other, exploit the potential of cooperation and its impact on building the company's value.

The aim of this study is to investigate the effects of cluster cooperation which might affect company value creation described with the productivity level measured by sold production per employee. The study has been developed among companies cooperating and competing within two Polish business clusters: aviation and fish products. Due to the fact that the data used was from the questionnaire in which the authors attempted to measure latent variables, such as competitiveness or cluster awareness, the results of the survey were subject to the partial least squares (PLS) analysis.

2 Literature Review

The modern concept of industrial clusters derives from the early 1990s and is strictly connected with the publications written by Michael Porter (1990, 1998a, b, 2001). In literature, there are many definitions of industrial clusters and related concepts, such as industrial districts (Becattini 1990; Brusco 1989; Markusen 1996), new industrial spaces (Scott 1988), local production systems (Crouch et al. 2001), local innovative *milieu* (Keeble and Wilkinson 2000), regional innovation systems (Cooke 2001), and learning regions (Florida 1995; Morgan 1997). The primary definition is the one developed by Porter (2001), which says that "Clusters are geographic concentrations of interconnected companies, specialized suppliers, and service providers, firms in related industries, and associated institutions (e.g. universities, standard agencies, and trade associations) in particular fields that compete but also cooperate". According to the above definition, clusters are characterised by a geographic concentration of entities, interactions between those entities, systematic relationships between them, as well as co-opetition.

The literature on the internal effects of cooperation within clusters has its beginnings in a research conducted by Marshall at the end of the nineteenth century, in which he established correlations between the co-location of companies and their economic efficiency. Companies cluster together to gain benefits from co-location—they can exploit the full potential of entities located in the same or similar economic sector. Marshall defines the following benefits arising from co-location (Marshall 1890): access to specific natural resources, lowering transaction costs, knowledge spillovers, optimisation of the economies of scale and its range, specialisation, access to knowledge and exchanges of information about the market and technological changes, as well as a faster learning process and creating a more sophisticated demand.

In the following years, Marshall's idea was developed and completed by many scholars. They focused on the correlation between geographical agglomeration and achieving economies of scale. Weber (1909) explains individual decisions of the producers regarding the location. They are motivated by minimisation of production and delivery costs within a concentrated group of producers. Modern-day researchers (Rodriguez-Clare 1996; Ciccione and Matsuyama 1996) have created models explaining that the presence of the benefits of Marshall's concept, combined with achieving economies of scale, leads to multiplying (maintaining) optimal production conditions and prohibits an underdevelopment trap. Krugman (1991) points out that knowledge spillovers and external financial factors have a great influence on the presence of the benefits. Rosenthal and Strange (2003) add that knowledge spills over especially heavily in the high technology sectors. Rodriguez-Clare (2005) indicates that the promotion of clusters should be intensive, but only in those sectors for which, besides the Marshall's benefits, there is comparative advantage. Schumpeter's (1943, 1996) contribution to the research underlies the role of process, product, organisational and marketing innovations, as well as the changes in technical industrial development. Lall (1980), Mairesse and Sassenou (1991), and Kravis and Lipsey (1988) argue that the cooperation of the coexisting entities and institutions of a milieu has a positive influence on the pace at which new technological solutions are implemented. Andersson et al. (2004) present three areas of positive influence of cooperation: greater innovativeness, greater productivity, and greater flexibility in business development.

The ideas presented above became even more popular in the 1980s, when the first concepts of cluster cooperation based on the example of the so-called Third Italy (North-Eastern and Central Italy) arose. A characteristic feature of this region is high industrial concentration in specialised sectors, recognised internationally, for example, the footwear industry, furniture industry, garment industry, musical instruments industry, and others. Alongside these processes, there was a rapid development in the area of production, innovation, and continuous quality improvement (Andersson et al. 2004; Brusco 1982, 1990; Dei Ottani 1994). From that moment, the main focus of source literature shifted to the cooperation, flexibility, and specialisation of small and medium-sized companies. There is not only a high significance of the cooperation between companies, based on economic policy, but also the creation of a network of interrelations between companies that are created "naturally" and are determined by historical and traditional conditions (Piore and Sabel 1984; Brusco and Righi 1989; Becattini 1990; Best 1990; Porter 1990).

The theories presented above are a methodological basis for the concept of clusters, and their postulates function as premises for creating clusters. However, not all theories complete one another. Some of them focus on supply (including factors generating technical development and innovation), others on demand—market forces and the role of entrepreneurship and marketing and management skills. One concentrates on the role of market operators, another on the mechanisms and market principles.

The general approach to identifying positive effects of cluster cooperation considers different aspects of the works discussed above. It shows effects that influence the greater productivity of companies—economies of scale (having regard to Marshall's factors and agglomeration benefits), reduction of transaction costs,

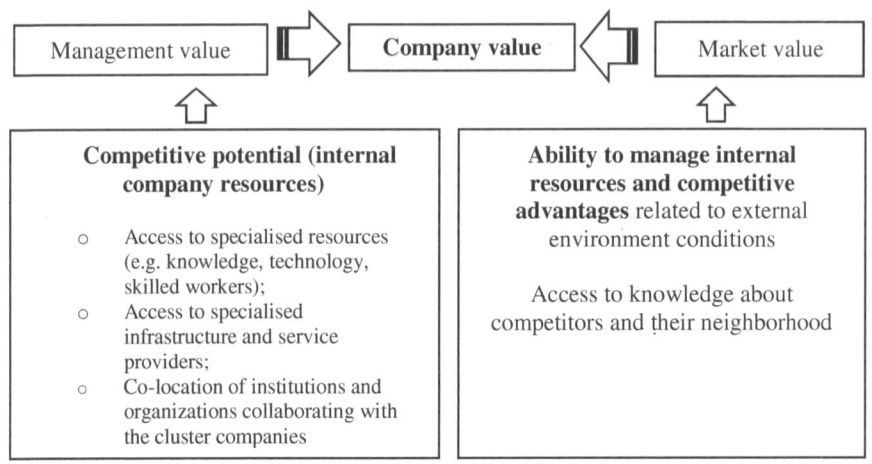

Fig. 1 Advantages of cluster cooperation affecting company value creation (self-study based on Gorynia and Jankowska (2008) and Kuczewska et al. (2012), pp 130–176)

greater innovativeness, stimulating entrepreneurship, and the role of social capital for knowledge spillovers (Gorynia and Jankowska 2008; Brodzicki et al. 2004).

It is, therefore, possible to identify the internal effects of cooperation within clusters in reference to creating companies' value. Gorynia and Jankowska (2008) analyse the benefits of cluster cooperation and its influence on value creation (see Fig. 1). Competitive potential is defined by access to specialised resources, access to specialised infrastructure and service providers, and co-location of institutions and organisations collaborating with the cluster companies. The ability to manage internal resources and competitive advantages is determined by the ability to apply knowledge about competitors and their neighbourhood, arising from co-location and knowledge spillover. The most important factors which define the value of the benefits of cluster cooperation are considered as the following: spillover effects and the strength of intercompany relations.

A successful cluster is the specialisation of its entities based on one main business, enabling a repetitiveness of processes, synergy, and the learning process (Audretsch 1995; Dunning 2000). Clusters also collaborate with other businesses/clusters and are open for cooperation opportunities instead of focusing solely on specialised internal value chains. Getting positive effects, knowledge spillovers, and the significant role of social capital depend on the entities within a cluster, on their co-opetition, and on achieving critical mass. The entities in a cluster are not only companies but also public institutions and research centres (Roelandt and den Hertog 1999) within the triple helix model of innovation (Etzkovitz and Leydesdorff 2000). Ensuring external financial resources is the responsibility of specialised financial institutions and cluster coordinators with the important role of effective cluster management. They are often called institutions for collaboration (Sölvell et al. 2003).

3 Methodology

The identification of effects of cooperation within clusters and their influence on creating value is based on a statistical survey carried out in 2018, among Polish enterprises, representing two geographically concentrated industries which form functioning industrial clusters and cluster initiatives. The chosen entities are the aviation sector, functioning mainly in the Subcarpathian Voivodeship and the Lublin Voivodeship, and the fish products sector, functioning in the Pomeranian Voivodeship and the West Pomeranian Voivodeship. In the case of the aviation sector, 47 entities responded, and in the case of the fish products sector, the number of responses was 19. The survey uses the methodology and results of a research project carried out in 2010–2012, regarding identification of industrial clusters and their economic effects in Poland[1] (Brodzicki and Kuczewska 2012).

The research carried out in 2010–2012 applies different methods using LQ (location quotient). It allowed concentration groups in Poland to be identified at the NUTS 3 level. Altogether, 35 groups were identified. The SQ (specialisation quotient), DIV index, and SIGMA index were calculated in order to determine potential external and internal effects of cluster cooperation. Then, on the basis of a qualitative analysis (a survey), the effects of cooperation within a cluster were verified. The survey consisted of 30 key questions within the Likert scale, regarding the revealing of effects, such as business results, productivity, innovativeness, average cost, and competitiveness. The role of control questions was assigned to the questions regarding different aspects of clusters' activity in the area of the job market, knowledge spillovers, and relationships—the links within the economic system, competitive pressure, tradition, cooperation, and self-awareness.

The survey presented above unambiguously shows that the presence of enterprises in geographic concentrations on its own does not indicate any direct and visible effects of cluster cooperation. Positive results on the improvement of business results, competitive position, knowledge availability, and lowering of the average cost were found. Clustering did not, however, have a direct influence on building relationships with other entities, nor was co-opetition revealed. Tradition had no influence on choosing a location, and there was no formalisation of cooperation (Kuczewska et al. 2012).

Recently, in order to verify the effects of cluster cooperation and its influence on value creation described with the productivity level measured by sold production per employee, a statistical survey has been carried out. Its analysis regards enterprises isolated in the research carried out in 2010–2012 which meet the requirements

---

[1]Research project carried out at the University of Gdansk, Economics of European Integration Chair, financed by the National Science Centre in Poland (1649/B/H03/2010/38, principal investigator: Tomasz Brodzicki). Title of the project "Identyfikacja klastrów przemysłowych w Polsce. Próba oceny ich efektów ekonomicznych. Implikacje dla polityki i rozwoju gospodarczego" (Identification of business clusters in Poland. Assessment of the potential internal effects of cluster cooperation. Implications for policy of regional development).

of geographic concentration (two NUTS 2 regions in both cases) and of existing and functioning formalised clusters or cluster initiatives. The research uses selected questions from a questionnaire also used in the 2010–2012 research, with the aim of verifying possible changes in the effects of cluster cooperation. For the analysis, variables were chosen which describe the productivity of enterprises belonging to the analysed industries, having the primary Marshall effects (competitive position, innovativeness, lowering the average cost, knowledge availability, formal and informal relationships with other entities, cooperation with research centres, cooperation with competitors, and the formalisation of a cluster—see Appendix).

Due to the characteristics of variables used for the study—Likert scale variables—the partial least squares (PLS) method was used. This method enables estimating connections between individual explanatory variables and determining the impact of exogenous variables on the explained variable simultaneously. The estimation was carried out with the SmartPLS 3 package using the bootstrapping method, which allowed the significance of the impact of individual variables on each other to be estimated (Ringle et al. 2015). The value of t-statistic >1.96 indicates the significance of the impact of an exogenous variable on an endogenous one.

After the rejection of variables that are not statistically significant, the structural formative model includes indices and latent variables that are consistent with the theory of economy. The following hypotheses were formulated:

Hypothesis 1 The level of productivity of a company is affected by the overhead costs.

Hypothesis 2 Networks and cooperation have an impact on the productivity level.

Hypothesis 3 The level of innovativeness of a specific company affects the level of productivity of the company.

Hypothesis 4 The level of productivity of the company is affected by the type and intensity of competition.

4   Results

In the case of companies from the aviation sector, functioning mainly in the Subcarpathian Voivodeship and the Lublin Voivodeship, a highly formalised cluster could be observed for many years (Aviation Valley). In the case of companies from the fish products sector, functioning mainly in the Pomeranian Voivodeship and the West Pomeranian Voivodeship, there are a few formalised clusters in the maritime industry, but they are not of as long a tradition and developed infrastructure as the Aviation Valley. A high concentration of entities within this industry is not accompanied by an advanced, long-term form of highly formalised cluster cooperation.

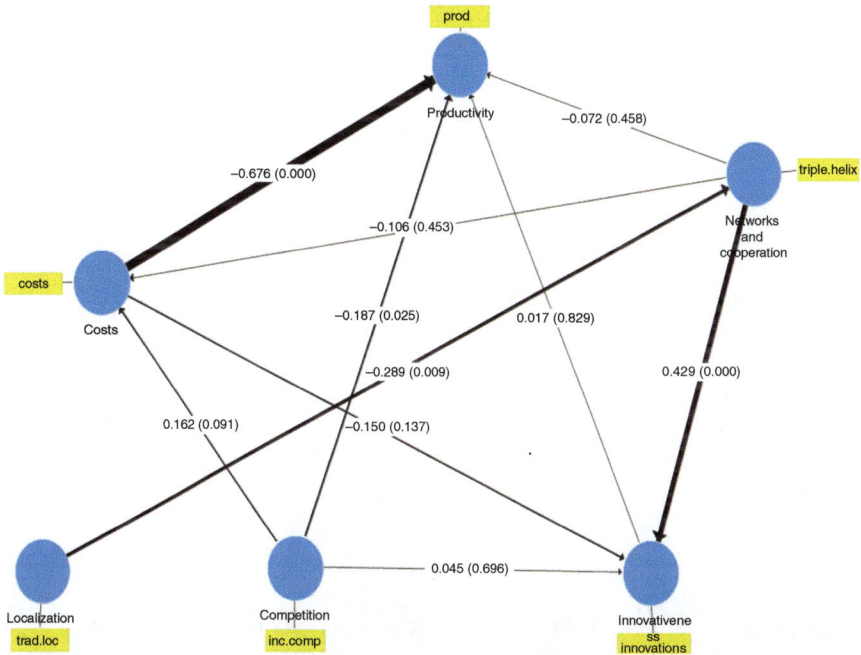

Fig. 2 Diamond graph of coefficients of significance (self-study based on SmartPLS 3)

The graph and table presented below show the results of selected questions, which indicate a significant level of relationship between a specific feature and productivity (see Fig. 2 and Table 1).

Analysing the influence of different indicators on productivity, generally two results can be observed. Firstly, there is a negative impact of competition on productivity (always indicated by companies in the short term). Secondly, also cogent and most significant, there is a negative influence of costs on productivity. As the overhead costs increase, average productivity will decrease (ceteris paribus). Overhead cost is the variable that has the strongest impact on the explained variable. Thus, the H1 and H4 hypotheses are statistically proved and accepted.

There is no significant impact of networks and cooperation on productivity. Moreover, the implementation of innovations does not affect the level of productivity. Thus, the hypotheses H2 and H3 are rejected.

The analysis of the relations between explanatory variables shows the following results. There is a negative influence of localisation on cooperation and companies' networks. It is more difficult to cooperate and be more open to mutual relations between enterprises at the moment when a given business activity is strongly historically embedded in a specific location. What is more, there is a positive and statistically significant relation between cooperation and companies' networks and companies' innovativeness. This proves that the number of innovative entities in clusters is simply higher (see also Beaudry and Breschi (2003)).

Table 1 Coefficients of significance for both clusters: aviation sector and fish products sector

	Original sample (O)	Sample mean (M)	Standard deviation (STDEV)	T-statistics (|O/STDEV|)
Competition → costs	0.162	0.160	0.095	1.694
Competition → innovativeness	0.045	0.038	0.116	0.390
Competition → productivity	**−0.187**	−0.188	0.084	**2.243**
Costs → innovativeness	−0.150	−0.152	0.101	1.487
Costs → productivity	**−0.676**	−0.688	0.083	**8.103**
Innovativeness → productivity	0.017	0.018	0.076	0.217
Localisation → networks and cooperation	**−0.289**	−0.288	0.110	**2.617**
Networks and cooperation → costs	−0.106	−0.111	0.142	0.752
Networks and cooperation → innovativeness	**0.429**	0.427	0.101	**4.259**
Networks and cooperation → productivity	−0.072	−0.088	0.097	0.742

Source: Self-study based on SmartPLS 3

Summing up the results presented above, the analysed entities do agree with the statement that the rise in productivity co-occurs with the geographic concentration of entities, but is independent from strengthening of isolation with relation to other entities (the distance between localisations of co-operators does not influence productivity, and what is more, the relation is negative). Significant productivity coexists with a lack of cooperation between different entities within the same area, which does not confirm the need of simultaneous competition and cooperation between entities within the same cluster.

5 Summary

The most important observation is the fact that the mere presence of the geographical concentration of enterprises is not enough to reveal the benefits of cluster cooperation affecting productivity. There are natural economic effects related to business results, competitive position, or access to knowledge, while the lack of formalisation of cooperation does not allow for additional benefits related to cooperation and competition, as well as building formal and informal market relations.

However, the lesser closeness of formal and informal relations with business partners does not always clearly go with productivity. This means that in some cases close relations with business partners do matter, but their localisations are not relevant for cooperation. Therefore, the cluster effect is ambiguous.

The closeness of formal and informal relations between enterprises and research centres and R&D organisations does not affect building relations between entities. In extreme cases, it negatively correlates with productivity. Hence, the conclusion is that a strong concentration and specialisation of entities in a certain region does not always result in a highly functioning cluster with global extensions (within Porter's definition), but either in the development of cluster initiatives or an earlier stage of formal cluster development.

In general, studies reveal that entities located in a cluster are characterised not only by high productivity but also an intensive drive of innovation in the field (Breschi et al. 2007). This does not mean, however, that each entity belonging to a cluster is more innovative than those outside of clusters. The number of innovative entities in clusters is simply higher (Beaudry and Breschi 2003). This is confirmed by the results from the research conducted by the authors, which indicate a clear lack of correlation between innovation and business results of entities within a cluster.

The results of this research, concerning the effects of cluster cooperation and its influence on the productivity of entities, raise a number of questions that are similar to those arising from the research conducted in 2012. Firstly, is it truly necessary for the emergence of internal effects resulting from co-localisation and high specialisation of entities to implement a formal structure responsible for the coordination of actions within a cluster or cluster initiatives? Secondly, should the formalisation of a cluster be a formal act (proposed by executives or research centres), or should it be a natural stage in the development of a cluster initiated by its entities? Thirdly, how then should clusters be supported in order to maximise the revealing of further positive effects resulting from co-location of the entities creating their business value?

In attempt to answer these questions, applying the *principle* of *subsidiarity* seems to comply with managing cluster groups. Undoubtedly, it is necessary to formalise clusters when working together on common projects, often initiated by public authorities or research centres (such as EU funds), and also while designing a clear development strategy for a given cluster. However, for revealing benefits for the entities within a cluster, directly connected with the execution of their business strategies (such as lowering average costs, achieving economies of scale, access to specialised employees, access to knowledge, etc.), a formal external organisation seems to be inessential (Andersson et al. 2004; Brodzicki and Kuczewska 2012). This can be confirmed by the remarkably high dynamic of creating and closing formal organisations within clusters in Poland, which are often implemented by public authorities in order to execute regional development strategies. Many times, formal structures of the organisers expand their scope of activity after finalising common projects co-financed by EU funds.

In conclusion, cooperation between specialised and geographically concentrated entities shows benefits affecting the increase in productivity. However, the enterprises' awareness of them benefiting from cluster cooperation, or the formalisation of a cluster, is not an essential factor in the process of achieving additional benefits affecting value creation. Indeed, it is often that the lack of cluster formalisation, or of the awareness of belonging to a cluster group, does not lead to absence of benefits arising from co-location.

Appendix

Questionnaire: The Survey Carried Out Among Cluster Companies
(Selected questions from the research project *Identification of business clusters in Poland. Assessment of the potential internal effects of cluster cooperation. Implications for policy of regional development*—questions' numbers according to the previous survey)

3. The level of productivity measured by sold production per employee in your company is:

1	2	3	4	5
definitely lower than the average for your industry		comparable to or the same as the average for your industry		definitely higher than the average for your industry

5. Within 3 years you have noticed:

1	2	3	4	5
a clear upward trend of the average cost (relation of the total cost to sold production or turnover)		an unchanged/stable trend of the average cost (relation of the total cost to sold production or turnover)		a clear downward trend of the average cost (relation of the total cost to sold production or turnover)

7. How do you assess your competitive position in the market?

1	2	3	4	5
definitely lower than your competitors' competitive position		comparable to or the same as your competitors' competitive position		definitely higher than your competitors' competitive position

8. The ability to introduce innovations determines the company's competitive position from a long-term perspective. Have you introduced a minimum of one new or improved product or process within the last 3 years?

1	2	3	4	5
definitely agree		difficult to say		definitely disagree

10. One of the most important issues determining the competitive position of the company is access to highly skilled employees. Localisation of your company:

1	2	3	4	5
definitely does not help to acquire highly skilled employees		does not affect acquiring highly skilled employees		definitely helps to acquire highly skilled employees

12. The average costs of acquiring skilled employees in your market are:

1	2	3	4	5
definitely higher than the national average		difficult to say		definitely lower than the national average

13. The level of employee rotation in your market is:

1	2	3	4	5
definitely higher than the national average		difficult to say		definitely lower than the national average

14. Knowledge spillover and wide access to professional knowledge determine the company's competitive position. Based on your experience, the localisation of your company:

1	2	3	4	5
definitely does not allow wide and relatively low-cost access to technological (patents and new technology) and market knowledge		does not affect getting wide and relatively low-cost access to technological (patents and new technology) and market knowledge		definitely allows wide and relatively low-cost access to technological (patents and new technology) and market knowledge

15. The formal and informal relations with science and R&D sectors are increasingly important to gain a competitive advantage. Based on your experience, the localisation of your company:

1	2	3	4	5
definitely does not help to develop such relations		does not affect developing such relations		definitely helps to develop such relations

16. Geographical concentration of the specialised companies in the same market increases the threat of imitation of technological solutions and business strategies. Based on your experience:

1	2	3	4	5
the threat of imitation is definitely low in your market		localisation does not affect the imitation		the threat of imitation is definitely high in your market

17. The formal and informal relations with your business partners are increasingly important to gain a competitive advantage. Based on your experience, the localisation of your company:

1	2	3	4	5
definitely does not help to develop such relations		does not affect developing such relations		definitely helps to develop such relations

18. Wide and low-cost access to new specialised subcontractors and suppliers helps to reduce total costs. Based on your experience, within your market:

1	2	3	4	5
it is definitely difficult to find new subcontractors and/or suppliers		localisation does not affect it		it is definitely easy to find new subcontractors and/or suppliers

21. Do you agree that competitive pressure is constantly rising in your market?

1	2	3	4	5
definitely disagree		difficult to say		definitely agree

25. The formal and informal relations with your competitors are increasingly important to gain a competitive advantage. Are such relations with competitors common practice in your market?

1	2	3	4	5
definitely disagree		difficult to say		definitely agree

26. Geographical concentration of the specialised companies in the same market increases the new entries. Do you observe a higher number of new entries in your market?

1	2	3	4	5
definitely disagree		difficult to say		definitely agree

27. In the case of some business sectors, localisation of the company depends on the long-standing tradition of running a business in a given area. Did business tradition play a big role in the decision on the location choice?

1	2	3	4	5
definitely disagree		difficult to say		definitely agree

References

Andersson T et al (2004) The cluster policies whitebook. IKED, Malmö

Audretsch D (1995) Innovation and industry evolution. MIT, Cambridge, MA

Beaudry V, Breschi S (2003) Are firms in clusters really more innovative? Econ Innov New Technol 12(4):325–342

Becattini G (1990) The Marshallian industrial district as a socio-economic notion. In: Pyke F et al (eds) Industrial districts and inter-firm co-operation in Italy. IILS, Geneva

Best MH (1990) The new competition: institutions of industrial restructuring. First Harvard Press, Cambridge, MA

Breschi S et al (2007) Clusters, networks and innovation. Oxford University Press, Oxford

Brodzicki T, Kuczewska J (eds) (2012) Klastry i polityka klastrowa w Polsce. Konkurencyjność przedsiębiorstw, sektorów i regionów. Wydawnictwo Uniwersytetu Gdańskiego, Gdańsk

Brodzicki T et al (2004) Polityka rozwoju oparta o klastry, najlepsze praktyki, rekomendacje dla Polski, Niebieska Księga PFSL nr 11. IBnGR, Gdańsk

Brusco S (1982) The emilian model: productive decentralization and social integration. Camb J Econ 6:167–184

Brusco (1989) A policy for industrial districts. In: Goodman E, Bamford J (eds) Small firms and industrial districts in Italy. Routledge, London

Brusco S (1990) The idea of the industrial district: its genesis. In: Pyke F et al (eds) Industrial districts and inter-firm cooperation in Italy. International Labour Office, Geneva

Brusco S, Righi E (1989) Local government, industrial policy and social consensus: the case of Modena (Italy). Econ Soc 18(4):405–424

Ciccione A, Matsuyama K (1996) Start-up costs and pecuniary externalities as barriers to economic development. J Dev Econ 49(1):33–59

Cooke P (2001) Regional innovation systems, clusters and the knowledge economy. Ind Corp Chang 10(4):945–974

Crouch et al (2001) Local production systems in Europe: rise or demise? Oxford University Press, Oxford

Dei Ottani G (1994) Cooperation and competition in the industrial district as an organisational model. Eur Plan Stud 2:463–483

Dunning JH e (2000) Regions, globalization, and the knowledge-based economy. Oxford University Press, Oxford

Etzkovitz H, Leydesdorff L (2000) The dynamics of innovation: from national systems and "mode 2" to triple helix of university-industry-government relations. Res Policy 29(2):109–123

Florida R (1995) Towards the learning region. Futures 27:527–536

Gorynia M, Jankowska B (2008) Klastry a międzynarodowa konkurencyjność i internacjonalizacja przedsiębiorstwa. Difin, Warszawa

Keeble D, Wilkinson F r (2000) High-tech clusters: networking and collective learning. Ashgate, Aldershot

Kravis I, Lipsey R (1988) The effects of multinational firms' foreign operations on their domestic employment, national bureau of economic research working paper no. 2760, Cambridge

Krugman P (1991) Increasing returns and economic geography. J Polit Econ 99:483–499

Kuczewska J, Kujawski M, Brodzicki T (2012) Efekty wewnętrzne klastrów. In: Brodzicki T, Kuczewska J (eds) Klastry i polityka klastrowa w Polsce. Konkurencyjność przedsiębiorstw, sektorów i regionów. Wydawnictwo Uniwersytetu Gdańskiego, Gdańsk

Lall S (1980) Developing countries as exporters of technology and capital goods; the Indian experience. Oxford University Institute of Economics and Statistics, Oxford

Mairesse J, Sassenou M (1991) R&D and productivity: a survey of econometric studies at the firm level, science-technology-industry review, no. 8 Pans, OECD

Markusen A (1996) Sticky places in slippery space: a typology of industrial districts. Econ Geogr 72(3):293–313

Marshall A (1890) Principles of economics. Macmillan, London

Morgan K (1997) The learning region: Institutions, innovation and regional renewal. Reg Stud 31:491–504

Piore MJ, Sabel CF (1984) The second industrial divide: possibilities for prosperity. Basic Books, New York

Porter ME (1990) The competitive advantage of nations. The Free Press, New York

Porter ME (1998a) On competition. Harvard Business School, Boston

Porter ME (1998b) Clusters and new economics of competition. Harv Bus Rev 76:77–90

Porter ME (2001) Porter o konkurencji. PWN, Warszawa

Ringle CM, Wende S, Becker J-M (2015) SmartPLS 3. SmartPLS GmbH, Boenningstedt. http://www.smartpls.com

Rodriguez-Clare A (1996) The division of labour and economic development. J Dev Econ 49(1):3–32

Rodriguez-Clare A (2005) Clusters and comparative advantage: implications for industrial policy, Inter-American Development Bank, working paper no 523

Roelandt TJA, den Hertog P (1999) Cluster analysis and cluster-based policy making: the state of the art. In: Boosting innovation: the cluster approach. OECD, Paris

Rosenthal SS, Strange WC (2003) Evidence on the nature and sources of agglomeration economies. Handb Urban Reg Econ 4:2119–2171

Schumpeter JA (1943) Capitalism, socialism and democracy. Routledge, London

Schumpeter JA (1996) The theory of economic development. Transaction Books, London

Scott A (1988) New industrial spaces. Pion, London

Sölvell O et al (2003) The cluster initiative greenbook. Ivory Tower AB, Stockholm

Weber A (1909) Theory of the location of industries. University of Chicago Press, Chicago

Entering a Foreign Market: Exports, FDI or Strategic Alliance?

Karl Morasch

Abstract The decision over exports vs. foreign direct investment (FDI) is usually discussed in an extension of the so-called Melitz model where firms with heterogeneous costs compete in a monopolistically competitive industry. The present paper starts from a situation where a potential foreign entrant would be just indifferent between exports and FDI in such a setting. However, by assuming oligopolistic interaction, strategic considerations are also taken into account. It is shown how the strategic impact of lower marginal cost makes FDI more attractive in a Cournot setting while exports are preferable under price competition in a market with differentiated goods. Beyond that it is also explored how a strategic alliance with a local incumbent could be a superior alternative for market entry.

1 Introduction

While relatively unproductive firms only produce for the home market, the more productive competitors tend to also export or even invest in production facilities in foreign countries. In the theory of international trade this behavior can be explained by the so-called Melitz model (Melitz, 2003). Extensions of the model state that the most productive firms prefer FDI (foreign direct investment) to exports (see Helpman et al., 2004). Beyond that, it is also possible to use the Melitz model to tackle questions concerning decisions about outsourcing and offshoring (see e.g. Helpman, 2006).

However, the Melitz model is based on monopolistic competition and therefore does not consider strategic interactions between oligopolistic competitors. As foreign market entry often takes place in oligopolistic industries, it seems to be important to understand these strategic considerations as well. Beyond that, such

K. Morasch (✉)
Bundeswehr University Munich, Neubiberg, Germany
e-mail: karl.morasch@unibw.de

© Springer Nature Switzerland AG 2019   353
J. Windsperger et al. (eds.), *Design and Management of Interfirm Networks*,
Contributions to Management Science,
https://doi.org/10.1007/978-3-030-29245-4_18

a setting also allows to analyze whether some sort of strategic alliance might be a superior alternative for market entry.

In order to deal with these questions, an oligopoly model is considered. The starting point is a Cournot duopoly with a domestic incumbent and a foreign entrant. If the foreign firm enters with the export strategy, it has a variable cost disadvantage due to trade costs. Entering by FDI avoids this cost disadvantage; however, there is a higher fixed cost as the firm has to set up another facility. Due to these cost differences, a firm entering by FDI is a more aggressive competitor. This is a strategic advantage in the Cournot setting as the other firm reacts with an output contraction. The analysis is then extended in two directions. By assuming more than one local competitor (Cournot oligopoly) the impact of the number of firms and the possibility of forming a strategic alliance with a local firm can be considered. Another extension considers product differentiation which allows to compare price and quantity strategies.

What happens if the entrant forms a strategic alliance with one of the competitors? Within such an alliance the entrant could transfer the know-how via licensing or franchising to one of the foreign firms that will then produce the additional variety. As another option, the two cooperating firms could set up a joint venture in order to produce and market the good. A strategic alliance might differ from exports and FDI with respect to production and transaction cost parameters. Depending on the specific circumstances, the alliance strategy might be more or less efficient than any of the two alternatives. However, beyond the impact on efficiency, such a cooperative venture could also affect incentives in a way that transforms to a strategic advantage for the cooperating firms. In particular, following a concept developed in Morasch (2000), the contract between the firms may be used as a strategic device that can be adapted to the specific situation in the product market.

While being more aggressive is a strategic advantage if the oligopolistic firms compete in quantities, the reverse is true under price competition. As price competition with homogeneous products yields marginal cost pricing even in duopoly and a limit pricing monopolist under heterogeneous cost, the analysis has to be extended to a market with horizontally differentiated goods. Using a linear specification, it is straightforward to compare price and quantity competition in this setting.

Recently there have been a couple of papers who also consider oligopolistic competition in the context of the Melitz model or similar approaches. Bekkers and Francois (2013) and Collie (2016) both show that under oligopoly with differentiated products a positive welfare effect of trade is not assured even with free entry. Of these two papers, Bekkers and Francois (2013) is more closely related to the initial Melitz model and the variant with an endogenous distribution of markups in Melitz and Ottaviano (2008). However, while both these models consider oligopolistic competition, they do neither deal with individual entry decision nor with the potential strategic impact of the entry mode under oligopoly. More closely related to our paper is Barac and Moner-Colonques (2016) who consider simultaneous entry of two firms with FDI versus exports in an oligopolistic industry under cost heterogeneity. However, among other things their analysis differs from ours in considering technological spillovers from the more efficient incumbent firm to the less efficient foreign entrants. Finally, in a quite recent paper Bernard et al. (2018) develop an alternative to the Melitz model that allows for large firms that consider their impact on market aggregates when deciding about their strategies. This quite complex general equilibrium model is used to provide testable predictions about international trade and competition. However, due to the complexity of interactions in this model, it cannot easily be adapted to analyze the specific impact of strategic interactions and alliance formation in the context of the entry decision of a single firm.

Given the received literature, what is the specific contribution of the present analysis? By considering a situation where a firm in the Melitz setting would be just indifferent between entry strategies, we are able to isolate the strategic impact of the differences in the cost structure between the export and the FDI strategy. Beyond that, we consider the possibility of a strategic alliance with one local competitor and show that forming such an alliance dominates the other entry strategies with respect to the strategic impact.

The rest of the paper is organized as follows. Section 2 starts with a setting where a firm would be indifferent between entering a foreign market with exports or FDI in a static version of the Melitz model. Analyzing a Cournot duopoly, it is shown how the strategic effect due to lower marginal cost makes FDI more attractive. Using a linear specification, it is then explored whether and when this effect is likely to be of relevant magnitude. Section 3 extends the analysis to a Cournot oligopoly with more than one incumbent firm. This allows us to analyze how the number of competitors affects the strategic impact. And, as the central aspect of this section, we consider forming an alliance with one of the incumbents as an alternative entry strategy and compare it with exports and FDI. Section 4 assumes a market with differentiated products and shows how the strategic impact differs between price and quantity competition. Section 5 concludes.

2 Export vs. FDI in Cournot Duopoly

In a market with heterogeneous firms it depends on relative productivity whether a firm decides to enter a foreign market via exports or FDI. This can be shown in a static version of the Melitz model as proposed in Helpman (2006). In this setting firms compete in a monopolistically competitive industry, and a more productive firm with lower marginal cost will produce a higher quantity in equilibrium and earn higher profits. However, firms are assumed to be of negligible size relative to the size of the industry. This implies the absence of strategic considerations in such a setting.

There are two kind of costs if a firm wants to sell to a market. There is a fixed cost which is identical for all firms and a variable cost which depends on the specific productivity θ_j of a given firm j. The fixed cost for selling to the domestic market is given by f_D. The rising straight line in Fig. 1 that starts at $-f_D$ indicates the

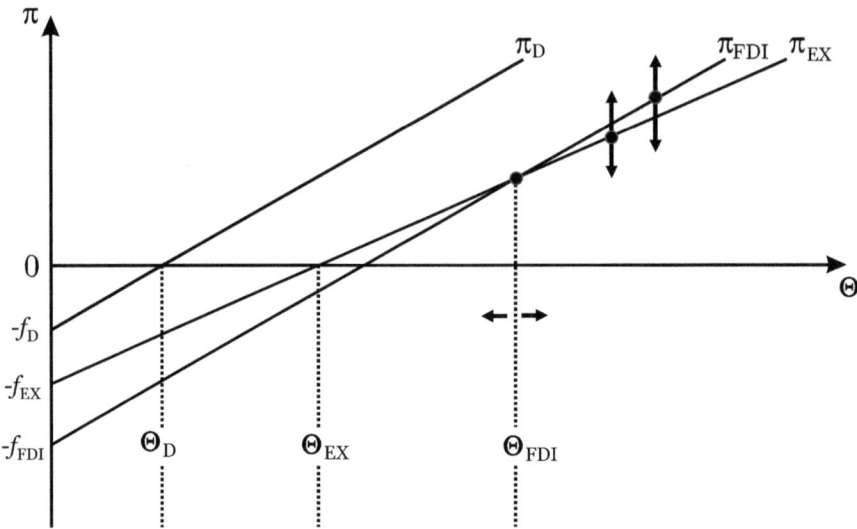

Fig. 1 Exports vs. FDI in the Melitz model

domestic profits π_D of a firm as a function of the productivity measure Θ.[1] A firm with a higher productivity will choose a lower profit maximizing price which yields higher sales and lower average cost. Together this implies higher profits for a more productive firm. Only firms to the right of the threshold level Θ_D will produce for the domestic market.

Beyond selling to the domestic markets, firms could also sell to foreign markets. This could either be done by exporting or by setting up a production facility in the foreign country (FDI). For simplicity we assume that there is only one foreign market which has the same demand elasticity as the domestic market. The fixed cost for exporting to the foreign market, f_{EX} is assumed to be higher than f_D, and the exporting firm must incur iceberg trading costs. This implies that π_{EX} is below π_D and also flatter due to the variable trading cost. The fixed cost for FDI is even higher. However, in this case there is no trading cost and therefore π_{FDI} is as steep as π_D. As a result, firms with a productivity above Θ_{EX} will not only produce for the local market but also sell to the foreign market. If the productivity is below Θ_{FDI}, they will do so by exporting; if the productivity is above this threshold, they opt for FDI.

The Melitz model tries to explain important empirical facts in international trade and investment across markets. Our question is much narrower, as we want to explore the foreign market entry strategy of a single firm. The analysis in the Melitz model is already quite complex with monopolistic competition and it would be

---

[1] Assuming a demand function with constant demand elasticity ϵ derived from a constant elasticity of substitution utility, and variable production costs given by c/θ_j, setting $\Theta \equiv \theta^{\epsilon-1}$ yields a linear function $\pi(\Theta)$. See Helpman (2006, p. 593) for details.

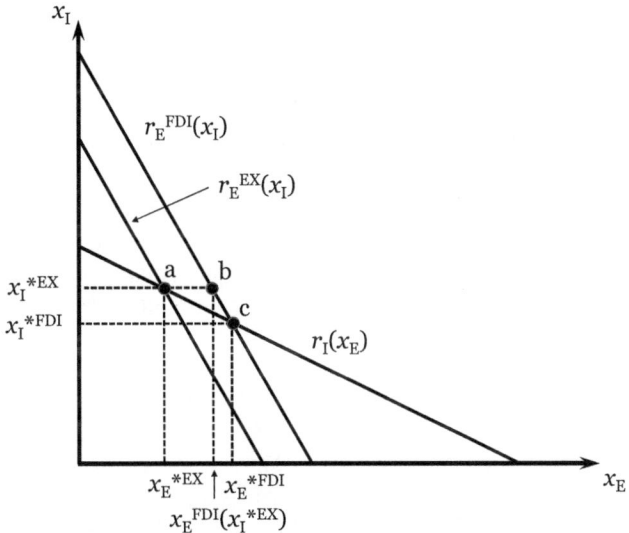

Fig. 2 Exports vs. FDI in a Cournot duopoly

hardly tractable if oligopolistic interaction should be considered as well.[2] While sticking to the basic cost structure with respect to fixed and variable costs, the actual analysis will therefore be performed in standard partial equilibrium oligopoly models. In a first step the basic strategic forces will be presented in a graphical analysis. Afterwards a linear specification will be used to shed some light on the quantitative importance of strategic aspects.

The impact of strategy considerations can most easily be illustrated in a Cournot duopoly setting as displayed in Fig. 2.[3] We assume that the entering firm E and the domestic incumbent I have identical and constant marginal cost c if firm E uses the FDI strategy. With the export strategy the marginal cost of firm E is higher due to the trading cost t. The reaction curves in the diagram depict profit maximizing quantities for a given quantity of the other firm. For each value of x_I, an exporting firm will choose a lower quantity x_E than a firm that entered with the FDI strategy.

---

[2]The additional complexity introduced by oligopolistic competition can be observed in Bernard et al. (2018) who develop an alternative model for international trade under imperfect competition that considers the possibility of large firms. This model is quite helpful to analyze some empirical facts that cannot be addressed in the Melitz model. However, due to the large number of additional interactions, such a general equilibrium setting is less well suited to deal with the question how strategic considerations affect the entry mode of a single firm for a given market.

[3]In Fig. 2 the reaction curves are straight lines, which will be the case with linear demand. However, this assumption is not necessary: as long as the reaction curves are downward sloping and the reaction curve of the entering firm E is steeper than the reaction curve of the incumbent I, we obtain identical qualitative results.

This is due to the higher marginal cost $c + t$. Accordingly the reaction curve of a firm entering with the export strategy, $r_E^{EX}(x_I)$, is to the left of the reaction curve under FDI, $r_E^{FDI}(x_I)$.

At the intersection between $r_E^{EX}(x_I)$ and $r_I(x_E)$ we obtain the Cournot-Nash equilibrium **a**. At this equilibrium the quantity of the incumbent, x_I^{*EX}, exceeds the quantity of the entrant, x_E^{*EX}. Now consider that the entrant contemplates about changing his entry strategy. Choosing FDI, the marginal cost would be lower but the fixed cost higher. Producing x_E^{*EX} is therefore no longer profit maximizing. Assuming that the incumbent does not change its quantity, it would be optimal to depart to point **b** on the reaction curve $r_E^{FDI}(x_I)$ and produce quantity $x_E^{FDI}(x_I^{*EX})$. This kind of reaction would also be observed under monopolistic competition: for given demand, a firm with lower marginal cost maximizes its profit by choosing a higher quantity (or charging a lower price). However, in the oligopoly setting there is an additional strategic effect. When determining the equilibrium quantity, the incumbent will now consider that the reaction curve of the entrant has shifted outward. This yields an output reduction to the new equilibrium quantity x_I^{*FDI}, and as residual demand for the entrant increases, an additional output expansion to x_E^{*FDI} is profitable. Together this yields the equilibrium under FDI in point **c**. If an entrant is indifferent between exporting in **a** and FDI in **b**, we would be exactly at the intersection between the profit schedules for exporting and FDI in Fig. 1. However, the strategic effect renders the FDI strategy more profitable as the incumbent firm reduces output relative to the equilibrium with an exporting entrant.

To get an idea about the magnitude of the strategic effect, we will now consider a linear Cournot duopoly. As we are only interested in the relative impact on profits, we could use the easiest formulation with demand $p(x_I, x_E) = 1 - (x_I + x_E)$, and normalized marginal production cost $c = 0$. If we also normalize fixed cost for domestic production and for exporting to $f_D = f_{EX} = 0$, we get the following profit functions for the incumbent firm and the exporting entrant:

$$\pi_I(x_I, x_E) = [1 - (x_I + x_E)]x_I \tag{1}$$

$$\pi_E(x_I, x_E) = [1 - (x_I + x_E)]x_E - tx_E. \tag{2}$$

The resulting equilibrium quantities for the incumbent and the exporting firm are:

$$x_I^{*EX} = \frac{1 + t}{3} \tag{3}$$

$$x_E^{*EX} = \frac{1 - 2t}{3} \tag{4}$$

In equilibrium, profits of the incumbent and an entrant with the FDI strategy only differ with respect to the fixed cost f_{FDI}. To determine the profit impact of the strategic effect—the move from point **b** to point **c** in Fig. 2—this fixed cost must be set in a way that profits with the export strategy in point **a** are equal to profits that would result with the FDI strategy in point **b**. Therefore we must set

$\pi_E^{EX}(x_I^{*EX}, x_E^{*EX})$ equal to $\pi_E^{FDI}(x_I^{*EX}, r_E^{FDI}(x_I^{*EX}))$ and solve for f_{FDI}. To obtain this equation, we must first determine $r_E^{FDI}(x_I^{*EX})$ by inserting x_I^{*EX} into the profit function of the firm entering with the FDI strategy. Solving the first-order condition for profit maximization with respect to x_E^{FDI} yields

$$x_E^{FDI}(x_I^{*EX}) = \frac{2 - t}{6}. \tag{5}$$

Note that the quantity produced is higher than x_E^{*EX} but still declining in t. This stems from the fact that the incumbent chooses a higher quantity if faced by a less competitive exporting entrant. The resulting profit for the entrant with the FDI strategy is given by

$$\pi_E^{FDI}(x_I^{*EX}, x_E^{FDI}(x_I^{*EX})) = \frac{(2 - t)^2}{36} - f_{FDI}. \tag{6}$$

When solving for the fixed cost that equalizes profits under exporting with profits under FDI assuming the quantity of the incumbent remains unchanged, we obtain

$$\hat{f}_{FDI} = \frac{t(4 - 5t)}{12}. \tag{7}$$

Note that the exporting strategy is only viable for $t < 0.5$. While the fixed cost $\hat{f}_{FDI}$ that equalizes profits for the two entry strategies rises in t for values close to zero, it actually declines when approaching $t = 0.5$. This is due to the fact that the incumbent covers nearly the whole market in the asymmetric cost equilibrium, which implies that residual demand and consequently the profit potential for the entrant with the FDI strategy are relatively low.

Based on this information, we are now able to compare the profits in point **b** and **c**. Figure 3 displays profits as a function of t in the relevant range $t \in [0, 0.5]$. The thick line represents the equilibrium profits of a firm that enters with the FDI strategy. Note that revenue does not depend on t in this case. The reason for the slope of this curve is the impact of t on $\hat{f}_{FDI}$ (details see above). The declining gray line below displays profits for a firm entering with FDI without the strategic effect (the profits in point **b** in Fig. 2). Note that $\hat{f}_{FDI}$ has been determined in a way that these profits are identical to the profits of a firm that enters with the export strategy (the profits of such a firm in point **a** in Fig. 2). The downward sloping line in the upper part of the graph displays the variable part of the profits of an entrant with the FDI strategy in point **b** in Fig. 2. Although the fixed cost $\hat{f}_{FDI}$ is not subtracted from the revenue, this curve is nevertheless downward sloping because a higher t implies a higher equilibrium quantity x_I^{*EX} of the incumbent which implies a lower residual demand for the entrant. Finally, the upward sloping line that starts at the origin depicts the strategic effect (profit change due to the movement from **b** to **c** in Fig. 2).

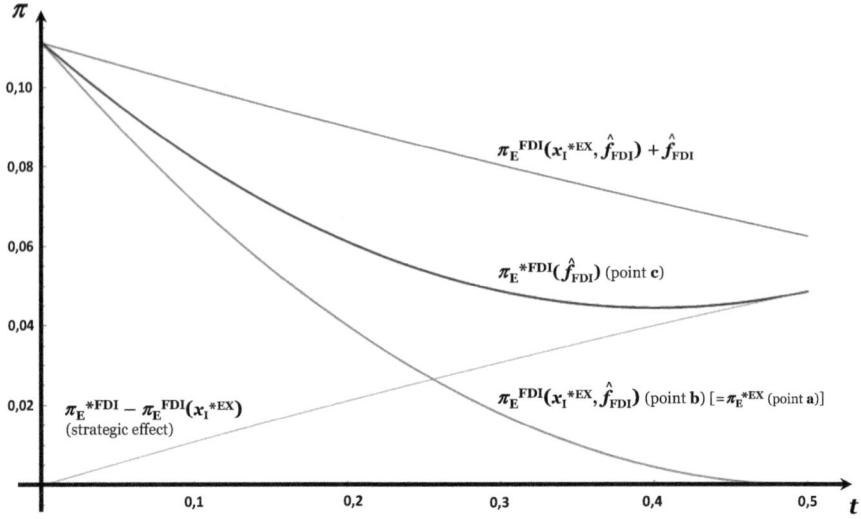

Fig. 3 Linear Cournot duopoly—exports vs. FDI

At first sight the impact of the strategic effect seems to be limited—the profit changes amount to about 1/10th of the trade cost t. However, if one considers the change in c that would be necessary to obtain the same profit without the strategic effect, i.e., for a constant quantity of the incumbent, the magnitude appears more relevant. Straightforward calculations show that the necessary reduction Δc would equal $t/2$. Therefore, we can state as a preliminary result from the duopoly analysis that the impact of the strategic effect is likely to be economically relevant.

3   Cournot Oligopoly and Alliance Formation

While there are situations with a monopolistic incumbent in a foreign market, it is much more likely that there are already some competing firms in this market. Therefore, we will now consider a Cournot oligopoly with $n \geq 3$ firms. To make the analysis as simple as possible, we still assume some entry barriers which yield a given number of domestic firms earning positive profit. We also still assume that all firms have identical production costs that are normalized to zero.

This setting allows us to work with aggregate reaction curves. Therefore a graphical representation is still feasible.[4] In the exporting vs. FDI scenario, the

---

[4]As only the joint reaction of all domestic firms together (or the outsiders if we consider the possibility of an alliance) is relevant, such a graphical representation would also be possible with heterogeneous costs as long as all firms produce in each equilibrium.

entrant is still a single player. However, its reaction curve $r_E(X_I)$ with $X_I = (n-1)x_I$ shows how it optimally responds to the joint output of all incumbent firms together. For the incumbent firms the aggregate reaction curve $R_I(x_E)$ displays the joint production of all incumbents at the given production of the entrant, assuming each incumbent firm behaves as a Cournot competitor relative to the other firms.

We are going to deal with two questions in the oligopoly setting. The first one is the impact of the number of domestic competitors on the strategic effect when comparing exporting and FDI. The second aspect is the possibility of another strategy for market entry: the entering firm may form some sort of alliance with one of the domestic competitors. Restricting attention to the strategic impact, we will assume that forming an alliance will neither affect fixed costs nor variable costs of the cooperating firms relative to entry with the FDI strategy.

The graphical representation for the export vs. FDI scenario in the Cournot oligopoly setting is qualitatively identical to the duopoly analysis. The only difference is that the aggregate reaction curve of the incumbents, $R_I(x_E)$, is steeper than the individual reaction curves and this steepness increases with the number of incumbent firms. As a graphical analysis of exports vs. FDI in the oligopoly setting would therefore not give any additional information relative to the duopoly analysis, we will now first restrict attention to the scenario with alliances and consider exports and FDI not until determining explicit solutions in the linear model.

To understand the proposed concept of a strategic alliance it is helpful to compare it with a non-strategic alliance. Such a kind of cooperation has been discussed in the context of merger analysis. In both cases the group of firms that forms an alliance or merges aims to maximize joint profits. However, only in a strategic alliance these firms are able to commit to a certain joint strategy before outsiders decide about their strategies. Under these circumstances joint profits of alliance members will never decline relative to the situation without an alliance: the cooperating firms behave together as a Stackelberg leader and thus may set their strategy in a way that is beneficial to them. However, if the cooperating firms and the remaining outsiders simultaneously decide about their strategic variable, an unintended strategic effect may eventually yield a profit reduction for the alliance members.

Salant et al. (1983) were the first to point out this negative consequence of a merger. In a Cournot oligopoly joint profit maximization of the merging firms calls for an output reduction relative to the sum of pre-merger outputs. As a reaction, outsiders will expand output which negatively affects the profits of the merger. This unintended strategic effect may dominate the internalization advantage of joint profit maximization. As a result mergers without synergies are only profitable if almost all firms in an industry join together.[5]

The situation may be visualized in a diagram with reaction curves showing the aggregate quantities of cooperating firms and remaining outsiders, respectively.

---

[5]Note that this result does not carry over to an oligopoly with price competition (strategic complements). Because outsiders raise their prices as a reaction to the price increase by the merger, mergers are always profitable (see Deneckere and Davidson, 1985).

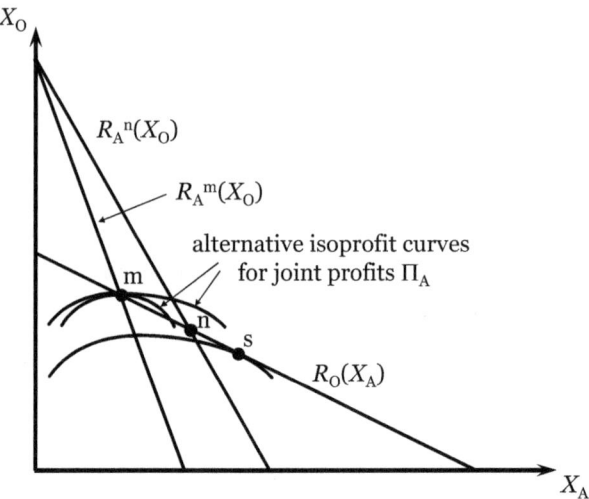

Fig. 4 Impact of strategic alliance vs. merger in Cournot oligopoly

Consider a Cournot market with n oligopolists and let two firms form an alliance. Variables which refer to cooperating firms are labeled by subscript A while subscript O indicates outsiders: X_A stands for the total quantity produced by the alliance members, Π_A for the joint profit of these firms, and X_O for total production of the other firms ("outsiders") in the industry. The different equilibria will be indicated by **n** for the initial non-cooperative Cournot equilibrium, **m** for the equilibrium where the alliance members behave like a merger (no commitment by cooperating firms), and **s** for the equilibrium with a strategic alliance (cooperating firms behave together as a Stackelberg leader relative to the rest of the industry).

Figure 4 displays three aggregate reaction curves: The reaction function $R_O(X_A)$ shows the aggregate output X_O of outsiders that results in a Cournot equilibrium between these oligopolists for a given level of total output produced by the cooperating firms. $R_A^n(X_O)$ refers to the total output of cooperating firms if they would behave like non–cooperating Cournot competitors—the intersection of the two reaction curves is the Cournot equilibrium **n**. Finally, $R_A^m(X_O)$ shows the total production of the cooperating firms that maximizes joint profits for a given total output of outsiders. The isoprofit contours refer to joint profits Π_A of the cooperating firms.

Note that $R_A^m(X_O)$ is left to $R_A^n(X_O)$ for $X_O > 0$ because cooperating firms consider the negative external effect of an output increase on the profits of their partners and thus reduce output relative to the initial Cournot equilibrium. Whether cooperation without commitment (i.e., a merger) is profitable depends on the isoprofit contour at the merger equilibrium **m**: If the isoprofit curve intersects with $R_O(X_A)$ to the left of the initial non-cooperative Cournot equilibrium **n**, profits are increased, otherwise they are lower than under Cournot competition.

The situation for the merging firms would be much more comfortable if they were able to commit to some output level: Like a Stackelberg leader they could then determine the tangential point of their joint isoprofit curve with the aggregate reaction curve of outsiders—in Fig. 4 this results in point **s**. This would yield profits that are at least as high as in the initial Cournot equilibrium. However, it is by no means clear how a merger could achieve such a commitment. As will be argued now, strategic alliances differ from mergers insofar as they offer a commitment device.

What should enable the alliance members to commit to an output level different from the Cournot solution? The idea is that the alliance contract may serve this purpose: incentives in the product market will be changed if the contract somehow leads to payments between alliance members which are based on their individual output decisions. Such a contract has to be binding and must usually be observed by the other firms in the industry, since a secret agreement might not induce the intended reaction by outsiders.[6]

In practice it is not common that firms forming a strategic alliance simply sign a contract which stipulates output based payments—one reason might be that such contracts would be banned by antitrust legislation in most countries. However, as shown in Morasch (2000) the same strategic effect will be achieved if the cooperating firms establish a production joint venture for an intermediate product, agree on an appropriate transfer price, and equally share in the resulting profits or losses of the joint venture. In this case a member firm will reduce output relative to the Cournot level if the transfer price exceeds the marginal costs of the intermediate product and expand output if it has to pay less than these marginal costs. In contrast to cartels such production joint ventures are usually allowed by antitrust authorities, especially if they are related to some innovation collaboration on earlier stages.

In a next step we demonstrate in the Cournot oligopoly with linear demand that a strategic alliance with one of the incumbent firms is preferable to the FDI strategy from a strategic perspective (assuming costs are the same in both settings). On the other hand it can easily be seen that a non-strategic alliance (like a merger) would be worse than the FDI strategy.

Solving the linear oligopoly model for exporting and FDI, respectively, is similar to the duopoly analysis. As we assume that domestic incumbents are symmetric, they will produce identical quantities in equilibrium. We can therefore just aggregate the $(n - 1)$ first-order conditions to one joint condition where $X_I = nx_I$. For the situation with exports as entry strategy this yields the following two first-order conditions:

$$1 - nx_I - x_E = 0 \tag{8}$$

$$1 - (n - 1)x_I - 2x_E - t = 0 \tag{9}$$

---

[6]See Katz (1991) for a thorough discussion of whether and when contracts may serve as commitment devices.

Solving for x_E and $X_I = (n-1)x_I$ would result in the reaction functions described above. Based on these reaction functions or by simultaneously solving the two equations, we obtain equilibrium quantities

$$x_I^{*EX} = \frac{1+t}{n+1}, \tag{10}$$

$$x_E^{*EX} = \frac{1-nt}{n+1}. \tag{11}$$

Similar to the analysis in the Cournot duopoly we must then determine the profit maximizing reaction of a firm that enters with the FDI strategy (this yields point **b** in Fig. 2):

$$r_E^{FDI}(X_I^{*EX}) = \frac{2-(n-1)t}{2(n+1)} \tag{12}$$

The resulting profit for the entrant with the FDI strategy is given by

$$\pi_E^{FDI}(X_I^{*EX}, r_E^{FDI}(X_I^{*EX})) = \frac{(2-(n-1)t)^2}{4(n+1)^2} - f_{FDI}. \tag{13}$$

When solving for the fixed cost that equalizes profits under exporting with profits under FDI, assuming the quantity of the incumbents remains unchanged, we obtain

$$\hat{f}_{FDI} = \frac{t(4-(3n-1)t)}{4(n+1)}. \tag{14}$$

Based on this, it is straightforward to calculate and compare profits for some values of n and t with and without the strategic effect in a similar fashion as in the Cournot duopoly. However, before we proceed with this analysis, we will also determine profits for a strategic alliance as this will allow us to compare this entry alternative with the export and the FDI strategy.

For a non-strategic alliance where the cooperating firms behave like a merger, we can just take the variable part of the equilibrium profits in the FDI setting in an industry with $(n-1)$ firms and divide the result by two (the fixed cost is not affected by the decision to cooperate). For a strategic alliance we need to take the joint reaction function of the $(n-2)$ outsiders and insert it in the joint profit function for the two alliance members:

$$\Pi_A(X_A, R_O(X_A)) = \left[1 - X_A - \frac{n-2}{n-1}(1-X_A)\right]X_A = \frac{1}{n-1}[1-X_A]X_A \tag{15}$$

Profit maximization then yields equilibrium quantities of alliance members and outsiders. Based on these quantities, the variable part of the profit is again given

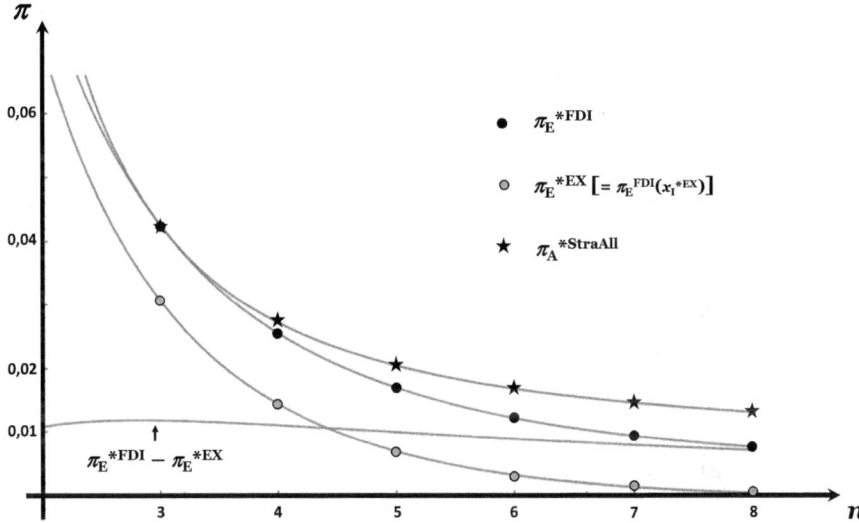

Fig. 5 Strategic alliance vs. FDI and exports in Cournot oligopoly for $t = 0.1$

by dividing the resulting alliance profit by two:

$$\pi_A^s = \frac{1}{8(n-1)} \tag{16}$$

The actual profits of the entrant are then determined by subtracting the appropriate value for $\hat{f}_{FDI}$ at the considered combination of t and n.

Figure 5 shows profits for industries with $n = 3$ to $n = 8$ firms for trade costs $t = 0.1$.[7] We compare the profits for entry with exports (indicated by a gray bullet), FDI (black bullet), and a strategic alliance (star). In all three cases the absolute profits get smaller with a larger number of firms. As expected, for all n profits under FDI are larger than profits of an exporting entrant. The absolute value of the profit gain from choosing FDI instead of exports as an entry strategy (indicated by the nearly horizontal gray line) is almost constant. However, as a higher number of competitors yields lower profits for an exporting entrant, the relative advantage of the FDI strategy is even more pronounced in an industry with a larger number of competitors. The strategic alliance solution yields the same profit as FDI for an

---

[7]The value $t = 0.1$ has been chosen as it results in positive profits for an exporting entrant as long as the number of incumbents does not exceed $(n - 1) = 8$. This allows us to show a reasonable amount of qualitatively different settings (including cases where an exporting entrant is only a marginal player).

industry with only one additional competitor (outsider). However, if four or more firms are active in the market, profits are higher with the strategic alliance and this profit difference increases with the number of competitors.[8]

4 Price and Quantity Competition with Heterogeneous Products

Extending the analysis to a situation with product differentiation does not yield qualitatively different results as long as we stick to quantities as the strategic variable. However, the strategic effect is qualitatively different if price strategies are considered. Whether it is plausible to assume price or quantity competition depends mainly on the importance of capacity decision in a given industry. While oligopolistic firms are not likely to be price takers (especially in markets with product differentiation), it may very well be the case that decision about capacity restricts the price setting game. As shown by Kreps and Scheinkman (1983), competition in a market with firms that first set quantities and afterwards decide about pricing is similar to Cournot competition. On the other hand, there are markets where capacity restrictions are less relevant. This is, for example, the case in market for information goods like software or movies. Therefore it is important to take a look at price setting games as well.

As can be seen in Fig. 6 reaction curves are upward sloping (strategic complements) in a heterogeneous good duopoly with price strategies: if one firm increases the price, the other firm would also react with a price increase. Considering our case with exports vs. FDI as an entering strategy, the entrant would choose a lower price under FDI. Starting from the export strategy equilibrium **a**, this will result in a move to **b** as long as the incumbent does not change its price. However, given the lower price of the entrant, the incumbent has an incentive to reduce its price as well. This yields the FDI equilibrium **c** with lower prices charged by both firms. Unlike the situation in the Cournot setting, the strategic effect yields a result with lower profits relative to point **b** for both incumbent and entrant. A potential entrant that is indifferent between exporting in point **a** and FDI in point **b** will now prefer the export strategy.

For the numerical analysis we start from a system of inverse demand that is properly rooted in a utility maximization problem. The setting is based on the love of variety approach of product differentiation pioneered by Spence (1976) and Dixit and Stiglitz (1977). Here the consumption side for the duopoly setting is given by a

---

[8]To keep the graphical representation as clear as possible, we did not include results for a non-strategic alliance. In the present setting with $t = 0.1$, an entrant forming a non-strategic alliance would fare better than an exporting entrant. However, for $t = 0.05$ the non-strategic alliance would be even worse than entering with the export strategy.

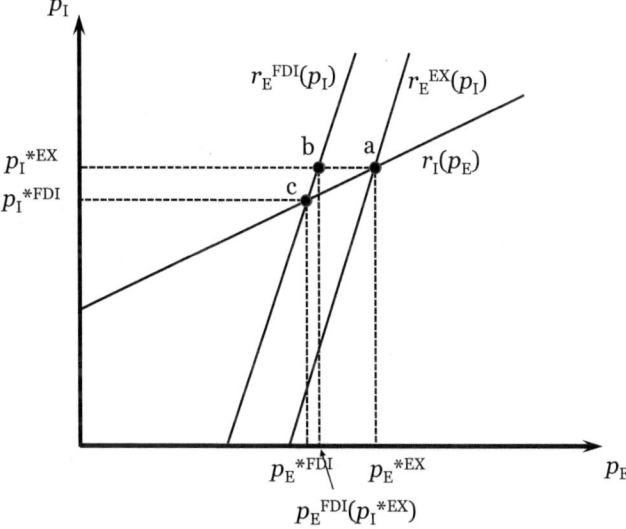

Fig. 6 Exports vs. FDI in a duopoly with price strategies

representative consumer with linear-quadratic utility

$$U(x_I, x_E; x_0) = \alpha(x_I + x_E) - \frac{1}{2}(x_I^2 + x_E^2 + 2bx_I x_E) + x_0 \qquad (17)$$

with x_I and x_E indicating the specific types of the differentiated good produced by firm 1 or 2, respectively, and x_0 a numeraire good which is assumed to be produced in another sector of the economy and has been added linearly to ensure that the marginal utility of income is equal to one. The parameter α is a measure of market size while b describes the degree of substitutability between the products of the two firms: If the products are perfect substitutes $b = 1$, if they are independent $b = 0$. For the ease of computation, the market size parameter is normalized to $\alpha = 1$. The consumer maximization problem then leads to the following linear inverse demand functions:

$$p_i = 1 - x_i - bx_j \quad \text{with} \quad j \neq i \qquad (18)$$

These inverse demand functions can be used to determine the equilibria in the quantity setting game similar to the Cournot analysis (for $b = 1$ we get the Cournot duopoly).

To analyze the price setting game the inverse demand system must be inverted. Based on the two inverse demand functions straightforward calculations yield demand functions expressing quantity demanded as a function of the two prices:

$$x_i(p_I, p_E) = \frac{1}{1 - b^2}[(1 - b) - p_i + bp_j] \quad \text{with} \quad j \neq \tag{19}$$

Note that this demand functions are not defined at $b = 1$ (this would be the Bertrand price duopoly with homogeneous goods).

Still assuming marginal production cost $c = 0$ and normalizing fixed cost for domestic production and for exporting to $f_D = f_{EX} = 0$, profit functions for the incumbent firm and the exporting entrant in the quantity setting game are given by

$$\pi_I(x_I, x_E) = [1 - (x_I + bx_E)]x_I, \tag{20}$$

$$\pi_E(x_I, x_E) = [1 - (bx_I + x_E)]x_E - tx_E. \tag{21}$$

This results in the following equilibrium quantities for the incumbent and the exporting firm:

$$x_I^{*EX} = \frac{2 - b + bt}{4 - b^2} \tag{22}$$

$$x_E^{*EX} = \frac{2 - b - 2t}{4 - b^2} \tag{23}$$

As in the Cournot analysis we must determine the quantity produced by the entrant in point **b** in order to calculate the value of $\hat{f}_{FDI}$. For this quantity we obtain

$$x_E^{FDI}(x_I^{*EX}) = \frac{4 - 2b - b^2t}{2(4 - b^2)}. \tag{24}$$

The resulting profit for the entrant with the FDI strategy is then given by

$$\pi_E^{FDI}\left(x_I^{*EX}, r_E^{FDI}(x_I^{*EX})\right) = \frac{(4 - 2b - b^2t)^2}{4(4 - b^2)^2} - f_{FDI}. \tag{25}$$

When solving for the fixed cost that equalizes profits under exporting with profits under FDI under the assumption that the quantity of the incumbent remains unchanged, we obtain

$$\hat{f}_{FDI} = \frac{4(4 - 8b + 5b^2 - b^3) + 4t(4 + 4b - 7b^2 + 2b^3) - t^2(16 + 8b - 8b^2 - b^4)}{4(2 - b)^2(2 + b)^2}. \tag{26}$$

For price competition the analysis has to be performed by using the demand functions. This yields the following profit functions:

$$\pi_I(p_I, p_E) = p_I \left[\frac{1}{1 - b^2}[(1 - b) - p_I + bp_E] \right] \tag{27}$$

$$\pi_E(p_I, p_E) = p_E \left[\frac{1}{1 - b^2}[(1 - b) - p_E + bp_I] \right]$$
$$- t \left[\frac{1}{1 - b^2}[(1 - b) - p_E + bp_I] \right] \tag{28}$$

This resulting equilibrium prices for the incumbent and the exporting firm, respectively, are:

$$p_I^{*EX} = \frac{2 - b - b^2 + bt}{4 - b^2} \tag{29}$$

$$p_E^{*EX} = \frac{2 - b - b^2 + 2t}{4 - b^2} \tag{30}$$

Note that equilibrium prices of both the entrant and the incumbent increase with rising trade costs. Similar to the previous analysis we need to determine the price chosen by the entrant in point **b** in order to calculate the value of $\hat{f}_{FDI}$. This price is given by

$$p_E^{FDI}(p_I^{*EX}) = \frac{4 - 2b - 2b^2 + b^2t}{2(4 - b^2)}. \tag{31}$$

The resulting profit for an entrant that enters with the FDI strategy is then given by

$$\pi_E^{FDI}\left(x_I^{*EX}, r_E^{FDI}(x_I^{*EX})\right) = \frac{(4 - 2b - 2b^2 + b^2t)^2}{4(4 - b^2)^2(1 - b^2)} - f_{FDI}. \tag{32}$$

We can now obtain the fixed cost that equalizes profits under exporting with the profits that result under FDI under the assumption that the quantity of the incumbent remains unchanged:

$$\hat{f}_{FDI} = \frac{t[8 - 4b - 4b^2 - t(4 - 3b^2)]}{4(4 - 5b^2 + b^4)^2}. \tag{33}$$

Based on this information, we are able to compare the profits in point **b** and **c** for both price and quantity competition. Figure 7 is similar to Fig. 3. It is based on a value of the substitutability parameter $b = 3/4$ and therefore considers a situation with relatively close substitutes. The dashed lines depict the situation

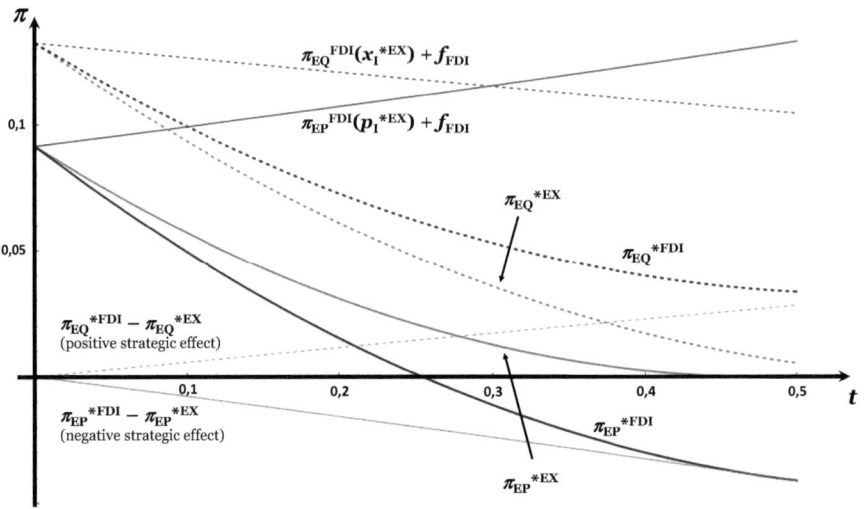

Fig. 7 Linear model—exports vs. FDI with price vs. quantity strategies

with quantity setting. These are qualitatively identical to the ones for the Cournot duopoly. The solid lines refer to price setting. Here the profits under FDI are lower than under exporting and consequently the strategic effect is negative. Also note that the variable part of the profit in point **b** is rising in t. This is due to the fact that an exporting entrant with a higher trade cost would be less aggressive which in turn induces the incumbent to raise its price. But this higher price is good news for the entrant with the FDI strategy.

5 Conclusion

How does the strategic impact in oligopoly competition affect the optimal strategy for entering a foreign market? Three options have been compared: Exporting, foreign direct investment (FDI), and the formation of a strategic alliance with one of the domestic incumbents.

We started from a situation where a firm would be indifferent between exporting and FDI as long as strategic considerations are absent (e. g., in a monopolistic competition setting). It has been shown that the additional strategic impact under oligopoly makes the FDI strategy more attractive in a Cournot oligopoly or a quantity setting oligopoly with heterogeneous products. This is due to the fact that lower marginal costs under FDI (no trade cost) yield higher output by the entrant that in turn induces a output reduction by the domestic incumbents. This result is reversed under price strategies where lowering the own price induces lower prices of the other firms.

Abstracting from any effects on cost, an alliance between the entrant and a domestic incumbent is the most preferable entry strategy as long as the cooperating firms are able to use the alliance contract as a strategic commitment device (alliance members behave together like a Stackelberg leader). However, if such a strategic contract is not feasible, the alliance has an unintended strategic effect: the cooperating firms internalize the negative impact of aggressive behavior on the partner and therefore reduce output or raise prices. While raising prices in a price setting oligopoly benefits both alliance members and outsiders, the output reduction of a non-strategic alliance in a Cournot setting yields an output expansion by outsiders that negatively affects the profits of the alliance members.

Beyond these qualitative results it has been shown that the strategic effect might have an order of magnitude that is economically relevant. In the Cournot duopoly setting the switch from exporting to FDI has a strategic impact that raises the profits of the entrant by the same amount as a reduction of the marginal cost by half of the trade cost. Therefore it seems fair to say that firms deciding about their entry strategy for a foreign market should not only look at the cost differences of different strategies but also consider the strategic effect.

To sum up, there are two central contributions of the present study to the theory of foreign market entry strategies. First, it is shown how the strategic impact of the cost structure can be taken into account when deciding about the preferable entry strategy. Second, forming a strategic alliance with a local firm is added as a possible additional entry option, and it is shown that this strategy dominates the other options with respect to the strategic effect.

What kind of managerial implications can be derived from these results? Generally, as in most kind of game theoretic analysis, the details of the situation are important and have to be considered appropriately. A first aspect is that the strategic impact will only be relevant if the entry strategies compared are close to each other with respect to cost considerations: for a firm that is barely productive enough to be able to export, the potential strategic advantage of FDI is most likely to be irrelevant. If we are in a situation where the two strategies are close, the kind of strategic interaction comes into play: if prices are the relevant strategic variables, the strategic impact favors the export strategy, while FDI has a strategic advantage when capacity decisions (quantities) are of strategic importance. Finally, in cases where a cooperation with a local firm is an option, it is important to understand whether a strategic alliance would be feasible or whether the firms could only form a non-strategic alliance. Considering the strategic impact, a strategic alliance dominates all other entry strategies and should be chosen as long as costs are not higher than under alternative entry strategies. On the other hand, for a cost efficient non-strategic alliance (as, for example, a merger) the negative strategic impact has to be considered.

References

Barac M, Moner-Colonques R (2016) Internationalization strategies in oligopoly with heterogeneous firms. Bull Econ Res 68(1):66–77

Bekkers E, Francois R (2013) Trade and industrial structure with large firms and heterogeneity. Eur Econ Rev 60:69–90

Bernard AB, Jensen JB, Redding SJ, Schott PK (2018) Global firms. J Econ Lit 56(2):565–619

Collie DR (2016) Gains from variety? Product differentiation and the possibility of losses from trade under Cournot oligopoly with free entry. Econ Lett 146:55–58

Deneckere R, Davidson D (1985) Incentives to form coalitions with Bertrand competition. RAND J Econ 16:473–486

Dixit A, Stiglitz J (1977) Monopolistic competition and optimum product diversity. Am Econ Rev 67:287–308

Helpman E (2006) Trade, FDI, and the organization of firms. J Econ Lit 44(3):589–630

Helpman E, Melitz MJ, Yeaple SR (2004) Exports versus FDI with heterogeneous firms. Am Econ Rev 94:300–316

Katz ML (1991) Game-playing agents: unobservable contracts as precommitments. RAND J Econ 22:307–328

Kreps DM, Scheinkman JA (1983) Quantity precommitment and Bertrand competition yield Cournot outcomes. Bell J Econ 14(2): 326–337

Melitz MJ (2003) The impact of trade on intra-industry reallocations and aggregate industry productivity. Econometrica 71:1695–1725

Melitz MJ, Ottaviano GIP (2008) Market size, trade, and productivity. Rev Econ Stud 75:295–316

Morasch K (2000) Strategic alliances as Stackelberg cartels — concept and equilibrium alliance structure. Int J Ind Organ 18:257–282

Salant SW, Switzer S, Reynolds RJ (1983) Losses from horizontal merger: the effects of an exogenous change in industry structure on Cournot–Nash equilibrium. Q J Econ 48:185–199

Spence M (1976) Product selection, fixed costs and monopolistic competition. Rev Econ Stud 43:217–235

Public-Private Partnerships in Latin America: Evidences from Healthcare Networks

Nathalie Colasanti, Rocco Frondizi, Marco Meneguzzo, and Noemi Rossi

Abstract The decision whether to invest is usually a very delicate one, and it requires the analysis of several aspects, first and foremost the risks associated with the investment. This is even more necessary when large infrastructure projects are at stake, as they require the identification of innovative strategies and tools for designing, financing and management activities. Consequently, the public sector has modified its financing methods, going from traditional debt instruments to new tools based on partnerships with the private sector. These are relatively new "alliances" between the public and the private sector referring to infrastructure investments, where the private sector partner cooperates in providing, managing and financing services and structures. These collaborations are called "public-private partnerships" (PPPs), and they have now become a commonly used investment strategy for all public administrations.

At international level, healthcare sector represents a promising field for the development of PPP. Latin American countries, after experimenting with public-private cooperation in several sectors, are now designing new healthcare infrastructures by using these innovative financing tools. This paper will analyse public-private partnerships, first at a more general level, and then by considering their application to the healthcare sector, providing a state of the art of relevant experiences in Latin America.

The final section will discuss future research perspectives, and it will introduce public network governance and management approaches as a theoretical framework to analyse existing experiences.

N. Colasanti · R. Frondizi (✉) · N. Rossi
University of Rome Tor Vergata, Rome, Italy
e-mail: nathalie.colasanti@uniroma2.it; rocco.frondizi@uniroma2.it; noemi.rossi@uniroma2.it

M. Meneguzzo
University of Rome Tor Vergata, Rome, Italy

Università della Svizzera Italiana, Lugano, Switzerland
e-mail: meneguzzo@economia.uniroma2.it

© Springer Nature Switzerland AG 2019
J. Windsperger et al. (eds.), *Design and Management of Interfirm Networks*,
Contributions to Management Science,
https://doi.org/10.1007/978-3-030-29245-4_19

1 Introduction

The decision whether to invest is a very complex one, and it requires the investor to carry out an in-depth analysis of numerous factors.

Large infrastructure projects call for specific studies and innovative strategies for the phases of construction, management and financing. This has led the public sector to change its financing strategies, going from traditional debt instruments to new financial tools based on partnerships with the private sector. These are a specific type of "alliance" between the public and private sector, relatively new in the field of infrastructure investment, and they require the private actor to intervene in the stages of designing, managing and financing activities, usually carried out exclusively by the public sector. These collaborative agreements, defined as public-private partnerships (PPPs), are now so common that they are regarded as a relevant investment strategy involving all public institutions, in all sectors and levels of government. When a PPP contract is signed, the local administration or central government entrusts the provision of a public service to a private agent through a long-term agreement that defines duties and obligations of all parties (the private actor is in charge for decisions regarding the construction of necessary infrastructure, as well as financial, managerial and maintenance aspects).

It is possible to highlight specific features of PPP operations, such as:

1. A PPP contract concerns various stages of an infrastructural project (from designing to building and delivering services).
2. A PPP contract usually lasts between 25 and 30 years, although there are examples of short-term PPPs.
3. The private sector is strongly involved in funding activities.
4. The public actors play the role of regulation, monitoring and control.
5. The allocation of risks between public and private sector, usually based on the analysis of factors such as user fees and contract length.

Over time a number of trends, such as the growing importance of knowledge in society, the evolution of the role of the State and the increased collaboration between different actors, have led to the creation and diffusion of networks, within which PPPs find relevant applications (Cristofoli et al. 2017). The creation of networks allows to face complex problems by using the interdependence between specific players and stakeholders (public and private) that, by definition, do not possess infinite knowledge. The use of network management within PPPs could lead to increased synergies between all actors involved, with positive impacts on information asymmetries, enhancing cooperation between public and private players, which is necessary for development in any advanced economy.

Over the last 20 years, important results have been observed in the healthcare sector, where different types of PPP, designed on the basis of juridical and healthcare systems, seem to be the best solution for carrying out infrastructure investments at national and international levels. At the European level, the first country to employ PPPs in healthcare was the United Kingdom: thanks to the use of private finance initiatives (PFI) to build new infrastructure, it has become a role model for many other countries. PPP schemes that were adopted in Europe were then used by countries all over the world, especially in Latin America, where over the last years many healthcare infrastructures have been built thanks to these innovative financial tools, following a period of experimentation with several types of public-private cooperation in different sectors.

The PwC report on PPPs in healthcare (Abuzaineh et al. 2018) indicates that 600 projects, most of which are PPPs, have been launched to build new healthcare infrastructure. Sixty percent of these are carried out in Europe, 15% in Asia and 15% in Northern and Latin America.

This work aims at answering the following research question: "How are PPPs carried out in different Latin American countries?" To do so, the chapter is organised as follows. In Sect. 2 we provide the theoretical framework on public-private partnerships, starting from a more general level and then moving to the healthcare sector. In Sect. 3 we describe the methodology utilised in the study. Section 4 is dedicated to findings. Finally, Sect. 5 presents future research perspectives and connects PPPs to the development of public healthcare networks.

2   Theoretical Framework: PPP in the Healthcare Sector

In this section, we will briefly discuss the main features of public-private partnerships and their diffusion in healthcare systems.

Public-private partnership is not a new concept, although lately it has received increasing attention. From Republican Rome to the mid-seventeenth century, governments involved their citizens in the provision of public services and, sometimes, in the construction of public works. At the time, the inclusion of private agents was the least expensive solution, both at economic and political levels.

Since 1980, OECD countries have begun to experiment with forms of collaboration between public and private sectors. The development and diffusion of New Public Management (NPM) introduced private sector techniques and tools in the public administration, with great emphasis on the concept of market as a space that drives better resource allocation and improved results.

In 2008, a joint conference by OECD, IMF and EIB highlighted how PPPs were turning into a global phenomenon. In fact the IMF delegate, Cottarelli (2008), presented a report indicating that, even 10 years ago, PPPs were spread across the globe.

All NPM reforms pushed for the transformation of the public sector from providing public services to buying and regulating their supply; the private sector, on the other hand, developed skills to provide public services thanks to outsourcing and privatisation processes. These new ways of providing public services developed over time in order to fix the inefficiency of traditional mechanisms (direct management, contracting out) that excluded the possibility of cooperation between partners from different sectors. During the Thatcher government in the United Kingdom, private actors were greatly involved in carrying out public infrastructure projects. The main objective was to reduce the share of public budgets dedicated to investments, in line with the fiscal consolidation process that was taking place in all European countries.

In 1992, the United Kingdom launched the private finance initiative (PFI), a tool to create collaborative relationships between public and private sectors, inspired to Ryrie Rules and based on transferring risks to the private sector (National Audit Office 2010). Many European countries enacted collaborative relationships based on the PFI, with the goal of reducing the impact of public investments on public budgets (which recorded excessively high debts in the 1980s and 1990s).

In the United States, a different form of collaboration between public and private sectors took place: while PFI schemes gave public administration and agencies' agents a large degree of autonomy in designing, defining and evaluating services to be provided, the Northern American version leaned more toward the autonomy of private actors and enterprises in providing public services.

Developing countries tend to use PPPs to compensate inefficiencies of the public sector in offering essential public services and goods, such as water, electricity, transportation, healthcare and education: private actors have more financial resources and competencies; thus, public administrations have an interest in engaging them in these processes. It is possible to say that PPPs in these countries usually lead to privatisation programmes aimed at improving the efficiency and effectiveness of public agencies, at redefining property rights so that private actors have greater incentives to cooperate with public administrations and at finding financial resources to maintain and renew old infrastructure.

In Europe the Green Paper (European Commission 2004) states that the concept of public-private partnership includes all cooperative relationships between public authorities and private companies that lead to financing, constructing, renewing, managing and maintaining a public infrastructure or providing a public service. Moreover, the European Commission defined the key elements of PPPs, such as the long-term duration of the contract, the collaboration between two types of actors, the existence of a unitary project, the provision of financial resources by the private sector with the possibility to add public funding, the clear separation of roles and finally the importance of risk sharing.

It is possible to outline key pillars of PPPs, such as long-term relationships, collaboration, sharing risks, costs and benefits and mutual value creation (Klijn and Teisman 2003). Moreover, PPPs display three main differences with respect to more general collaborative practices: first, there is no shared ownership structure; second, the outcome of PPPs is usually a public good that benefits users, not the partners; finally, PPP agreements tend to remain valid in the long term between specific partners (Zhang et al. 2009).

Public management scholars (Osborne 2000) analysed PPPs with the lenses of managerial reforms in the public administration, stating that "the word partnership includes contractual agreements, alliances, cooperative agreements, collaborative activities aimed at developing public policies, supporting and offering public programs and services".

Healthcare organisations and agencies work in a sector where needs and demand are constantly growing, with a continuous evolution toward new federative arrangements that lead to spreading responsibilities and decision-making power. Moreover, with increasing costs and decreasing public budgets, governments have started looking into PPPs (Blanken and Dewulf 2010).

In order to face this complex environment riddled with "wicked problems" (Mason and Mitroff 1981), intentional interventions have been experimented to redefine institutional structures and functioning mechanisms of healthcare organisations, with little success. At the same time, other phenomena have developed, not always intentionally, allowing to introduce new approaches based on effectiveness and functionality and to couple technical feasibility with social sustainability. There was also a mindset shift by private actors that started acknowledging that reaching public health goals is a pre-condition for their own long-term success and focusing on corporate social responsibility practices (Reich 2002).

Public governance represents a theoretical framework where public-private collaborations begin to work, becoming central in improving the efficiency of healthcare institutions and creating synergies between actors working in the field; the emphasis on social cohesion values also promoted network building, systemic governance and collaborative relationships (Newman 2004).

Public-private partnerships require the development of new governance models that allow an equal allocation of responsibilities among all actors involved. The large opportunities generated by these partnerships, especially in healthcare, can only be exploited if the public sector remains responsible for defining quality and quantity standards for the services delivered, as well as for establishing socially sustainable pricing policies and for monitoring managerial efficiency and effectiveness in satisfying citizens' needs (Cappellaro and Marsilio 2007). The role of the public sector changes from service provider toward promoter and catalyst of partnerships aimed at improving community health (Sofaer 1992). The key point is that the private actor is able to bring "high value added" for patients or "collective value for the public system", contributing to the cost reduction and to a higher service quality.

In the healthcare sector, public-private collaborations have followed different juridical and managerial models over time, such as mixed companies, leasing (operative, financial and real estate), foundations, project financing, general contractors, sponsorships, concessions of services/rights to build and manage and finally global service. The most commonly used model is the private finance initiative (PFI).

At international level, the managerial literature on involving private players in healthcare highlights theoretical debates and a lack of empirical analyses. At national level, on the other hand, the literature still presents relevant gaps.

According to Cuccurullo (2005), the academic literature indicates four research strands:

- Strategic analyses: the main objective is to study motivations behind the creation of networks. According to several authors, motivations include the improvement of competitive skills (Kogut 1988), the improvement of efficiency through the reduction of transaction costs (Hennart 1988) and knowledge accumulation (Hamel 1991).

– Organisational analyses, focused on studying institutional arrangements, risks and opportunities of different governance structures (Meneguzzo 1996).
– Economic analyses, used to evaluate network effectiveness through the identification of key factors that influence their performance (Koh and Venkatraman 1991).
– Social analyses, which consider the influence of the context on network behaviour, in terms of structural, institutional and cultural elements (Granovetter 1973).

Preker et al. (2000) aim at finding economic variables that are important for decision-making processes in providing healthcare services; to do so, they focus on specific features of services and institutional environments and they have identified two variables.

These variables are (1) contestability of the good, which is closely linked to the type of entrance and exit barriers in the market (in healthcare it is important to invest in knowledge as this strengthens entrance barriers and increases revenues) and (2) measurability of healthcare services (i.e. inputs, processes, outputs and outcomes of service provision).

Cuccurullo (2005) built a new model and defined collaborative relationships on the basis of their governance mechanisms. He finds three types of partnership:

– Informal collaboration, characterised by low level of specification, a relevant role performed by the public sector, very specific transactions and strong links with the territorial environment.
– Contractual collaboration, where the formal contract is important and allows gaining several advantages in terms of strategy, organisation, economic and operational aspects.
– Formal collaboration, characterised by the creation of mixed companies, foundations, associations and cooperatives that display specific corporate governance mechanisms.

Abuzaineh et al. (2018) indicate three main trends for the future of PPPs: infrastructure, integrated schemes and clinical services.

3   PPP in Latin America: A Multiple Case Studies Analysis

In order to answer our research question, we provide an in-depth overview of the application of PPPs to the healthcare sector by Latin American countries. First, we selected all Latin American countries that have carried out PPP projects in healthcare or that have drafted regulatory frameworks for their implementation. This restricts our analysis to six countries: Mexico, Chile, Peru, Argentina, Brazil and Colombia. Then, for each country, we examined secondary sources (formal and informal documents and communications issued by relevant stakeholders) and carried out a documentary analysis to identify the main features of the application of PPP to the healthcare sector. Then, we analysed data based on the theoretical framework of PPPs which was presented in Sect. 2 in order to outline the peculiarities of its implementation by Latin American countries, as well as potential future strategies.

3.1 Findings

The objective of this section is to present the main PPP experiences in the Latin American healthcare sector. We will only take into consideration countries that have provided regulation on the topic and/or that have carried out projects. For each of them, the degree of diffusion of PPPs will be evaluated, as well as their strengths, weaknesses and potential for future development.

Mexico

Mexico was the first Latin American country to carry out public-private partnership initiatives. Different PPP models were developed over time, with varying levels of engagement of the private sector in public projects, which did not always lead to the desired result. In 1952, concessions were implemented to build the first toll-payment highway that linked the Federal District with the town of Cuernavaca, funded with reimbursable resources from international institutions (the World Bank) and with toll payments (removed during the 1970s). This model was used again in the 1980s, when the Banco Nacional de Obras (BANOBRAS), through the programme called *Programa Nacional de Concesiones de Autopistas*, planned to deal with construction, financing and maintenance of toll-payment highways.

The first PPP models in Mexico date to 2006, when Vicente Fox's government (2000–2006) launched the *"Proyectos para la Prestación de Servicios"* (Projects for service provision—PPS), which were very similar to British PPP models. PPSs are juridically grounded in articles 3 and 24 of the *"Ley de Adquisiciones, Arrendamientos y Servicios del Sector Pùblico"*, and they are regulated by articles 32 and 50 of the law proposal *"Ley Federal de Presupuesto y Responsabilidad Hacendaria"*.

More precisely, PPSs are based on the *"Reglas para la Realización de PPS"* published in April 2004, and they were first used in highway infrastructure, education, security, airports and healthcare infrastructure. PPSs have made it possible to offer a wide range of services with high quality standards without increasing public spending, simply by improving the use of existing resources.

Since 2005, Mexico has launched many projects in different sectors, following the model of PPS. In healthcare, the *Plan Maestro* was developed, i.e. a plan for creating a very complex hospital network. More specifically, it established that numerous hospitals would be built across Mexico, offering services to local populations, with the most relevant displayed in Table 1.

The application of the PPS model allowed the country to improve its healthcare infrastructure, but there is still a gap between planning and actual implementation.

Table 1 Main experiences of PPPs in the Mexican healthcare sector

Infrastructure	Year
Hospital Regional de Alta Especialidad del Bajio	2005
Hospital Regional de Alta Especialidad de Ciudad Victoria	2007
Hospital Regional de Alta Especialidad de Chihuahua	2007
Hospital General de Alta Especialidad de Guerrero	2007
Hospital General de Alta Especialidad de Tamaulipas	2007
Hospital General de Alta Especialidad de Sinaloa	2007
Hospital General de Alta Especialidad de Torreon	2007
Hospital Regional de Alta Especialidad de Ixtapaluca	2008
Hospital Regional de Alta Especialidad de Zumpango	2009
Hospital Regional de Alta Especialidad de Toluca	2009
Hospital Regional de Tlalnepantla	2010
Hospital General de Ticul	2010

At first, in order to enact the PPS model, the Mexican government decided to change existing regulations. In addition to this, the government invested much in cost-benefit analyses before approving each project and in training employees. The results linked to the first phase were not those that the government had expected. There were many problems in organising a system of consulting activities and capacity building services in the assistance network, in managing healthcare services and in training public officers, who resulted unable to cooperate effectively with the private sector.

The PPS project was strongly improved over time, but current experiences indicate that additional adjustments are necessary. Glanc (2015) identifies the following areas for improvement:

– Training public officers so that they are experts on PPS
– A clear definition of the role of public actors and the introduction and diffusion of modern and advanced management models that is up to date with technologic and construction innovations
– Definition of a juridical framework that is homogeneous for all State levels, so federal and local programmes are consistent
– Improvement of monitoring methods and tools
– Availability of skilled people resources in the public sector that can contribute to any project
– Design of procurement processes that are based on clear demands in terms of technical features and quality standards, risk transfer mechanisms and evaluation tools
– Introduction of efficient communication mechanisms between public and private sectors and incentives that promote innovative processes throughout the contract duration
– Possibility for the private actor to define how quality standards can be achieved, so that there is an equal allocation of risks

Chile

In Chile, the public-private partnership model is known as "system of concessions". The country experienced great economic growth at the beginning of the 1990s, which shed light on the worrying situation of national infrastructure (especially airports and highways), showing large decreases in productivity. This situation led President Aylwin's government (1990–1994), through the involvement of the Ministerio de Obras Públicas (MOP), to allow the private sector to take part in financing public infrastructure by employing the system of concessions regulated by the *Ley Orgánica del Ministerio de Obras Públicas* and the *Ley Reglamento de Concesiones de Obras Públicas*. According to these laws, the MOP is responsible for building infrastructure through the use of concessions, although it is possible for private actors (either individuals or companies) to present proposals.

All projects carried out in Chile follow the traditional BOT model (build, operate, transfer), and the infrastructure is owned by the public sector at all times. According to the procedure, participants can also be consortia of national and international companies. The concessionaire has to respect all quality and quantity standards for the services it provides, throughout the duration of the concession, as they were established in the contract. Standards can only be modified for public interest reasons. The concession cannot last for more than 50 years and once it has expired the infrastructure goes back to the MOP.

The first project that was implemented concerned the development of the *Ruta 5—Panamericana* that connects the country from La Serena to Puerto Montt, the *Rutas Transversales* and many national airports. In the healthcare sector, two experiences are especially relevant: the *Programa Hospitalario de Maipù y La Florida* and the hospital of Antofagasta.

All began in 2003, when the Ministry decided to renew and rebuild the *Complejo Hospitalario Salvador Infante* in Santiago, applying the system of concessions to the Maipù and La Florida hospitals, which became "pilot projects" for the "*Programa de Concesiones II*". The Chilean model of PPP puts great emphasis on architectural and infrastructural aspects.

To solve this issue, the government approved the *Ley de Concesiones* (2010), which introduced service standards in concessions, similar to those applied in the United Kingdom and in Spain.

In general, sanctions for breach of contract are always well defined, as well as information regarding management indicators and acceptable standards.

The Chilean concession model, like the Mexican one, states that the private actor has to offer specific services (e.g. building maintenance and electricity provision); on the other hand, the provision of medical equipment is usually not outsourced. The Chilean concession model pays great attention to the characteristics of suppliers, which are screened and selected through a multiple-step process.

So far it is not yet possible to evaluate the Chilean experience with PPP in healthcare, because buildings are still under construction. However, the introduction of a flexible law has led to increasing the amount of projects that are carried out, and the fact that decision-making power to launch specific programmes is in the hands of a restricted number of actors (the Ministry of Finance and the Ministry of Public Works) has emerged as a key success factor.

Peru

During the 1990s, Peru carried out a large privatisation programme that focused on PPP models (based on Law 25.327 and Legislative Decree 674). In 1996 a Commission was created to organise all PPP projects; Legislative Decree 839 changed the framework of concessions, promoting their diffusion and allowing for the development of several models of public-private collaboration. Following this law, the "*Comisión de Promoción de Concesiones Privadas*" (PROMCEPRI) was created with the objective to guide the private sector in carrying out works and infrastructure for public service delivery.

During President Toledo's government (2001–2006), the POINVERSION was born, i.e. the Agency for the Promotion and Development of the National Policy for the Enhancement of Private Investment in Peru. The creation of this agency was a turning point for the organisational development of the country: it acted as a bridge between two worlds, private and public, which are very different, and it promoted the diffusion of PPP projects.

According to Peru's legal system, a concession regarding a public work always has to include its construction, renewal, functioning and maintenance; moreover, the law defines public works as all infrastructures in transportation, environmental protection, energy, healthcare, education, tourism, communications, etc. The PPP model in Peru is different from others with regard to payment models to the private actors. Thanks to its very clear legal framework, Peru is increasingly using concessions both at central and regional level to construct infrastructures in several sectors.

In healthcare, Law 29344 (*Ley de Aseguramiento Universal en Salud por el Seguro Integral de Salud*) allowed to develop the *Plan Esencial de Aseguramiento en Salud* (PAES), which is at the heart of all PPP projects. PPP is considered as the only solution to improve healthcare services, especially those addressed to the poorest citizens.

Healthcare services in Peru are provided by institutions managed by the Ministry of Healthcare (MINSA), by EsSalud (Insurance System for Social Healthcare), by the army and police, by municipalities (urban hospitals), by private clinics (EPS) and by NGOs.

EsSalud is a public agency characterised by administrative, economic, financial and tax decentralisation (Law 28006) that administers funds resulting from insurance payments. Based on the consideration that PPP is the only solution to face issues with the country's healthcare infrastructure, EsSalud has launched large campaigns, with international investments, that led to carry out several projects especially in 2008:

1. A DBOT project for the provision of healthcare services: the private for-profit player is responsible for design and construction, for providing medical and IT equipment and only partially for the provision of healthcare services, based on a 32-year long contract. The project plans the creation of a 30.000 m^2 hospital with 300 beds. Risks are equally distributed among all stakeholders.

2. The construction of a hospital based on the full concession of healthcare services to the private sector. This is the first example outside Spain and a unique experience in Latin America. It is the Hospital del Milagro in Salta Province, Argentina, built by the same private institution that manages the Hospital de la Ribeiro in Valencia based on the Alzira Model.
3. The Guillermo Kaelin de la Fuente and the Callao hospitals, two projects carried out with full concessions: it is not yet possible to evaluate them as they are under construction.

The Ministry of Healthcare has recently launched a PPP programme to build 15 new hospitals.

Colombia
Colombia presents a unique situation in terms of PPP, since it has not yet adopted any of the aforementioned models. The reform of the healthcare system (Law 100.1993) introduced competition between private and public agencies.

This model considers equally private and public healthcare operators, both of which have the goal of providing a "bundle" of healthcare services to citizens covered by Social Security, and they are paid for each provision. A consequence of the introduction of this model has been larger healthcare coverage for Colombians, as each institution aims at serving large amounts of people to get more revenues; however, this has caused broad inequalities.

Today there is not enough information to analyse the effectiveness of this type of involvement by the private sector in public healthcare. On the other hand, the Colombian government wants to launch PPP programmes in education, highways and airports and healthcare.

Brazil
The first PPPs were introduced thanks to the *Ley do Parcerias*, aimed at regulating private investments in public projects with the perspective of collaboration between the two sectors. The Brazilian experience with PPP is rather poor, even considering existing projects: the only one is the *Hospital do Suburbio* in Salvador de Bahia. The city is in the Northeast of Brazil and is characterised by high income inequality and difficulties in accessing healthcare services. The construction of this hospital through the use of PPP was supposed to solve this problem and ensure that the whole population would be able to obtain high-quality healthcare.

The tender was won by a consortium formed by Promedica, a leading company in healthcare assistance in Brazil, and Dalkia, a French company specialised in managing healthcare structures and offering non-medical services. The contract lasts 10 years and involves private actors in various stages, from maintenance to operations, with a 23 million US$ investment in equipment during the first year and 9 million US$ to spend during the rest of the contract. The agreement foresees that the private partner's revenues would be linked to 31 qualitative performance indicators, while monitoring would be carried out by a professional company. Other conditions established that risks would be equally distributed among partners. The negotiation closed on May 28, 2010 and resulted in a new hospital with 298 beds.

Recently, the Bahia State government entrusted private players with complete operations in 12 hospitals that were built and equipped by the State, which was in charge of performing healthcare and support activities. These exchanges were regulated by yearly contracts, renewable up to 5 years. These hospitals are created to satisfy demand, and gains are defined on the basis of predetermined production amounts; revenues will be obtained only if 80% of production objectives are reached.

Brazil does not provide enough information to make comparisons or to derive conclusions regarding its use of PPP due to the small amount of experiences that were carried out; however, the country has recently launched new forms of collaboration for healthcare investments. With the project of the *Hospital do Suburbio* alone, Brazil increased the provision of healthcare services (emergency ones included), created additional jobs for doctors, nurses, physiotherapists and other professionals; the project is considered one of the most innovative globally and has been an example for the realisation of similar initiatives.

Argentina
In Argentina, when the public sector decides to build infrastructures, it always refers to the traditional model of public work, regulated by Law 13.064, or to the model of concession of public works regulated by Law 17.250.

Private sector initiative is regulated by Law 17.520 and then amended by Law 23.696 which originally only referred to the concession of public works and then was extended to other fields. Then Decree 436/2000 was introduced in order to regulate private initiatives in public tenders and concessions of public services, as well as other types of privatisation. The decree defines a PPP model based on the duty of the private sector for what concerns public interest activities. This system is similar to those applied in Peru and Uruguay, and it establishes that the State receives proposals by private actors to carry out a public interest project, and only after the administrative procedure (which can lead to other competitors improving the proposal) it is possible to sign the contract.

There are not many PPP projects in healthcare; the only experiences are those of the *Hospital del Milagro*, in Salta Province, and the *Hospital El Cruce Dr. Néstor Carlos Kirchner*, in Florencio Varela, a town in the province of Buenos Aires. The new law on PPP in Argentina (Law 27.328) could enhance the development of new projects (Cardilli 2017).

4 Discussion

Our analysis indicates that the degree of application of public-private partnership models in Latin American healthcare is still low. All countries have shown interest and commitment to use PPP for carrying out infrastructure projects (see Table 2):

Table 2 Final comparison

Country	Main features	Level of adoption of healthcare PPPs
Mexico	• First Latin American country to adopt PPP • Clear regulatory framework • High commitment to application of PPP to healthcare • Attentive planning, difficult implementation • Issues with organising networks and training employees • Results: low employment, high costs	Medium
Chile	• Clear regulatory framework (with flexible laws) • Three relevant projects so far • Great emphasis on architectural aspects • Private actors undertake more risks than they do in other countries/models • Risk of corruption in the public sector	Low
Peru	• Clear regulatory framework • Specific rules for paying the private partner • PPP seen as only solution to improve public healthcare • One case of full healthcare provision by the private partner • Strong investment on PPP in healthcare	Low
Colombia	• No models of PPP adopted • Willingness to launch PPP programmes in education, highways and airports, healthcare	Low
Brazil	• Only one relevant experience of PPP in the healthcare sector	Low, but increasing
Argentina	• Only two experiences of PPP in the healthcare sector • New law on PPP in Argentina, potentially enhancing the development of new projects	Medium, with great focus on regulation

especially in the healthcare sector, this could be a solution to the issues that affect this area of the world. Indeed, these countries have suffered high poverty rates and large inequalities in wealth distribution, which increase adverse selection in patient care.

Over the last years, Mexico was able to implement many PPP projects, many of which in healthcare. In fact, several hospitals were built through this new collaborative model between public and private sector. The framework that was used in all projects is known as *Proyectos Para la Prestación de Servicios* (PPS). The country was very effective in designing these initiatives, also because of the clarity of the legal framework; on the other hand, there were issues in implementing them. Despite many interventions aimed at training human resources in the public sector, the public administration was lacking the ability of collaborating with the private sector.

Chile is farther behind Mexico in the implementation of PPPs for healthcare services, but it was able to employ the concession system, which was successful in other fields and is slowly reaching the healthcare sector. Projects are not completed yet so it is not easy to evaluate them, but there are good chances that they give positive results.

Peru adopted both "pure" PPP models and a system of full concessions, leaving the concessionaire a high degree of autonomy in the stages of the project; this system, however, has not proven to be better than those of other countries.

There have not been fully positive experiences in Colombia and Brazil yet. The former has not carried out any healthcare project. In the past, the introduction of a law opening the public sector to competition with private players had paved the path for new possibilities and improved the country's medical coverage. Today, there are only good intentions expressed by the government to implement projects by using PPP in healthcare. For what concerns Brazil, the scarce material available indicates that there are little to none PPP projects in healthcare: there are no other projects than the *Hospital do Suburbio*, which was realised using PPPs and led to large improvements in healthcare. In this case as well, the assignment of 12 hospital projects to the private sector anticipates positive developments for the country.

So far, Argentina has very few projects aimed at creating healthcare infrastructure with PPPs, although the legal framework indicates that the government pays attention to these issues. The recent introduction of Law 27.328 on PPPs confirms the interest to carry out projects that adopt this approach: based on these considerations, Argentina can be described as one of the most active countries in Latin America.

Finally, there are no relevant projects in Uruguay, Paraguay, Bolivia, Ecuador and Venezuela.

5 Conclusions

Findings from our cross-country analysis on PPPs have interesting implications for studies on network governance and management. Indeed, for over 30 years the healthcare sector has been a relevant field of research and reflection on network studies, with contributions from European and American scholars (respectively, Kickert, Klijn and Koppenjan; Mandell, Kenis and Provan). Several international research networks dealing with public network management (such as EURAM with its Special Interest Group on Public Management, EGPA with its Permanent Strategic Group on Public Network Management and Governance and IRSPM) have committed to studying the healthcare sector (Cristofoli et al. 2017).

Scholars started relatively recently by focusing on network governance methods and exploring their relationships with network performance. It was in the well-known study on "Modes of Network Governance: Structures, Management and Effectiveness" by Provan and Kenis (2008) who identified three different forms of network governance: shared participant governance, lead organization governance and network administrative organization (NAO) governance. In a subsequent article, the authors looked in more detail into the relationships between these governance forms and network performance, arguing that the appropriateness and success of different governance forms can vary in different circumstances (Kenis and Provan 2009).

National case studies analysed in this chapter indicate the various roles of stakeholders involved in PPP projects and how networks are governed within each type of PPP.

To conclude, we can say that national PPP experiences yielding positive results are associated with the NAO model (i.e. Mexico and Peru) and with the lead organization governance model (Chile).

References

Abuzaineh N, Brashers E, Foong S, Feachem R, Da Rita P (2018) PPPs in healthcare: models, lessons and trends for the future, Healthcare public-private partnership series, no. 4. The Global Health Group, Institute for Global Health Sciences, University of California, San Francisco and PwC, San Francisco

Blanken A, Dewulf GP (2010) PPPs in health: static or dynamic? Aust J Public Adm 69(1):35–47

Cappellaro G, Marsilio M (2007) Le collaborazioni pubblico-privato per la gestione dei servizi sanitari: riflessioni alla luce della ricognizione delle esperienze internazionali e nazionali. Mecosan 63:9–35

Cardilli R (2017) La nuova legge argentina di partenariato pubblico privato. Quaderni C.R.I.A, Roma

Cottarelli C (2008) Public private partnerships. What are they? Theory and practice. https://www.oecd.org/gov/budgeting/41273943.ppt

Cristofoli D, Mandell M, Meneguzzo M (2017) The public network scholarly community in Europe: main characteristics and future developments. In: Ongaro E, Van Thiel S (eds) The Palgrave handbook of public administration and management in Europe. Palgrave, London

Cuccurullo C (2005) Le collaborazioni tra pubblico e privato in sanità: meccanismi di governance. Cedam, Padova

European Commission (2004) Green paper on public-private partnerships and community laws on public contracts and concessions, Bruxelles

Glanc M (2015) Modelos de asociación publico privada en el desarrollo de hospitales publicos en Latinoamerica. Analisis de una decada de experiencia. Isalud, Ciudad Autonoma de Buenos Aires

Granovetter M (1973) The strength of weak ties. Am J Sociol 78(6):1360–1380

Hamel GP (1991) Competition for competence and inter partner learning within international strategic alliance. Strateg Manag J 12:83–103

Hennart JF (1988) A transaction costs theory of equity joint ventures. Strateg Manag J 9(4):361–374

Kenis P, Provan KG (2009) Towards an exogenous theory of public network performance. Public Adm 87(3):440–456

Klijn EH, Teisman GR (2003) Institutional and strategic barriers to public-private partnerships: an analysis of Dutch cases. Public Money Manag 23(3):1–9

Kogut B (1988) Joint ventures: theoretical and empirical perspectives. Strateg Manag J 9(4):319–322

Koh J, Venkatraman G (1991) Joint venture formations and stock market reactions: an assessment in the information technology sector. Acad Manag J 34:869–892

Mason O, Mitroff I (1981) Challenging strategic planning assumptions: theory, case and techniques. John Wiley and Sons, New York

Meneguzzo M (ed) (1996) Strategie e gestione delle reti di aziende sanitarie. Egea, Milano

National Audit Office (2010) The performance and management of hospital PFI contracts, London

Newman J (2004) Constructing accountability: network governance and managerial agency. Public Policy Adm 19(4):18–35

Osborne SP (2000) Public-private partnerships, theory and practice in international perspective. Routledge, London

Preker AS, Harding A, Travis P (2000) Make or buy decisions in the production of health care goods and services: new insights from institutional economics and organizational theory. Bull World Health Organ 78(6):777–790

Provan KG, Kenis P (2008) Modes of network governance: structure, management and effectiveness. J Public Adm Res Theory 18(2):229–252

Reich MR (2002) Public-private partnerships for public health. Harvard Centre for Population and Development Studies, Cambridge

Sofaer S (1992) Coalitions and public health: a program manager's guide to the issues. Centers for Disease Control, Atlanta

Zhang Z, Wan D, Jia M, Gu L (2009) Prior ties, shared value and cooperation in public-private partnerships. Manag Organ Rev 5(3):353–374